BTEC LEVEL 2

First Sport

Second Edition

BTEC LEVEL 2

First Sport

Second Edition

Jennifer Stafford-Brown
Simon Rea
Chris Manley

HODDER
EDUCATION

Orders: please contact Bookpoint Ltd, 130 Milton Park, Abingdon, Oxon OX14 4SB.
Telephone: (44) 01235 827720. Fax: (44) 01235 400454. Lines are open
from 9.00 – 5.00, Monday to Saturday, with a 24-hour message answering
service. You can also order through our website www.hoddereducation.co.uk.

British Library Cataloguing in Publication Data
A catalogue record for this title is available from the British Library

ISBN: 978 1 444 111941

First Published 2010
Impression number   10 9 8 7 6 5 4 3 2
Year   2016 2015 2014 2013 2012 2011 2010

Hachette UK's policy is to use papers that are natural, renewable and
recyclable products and made from wood grown in sustainable forests.
The logging and manufacturing processes are expected to conform to the
environmental regulations of the country of origin.

Cover photo © Stockbyte/Getty Images

Typeset by Pantek Arts Ltd, Maidstone, Kent

Printed in Italy for Hodder Education, part of Hachette UK, 338 Euston Road,
London NW1 3BH

Contents

Acknowledgements
Figures

ACKNOWLEDGEMENTS

4.15 © Getty Images
4.16 © George Tiedemann/GT Images/Corbis
4.17 © Getty Images
4.18 (a) actionplus sports images (b) actionplus sports images
4.19 (a) actionplus sports images (b) actionplus sports images
4.20 (a) Richard Hutchings/Photolibrary
(b) Richard Hutchings/Photolibrary
4.37 (a) A. Glauberman/Science Photo Library
(b) uncredited
4.38 Maska/Shutterstock Images LLC

6.1 Jane Vernon/English Institute of Sport at Sheffield
6.4 Emmanuel Dunand/Staff/Getty Images
6.5 PhotosIndia RM/Photolibrary
6.6 AFP/Stringer/Getty Images
6.7 © Corbis
6.8 Fisher Hart/Photolibrary

7.1 Emely/Corbis

8.1 Getty Images
8.2 actionplus sports images
8.3 Getty Images
8.4 © Janine Wiedel Photolibrary/Alamy
8.5 *Mail on Sunday*/Rex Features

8.6 Chalkboard (© Guardian Newspapers Limited)
8.7 actionplus sports images
8.8 © Stock Connection Distribution/Alamy

15.2 Guildford Spectrum
15.3 Eye Ubiquitous/Alamy
15.4 Paul Miles/Getty Images
15.5 Safety/Alamy

16.1 Zero Creatives/Photolibrary
16.2 Owen Franken/Corbis
16.4 Alan Becker/Getty Images
16.5 © Annie Griffiths Belt/Corbis
16.7 Vegar Abelsnes Photography/Getty Images
16.8 © John Schweider/Alamy

18.4 AHMAD YUSNI/Stringer/Getty Images
18.5 (a) Novastock Novastock/Photolibrary
(b) Novastock Novastock/Photolibrary
18.6 actionplus sports images

19.1 Novastock Novastock/Photolibrary An exercise class
19.2 actionplus sports images
19.3 © Design Pics Inc./Alamy

Images used for opening chapters (numbers given in **bold**): **1** (Tips RF/Photolibrary), **2** (Rolfo Rolf Brenner/Getty Images), **3** David Madison/Getty Images, **4** (Niklas Bernstone/Getty Images), **5** (Barros & Barros/Getty Images), **6** (© Pete Saloutos/CORBIS), **7** (© MARC SEROTA, Reuters/Corbis), **8** (© Glowimages RM/Alamy), **9** (Paul Bradbury/Getty Images), **10** (Jamie McDonald/Getty Images), **11** (Mike Powell/Photolibrary), **12** Medioimages/Photodisc/Getty Images, **13** (Paul Miles/Getty Images), **14** (Neal Preston/CORBIS), **15** (© Glowimages RM/Alamy), **16** (© Tom Stewart/CORBIS), **17** (Frans Lemmens/Getty Images), **18** (© Image Source/Alamy), **19** (AFP/Getty Images), and **20** (Stuart Forster/Rex Features).

FIGURE LIST

Chapter 1
Fitness Testing & Training

This chapter gives an overview of the fitness requirements of different sports and the training methods that can be used to achieve a successful sporting performance. The chapter also explores other factors that will be related to the success of the performer, such as the effects of psychological and lifestyle factors.

Learning Goals

By the end of this chapter you should:

- Know the fitness and training requirements necessary to achieve excellence in a selected sport.
- Know the lifestyle factors that affect sports training and performance.
- Be able to assess own level of fitness.
- Know the effects of psychological factors on sports training and performance.

To achieve a PASS grade the evidence must show that the learner is able to:	To achieve a MERIT grade the evidence must show that, in addition to the pass criteria, the learner is able to:	To achieve a DISTINCTION grade the evidence must show that, in addition to the pass and merit criteria, the learner is able to:
P1 describe the fitness requirements for achieving excellence in a selected sport	**M1** explain the fitness requirements for achieving excellence in a selected sport	
P2 describe three different fitness training methods used to achieve excellence in a selected sport		
P3 describe four different lifestyle factors that can affect sports training and performance		
P4 carry out four different fitness tests for different components of fitness, recording the results accurately		
P5 interpret their test results and personal level of fitness	**M2** explain their test results and personal level of fitness, identifying strengths and areas for improvement	**D1** evaluate their test results and personal level of fitness, considering the level required to achieve excellence in a selected sport
P6 describe the effects of psychological factors on sports training and performance	**M3** explain the effects of psychological factors on sports training and performance	**D2** analyse the effects of psychological factors on sports training and performance

1.1 Fitness and Training Requirements to Achieve Excellence in Sport

Components of Fitness

When we look at fitness we need to examine it in a broad sense. When we think about fitness we need to ask the question: 'Fit for what?' Each individual will have their own individual fitness requirements.

Physical Fitness

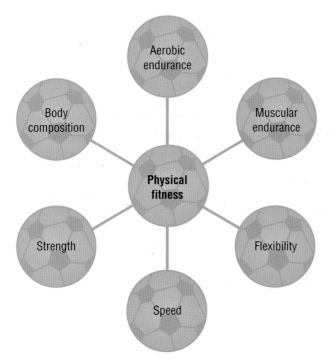

Figure 1.1   Different factors that make up physical fitness.

1. **Aerobic endurance** – this is the ability of the muscles to exercise for a long period of time without becoming tired. It is a measure of how well the lungs can take in oxygen, how well the heart and blood can transport oxygen and then how well the muscles can use oxygen.

2. **Muscular endurance** – this is how well the muscles can produce repeated contractions. When training for muscular endurance we usually do sets of 15–20 repetitions.

3. **Flexibility** – this is the range of motion that a joint or group of joints can move through.

4. **Speed** – this is how quickly the body or individual limbs can move.

5. **Strength** – this is the maximum force a muscle or group of muscles can produce. To train for strength we usually do sets of 1–5 repetitions.

6. **Body composition** – this is the make-up of the body in terms of how much of the body weight is fat and how much is not fat, which we call lean body weight (LBW).

Skill-related Fitness

This aspect of fitness relates to the production of skilled movement (see Figure 1.2). This is the coordination between the brain, nervous system and muscles. All movement will start in the brain, as it produces a nervous impulse that is transferred to the muscles through the nerves. The nervous impulse will travel down the spinal cord and out through the nerves that shoot off the spinal cord. These nerves bring the nervous impulse to the muscles, which then contract to produce movement.

When we learn a skill the brain sends the message to the muscles, but at the start it may not be the right message and may not produce a skilled performance. However, as we practise the skill we learn to send the right message and we develop a 'pathway' between the brain, nerves and muscles. All these skills need to have a strong pathway between the brain, nerves and muscular system.

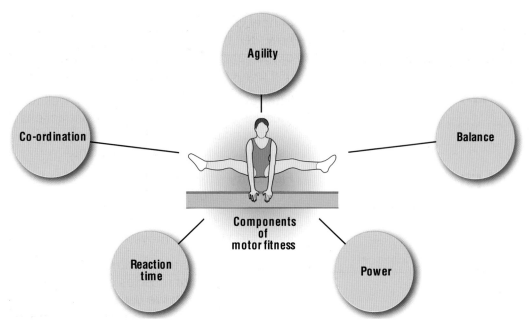

Figure 1.2   Components of motor fitness

1. **Agility** – this is a measure of how well you can control your body while moving through the air. It is particularly important when you have to change direction quickly.

2. **Balance** – this is how well you can keep your body weight over a central base of support.

3. **Power** – this is the production of strength at speed and can be seen when we throw an object or perform a sprint start.

4. **Coordination** – this is how well we can produce the skilled movement that is required of us.

5. **Reaction time** – this is how quickly we can pick up information, make a decision and then produce a reaction to it.

Achieving Excellence in Sport

Achieving excellence in sport demands a mixture of all the physical fitness and skill-related factors. In certain sports, such as track and field athletics, it is clear what performances will achieve regional, national and international status because the outcome of performance is measured in time or metres; however in most sports, performance is dependent upon many factors and while some of these can be measured (time over a certain distance or flexibility at a joint), it is not possible to state exactly what makes a regional, national or international performance. We can look at a sport and describe what components of fitness are important and what we would expect a performer at each level to be able to do. Performance is also dependent upon many psychological factors and performers become better the older they get, not necessarily because they are fitter, but because they have had more experience and understand the demands of the game better.

(k) Key learning points

- **Components of physical fitness:**
  - Aerobic endurance is a measure of how well the lungs can take in oxygen, how well the heart and blood can transport oxygen and then how well the muscles can use oxygen. Muscular endurance is how well the muscles can produce repeated contractions at low intensities.
  - Flexibility is the range of motion that a joint or group of joints can move through.
  - Speed is how quickly the body or individual limbs can move.
  - Strength is the maximum force a muscle or group of muscles can produce once.
  - Body composition is the ratio of body fat to lean body weight.

(k) Key learning points

- **Components of motor fitness:**
  - Agility is a measure of how well you can control your body while moving through the air.
  - Balance is how well you can keep your body weight over a central base of support.
  - Power is the production of strength at speed.
  - Coordination is how well you can produce the skilled movement that is required of you.
  - Reaction time is how quickly you can pick up information, make a decision and then produce a reaction to it.

Activity **1.1** 60 mins   P1   M1

Applying the components of fitness

Task

Look at each of these sports performers.

- Steven Gerrard
- Stuart Broad
- Beth Tweddle
- Ronnie O'Sullivan
- Jessica Ennis.

Select one sports performer, then pick out the five most important components of physical fitness and skill-related fitness for that sports performer and place them in the table below.

Now describe and explain why each component is important for that sports performer.

Component of fitness	Why is it important?

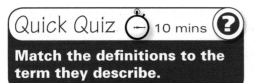

Term	Definition
Aerobic endurance	How well you can control your body as you move through the air.
Muscular endurance	The ability to produce strength at speed.
Strength	The ability of the muscles to use oxygen over a long period of time.
Speed	The maximum force a muscle can produce once.
Agility	How quickly the limbs can move.
Power	The ability of muscle to produce contractions repeatedly.

1.2 Fitness Training Methods P2

There are a number of different components of fitness and if you want to develop one particular aspect of fitness you will need to take part in different types of training.

Training Components of Physical Fitness

Training to Develop Strength

A person's strength depends upon the size of their muscles, so the larger muscles you have, the stronger you will be. In order to become stronger it is necessary to overload the muscles through resistance training. This basically means that you will need to carry out some form of weightlifting exercises that are specific to the muscle group you want to improve; for example if you would like to increase the size of your biceps you could perform bicep curls using dumbbells. The muscle is actually damaged during the exercise, then during the rest period that follows it is repaired and made bigger and better than before the resistance training. In order to build muscle mass you need to use heavy weights and repeat the lift 2–6 times (this is called the reps), have a rest and then repeat the process one or two more times (this is called the sets).

Training to Develop Aerobic Endurance

This type of training is designed to train the heart muscle and also the lungs. The heart is a muscle and will respond to exercise by getting stronger. The lungs also respond to training by becoming better at taking in more oxygen. Therefore, to exercise the heart and lungs effectively it is necessary to perform aerobic-type exercises, such as walking, jogging, swimming and cycling, at an intensity where you are only just able to carry on a conversation, for a period of at least 20 minutes three times per week.

Other types of training that train cardiovascular endurance are interval training, fartlek training and circuit training.

Training to Develop Muscular Endurance

Muscular endurance is the ability of a muscle, or a group of muscles, to continue performing contractions. In order to improve muscular endurance, it is necessary to exercise the specific muscle groups for periods of time. If a person wants to use resistance equipment to increase their muscular endurance, they should use low weights and high repetitions (12 or more) for two or three sets.

Circuit training can also be used to train muscular endurance. The circuit should be designed to consist of resistance exercises that use body weight as resistance, as in press-ups, and also resistance equipment such as dumbbells. Most circuits consist of a number of exercises set up in different areas of the room. The sports person exercises on each station for a period of around one minute, has a very short break (5 seconds) as they move on to the next station until the circuit is complete. The circuit is then repeated with less time spent on each station, for example 40 seconds.

Flexibility Training

This is probably the most neglected form of training but is very important indeed as it helps to prevent injury as well as improving a sports person's performance.

There is a range of different methods of flexibility training: active stretching, passive stretching and PNF (proprioceptive – pronounced 'prope-rio-ceptive – neuromuscular facilitation) training.

Active stretching involves holding a stretch for around 30 to 60 seconds, for example sitting down with your legs out straight in front of you and reaching to touch your toes.

Passive stretching involves relaxing the body and having a partner gently push or pull the body or limb into a stretched position. PNF was originally developed as a rehabilitation technique but is now widely used to improve flexibility in tight muscles. It is usually done with a partner and first involves a muscle being moved to the point where the stretch is initially felt. At this point the person being stretched is asked to

contract their stretched muscle to about 40–50 per cent of a maximum contraction and to hold it for 10 seconds. Once the 10 seconds is over the person relaxes and their muscle is stretched again to the point where they feel the new stretch (it will be further than the initial point of stretch). This is repeated three or four times, with the muscle being stretched further each time. This type of stretching is very effective and improves flexibility more quickly than developmental stretching without a contraction.

Speed Training

Speed can be trained by practising the technique of sprinting at slow speeds then running at maximal sprinting speed. You can also train for speed by sprinting down a hill with a suitable surface (a hill with a decline of 15 degrees is best; any steeper would be dangerous).

Power Training

Plyometrics is a good method of training for power – it works by quickly stretching the muscle (eccentric) followed by a very quick muscle contraction (concentric). This results in the body learning to create a faster and greater muscle contraction. Examples of plyometric training are hopping, jumping, drop-jumping from a bench up onto another bench.

Activity 1.2 40 mins · P2

Fitness training methods to achieve excellence in sport

Task 1

Choose three different components of fitness from the list below:

- Flexibility
- Strength
- Power
- Aerobic endurance
- Muscular endurance
- Speed.

Task 2

Select and describe three different training methods that can be used for each of your selected components of fitness.

Quick Quiz 🕐 10 mins ?

Match the training method to the component of fitness.

Component of fitness	Training method
Flexibility	Plyometrics
Strength	Running at maximal speed
Power	Interval training
Aerobic endurance	Heavy weights with low repetitions
Muscular endurance	PNF
Speed	Low weights with high repetitions

1.3 Lifestyle P3

The way in which a person lives their life has a huge impact upon their health and consequently their sports performance. For example, factors such as smoking or drinking alcohol adversely affect performance. Research clearly indicates that smoking over a period of time will adversely affect health and, in most cases, will decrease sporting performances, especially in sports that use the aerobic energy system.

Once sports participation has finished for the day, alcohol consumption in moderation is thought not to have too much of a detrimental effect on a player's health or sports performance. However, if alcohol is consumed in excess, the 'hangover' effects and damage to the liver will reduce sporting performance. Alcohol consumed prior to or during sports performance will negatively affect performance

by slowing down reaction times and affecting balance and coordination, which could lead to accidents or injuries.

Most sports performers will experience some levels of stress prior to, during and even after their event. They will need to learn to deal with this stress so that it does not start to affect their health. If a person is feeling stressed it may prevent them from sleeping properly and thereby not giving the body and mind a chance to relax and recuperate.

All sports performers should ensure they are eating a diet that provides them with the right quantities of nutrients, vitamins, minerals and calories. If they are eating too much food, they will start to put on weight, which will adversely affect performance. Alternatively, if they eat too little, they will lose weight and probably not provide their body with the fuel it requires to recover from training and competition.

Activity 1.3 🕐 20 mins   P3

The effect of lifestyle factors on performance

Task

Take an individual of your choice and describe how the following lifestyle factors may affect their training or performance.

Lifestyle factor	How it affects performance
Stress	
Excess alcohol	
Smoking	
Diet	

Quick Quiz ⏱ 10 mins ?

Which of the following statements are True and which are False in relation to the advice you would give an athlete?

1. Smoking in moderation will not affect your performance.
2. Because alcohol is a carbohydrate it is important to include it in your daily diet.
3. Stress can affect how well you sleep and prevent you from relaxing.
4. The correct diet is important in maintaining your correct weight.

1.4 Assessing   Individual Fitness Levels

It is important to have a variety of tests that you can use with athletes and the general public. These tests should include the following:

- Sit-and-reach test (flexibility)
- 1-repetition maximum (strength)
- Grip-strength dynamometer (strength)
- Multi-stage fitness test (aerobic endurance)
- 1.5 mile run (aerobic endurance)
- 40 m sprint (speed)
- Vertical jump (power)
- 1-minute sit-ups (muscular endurance)
- 1-minute press-up test (muscular endurance)
- Skin-fold test (body composition)
- Bioelectrical impedance (skin fold).

While you are able to use all these tests, it is vital that you ask yourself which tests are appropriate for each athlete. Rather than doing all the tests, select the appropriate ones.

Informed Consent

An informed consent form makes the athlete aware of what is involved in the exercise testing and any risks there may be. Once they become aware they can then give their agreement or consent to undertake the tests and the risks that are involved.

Validity and Reliability

These two terms must be considered before a test is conducted. The two questions you must ask yourself are:

1. Does this test actually test what I say it tests?

2. If this test were to be repeated, would I get the same results?

The first question tests validity. For example, a speed test using a shuttle run may actually test an athlete's ability to turn; this is agility rather than speed. The second question tests reliability: the conditions of the test must always be identical, and then it is likely that the same results will be produced. However, there are many factors that may change, such as the temperature of the environment, the physical state of the athlete, the technique of the tester. All these may alter the results.

Test Protocols

When testing for fitness it is important to follow the correct protocols. We look here at the protocols for the following fitness tests:

- Body mass index
- Skin folds
- Bioelectrical impedance
- Sit and reach
- Vertical jump
- T-test
- Grip strength dynamometer
- 40 m sprint
- 1-minute sit-up test
- Multistage fitness test or 1.5 mile run.

Body Composition

Fat mass	Lean body weights
Fat (adipose tissue)	Muscle
	Water
	Bone
	Organs
	Connective tissue

In very simple terms, a person's body weight or mass can be split into two types: fat mass and lean body weight (all that is not fat) (see Table 1.1).

From Table 1.1 we can show that you can lose weight by reducing any of the components of the body. However, lean body weight can be seen as 'healthy' weight as it contributes to the performance of the body; fat weight in excess is 'unhealthy' weight, as it can cause a loss in performance because it requires oxygen without giving anything back to the body.

It is necessary to measure body fat to show that the weight loss is fat and not muscle.

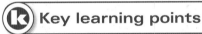 **Key learning points**

It is impossible to turn muscle into fat or fat into muscle. This is because they are completely different types of tissue in the body. A good training programme will produce a loss of fat or excess fat and a gain in muscle tissue. So while it may look like one is turning into the other, it is not true. This particularly will happen when an athlete does weight training. There is a range of tests available to estimate a person's body composition. The ones we look at here are: BMI, skin-fold assessment and bioelectrical impedance.

Body Mass Index (BMI)

This is worked out by using the following formula:

$$\text{Body mass index (BMI)} = \frac{\text{Weight (in kg)}}{\text{Height in m x height in m}}$$

For example, a male who is 75 kg and 1.80 m tall

$$\frac{75}{1.80 \times 1.80} = \frac{75}{3.24} = 23.1$$

Their body mass index will be 23.1 kg/m^2.

(*Source*: Baechle and Earle, 2008)

Results

Classification of overweight and obesity	Obesity class	BMI (kg/m^2)
Underweight		<18.5
Normal		18.5–24.9
Overweight		25–29.9
Obesity	I	30–34.9
Obesity	II	35–39.9
Extreme obesity	III	>40

(*Source*: Baechle and Earle, 2008)

The body mass index has serious limitations because it does not actually measure body composition. It can be used as a quick measure to see if a person is over fat. However, it is inaccurate because it does not make a difference between muscle and fat. Thus, someone with a lot of muscle may come out as fat! (The test does not apply to elderly populations, pregnant women or very muscular athletes.)

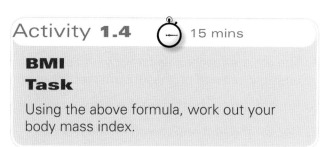

Activity **1.4**   🕐 15 mins

BMI
Task

Using the above formula, work out your body mass index.

Skin-fold Assessment

This test is done using skin-fold callipers. It is done using the Durnin and Wormsley sites, which are as follows:

Area	Description of site
Triceps	This is taken halfway between the shoulder and elbow on the back of the arm. It is a vertical pinch.
Biceps	This is taken 1 cm above the site for the triceps on the front of the arm. It is a vertical pinch.
Subscapular	This is taken 2 cm below the lowest point of the shoulder blade. It is taken at a 45-degree angle.
Suprailiac	This is taken just above the iliac crest (hip bone) directly below the front of the shoulder. It is a horizontal pinch.

The test protocol is as follows:

1. Take the measurements on the left.

2. Mark up the client accurately.

3. Pinch the skin 1 cm above the marked site.

4. Pull the fat away from the muscle.

5. Place the callipers halfway between the top and bottom of the skin fold.

6. Allow the callipers to settle for 1–2 seconds.

7. Take the reading and wait 15 seconds before repeating for accuracy.

8. Add up the total of the four measurements.

9. Calculate body-fat percentage using the following table.

Male Sum of skin folds	Male Body fat %	Female Sum of skin folds	Female Body fat %
		14	9.4
		16	11.2
		18	12.7
20	8.1	20	14.1
22	9.2	22	15.4
24	10.2	24	16.5
26	11.2	26	17.6
28	12.1	28	18.6
30	12.9	30	19.5
35	14.7	35	21.6
40	16.3	40	23.4
45	17.7	45	25.0
50	19.0	50	26.5
55	20.2	55	27.8
60	21.2	60	29.1
65	22.2	65	30.2
70	23.2	70	31.2
75	24.0	75	32.2
80	24.8	80	33.1
85	25.6	85	34.0
90	26.3	90	34.8
95	27.0	95	35.6
100	27.6	100	36.3
110	28.8	110	37.7
120	29.9	120	39.0
130	31.0	130	40.2
140	31.9	140	41.3
150	32.8	150	42.3
160	33.6	160	43.2
170	34.4	170	44.6
180	35.2	180	45.0

Results

Using the following table you can categorise your body-fat percentage.

Classification (% body fat)	Males (% body fat)	Females (% body fat)
Under fat	<6%	<14%
Athletes	6–13%	14–20%
Fitness	14–17%	21–24%
Acceptable	18–25%	25–30%
Overweight	26–30%	31–40%
Obese	>30%	>40%

(*Source*: Franklin, 2000)

Bioelectrical Impedance

This technique involves placing electrodes on one hand and one foot and then passing a very small electrical current through the body. The theory is that muscle will conduct the electricity while fat will resist the path of the electricity. Therefore, the more electricity that comes out of the body, the more muscle a person has; also, the less electricity that comes out, then the more fat they have.

This technique has benefits over skin-fold measurements because it is easier to do and the client does not have to remove or adjust any clothing. However, it has been shown to be a less accurate measure of body-fat percentage.

Flexibility

Each flexibility test is specific to a particular movement or joints; therefore there is no one set test to determine a person's flexibility. We look here at the sit-and-reach test.

Sit-and-reach Test

This test measures the flexibility of the muscles in the lower back and hamstrings. This test is

safe to perform unless the athlete has a lower back injury, particularly a slipped disc. The test is performed in the following way:

1. Warm up the athlete with 5 minutes' jogging or cycling.

2. Ask the athlete to take off their shoes and any clothing that will limit movement.

3. The athlete sits with their legs straight and their feet against the board. Their legs and back should be straight.

4. The athlete reaches as far forward as they possibly can and pushes the marker forward.

5. Record the furthest point the marker reaches.

6. Repeat the test and record the best score.

Results

Category	Men (cm)	Women (cm)
Elite	>27	>30
Excellent	17 to 27	21 to 30
Good	6 to 16	11 to 20
Average	0 to 5	1 to 10
Fair	–8 to –1	–7 to 0
Poor	–9 to –19	–8 to –14
Very poor	<–20	<–15

(*Source*: Adapted from Baechle and Earle, 2008)

Power

Power is the production of strength at speed and can be seen when we throw an object or perform a sprint start. We look here at the vertical jump test.

Vertical Jump

This is a test of power, with the aim being to see how high the athlete can jump. It is important that you find a smooth wall with a ceiling higher than the athlete can jump. A sports hall or squash court is ideal. The test is conducted in the following way:

1. The athlete rubs chalk on their fingers.

2. They stand about 15 cm away from the wall.

3. With their feet flat on the floor they reach as high as they can and make a mark on the wall.

4. The athlete then rubs more chalk on their fingers.

5. They bend their knees to 90 degrees and jump as high as they can up into the air.

6. At the top of their jump they make a second chalk mark with their fingertips.

7. The trainer measures the difference between their two marks; this is their standing-jump score.

8. This test is best done three times so the athlete can take the best of their three jumps.

Results

Rating	Men (cm)	Women (cm)
Excellent	>70	>60
Very good	61–70	51–60
Above average	51–60	41–50
Average	41–50	31–40
Below average	31–40	21–30
Poor	21–30	11–20
Very poor	<21	<10

(*Source*: Adapted from Chu, 1996)

Strength

Strength tests involve working against a resistance. We look here at the grip-strength dynamometer test.

Grip-strength Dynamometer

This is a static test to assess muscular strength in the arm muscles. Unfortunately, it gives no indication of the strength of other muscle groups. The test involves squeezing a hand-grip dynamometer as hard as possible. The test is conducted in the following way:

1. Adjust the handle to fit the size of your hand.

2. Hold the dynamometer in your stronger hand and keep the arm hanging by your side with the dynamometer by your thigh.

3. Squeeze the dynamometer as hard as you can for around 5 seconds.

4. Record the results and repeat after about a minute.

5. Take your best result.

Results

Rating	Men (cm)	Women (cm)
Excellent	>64	>38
Very good	56–64	34–38
Above average	52–56	30–34
Average	48–52	26–30
Below average	44–48	22–26
Poor	40–44	20–22
Very poor	<40	<20

(*Source*: Baechle and Earle, 2008)

Speed

Speed is how quickly the body or individual limbs can move. We look here at a simple sprint test.

40 m Sprint

This is a test for pure speed and you will need a flat running surface and a tape measure to ensure the distance is correct. You also require a stopwatch and a person who can time the run. The test is conducted in the following way:

1. The athlete warms up for several minutes.

2. They then do the 40 m run at a speed of less than their maximum.

3. The athlete starts the test behind the line with one or two hands on the ground.

4. The starter shouts 'go' and the athlete sprints the 40 m as quickly as possible.

5. This run should be repeated after 2 or 3 minutes and the average of the two runs taken.

Results

Category	Men	Women
Elite	<4.6s	<5.5
Excellent	4.6–4.7	5.5–5.7
Good	4.8–5.0	5.8–6.3
Average	5.1–5.5	6.4–6.7
Below average	5.61+	6.71+

(*Source*: Baechle and Earle, 2008)

Muscular Endurance

Muscular endurance is how well the muscles can produce repeated contractions. We look here at the 1-minute sit-up test.

1-minute Sit-up Test

This is a test of muscular endurance in the abdominals, and you will need a mat and a stopwatch. The test procedure is as follows:

1. The athlete lies on the floor with their fingers on their temples and their knees bent.

2. On the command of 'go' the athlete sits up until their elbows touch their knees.

3. They return to the start position with the back of their head touching the floor. This constitutes one repetition.

4. The athlete does as many as they can in 1 minute.

Results

Age	Males			Females		
	17–19	20–29	30–39	17–19	20–29	30–39
High	49	44	39	42	36	30
Above average	44–48	39–43	34–38	32–41	27–35	22–29
Average	37–43	32–38	37–33	35–31	21–26	17–21
Below average	24–36	20–31	16–26	19–24	15–20	11–16
Low	<24	<20	<16	<19	<15	<11

(*Source*: Franklin, 2000)

Aerobic Endurance

Aerobic endurance is the ability of the muscles to exercise for a long period of time without becoming tired. We look here at the multistage fitness test.

Multistage Fitness Test

This test was developed at Loughborough University and is known as the 'bleep' test because athletes have to run between timed bleeps. The test will give you an estimation of VO_2 max, which is the measure of aerobic fitness level. You will need a pre-recorded CD that contains the instructions and timing for the test and a flat area of 20 m with a cone at either end. This test can be used with large groups, as all the athletes will run together. The procedure is as follows:

1. Mark out a length of 20 m with cones.

2. Start the CD; the athletes run when the first bleep sounds. They run the 20 m before the second bleep sounds.

3. When this bleep sounds they turn around and run back.

4. As they continue to do this, the time between the bleeps gets shorter and shorter so that they have to run faster and faster.

5. If an athlete fails to get to the other end before the bleep on three consecutive occasions, then they are out.

6. Record at what point the athlete dropped out.

7. Using the table, assess the predicted VO$_2$ max.

Results

Category	Male	Female
Extremely high	70	60
Very high	63–69	54–59
High	57–62	49–53
Above average	52–56	44–48
Average	44–51	35–43

(*Source*: Adapted from Baechle and Earle, 2008)

(k) Key learning points

- Before fitness testing, you must follow pre-test procedures to ensure the athlete is in an appropriate state for testing and that the environment is suitable.
  The athlete should:
  - Have medical clearance for any health conditions.
  - Be free of injuries.
  - Be wearing appropriate clothing.
  - Not have had a heavy meal in the three hours before the test.
  - Have had a good night's sleep.
  - Not have trained on the day and be fully recovered from previous training.
  - Have avoided stimulants such as tea, coffee or nicotine for two hours before the test.
- The following should be taken into consideration regarding the environment:
  - Heat – the area should be at room temperature (around 18 degrees Celsius (64 degrees Fahrenheit)).
  - The room should be well ventilated.
  - The room should be clean and dust free.
- Validity and reliability:
  - Does this test actually test what I say it tests? (Validity)
  - If this test were to be repeated, would I get the same results? (Reliability)
- Appropriate tests for fitness are as follows:
  - Body mass index to work out weight in relation to height and compared with normal tables.
  - Skin folds and bioelectrical impedance to work out percentage body fat and percentage lean body weight.
  - Sit-and-reach to assess flexibility of hamstrings and lower back.
  - Vertical jump to measure power.
  - T-test to assess speed, power and agility.
  - Grip-strength dynamometer to measure pure strength.
  - 40 m sprint to assess sprinting speed.
  - 1-minute sit-up test to assess local muscular endurance in the abdominal muscles.
  - Multistage fitness test or 1.5 mile run to determine aerobic fitness.

Activity 1.5 60 mins

Record of test scores

Task

Part 1

Using a sport of your choice, fill in the following table to present your own fitness test scores and then compare them against the score needed to achieve excellence. The following example is a score for an 800 m female swimmer.

Test completed	Score achieved	Category of score	Score needed to achieve excellence
E.g. Multistage fitness test	49.3 ml/O^2/kg/min	High	60 ml/O^2/kg/min

Part 2

Explain your test results and what you see as being your strengths and weaknesses.

Part 3

Evaluate your results by saying why you achieved the scores that you did – was it down to your training, natural level of fitness or how well or badly you did the test? How can you improve your test scores to get closer to the scores needed for excellence in your sport?

Quick Quiz 15 mins ?

1. **Give four pre-test procedures.**
2. **Give three conditions that need to be referred to the doctor for clearance.**
3. **What are validity and reliability?**

1.5 The Effect of Psychological Factors on Sports Training and Sporting Performance

How a sports person thinks and feels before, during and after an event can have a big impact on their performance.

The Impact of Motivation on Sports Performance

Definition

Motivation the stimulus for a sports person to continue training and competing in their chosen sport.

There are two main types of motivation:

- Intrinsic
- Extrinsic.

Intrinsic Motivation

Behaviour which is intrinsically motivated has the following features:

● Behaviour is chosen for the pleasure of participating.

● Behaviour provides its own satisfaction.

● There is no reward outside participating in the activity.

Extrinsic Motivation

Behaviour that is extrinsically motivated has the following features:

● Behaviour where the goal of participation is outside the activity.

● Behaviour in the activity is a means to an end rather than for the pleasure of being involved – this can be in the form of rewards such as a trophy, money or praise.

● Success is needed to ensure maximum results.

Ⓚ Key learning points

● Extrinsic motivation comes from sources outside the activity and could include financial rewards or physical rewards such as medals or trophies.

● Intrinsic motivation comes from within, and behaviour that is intrinsically motivated provides its own satisfaction as reward.

Arousal and Anxiety

Arousal and anxiety are terms related to stress. Arousal is seen as being a positive aspect of stress and shows how motivated we are by a situation. The more aroused we are, the more interested and excited we are by a situation. Anxiety can be seen as a negative aspect of stress, and it may accompany high levels of arousal. It is not pleasant to be anxious and to experience feelings of nervousness and worry.

Again, the stress and anxiety responses are unique to each individual. Arousal levels will have an influence on performance. In some cases as arousal levels increase, performance will also increase (Drive theory) – this can be seen mainly in strength-related sports such as weightlifting. However, sports such as snooker or archery that require a lot of concentration and precision can be negatively affected by high levels of arousal.

The inverted-U hypothesis suggests that arousal does improve performance, but only up to a point, and once arousal goes beyond this point performance starts to decline (see Figure 1.3).

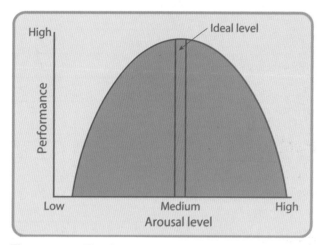

Figure 1.3   The inverted U-hypothesis

This theory's main point is that there is an optimum level of arousal before performance starts to diminish.

Personality and Sport

Personality is how we present ourselves to the outside world. Each person is unique in this respect and while we compare ourselves to others, we are not really like anyone else. However, although we are all different, we can still place people in certain categories that will give us an indication of how they may react in certain situations.

The most basic approach looks at whether we are a type A or type B personality. You can work out your personality type by completing the following questionnaire.

Are You a Type A or Type B Personality?

Instructions: Give yourself a score between 1 and 7 to show which of the two statements applies to you best.

Statement	Score	Statement
Don't mind leaving things temporarily unfinished	1 2 3 4 5 6 7	Must get things finished once started
Calm and unhurried about appointments	1 2 3 4 5 6 7	Often late for appointments
Not competitive	1 2 3 4 5 6 7	Highly competitive
Listen well, let others finish speaking first	1 2 3 4 5 6 7	Anticipate others in conversation, interrupt by finishing their sentences
Never in a hurry, even when pressured	1 2 3 4 5 6 7	Always in a hurry
Able to wait calmly	1 2 3 4 5 6 7	Uneasy when waiting
Easy going	1 2 3 4 5 6 7	Always going at full speed
Take one thing at a time	1 2 3 4 5 6 7	Always trying to do more than one thing at once
Slow and deliberate in speech	1 2 3 4 5 6 7	Speak fast and forcefully using a lot of gestures
Concerned with satisfying yourself and not others	1 2 3 4 5 6 7	Want to get recognition from others for doing things well
Slow at doing things	1 2 3 4 5 6 7	Fast at doing things
Relaxed	1 2 3 4 5 6 7	Always active
Express feelings openly	1 2 3 4 5 6 7	Keep feelings to yourself
Have a large number of interests	1 2 3 4 5 6 7	Only have a few interests
Satisfied with life	1 2 3 4 5 6 7	Always want more from life
Never set own deadlines	1 2 3 4 5 6 7	Always work to deadlines
Feel limited responsibility	1 2 3 4 5 6 7	Always feel responsible
Never judge things in terms of quantity, only quality	1 2 3 4 5 6 7	Quantity is more important than quality
Casual about work	1 2 3 4 5 6 7	Take work very seriously
Not very precise	1 2 3 4 5 6 7	Very precise and careful about detail

Total _____

Scoreboard

21–59 means you have a type B personality. You are relaxed and contented and deal well with stress. You enjoy life and are happy with what you have.

60–79 means you have a type A/B personality. You have a mixture of both personality types. This is a happy balance.

80–109 means you have a type A personality. You are a very driven person who is competitive and has to succeed. You are also likely to experience stress and changes in mood. You may have a quick temper and get angry easily.

110–140 means you are an extreme type A personality. This means you are very likely to experience stress and it may affect your health.

Another method of categorising people is to decide if they are an introvert or extrovert. An introvert is a person who is shy, quiet and inward looking; they are not so good in social situations and like to spend time on their own. Many long-distance runners have been found to have such a personality and this makes sense as they spend a lot of time training on their own. An extrovert is someone who is outgoing, likes talking and mixing with people and is good in social situations; they do not like to spend too much time on their own and are easily bored. People who take part in team sports are more likely to have an extrovert personality as these sports usually provide action and excitement.

Concentration

When playing sport it is important to focus on the correct information. This is more difficult than it sounds because there is so much happening at any point. For example, if you take a golfer playing a shot they will be presented with the following information:

- Where the hole is
- Where the hole is in relation to the green
- The lay of the land between the ball and the hole
- Any water, rough or bunkers
- Wind and rain
- The hardness or softness of the grass
- Spectators
- Opponents
- Wildlife.

They then have to make a decision about what information here is relevant and cut out all the irrelevant information to produce a good shot. Most golfers focus on avoiding a bunker or water and try so hard to not get the ball in them that it is all they can think of and they end up putting the ball in the bunker or water!

Concentration is about focusing on what is relevant in playing your sport and ignoring everything else that is irrelevant.

Key learning points

- A certain amount of arousal enhances sports performance. High levels of arousal are good in strength-related sports but have a negative impact on sports that require a significant level of concentration.
- Introverts enjoy their own company.
- Extroverts are outgoing and enjoy social situations.
- Concentration is about focusing on what is important and ignoring everything else.

Activity **1.6** 60 mins   **P6**

The effect of psychological factors on performance   **M3**

Task

Part 1

Using yourself as a case study describe how the following psychological factors affect your own performance.

Psychological factor	Description and explanation of how this affects my performance
Motivation	E.g. Sometimes I need to be motivated by a reward and other days I am motivated to succeed for my own satisfaction
Arousal	
Anxiety	
Personality	
Concentration	

  10 mins   **?**

Which of these statements are True and which are False?

1. **My intrinsic motivation means I don't need to win trophies and medals for motivation.**
2. **My extrinsic motivation means I like getting praise from my coach.**
3. **When I play golf I know that it is important to have high levels of arousal to improve my performance.**
4. **When you are concentrating it is important to think about things that are relevant and irrelevant to your performance.**

Useful websites

www.topendsports.com/testing/tests.htm
Over 100 fitness tests to try, all divided into different fitness categories.

www.teachpe.com
Extensive range of online resources that cover the major sports, their skills and techniques, coaching tips, and physiology and anatomy.

Further Reading

Dagleish, J. and Dollery, S., 2001, *The Health and Fitness Handbook*. Harlow: Pearson Education.
Sharkey, B.J. and Gaskill, S.E., 2006, *Fitness and Health*. Champaign, IL: Human Kinetics.

References

Baechle, T.R. and Earle, R.W., 2008, *Essentials of Strength Training and Conditioning*. Champaign, IL: Human Kinetics.
Chu, D., 1996, *Explosive Strength and Power: Complex training for maximum results*. Champaign, IL: Human Kinetics.
Franklin, B.A. (ed.), 2000, *ACSM's Guidelines for Exercise Testing and Prescription*, 6th Edition. Baltimore, MD: Lippincott, Williams and Wilkins.

Chapter 2
Practical Sport

The number of people participating in sport is continuously growing. There are many reasons for this including increased opportunities for sports activities and greater awareness of the health benefits associated with exercise. There are many different types of sports, and this chapter will include details on how to improve your performance in sport and how to improve your knowledge of the rules and regulations.

Sports are enjoyed and played by many across the world. Participation in sport is normally as an individual in sports such as tennis and golf or as part of a team in games such as volleyball or basketball. Individuals normally play specific roles in team sports; however, to be successful, individuals need to play together as a team.

Learning Goals

By the end of this chapter you should:

- Be able to demonstrate a range of skills, techniques and tactics in selected sports.
- Know the rules, regulations and scoring systems of selected sports.
- Know the roles and responsibilities of officials in selected sports.
- Be able to review sports performance.

To achieve a PASS grade the evidence must show that the learner is able to:	To achieve a MERIT grade the evidence must show that, in addition to the pass criteria, the learner is able to:	To achieve a DISTINCTION grade the evidence must show that, in addition to the pass and merit criteria, the learner is able to:
P1 demonstrate use of practical skills, techniques and tactics appropriate for one team sport		
P2 demonstrate use of practical skills, techniques and tactics appropriate for one individual sport	**M1** describe use of tactics appropriate for one team and one individual sport	**D1** justify use of tactics appropriate for one team and one individual sport, identifying areas for improvement
P3 describe the rules, regulations and scoring systems for one team sport		
P4 describe the rules, regulations and scoring systems for one individual sport	**M2** assess, using appropriate examples, the rules, regulations and scoring systems for one team and one individual sport	
P5 describe the main roles and responsibilities of officials in one team sport		
P6 describe the main roles and responsibilities of officials in one individual sport		
P7 produce, with tutor support, an observation checklist that could be used to review the sports performance of an individual or a team	**M3** independently produce an observation checklist that could be used to review the sports performance of an individual or a team	
P8 use the observation checklist to review the sports performance of an individual or a team, identifying strengths and areas for improvement	**M4** explain the strengths and areas for improvement of an individual or a team, in one individual sport or one team sport, justifying recommendations for improvement	
P9 use the observation checklist to review own sports performance in an individual sport or team sport, identifying strengths and areas for improvement	**M5** explain own strengths and areas for improvement in an individual sport or team sport, providing recommendations for improvement	**D2** analyse own strengths and areas for improvement in an individual sport or team sport, justifying recommendations for improvement

2.1 Different Types of Sports

There are many different types of sports and most can be classified as team or individual sports:

1. **Team sports**

   Invasion sports – these are games such as football, netball, basketball and rugby where the object of the sport is to invade the opponent's territory.

   Court sports – these are non-contact because opponents are normally on opposite sides of a net, for example badminton, volleyball and tennis.

   Striking/fielding sports – games that have a batting and a fielding team. These include cricket, baseball and rounders.

   Water sports – water sports are activities that are undertaken on or within water, including swimming, sailing and water polo.

2. **Individual sports**

   Court sports – essentially non-contact because opponents are normally on opposite sides of a net, for example squash and singles tennis.

   Target sports – target sports involve the use of marksmanship and include sports such as golf and archery.

   Martial arts – martial arts come from different ancient fighting methods. Many of these originate from the Far East, such as judo, taekwondo and karate.

   Water sports – water sports are activities that are undertaken on or within water, including swimming, sailing and water polo.

   Field sports – hunting sports associated with the outdoors, for example shooting and fishing.

Most sports involve elements of attack, as you go in search of winning points or scores. At the same time you are defending and trying to stop your opponents from scoring. Other sports require the competitors to produce a movement or series of movements. These include gymnastics, figure skating and diving, where performance is judged on aesthetics and difficulty.

In addition to this, there are sports that are just a competition of who is the fastest. These include some athletics events, swimming and cycling. Other athletics events are judged on who can throw the furthest or on who can jump the highest or furthest.

> Definition
>
> **Aesthetics refers to how pleasing something is to look at.**

2.2 Skill, Techniques and Tactics

> Definition
>
> **Skill the ability to do an activity well, because it has been practised.**

All sports are made up of a range of specific skills. For example, in badminton there are a number of different shots that you can play at different times during a game. Playing these effectively will allow you to win points. These include:

- The **drop shot** – a shot that just falls gently over your opponent's side of the net.

- The **overhead clear** – a defensive shot that is used to move your opponent around the court and allow you time to move around the court.

- The **smash** – a powerful shot played down into the ground in your opponent's half of the court.

> Definition
>
> **Technique a way of undertaking a particular skill.**

If a badminton player is able to play the smash shot well, then it is said that they have a good technique in playing the shot.

There are many shared skills in different team sports, and having the awareness and ability to undertake them will be an advantage to your team. These include:

- **Passing** – moving the ball from one teammate to another.
- **Receiving** – being able to receive a pass from a teammate.
- **Shooting** – aiming at a specific target such as a goal or a basket.
- **Dribbling** – moving around in close contact with the ball.
- **Throwing** – there are many ways of throwing an object; these are normally specific to the sport being played.
- **Intercepting** – this is where a player stops the ball from reaching its intended place. This could be through a block or a tackle.
- **Creating space** – this means moving away from opponents so that you are in a position in which you can receive a pass or create a shooting opportunity.

Tactics in Sport

In addition to the skills and techniques, it is important to have a good understanding of different tactics when playing sport.

Definition   ⓓ

Tactics methods used to improve performance and gain an advantage over your opponent.

Tactics are used to gain an advantage over your opponent and can include a number of specific factors, for example if you are a badminton player who has a good smash shot, you may look at playing certain shots that will help create the opportunity to play the smash.

Tactics can include playing precise formations against specific opponents. Football teams may play more defensively away from home and opt to play with more defending players rather than strikers. In certain sports opposing players may be marked so as to stop them having a positive effect for their team. Other tactics may include working on specific set plays such as line-outs in rugby and corners and free kicks in football.

Recording Evidence of Your Performance

In order to improve your performance, it is a good idea to watch yourself perform the skills. Have a friend or a coach video you using a camcorder while you perform a set skill. You can then analyse your performance and see what you are doing; you may be surprised and realise your body is not actually doing what you think it is doing! You will then need to amend the skill, practise it and video yourself again in order to check that you are now performing the skill properly.

The use of video is only one way to record evidence of how you are performing; you could also use:

- a logbook
- a diary
- witness testimony
- feedback sheets.

ⓚ **Key learning points**

- Skill – the ability to do an activity well, because it has been practised.
- Technique – a way of undertaking a particular skill.
- Tactics – methods used to help you perform better and gain an advantage over your opponent.

Activity 2.1 3 hours

P1   P2   M1   D1

Logging your practical sessions

To achieve P1 and P2 you need to be involved in practical sessions for one individual sport and one team sport. The sessions will be led by your tutor or a qualified instructor. You need to be actively involved and in the development of your skills, techniques and tactics and keep a diary of your involvement.

Task

Part 1

Before recording your involvement in sessions you need to break down the sports into their skills/techniques and tactics. Then you can record which skills/techniques and tactics that you demonstrated in each session. You can use tables such as the ones shown below and they can form the basis of your logbook or diary.

You will need two logs – one for your individual sport and one for your team sport.

Part 2

To achieve M1 you need to describe the tactics that were used.

Part 3

To achieve D1 you need to justify why these tactics were chosen and why other tactics were not used. You may talk about your strengths or the strengths and weaknesses of your opposition.

Skill/ Technique	Session 1: (Date)	Session 2:	Session 3:	Session 4:	Session 5:	Session 6:
E.g. Passing						
Receiving						
Shooting						
Dribbling						
Striking						
Throwing						
Tackling						

Table 2.2 Log of tactics used

Tactics	Session 1: (Date)	Session 2:	Session 3:	Session 4:	Session 5:	Session 6:
E.g. Defensive plays						
Offensive plays						
Set plays						
Formations						
Marking						
Communications						
Tackling						

2.3 Rules, Regulations and Scoring Systems

P3 P4 M2

Rules

The rules are a set of agreed standards that are laid down to standardise how a sport is played. The rules of a sport are normally set and amended by its national governing body (NGB) and international sports federation (ISF). These are set to ensure that the sport is played fairly and that the opponents are aware of how to win. Different governing bodies may call these rules by a different name; for example in cricket and football they are known as the 'laws'.

International sports federations and national governing bodies may change the rules and regulations periodically as they look to improve the sport. For example, the Fédération Internationale de Football Association (FIFA) recently changed the offside law to encourage more attacking football. The English Football Association (national governing body for football) ensured that both referees and the teams playing in this country understood the change.

CASE STUDY

Laws of football

Football rules are known as the 'Laws of the Game'. There are 17 laws in football, which have changed marginally over the years. The international sports federation (FIFA) adapts them as it thinks necessary. Recent examples of this include changing the offside law to encourage more attacking football. The following is a summary of the 17 laws:

1. The field of play – this law looks at the surface, dimensions, layout and markings of the football pitch.
2. The ball – the shape and dimensions of the football are covered, as well as replacing the ball should it burst during a match.
3. The number of players – there should be eleven players at the start of a match, including a designated goalkeeper; the use of substitutions is also covered.
4. The players' equipment – first the health and safety considerations of what players wear is considered. No jewellery should be worn and all players must wear shin pads.

The goalkeeper must also wear a top that distinguishes him from the other players.

5. The referee – this law looks at the responsibilities of the referee, which include enforcing the laws, taking responsibility for the safety of the players, acting as a timekeeper, punishing serious offences and providing a match report to the relevant authority.
6. The assistant referees – assistant referees assist the referee to control the game. They will signal when the ball goes out of play and signal for any offences that the referee may miss.
7. Duration of the match – a football match is played over two equal periods of 45 minutes. This time may be reduced for youth football. Time can be added for substitutions, injuries and time-wasting at the referee's discretion.
8. The start and restart of play – the team that wins the toss of a coin can choose which goal they want to attack. The game starts with a kick-off, where all players must be in their own half of the pitch; this method is also used after a goal has been scored.
9. The ball in and out of play – the ball is out of play when the whole ball crosses one of the perimeter lines or when the referee blows his whistle to stop play.
10. The method of scoring – the rule states that a goal is scored when the ball crosses the line between the posts and

under the cross bar. The team with the most goals wins.

11. Offside – a player is offside if 'he is nearer to his opponent's goal line than both the ball and the second-last opponent' and receives a pass from one of their teammates. The player also needs to be in his opponent's half and interfering with the game. However, he cannot be offside if he receives the pass from a goal kick or throw-on.

12. Fouls and misconduct – fouls and misconduct are penalised by either a direct or indirect free kick. There are ten offences that result in a direct free kick, including kicking, tripping or pushing an opponent. Indirect free kicks are given for infringements such as a goalkeeper picking up a back pass or throw-on or for impeding an opponent. Direct free kick offences that are committed by a player in their own penalty box are awarded as a penalty kick.

13. Free kicks – following a foul, a free kick is awarded, which will be either direct or indirect. Opponents must be a minimum of ten yards away from the ball. A direct free kick shot directly into the opponent's goal will be awarded a goal, while a goal can only be scored from an indirect free kick if it has touched another player before going into the goal. A referee will signal an indirect free kick by raising one arm into the air above his head.

14. The penalty kick – awarded when an offence is committed by a player in his or her own penalty area. The goalkeeper must remain on his line until the ball has been kicked. A penalty taker cannot touch the ball until it has touched another player if his kick misses.

15. The throw in – the ball is thrown back onto the pitch when it goes out of play on either side of the pitch. A throw-on is taken with two hands on the ball, and the ball must be released from behind the player's head.

16. The goal kick – the ball is kicked back into play from within the goal area when the ball crosses the goal line and was last touched by an attacking player. The ball must leave the penalty area before it can be played again.

17. The corner kick – a corner is awarded when the ball crosses the goal line and was last touched by a defending player. The kick is taken from within the corner arc. A goal can be scored direct from a corner kick.

The Football Association (FA) has also set a number of regulations to help the running of football in England. Regulations are rules controlled by the organising bodies. The FA has included regulations on the following:

● The control of youth football

● The doping control programme

● Disciplinary procedures.

Regulations

Regulations relate to specific aspects of the laws or rules, such as the number of players and the accepted playing surfaces. Guidelines for timing, scoring, facilities and equipment are examples of regulations.

Time

Many team sports have time constraints, and are split into periods of play. The team with the most points or goals is declared the winner, while if the scores are tied then the game is normally declared a draw. Time can be stopped for minor stoppages such as injuries or the ball being out of play. In basketball the clock is stopped every time the ball is out. Some sports may have periods of extra time to declare a winner. In some sports a winner can be declared before the allocated time has elapsed. For example, in test match cricket, a team may have bowled out the opposing team twice and scored the required number of runs before the five days are over. Time has a major effect on sports even if the sport does not have time constraints.

The longer a game goes on, the more tired the players will become. This can be a problem as players are usually trained to withstand the usual game time constraint.

Scoring

Each sport has a different scoring system, with the team or individual with the most points usually being declared the winner. An exception to this is golf, where the player who has had the least number of strokes is the winner. Scoring may include putting the ball into a goal in football and handball or downing the ball in rugby or downing a shuttlecock into your opponent's court in badminton.

Many sports give a different number of points for certain scoring actions. In rugby there are different methods of scoring and different points are given for tries, drop goals and conversions. In basketball successfully shooting outside the 3-point arc will give you an extra point compared to scoring a lay-up. In cricket a batsman can score anywhere between one and six runs off a single ball.

Facilities and equipment

Specific sports require certain facilities to enable play to take place. Different surfaces can be used for different sports and often sports are played on a range of surfaces. Tennis is a good example of this as it can be played on grass, clay and hard surfaces and can be played inside or outdoors. Occasionally rules may be adapted for sports played on different surfaces.

Many sports require the participants to wear or use specialist equipment. In football the laws of the game insist that all players must wear shin guards to protect their lower legs. In sports such as hockey, rugby and cricket, players may wear specific equipment to reduce the risk of injury. This could include arm guards, helmets and padding.

You can find the rules and regulations of each sport via its national governing body. The national governing body looks after many aspects of a sport including organising major competitions, running coaching schemes and dealing with the development of the sport at all levels.

 Key learning points

- Rules – a list of set instructions that must be followed.
- Regulations – an official rule or taking control of something.
- National governing body – the organisation responsible for a sport in England. For example, the FA is responsible for football in England.
- International sports federation – the organisation responsible for a sport globally. For example, FIFA is responsible for world football.

Activity **2.2** 90 mins   P3

Rules of sport   P4

Tasks

M2

Part 1

Choose one individual and one team sport and then find the rules/laws for each activity. Produce a document aimed at a beginner that summarises the rules/laws so that are able to play the chosen sports.

Part 2

Choose the key rules/laws from your individual and team sports and present examples of these key rules to show the beginner how they are used in practice by the participants and officials.

2.4 The Roles and Responsibilities of Officials in Sport P5 P6

The role of the official in sport is to ensure that the participants adhere to the set rules, and that fair play is present. Other additional responsibilities include timekeeping, starting play and scoring.

Officials may be known by different names in certain sports, such as referee, umpire or judge, but they all play similar roles in their individual sports. Sometimes officials are supported by additional assistants, each with designated responsibilities. Examples of this include line judges in tennis and timekeepers in basketball.

The official's decision is final in all sports and players who fail to adhere to the rules may have disciplinary action taken against them. This may include being sent off or being put in a sin bin for a period of time.

Officials will have a good understanding of their sport and will have undergone training to allow them to become a qualified official. Certain sports require the officials to have good fitness levels so they can move around the area of play. Premiership referees have to reach certain levels of fitness due to the demands of the sport and must retire from the league at the age of 48.

The health and safety of the participants are also the responsibility of the official, who will need to check the equipment, surface and facilities prior to starting the game and ensure that the participants do not endanger each other.

Technology is being used more to assist officials with their decision making and ensure that these decisions are correct. Video referees are used in rugby to decide on whether a try has been scored. A third umpire will assist with closed decisions in cricket, such as run outs and whether a ball has cleared the boundary. Other technological advances include the use of headsets so that officials can communicate effectively with each other. Officials require very good communication skills as their role often involves dealing with heated performers who may not agree with their decisions. Many other sports are now contemplating the use of technology to enhance the sport and ensure more consistency with decisions.

Officials use a variety of methods to communicate with the performers. Whistles are used to alert the players of decisions, and assistant officials in football and rugby use flags to alert the main official of an infringement. Hand signals are also used in many sports to highlight a decision to the players.

Activity **2.3** 🕒 30 mins P5 P6

Roles and responsibilities of officials

Task

Research the roles and responsibilities of the official/s in one individual and one team sport of your choice by using the following grids.

Chosen sport: Football

Roles of Officials	Description of each role	Responsibilities
Referee		
Assistant referee		
Fourth official		

2.5 Reviewing Sports Performance

Reviewing sports performance is a vital skill to develop if you are going to be able to improve your performance or help others to improve theirs. When you consider the process of review you need to think why you are doing it. The following are some of the reasons you may have for reviewing performance:

- to review their current level of competence;
- to review specific aspects of their performance;
- to identify what they are doing well;
- to identify what they are doing badly.

A good review will take an activity and break it down into its smaller parts. You could divide a sport into four categories:

- Sport specific skills
- Sport specific fitness
- Tactical skills
- Psychological skills.

Rachel has reviewed her own performance here in a general way. She could also rate these factors for each match that she plays and also she could get her coach to rate these factors as well. It would be interesting to see if they agreed or differed!

An analysis could cover more ground than the four categories explained earlier. It could include areas such as:

- Respect of the rules and regulations
- Knowledge of the sport
- Appreciation of health and safety issues.

This way of reviewing performance is slightly limited because it does not tell us exactly what is good about something or what needs to be improved – a comprehensive review would need more detail. For example, with Rachel the tennis player, we would want to know more about what she thinks is good about her forehand shots.

Feedback from Others

When you are conducting a review of yourself or another performer you can include the views of other significant people in your review. Significant people could include some of the following people:

- The coach
- Team mates
- Other participants
- Peers
- Other observers.

CASE STUDY

Rachel is a county standard tennis player and she has been asked to decide what are the ten most important factors for a successful performance in her sport. She has been asked to rate their importance from 1 to 10.

where 1 is the most important and 10 is the least important. Once she has done that she will rate herself from 1 to 10 where 1 is very poor and 10 is excellent. This is what she came up with.

Rating of importance	Factor	Score out of 10
1	Serving	6
2	Stamina	8
3	Returning the serve	7
4	Forehand shots	8
5	Power	3
6	Mental toughness	5
7	Reading the opponent	8
8	Backhand shots	5
9	Controlling anxiety	2
10	Choosing correct shots	4

Identifying Strengths and Areas for Improvement P7 P8 M4 M5

By using your checklist and gaining the views of other people you can now analyse the information that you have gathered. You can pick out the most important information and divide them up into:

● Areas of strength

● Areas for improvement.

A good sports coach will not only be able to analyse the sports player's performance but should be able to prescribe methods that can help improve areas of weakness.

Depending on the weakness, a coach will use different methods to improve a team or individual's performance.

If the problem is linked to a player's inability to undertake a skill, the coach may give demonstrations and guidance to help the player improve. If a team is not performing tactics correctly, then a coach may create drills to recreate them and help the players improve.

Sometimes a performer's fitness may be the cause of their weakness. If this is the case the coach should look to incorporate specific training methods into practice sessions or write training programmes for players to follow. A player may need to work on fitness areas such as strength, flexibility or cardiovascular endurance.

Once the review has taken place then short term and long-term goals can be set to address the areas where improvement is needed. Again these goals could be divided up into specific areas, such as skills, tactics, physical fitness or psychological skills.

Activity **2.4** 90 mins   P7 P8 **P9** M3 M4 M5 D2

Preparing to review performance

Task

Part 1

Prepare an observation checklist for a sport of your choice to include aspects of:

- Sport specific skills
- Sport specific fitness
- Tactical skills
- Psychological skills.

Also, give yourself space to write comment about each of the factors. You could use the following table.

To achieve M3 this needs to be done without the help of your tutor.

Part 2

To achieve P8 and M4 you need to use your checklist to review the performance of an individual and a team.

Part 3

To achieve P9, M5, D2 you need to use the checklist to analyse your own performance in an individual and a team sport and provide recommendations for how you can improve your performance. To achieve a distinction you need to justify how these recommendations will improve your performance/s.

Factor	Score out of 10	Explain strengths	Explain weaknesses

Useful websites

www.1st4sport.co.uk

A one-stop shop for sports coaches, training and physical education books and resources.

www.sportsofficialsuk.com

Provides a gallery of officiating images from football, American football, netball and Rugby Union, as well as offering general articles to support those officiating sporting events.

www.uksport.gov.uk

A good source of wide-ranging topics that affect UK sport, such as drugs testing, performance and the Olympic Games.

Chapter 3
Practical Outdoor & Adventurous Activities

Outdoor and adventurous activities are becoming more and more popular and part of their appeal is because of the element of danger and potential risks that they involve. This increase in demand has been met by the development of many new outdoor activity centres. There is also a large increase in the number of organisations promoting outdoor and adventurous activities.

Learning Goals

By the end of this chapter you should:

- Know the organisation and provision of outdoor and adventurous activities.
- Know health and safety considerations and environmental impacts associated with participation in outdoor and adventurous activities.
- Be able to demonstrate techniques and skills associated with selected outdoor and adventurous activities.
- Be able to review performance in outdoor and adventurous activities.

To achieve a PASS grade the evidence must show that the learner is able to:	To achieve a MERIT grade the evidence must show that, in addition to the pass criteria, the learner is able to:	To achieve a DISTINCTION grade the evidence must show that, in addition to the pass and merit criteria, the learner is able to:
P1 describe the organisation and provision of two outdoor and adventurous activities	**M1** compare the organisation and provision of two outdoor and adventurous activities	
P2 describe the health and safety considerations associated with participation in two outdoor and adventurous activities	**M2** explain health and safety considerations associated with participation in two outdoor and adventurous activities, identifying precautions and actions that can be taken, or used, in relation to them	**D1** explain precautions and actions that can be taken, or used, in relation to health and safety considerations associated with participation in two outdoor and adventurous activities
P3 produce a risk assessment for a selected outdoor and adventurous activity		
P4 describe environmental impacts associated with participation in two outdoor and adventurous activities	**M3** explain the environmental impacts associated with participation in two outdoor and adventurous activities, identifying precautions and actions that can be taken, or used, to reduce them	**D2** explain precautions and actions that can be taken, or used, to reduce the environmental impacts associated with participation in two outdoor and adventurous activities
P5 demonstrate techniques and skills appropriate to two outdoor and adventurous activities	**M4** review and justify choice of techniques demonstrated in outdoor and adventurous activities	
P6 review the performance of another individual participating in two outdoor and adventurous activities, identifying strengths and areas for improvement		
P7 carry out a review of own performance in outdoor and adventurous activities, identifying strengths and areas for improvement	**M5** explain identified strengths and areas for improvement in own performance in outdoor and adventurous activities, making recommendations for further development of identified areas for improvement	**D3** justify recommendations relating to identified areas for improvement in own performance in outdoor and adventurous activities

3.1 Organisation and Provision of Outdoor and Adventurous Activities [P1] [M1]

There are many providers of outdoor and adventurous activities in the UK. Most activities have their own governing bodies that are responsible for the activity in Great Britain.

General Provision

The Countryside Agency

There are many organisations in England, like the Countryside Agency and the National Park Authorities, which encourage people to enjoy the outdoors for leisure, sport or relaxation. They work alongside others like the Ramblers Association, the British Mountaineering Council and Sustrans to let people know where they can go and what's on offer.

There are currently 12 National Parks in England and Wales. These include: the New Forest, Snowdonia, the Brecon Beacons, Dartmoor, Exmoor, the Peak District, the Lake District, the North York Moors and the Yorkshire Dales (see Figure 3.1). All of these areas provide excellent opportunities to participate in a range of outdoor and adventurous activities.

National Sports Centres

National Sports Centres also exist to provide top-level participants with the opportunity to train and prepare for competition. Holme Pierrepont in Nottingham is the National Water Sports Centre, and has a regatta lake and slalom course among its facilities. Plas y Brenin is the National Mountain Centre and is located near Snowdonia in North Wales. Its location means that it can offer some of the best places to participate in mountaineering, climbing and canoeing. It also has a climbing practice wall, ski slope and indoor canoe pool.

National Governing Bodies

Each sport is regulated by its own authority, which are known as national governing bodies (NGBs). NGBs are responsible for the provision of the rules and regulations for their respective sports. The NGBs play an important role and undertake many duties for the activity they represent: they traditionally look at aspects such as promoting the activity, liaising with other agencies and organising coaching and leadership qualifications. Many governing bodies provide job opportunities either through coaching and educating or in administration. Researching different national governing bodies' websites will allow you to find out more details on what the different organisations are responsible for.

The British Orienteering Federation

The British Orienteering Federation (BOF), situated in Matlock, Derbyshire, is the official governing body for orienteering in the UK. Formed in 1967, it is a member of the International Orienteering Federation, which is based in Helsinki, Finland. Its responsibilities include overseeing development and coordinating a range of orienteering events.

The BOF has a national badge scheme, which awards badges on the basis of performance over a series of events. It also runs five coaching awards, which specialise in teaching orienteering in a range of different environments, and cater for beginners through to experts.

The British Canoe Union

The British Canoe Union (BCU) was formed in 1936 to prepare a team for the Olympic Games in Berlin. It is now the governing body responsible for canoeing and kayaking in the UK, with a membership of over 25,000 individual and 25,000 club members. Its prime aim is to encourage and provide opportunities for people to participate in canoeing. The BCU is currently working on improving access to more rivers in England and Wales.

It is also responsible for developing policies on areas such as child protection, members' code of conduct and risk assessment.

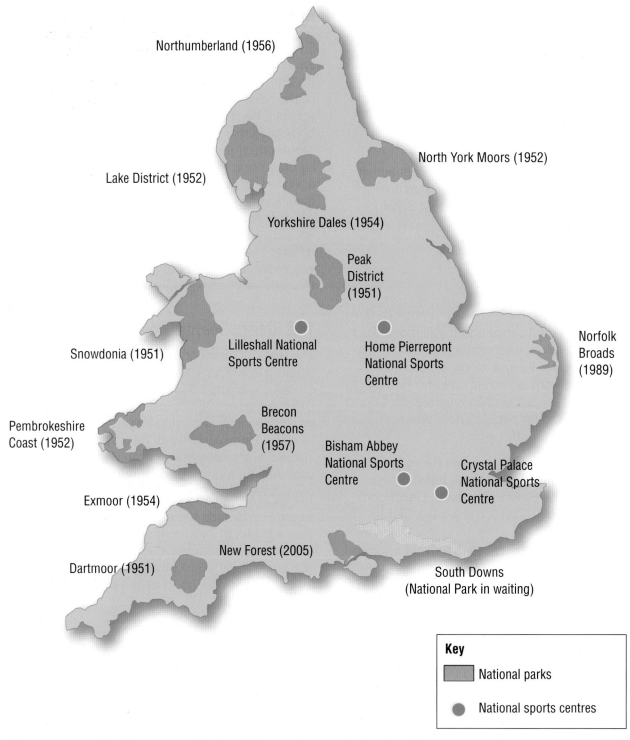

Figure 3.1 National Parks and National Sports Centres in England & Wales

The BCU operates a widespread range of coaching and education courses. These courses are designed to ensure that coaches and participants are sufficiently prepared to take part in the sport and that the coaches have the relevant qualifications to instruct participants in all aspects of technique, safety and understanding.

The Duke of Edinburgh Award

The Duke of Edinburgh Award is a programme that includes practical, cultural and adventurous activities. It is designed for males and females aged between the ages of 14 and 25 to help their social and cultural development. The Award offers many individual challenges, and encourage young people to undertake a range of new and exciting challenges and activities in their leisure time.

Where Do Outdoor Adventure Activities Take Place?

Most outdoor and adventurous activities are set in rural settings with natural resources. Examples of these include the countryside, hills, rocks or coastal areas. These natural resources provide the best facilities to enjoy participating in outdoor and adventurous activities.

Areas such as the Peak District, Snowdonia and the Lake District provide the environment to participate in many outdoor and adventurous activities. This helps attract many visitors to these areas.

Due to the increase in the number of people living in more urban areas (built-up towns and cities), there has been an increase in the number of facilities offering opportunities for urban dwellers to participate in outdoor and adventurous activities. For example, somebody who participates in rock climbing and lives in London will find it difficult to get to natural rocks regularly to practise. As technology has advanced, many man-made facilities have been created that replicate natural resources. Indoor climbing walls and man-made lakes have meant that more people gain the opportunity to participate in a bigger range of activities. An example of modern technology can be seen

where artificial ski slopes are being replaced by real-snow indoor skiing facilities, for example Xscape in Milton Keynes and Castleford. So the construction of man-made facilities has increased participation in many activities that otherwise would not be easily accessible to some people.

Key learning points

- A range of different organisations provides places for outdoor and adventurous activities to take place. These include the Countryside Agency and national sports centres.
- A national governing body is the organisation responsible for the running of an activity in this country, for example the British Canoe Union. Most activities have their own specific national governing body and provide details of where people can go to take part in their sport.

Activity 3.1 60 mins P1

Organisation and provision of outdoor and adventurous activities

M1

Think about the different types of outdoor and adventurous activities that you like to take part in. Select two of these activities and carry out the following tasks.

Task 1

Using the internet, find out who the governing bodies are for both of your selected outdoor and adventurous activities. Find out where you can take part in each of your selected activities in both your local area and further afield.

Task 2

Design a poster that shows the organisation and provision of each of your selected activities which also includes a written description of the organisation and provision for each.

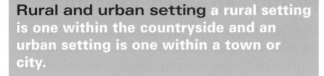

Definition

Rural and urban setting a rural setting is one within the countryside and an urban setting is one within a town or city.

Activity **3.1** continued

Task 3

Write a few paragraphs to compare the organisation and provision of each of your selected outdoor and adventurous activities, for example, is there more access for one, are there similar coaching schemes available for each?

Quick Quiz   5 mins   ?

National governing body	12	Rural	14
Holme Pierrepont	Urban	Snowdonia	Plas y Brenin

Choose a word(s) from the boxes above to answer the following questions.

1. **There is this number of National Parks in England and Wales.**
2. **You have to be this age or over to take part in the Bronze Duke of Edinburgh Award.**
3. **This is the name of a national sports centre based in Nottingham.**
4. **This is the name of a place within the countryside.**
5. **This is the name of a national sports centre in Wales.**
6. **This is the name of the organisation that represents each sport.**
7. **This is the name of a place that is situated within a town or city.**
8. **This is an example of a rural setting which has its own natural resources for participation in outdoor and adventurous activities.**

3.2 Health and Safety Considerations   P2   M2   D1

The Adventure Activities Licensing

The Adventure Activities Licensing Authority (AALA) was founded in 1996 and works in conjunction with the Adventure Activities Licensing Service, which are both run by the Health and Safety Executive (HSE) to form the Adventure Activities Licensing. The Adventure Activities Licensing is reponsible for inspecting activity centres and other outdoor and adventurous activity providers. If the Adventure Activities Licensing is satisfied that the provider meets nationally accepted standards of good practice, then it will issue a license. This helps to provide the public with assurances that the activities are not exposing participants to unnecessary danger or risks of injury.

Health and Safety Executive

The Department for Education and Skills created the Health and Safety Executive which is responsible for the regulation of all risks to health and safety. It has produced guidelines on arranging and undertaking risk assessments for outdoor activities and educational visits.

Most outdoor adventurous activities governing bodies also provide support, advice and guidelines on health and safety matters relevant to their activity.

What Is a Risk Assessment?

Risk assessment is a technique for preventing any potential accidents, injury or ill health by helping people to consider what could go wrong while undertaking an activity (in this case an outdoor adventurous activity). A risk assessment looks at the possible hazards that may occur, the likelihood of them happening and how the hazards could be prevented.

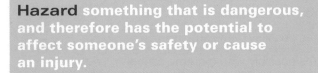

Definition

Hazard something that is dangerous, and therefore has the potential to affect someone's safety or cause an injury.

Most outdoor pursuit activities contain many hazard factors that could affect a person's general health and safety. Therefore the participants must ensure that they remain safe and avoid the possibility of injury or even death. This is normally the responsibility of the person leading the session.

An example of a hazard could include:

- Climbing in a new area.
- A strong current in the sea, used for sailing.

Definition   (d)

Risk a risk is linked to the chance of somebody being harmed by the potential hazard.

A risk is linked to the chance of somebody being harmed by the potential hazard. Risks are often categorised into how likely they are to happen. Something that is a low risk means that the likelihood of it happening is low, whereas something that is high risk means that it is likely to happen.

Undertaking a Risk Assessment

We have established that a risk assessment is about identifying hazards and assessing the risks associated with them. How do we undertake a risk assessment?

Risk Assessment

After you have highlighted a particular hazard you can use the formula on page 40 to assess the potential problems that may arise.

In the example shown, the likelihood of the risk happening multiplied by the severity results in a score of 3 which means that the risk is worth taking but with extreme caution. In order to minimise the risk, participants can wear specialist equipment such as a helmet which will reduce the severity of the injury should a person capsize when kayaking down rapids.

Control Measures

Outdoor and adventurous activities often contain an element of risk, so it is important that a thorough risk assessment is undertaken prior to undertaking the activity. This includes setting control measures to help avoid any major injuries or accidents. Many outdoor and adventurous activities require the participants to use a variety of safety equipment. Using this correctly will also help reduce the risk of any injuries occurring.

LIKELIHOOD x SEVERITY

LIKELIHOOD – Is it likely to happen?

1 Unlikely
2 Quite likely
3 Very likely

SEVERITY – How badly someone could be injured.

1 No injury/minor incident
2 Injury requiring medical assistance
3 Major injury or fatality

Example: Kayaking down rapids, capsizing and hitting head on a rock

| Likelihood of happening? | 1 Unlikely |
| Severity? | 3 Major injury or fatality |

By multiplying the likelihood by the severity you will be able to set a chart that looks at the potential problems and make a decision on whether you want to take the risk or whether it is too much of a hazard.

Likelihood x Severity	Is the risk worth taking?
1	Yes with caution
2	Yes possibly with caution
3	Yes possibly with extreme caution
4	Yes possibly with extreme caution
5	No
6	No

Activity 3.2  60–90 mins

P2   M2   D1   D2

Health and safety considerations for outdoor and adventurous activities

Select two outdoor and adventurous activities of your choice, then carry out the following tasks.

Task 1

Using the internet, go to the website for the national governing body of each of your selected outdoor and adventurous activities and also other websites which detail the protective clothing or equipment that should be worn and used in order to take part in each of your selected sports.

Task 2

Design a leaflet that describes and explains the health and safety considerations that are associated with people taking part in your two selected outdoor and adventurous activities.

Task 3

Include in your leaflet details to identify and explain precautions and actions that can be taken or used to help to increase the health and safety of participants in your two selected outdoor and adventurous activities.

Example of a Risk Assessment Form

Location of Risk Assessment: Grade 3 Rapids

Risk Assessor's name: O. Opsudaisy

Date: 28.09.10

Hazard observed	People at risk	Level of risk (likelihood x severity)	Use of specialist equipment	Risk rating with specialist equipment
Rocks in river	Kayakers when they capsize	4	All kayakers to wear helmets to protect their heads	2

Activity 3.3 45 mins   P3

Carrying out a risk assessment

You have been asked to assist leading an outdoor activity of your choice to a group of 14-year-old children.

Task 1

List the hazards that may be associated with your outdoor and adventurous activities that may be a danger to participants.

Task 2

Produce a risk assessment for your selected outdoor and adventurous activity that includes measures that you can use to minimise the risks identified.

3.3 The Environmental Impact of Outdoor and Adventurous Activities

Participating in outdoor and adventurous activities cause some impact on the natural environment. It is therefore important that participants are aware of how they can preserve the environment, so that people can continue to enjoy it. If the activities or our own mistreatment continues to damage these areas, then authorities will use control measures to reduce the impact.

The Countryside Agency is the government's advisory body responsible for all aspects of the countryside. The Countryside Agency states in its vision statement that it aims to:

'Make life better for people in the countryside and to make the quality of the countryside better for everyone.'

The Countryside Agency is responsible for improving and conserving the countryside and looking at the social and economic impact it has on people.

There are many ways in which participants can help look after these environments, and the national governing bodies all prioritise looking after the countryside, and set recommendations to follow, to help avoid impacting on the environment.

Types of Environmental Impact

Erosion

Erosion is a major factor in the outdoors, so what is it and what does it affect?

Erosion affects paths and tracks. It is a natural process where soil wears away due to heavy exposure to rain and wind. Because of the slope on hills the soil moves down the slope towards the streams and rivers. Human activity can also increase the rate of erosion. Many major paths have been formed over the years and many have been treated to combat the effects of erosion. Sometimes paths will be closed as they are treated.

There are often dry-stone walls in the countryside, which act as boundaries and markers. Walkers should ensure that they use the gates and stiles rather than trying to climb over these as dry-stone walls are easily damaged and difficult to put back together. It is also important to close all gates after use, so that livestock cannot escape from their allocated space.

Pollution

Pollution is another factor that has increased in the countryside. This has come mainly from the increase in cars visiting the areas. There is often limited car parking, and parking should be considered before travelling. There has also been an increase in the number of motorised activities taking place in rural settings, for example quad biking. Many countryside users have complained about the noise and pollution that these activities cause. The Countryside Agency is monitoring this closely, and has clamped down on groups doing these types of activities in public spaces.

Rubbish and litter should be taken home with you and not dumped in the countryside. Not only does rubbish look untidy but it is also harmful to livestock and wildlife. Rubbish can also attract scavengers, which can displace the species of the area.

Human Disturbance

Both plants and wildlife are easily disturbed by human behaviour. Humans should not touch wildlife or pick plants, as many are rare and even protected. It is important that dogs are also kept on leads, as they may worry animals. Rare species of birds often leave their nests through fright and do not return to hatch their eggs.

Often competitions are in conservation areas and involve getting off the main paths to find specific checkpoints, therefore trampling plants and disturbing the wildlife.

The British Orienteering Federation is committed to preserving the environment, as research has shown that orienteering has a low impact on the environment. The BOF has responded to some criticism by:

- Its members declaring a high commitment to conservation principles.

- Using a qualified environmental scientist as its Environmental Officer.

- Commissioning independent scientific researchers to look at the environmental impact of orienteering.

Activity 3.4 45–60 mins

Environmental impact of outdoor and adventurous activities

Outdoor and adventurous activities can have some negative impact on the environment. However, once people are aware of these impacts they are more able to try to reduce them.

Task 1

Design two leaflets for two different outdoor and adventurous activities that can be given to people who take part in each activity to make them aware of the environmental impact of that activity.

Your leaflet should:

- describe and explain the environmental impacts associated with participation in each outdoor and adventurous activity;
- explain precautions and actions that can be taken or used to help to reduce the environmental impact of each outdoor and adventurous activity that you have selected.

Key learning points

- Hazard – something that has the potential to cause injury or compromise safety.
- Risk – the likelihood of something bad happening.
- Risk assessment – a list of possible hazards that states the likelihood of them happening, and ways of controlling them.
- Environmental impact – something that can affect the natural environment.
- All people visiting the countryside should adhere to the Countryside Code.

Quick Quiz 10 mins

Answer the following questions with True or False.

1. An example of a hazard could be slippery rock.
2. Risk assessments should only be carried out if the Adventure Activities Licensing Authority is coming to a centre for an inspection.
3. A national governing body provides the rules and regulations for a sport.
4. Safety equipment only needs to be worn by people who have not taken part in outdoor and adventurous activities before.
5. Pollution is a natural process where soil wears away due to heavy exposure to rain and wind.
6. Rubbish and litter should be taken home with you and not dumped in the countryside.
7. A risk is linked to the chance of somebody being harmed by the potential hazard.
8. Walkers can climb over dry-stone walls rather than using the gates and stiles.
9. In a risk assessment, the severity is how badly someone could be injured.
10. An activity with a level of risk value of 9 should not be undertaken.

3.4 Skills and Techniques

Definition

Skill the ability to do an activity well, because it has been practised.

Generic Skills and Techniques

Many outdoor adventure activities require competent use of specialist equipment and accessories. Much of this equipment is designed for the safety of the participant; this could include buoyancy aids for water-based activities such as canoeing and windsurfing, or ropes and harnesses for activities such as abseiling and potholing.

Experience is vital in all outdoor adventure activities. By doing something regularly you will become better at it and eliminate the risk of injury or potential accidents. Experience improves a person's knowledge and allows them to make important decisions or judgements. Decision making and judgement are very important in outdoor pursuits. For example, it is important to know when it is not appropriate to undertake the activity. Extreme weather conditions could mean that it is unsafe to undertake the activity or that the conditions are not suitable for

Definition

Technique a way of undertaking a particular skill and includes how the person performs that skill and the method they use to do it. For example, a skill required in rock climbing is your hand contact on the surface, while the technique is how you hold on to the surface (the type of hand grip you use).

beginners. Judgement could include making a decision on what may be the quickest route off a mountain.

A good awareness of health and safety is a very important skill. Safety checks prior to undertaking outdoor adventure activities are essential; these include assessing any potential hazards that could occur during the activity and ensuring that the equipment is in good working condition. The nature of these activities means there are often many potential hazards, and during the preparation stages safety should be a top priority.

Outdoor adventure activities will help participants develop leadership skills. Some outdoor adventure activities require people to make important decisions or take responsibility for others around them. Outdoor pursuit activities are also associated with developing an individual's character, by improving their personal qualities. People undertaking these types of activities gain characteristics such as responsibility, leadership qualities, awareness, personal achievement, respect for others, overcoming fears and dealing with extreme circumstances.

Outdoor activities are a good vehicle for learning the skill of communication. Most activities require interaction, while others allow people to express themselves. Different communication methods are used in different settings and outdoor activities.

Teamwork is a vital part of many outdoor adventure activities. For example, hill walkers must walk at the pace of the slowest team member and between them carry the equipment required. Many organisations will send their employees to outdoor activity centres, so that they can learn to work as a team.

A good level of physical fitness is required to undertake many outdoor adventure activities. Certain activities need good basic fitness levels before participation in order to reduce the risk of the person sustaining an injury.

Specific Skills and Techniques

Each outdoor activity that one chooses to undertake will have a range of skills and techniques specific to the sport. It is necessary to practise these skills and techniques in order to carry out these outdoor activities successfully. Below are some examples of specific skills and techniques related to a range of outdoor activities.

Rock Climbing

Rock climbers require strength, muscular endurance and flexibility. Strength is required to lift your bodyweight, while muscular endurance is also required as the muscles are working for long periods of time. Flexibility comes into action when climbers have to stretch out to reach for potential hand or footholds.

A good rock climber will have the ability to lead other climbers through a chosen climb. If the climb has not been set up prior to starting, the lead climber takes responsibility for placing protection as they go. This includes fixing the rope to the rock face, which is often known as anchoring.

The setting up of a climb is a very important skill, as you must ensure that it is safe for people to undertake. This includes having a good understanding of the ropes and how to tie specific climbing knots. Belaying is undertaken by an experienced climber and is the term used for fastening the climbing rope around a metal device which is secured to the inexperienced climber in order to stop them falling. By feeding the rope as the climber moves up the surface, the climber is kept secure and safe should they lose their grip on the rock face. This person will also be able to call out advice to other climbers on where they should place their hands and feet while climbing. These are known as contact skills as this hand and foot contact will allow a person to hold their body to the rock face and move up to the summit.

Orienteering

Orienteering originates from Scandinavia and is an outdoor activity that requires you to use a map to locate set controls (markers).

The main skill required to be successful is a good understanding of map work and the ability to use a compass. An orienteering participant will need to be able to recognise the different map symbols, understand contour lines and know the difference between the types of paths and tracks. The use of a compass will also assist in finding the control checkpoints. A compass is used to support the map work and to take bearings. This is useful when looking for controls, which are located away from main paths. It is also helpful to have good awareness, especially when looking for the controls. These are often hidden in dells, woods or behind obstacles, but do come with a description of where they can be found.

Orienteering requires a good level of aerobic fitness to compete at a high standard and it is important for competitors to be able to pace themselves during long-distance events. The terrain that competitions are held on can vary and therefore it is important to have a good general fitness level.

Mountain Biking

A range of skills and techniques is required for mountain biking. Good aerobic fitness is necessary to overcome the hills and rough terrain, while good balance is also required to stop you falling off your bike.

More specific skills include braking, turning and knowing when to change gears. It is important to shift your bodyweight backwards when braking as most of the brake power goes to the front wheel. This will also stop the rider from being thrown over the handlebars! A cyclist will learn when to stand and when to sit down while riding. Standing is also known as coasting and is often done when descending. It is important to change gears at the right time to avoid overexerting yourself. It is harder to cycle in a higher gear, and easier if the bike is in a lower gear. It is easier to change gear prior to going up a hill than trying to change your gear halfway up the ascent; this can also increase the chance of the bike's chain coming off.

It is important that a cyclist has some knowledge of basic bicycle maintenance. Fixing a flat tyre and repairing punctures are common issues to contend with when cycling in rough terrain. Repairing the chain and replacing brake pads and cables are also common fixes required.

Activity 3.5   1–2 hours   P5   M4

Skills and techniques in outdoor and adventurous activities

For this activity you will need to have spent some time practising the appropriate skills and techniques required for two outdoor and adventurous activities.

Task 1

You will need to be observed by your teacher/tutor or outdoor and adventurous activity instructor for this task. Demonstrate all of the necessary skills and techniques required to competently take part in two different outdoor and adventurous activities.

Task 2

Through a discussion with the person who has carried out the observation of your demonstrations, review your performance (including techniques) and justify the techniques that you chose to demonstrate.

Recording Evidence

You should investigate different methods of recording your skills and determine which ones are most appropriate to you.

A diary or a logbook would ensure you are keeping an accurate and daily or weekly account of your progress.

If you have a camcorder or access to one, it would be a good idea to video yourself performing each skill. You will then be able to watch it and gain a better understanding of your ability. This will also act as a record to refer back to in order to determine how you have improved certain skills and techniques.

You may wish to consider asking a tutor, coach, friend or family member to complete an observation checklist which could be used to highlight techniques and tactics that you are performing well in and areas that could be improved upon.

Activity **3.6**   ⏱ 1 week – 3 months      P7 M5 D3

Allow from one week to a few months

Participation in outdoor and adventurous activities

Task

Keep a logbook of your participation in outdoor and adventurous activities. Highlight the different skills that are important in the activity and any tactics that are commonly used. Note your strengths and weaknesses so that you can review your performance in these activities.

See the table below for an example.

Activity	Date	Skill	Tactic	Strengths/ Weaknesses
Windsurfing				
Snowboarding				
Canoeing				

3.5 Review Performance in Outdoor and Adventurous Activities

P6 P7 M4 M5 D3

Create an observation checklist that can be used to analyse your and another person's performance in a range of activities. Remember to consider specific skills required, strengths, weaknesses and how these can be improved. When assessing yourself, try to obtain feedback from both instructors and your classmates on how you did.

SWOT analysis allows you to pinpoint your strengths, weaknesses, opportunities and threats. This is often mapped out using a template similar to that shown in Figure 3.2.

Strengths	Weaknesses
Opportunities	**Threats**

Figure 3.2   SWOT analysis template

Activity **3.7** 30 mins

P6
P7
M5
D2

SWOT analysis
Task

Using the SWOT analysis template, review another person's performance in two outdoor and adventurous activities of your choice:

- Strengths – what are their strengths?
- Weaknesses – what impedes their performance?
- Opportunities – what openings have they got to improve?
- Threats – what are the obstacles in their way that are stopping them from doing something?

Now carry out the same SWOT analysis to help to review your own performance.

Setting Targets

It is good to set yourself targets when undertaking any outdoor and adventurous activities. You might want to climb Mont Blanc, but without any prior training this would be impossible.

There is an acronym for setting goals that is believed to motivate people in achieving their targets. These are known as SMARTER targets:

Specific – your target must be specific.

Measurable – how can you measure it?

Achievable – it must be possible to achieve the goal.

Realistic – be realistic with your targets; are they achievable?

Timed – set yourself a time period within which to achieve your goal.

Exciting – this will help motivate you to achieve your targets.

Recorded – record your targets; this will help you stick to them.

Activity **3.8** 25 mins

P7
M5
D3

SMARTER targets
Task

Using the SMARTER targets, develop training plans that will allow you to improve in two outdoor or adventurous activities of your choice. Remember to consider what resources you would require to undertake your plan.

Quick Quiz 10 mins (?)

N	R	E	V	I	E	W	U	T	O	A	K
O	P	A	I	E	H	I	G	T	V	I	C
I	T	E	C	H	N	I	Q	U	E	S	A
T	A	T	G	S	S	T	S	E	O	M	B
A	V	I	N	R	R	K	B	W	P	A	D
V	S	U	P	E	R	V	I	S	O	R	E
R	O	C	N	E	M	S	F	L	O	T	E
E	U	C	N	P	T	P	S	D	L	S	F
S	F	T	R	A	I	N	I	N	G	S	D
B	S	M	A	R	T	E	R	U	H	T	H
O	L	O	G	B	O	O	K	E	Q	W	Y
S	H	T	G	N	E	R	T	S	D	E	P

Find the following words in the wordsearch above:

OBSERVATION   SMARTER
TECHNIQUES   LOGBOOK
SUPERVISOR   SKILLS
EQUIPMENT   REVIEW
STRENGTHS   PEERS
FEEDBACK   SWOT
TRAINING

(k) Key learning points

- Outdoor adventurous activity – an activity that contains an element of danger and normally takes place in a rural setting.
- Skill – the ability to do an activity well, because it has been practised.
- Technique – a way of undertaking a particular skill.
- SWOT analysis helps to identify strengths and areas for improvement
- SMARTER targets should be set to try to improve performance.

Useful websites

www.bcu.org.uk

Provides information on canoeing for coaches, beginners and advanced participants, including how to stay safe and details of forthcoming canoeing events.

www.thebmc.co.uk

Provides information on equipment, safety, and details of forthcoming events for climbers, mountaineers and hill walkers in the UK.

www.ramblers.org.uk

Provides information such as walking routes and sound advice suitable for walkers of all ages.

www.rya.org

Comprehensive and unstuffy source of invaluable information for anyone who enjoys sailing, wind-surfing, even model yachting. Includes advice and tips on getting started in the sport, up-to-date data on weather and tides, and a downloadable information pack.

References

Cox, D., 2002, *The Sailing Handbook*. London: New Holland Publishers.

Hanson, J. and Hanson, R., 1997, *Ragged Mountain Press Guide to Outdoor Sports*. Maidenhead: McGraw-Hill.

Lockren, I., 1998, *Outdoor Pursuits*. Cheltenham: Nelson Thornes.

Long, S. and Cousins, J., 2003, *Hill Walking: The Official Handbook of the Mountain Leader and Walking Group Leader Schemes*. Capel Curig: UKMTB

Rowe, R.,1989, *Canoeing Handbook: Official Handbook of the British Canoe Union*. Bangor: Pesda Press.

Chapter 4
Anatomy & Physiology for Sport

This chapter explores the foundations of anatomy and physiology. This chapter will cover both the structure and function of the:

- skeletal system
- muscular system
- cardiovascular system
- respiratory system.

Learning Goals

By the end of this chapter you should:

- Know structure and function of the skeletal system
- Know structure and function of the muscular system
- Know structure and function of the cardiovascular system
- Know structure and function of the respiratory system

To achieve a PASS grade the evidence must show that the learner is able to:	To achieve a MERIT grade the evidence must show that, in addition to the pass criteria, the learner is able to:	To achieve a DISTINCTION grade the evidence must show that, in addition to the pass and merit criteria, the learner is able to:
P1 describe the structure and function of the skeletal system		
P2 describe the different types of joint and the movements allowed at each	**M1** explain the movements occurring at two synovial joints during four different types of physical activity	
P3 identify the major muscles of the body		
P4 describe the different types of muscle and muscle movements	**M2** give examples of three different types of muscular contraction relating to three different types of physical activity	**D1** analyse the musculoskeletal actions occurring at four synovial joints during four different types of physical activity
P5 describe the structure and function of the cardiovascular system		
P6 describe the structure and function of the respiratory system	**M3** explain how the cardiovascular and respiratory systems work together to supply the body with oxygen	**D2** evaluate how the cardiovascular and respiratory systems work together to supply the body with oxygen and remove carbon dioxide

4.1 The Skeletal System

Structure of the Skeletal System

Major Bones

You are born with around 350 bones. However, as you grow, some of these bones join together to form one bone. Once you become an adult your skeleton will consist of 206 bones.

Skull

The skull consists of the cranium that protects the brain and facial bones, which include the upper and lower jaw and other facial structures.

Sternum (breast bone)

This is located in the middle of the chest.

Ribs

Adults have 12 pairs of ribs. The ribs are flat bones that are joined to the sternum to form a protective cage around the heart and lungs.

Clavicle (collar bone)

This bone connects the upper arm to the trunk of the body. One end is connected to the sternum (breast bone) and the other is connected to the scapula (shoulder blade).

Scapula (shoulder blade)

This bone is situated on the back of the body.

Arm

This consists of three bones: the humerus (upper arm), the radius and the ulna (lower arm).

Pelvis (hips)

The pelvis protects and supports the lower internal organs, including the bladder, the reproductive organs and also, in pregnant women, the developing foetus.

Leg

The leg consists of four bones: the femur (thigh bone), tibia (shin bone), fibula (lower leg) and patella (kneecap).

Function of the Skeletal System

There are five main functions that the skeleton performs: shape, movement, protection, blood production and mineral storage.

Shape

Without a skeleton we would not have the human form; we would be a shapeless structure like a jelly on the floor. Our skeleton forms a frame under the skin to which muscles attach and within which internal organs can sit.

Movement

The skeleton is made up of lots of bones that are connected by joints that allow different degrees of movement. Muscles are then attached to these bones, which pull on them and produce movement.

Protection

Internal organs are delicate in comparison to bones and muscles, and they would not be able to withstand the many everyday stresses we place on our bodies unless they were protected by the skeleton. Various areas of the skeleton protect different vital organs, for example the ribs and sternum protect the heart and lungs, the brain is protected by the skull, the vertebral column protects the spinal cord and in pregnant females the pelvis protects the developing foetus.

Blood Production

Red bone marrow makes red and white blood cells. The centres of some bones in the skeleton contain red bone marrow and therefore are the site of blood production. The main bones that are responsible for blood production are the sternum, vertebral column and pelvic girdle.

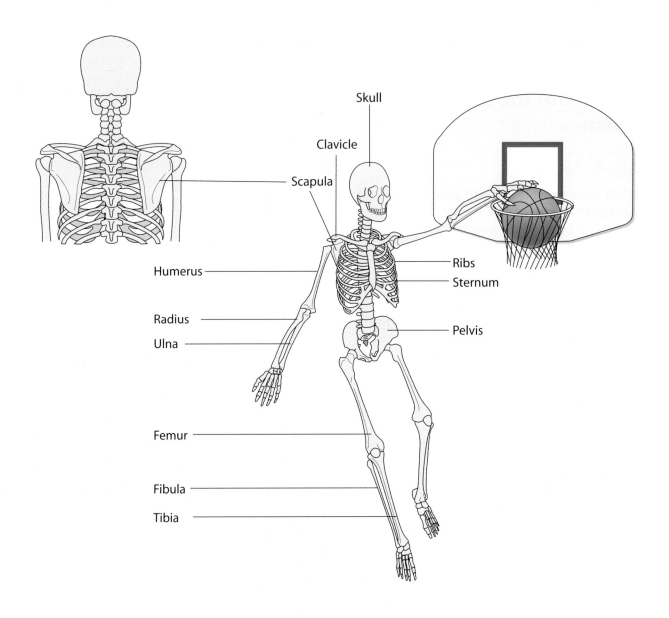

Skull

Clavicle

Scapula

Humerus

Radius

Ulna

Femur

Fibula

Tibia

Ribs

Sternum

Pelvis

Figure 4.1   Major bones of the body

Mineral Storage

The bones in the skeleton store minerals, which include phosphorus and calcium, the main and most important one being calcium. The calcium in our bones is largely responsible for ensuring they remain hard and are able to withstand impact, that is, they do not break when we fall over. As our bones are continually being broken down and replaced, we require a constant supply of calcium to ensure the 'new' bones are tough and durable.

Activity **4.1** 30 mins

The skeletal system

Task 1

Examine the skeleton below and label all the major bones. For help, take a look at the labelled skeleton on page 52.

Task 2

Make a list of all of the major bones and write next to the name something about where it can be found or its main function.

For example:

The skull – this is at the head of the body and helps to protect the brain.

Task 3

The skeleton has five main functions. List each function and describe what it means.

Function	Description
For example: Protection	The skeleton helps to support our body's internal organs, which are delicate in comparison to bones and muscles. For example the ribs and sternum protect the heart and lungs, the skull protects the brain and the vertebral column protects the spinal cord

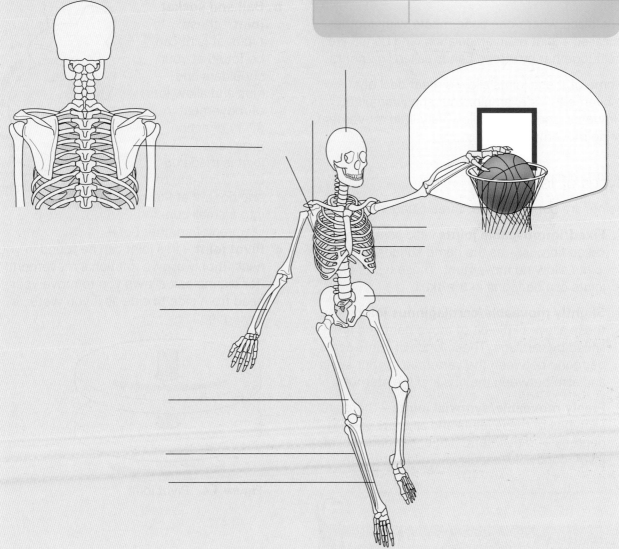

Joints

Definition

Joint the place where one bone meets with another.

The place where one bone meets with another is called a joint or an articulation, and bones are held together by strong bands called ligaments.

Some of these joints allow a great deal of movement (for example, your shoulder joint). However, some joints allow very little movement or no movement at all.

Types of Joint P2

Joints are put into one of three categories:

1. **Fixed/immoveable joints** (also sometimes called fibrous) – as the name suggests, these joints allow no movement. These types of joints can be found in the skull.

2. **Slightly moveable/cartilaginous joints** – these allow a little bit of movement and are linked by cartilage. These kinds of joints can be found between the vertebrae in your spine and also between the ribs and the sternum.

3. **Freely moveable/synovial joints** – there are six types of these joints and all allow varying degrees of movement: hinge, ball and socket, pivot, condyloid, saddle and gliding.

Definition

Ligament joins bones to other bones.

a **Hinge joint** – these can be found in your elbows and knees, and they allow you to bend and then straighten your arms and legs. Hinge joints are like the hinges on a door, and allow you to bend your arms and legs in only one direction.

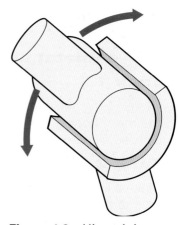
Figure 4.2   Hinge joint

b **Ball and socket joint** – these types of joint can be found at your shoulders and hips and allow lots of movement in every direction. A ball and socket joint is made up of a round end of one bone that fits into a small cup-like area of another bone.

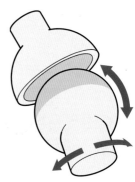
Figure 4.3   Ball and socket joint

c **Pivot joint** – this joint can be found in your neck. It only allows rotational movement (for example, it allows you to move your head from side to side as if you were saying 'no').

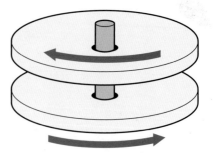
Figure 4.4   Pivot joint

d Condyloid joint – this type of joint can be found at the wrist. It allows movement in two planes. It allows you to bend and straighten the joint, and move it from side to side.

e Saddle joint – this type of joint can only be found in your thumbs. It allows the joint to move in two planes, backwards and forwards, and from side to side.

Figure 4.5 Condyloid joint

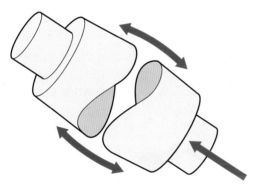

Figure 4.6 Saddle joint

f Gliding joint – this type of joint can be found in the carpal bones of the hand. These types of joints occur between the surfaces of two flat bones. They allow very limited movement in a range of directions.

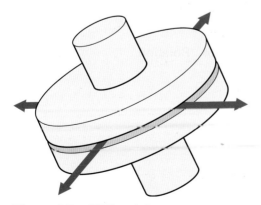

Figure 4.7 Gliding joint

Structure of a Joint

Figure 4.8 shows the structure of a synovial joint.

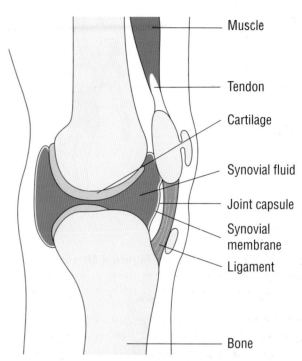

Muscle

Tendon

Cartilage

Synovial fluid

Joint capsule

Synovial membrane

Ligament

Bone

Figure 4.8 Structure of a synovial joint

Types of Joint Movement   P2 M1 **D1**

There are a number of different types of joint movement:

● **Flexion** – this means bending the joint. This occurs at the knee when one is preparing to kick a football.

Figure 4.9 Flexion

- **Extension** – this means straightening the joint. This occurs at the elbow when one is shooting in netball.

Figure 4.10   Extension

- **Adduction** – this means movement towards the body. This occurs at the shoulder when one is in the pulling phase of the breast stroke.

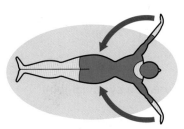

Figure 4.11   Adduction

- **Abduction** – this means movement away from the body. This occurs at the hip during a star jump.

Figure 4.12   Abduction

- **Circumduction** – this means that the limb moves in a circle. This occurs at the shoulder joint during an overarm bowl in cricket.

Figure 4.13   Circumduction

- **Rotation** – this means that the limb moves in a circular movement towards the middle of the body. This occurs in the hip while performing a drive shot in golf.

Figure 4.14   Rotation

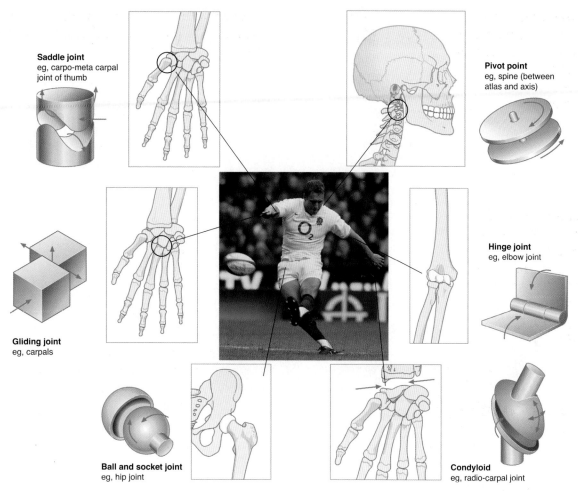

Figure 4.15   Synovial joints in action

(k) Key learning points

There are three categories of joint: fixed, slightly moveable and freely moveable/synovial.

Type of joint	Type of movement	Examples in the body
Fixed joint	None	Skull
Slightly moveable	Slight movement	Between ribs and sternum
Freely moveable/synovial	See below	See below
Hinge joint	Flexion and extension	Elbow, knee
Ball and socket	Flexion and extension Abduction and adduction Circumduction and rotation	Hips and shoulders
Pivot	Rotation	Neck
Condyloid	Flexion and extension Abduction and adduction	Wrist
Saddle	Flexion and extension Abduction and adduction	Thumb
Gliding joint	Limited movement in all directions	Carpals

Wrist
(flexion, extension,
abduction, adduction)

Elbow joint
(flexion, extension)

Knee joint
(flexion, extension)

Figure 4.16   Joints and their associated movement patterns

Activity **4.2**   40 mins   P2   M1

Joints and movement

Without joints we would not be able to move our bodies in the way that we do. If you consider all of the different sports that people can take part in (e.g. swimming, tennis, basketball, hurdles, high jump etc.) we have to move our bodies in different ways to be able to perform them. When Rebecca Adlington won her gold medals at the Beijing Olympics in 2008, she swam front crawl. To swim front crawl your shoulder joint is moving in an overarm action which you now know is called **circumduction**. Her hip joints would have been flexing and extending as she kicked her legs to help to propel her through the water. To help you answer the following task, have a think about other different types of sports and the types of movements that would be occurring at each joint.

Task 1

(a) Describe the three different categories of joint and give examples of where you could find each.

(b) Name the six different types of synovial joint and describe the types and range of movement that is allowed at each.

(c) Think about the following different types of movement:

- a netball shot
- a rugby kick
- an overarm tennis serve
- a squat.

Activity 4.2 continued

Figure 4.17 Netball shooting: (a) elbows and (b) wrists

Figure 4.18 (a) Kicking: knee

Figure 4.18 (b) Kicking: hip

Figure 4.19 (a) The tennis serve: shoulder

Figure 4.19 (b) The tennis serve: elbow

Figure 4.20 Squat: (a) knee (b) hip

Task 2

(a) Select two different joints for each movement, then complete the table below to show which movement is occurring at each joint.

For example:

Type of activity	Joint 1: Name and type of joint	Type of movement	Joint 2: Name and type of joint	Type of movement
Star jump	Shoulder ball and socket	Abduction	Hip ball and socket	Abduction

Activity **4.2**   continued

Your turn:

Type of activity	Joint 1: Name and type of joint	Type of movement	Joint 2: Name and type of joint	Type of movement
Netball shot	Elbow		Wrist	
Football kick	Knee		Hip	
Overarm tennis serve	Shoulder		Elbow	
Squats – down phase	Knee		Hip	

(b) Write one to two paragraphs to explain the table above, what is happening during each activity and how it is happening.

For example:

During a star jump, both the arms and legs move outwards and away from the mid-line of the body. This happens through the shoulder joint performing a movement called abduction. The shoulder joint moves upwards and outwards away from the body so that arm travels out to the sides. The hips also produce the same type of movement called abduction, which takes the legs and feet away from the mid-line of the body. Both the shoulder and hip joints are ball and socket joints, which allow a great deal of movement including abduction.

Now your turn...

Quick Quiz   ⏱ 5–10 mins   ❓

bone marrow	calcium	flexion	the leg	ball and socket
ribs	abduction	wrist	pivot	immoveable

Choose a word(s) from the boxes above to answer the following questions.

1. **What is the name of a mineral stored in bones?**
2. **Where would you find a condyloid joint?**
3. **Where are blood cells produced?**
4. **Which limb consists of four bones?**
5. **A hinge joint is shaped to allow which type of movement to take place?**
6. **Which term describes movement away from the body?**
7. **This type of joint can be found in the neck.**
8. **This type of joint can be found in the skull.**
9. **This type of synovial joint allows the greatest range of movement.**
10. **Which bones protect the heart and lungs?**

4.2 The Muscular System

Major Muscles

Figure 4.21 shows the major muscles that can be found in the human body.

Types of Muscle Tissue

There are three types of muscle tissue: smooth, skeletal and cardiac.

Smooth Muscle

Smooth muscles are also called involuntary muscles. You cannot consciously control this type of muscle; your brain and body tell these muscles what to do without you even having to think about it. Smooth muscle can be found all over your body, for example in your digestive system, in your bladder and in your eyes.

Cardiac Muscle

The heart is made up of cardiac muscle (also known as the myocardium). Cardiac muscle is

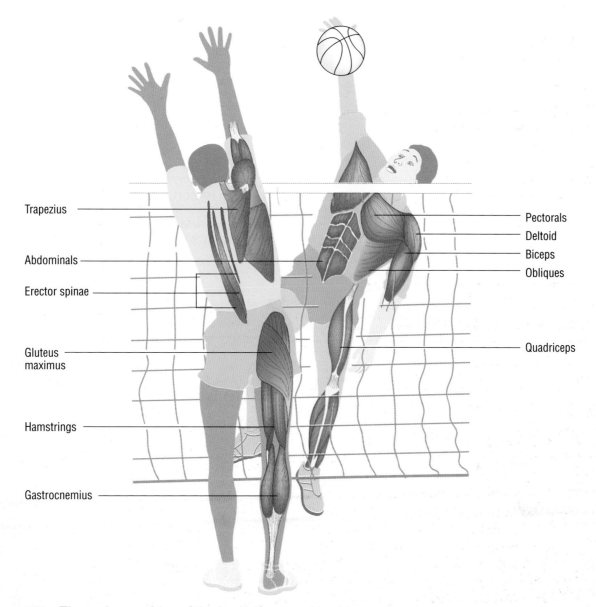

Trapezius

Abdominals

Erector spinae

Gluteus maximus

Hamstrings

Gastrocnemius

Pectorals

Deltoid

Biceps

Obliques

Quadriceps

Figure 4.21   The major muscles of the body (front and back)

Type of muscle	Smooth	Skeletal	Cardiac
Voluntary or involuntary	Involuntary	Voluntary	Involuntary
Found	Digestive system, bladder, eyes	External muscle	Heart

also called an involuntary muscle as it contracts without you consciously having to control it. Cardiac muscle consists of specialised fibres that do not tire.

Activity **4.3**   40 mins   **P3**

Major muscles

Task

Identify the major muscles below.

Figure 4.22   What are the major muscles?

Skeletal Muscle

You are probably familiar with this type of muscle as they are responsible for allowing us to move and take part in sports. As you know, if you 'work out' you will gain good muscle tone and shape and it is this skeletal muscle you are training. This type of muscle is also known as striated muscle, which basically means that if you were to look at it under a microscope you would see that it has a striped appearance.

Skeletal muscles are also known as voluntary muscles. This means you can control what they do, so if you want to kick a ball, you have to think about it and this will make your skeletal muscles contract to allow the movement to happen.

(k) Key learning points

- There are three types of muscle tissue: smooth, skeletal and cardiac.
- Smooth muscles and cardiac muscles are involuntary muscle.
- Skeletal muscles are voluntary muscle.

Muscle Movement   **P4**   **M2**   **D1**

Tendons are responsible for joining skeletal muscles to your skeleton.

Tendons are cords made of tough tissue, and they work to connect muscle to bones. When a muscle contracts, it pulls on the tendon which in turn pulls on the bone and makes the bone move.

Definition

Tendons join muscles to the skeleton.

Muscles can only produce a pulling movement, so each muscle has a 'partner' that can return the body part back to its original position. These are called antagonistic muscle pairs.

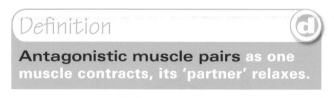

Definition   (d)

Antagonistic muscle pairs as one muscle contracts, its 'partner' relaxes.

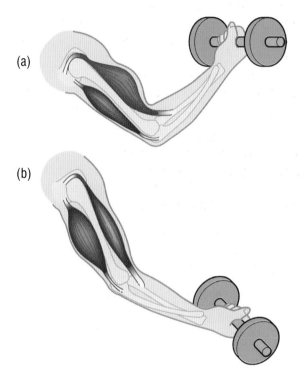

(a)

(b)

Figure 4.23 The biceps and triceps in (a) upwards and (b) downwards phase of bicep curl

Activity 4.4   30 mins   P4

Muscles and movement

Task 1

There are three different types of muscle in the human body. Describe each, giving examples of where you would find them in your body.

Task 2

Copy out the table below, then draw a line to link the correct muscle next to its antagonistic pair.

If you are not sure, identify where you would find each muscle on your body and then try to work out where its partner is.

Biceps	Trapezius
Hamstrings	Erector spinae
Abdominals	Quadriceps
Deltoids	Triceps

Task 3

Describe the process of how muscles work in antagonistic pairs to produce movement.

Remember – muscles can only 'pull'.

Types of Muscle

Contraction   M2   D1

There are three main types of muscle contraction.

1. Concentric Contraction

This is the main type of muscle contraction. In this type of contraction, the muscle gets shorter and the two ends of the muscle move closer together. For example, flexing the knee in preparation for kicking a ball.

Figure 4.24 Knee flexion

2. Eccentric Contraction

In this type of muscle contraction, the muscle actually increases in length while still producing tension. The two ends of the muscle move further apart. For example, in the lowering phase of a bicep curl, the biceps are working eccentrically to control the lowering of the weight.

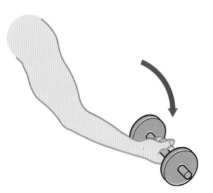

Figure 4.25   Eccentric contraction

3. Isometric Contraction

In this type of contraction, the muscle actually stays the same length, so there is no movement of the muscle or body part that is attached. For example, in gymnastics, holding the Iron Cross on the rings.

Figure 4.26   Isometric contraction

	Concentric	Eccentric	Isometric
Muscle action	Muscle shortens	Muscle lengthens but still produces tension	Muscle remains the same length but still produces tension
Name of muscle contracting	Biceps	Biceps	Quadriceps
Example	Upwards phase of a bicep	Downwards phase of a bicep	Ski squat

Activity 4.5   20 mins

Muscle contraction
Task 1

Try to think of three different sporting activities from the examples shown that involve each of the different types of muscle contraction, and complete the table below.

It may help you to actually perform the movement so that you can work out if the muscle is getting shorter, longer or staying the same length.

Task 2

Write a sentence or two for each example that you have given to describe how the muscle is contracting and why this is necessary in each sporting example.

	Concentric	Eccentric	Isometric
Name of muscle contracting			
Example of a sporting activity			

Activity 4.6 40 mins

Musculoskeletal actions

Task 1

Examine and complete the table below.

Name of physical activity	Joint	Joint type	Movement produced	Muscle	Type of muscle contraction
Netball shot	Elbow	Hinge	Extension	Triceps	Concentric
Football kick – preparation phase	Knee				
Sit-up – downwards phase	Vertebral column				
Squats – downwards phase	Knee				
Star jump – jumping outwards phase	Shoulder				

Task 2

Write a few paragraphs to analyse each of the muscular and skeletal actions that have occurred during each of these four different activities.

In your analysis you will need to include the following points:

- The structure of each of the synovial joints that you have examined and how they allow the different types of movement.
- The muscle name and type of muscle involved in producing the movement.
- An explanation of the different types of movement.

It is also a good idea to try to use quotes in your work to 'back up' or reinforce your point.

You can also use diagrams to help to illustrate your answer.

For example:

In a netball shot, when the person is 'shooting' the netball towards the goal post, their elbow extends. The elbow is a hinge joint, which allows movement 'like the hinges on a door, and allows you to bend your arms in only one direction' Stafford-Brown et al. (2003).

Extension means that the joint is being straightened. In a netball shot, the elbow is flexed in preparation for the shot and then extends in the 'shooting' phase.

The muscle that makes the elbow extend is the triceps. This type of muscle is a skeletal muscle and is under voluntary control, which means we can think about when and how we want to use it. The type of contraction is called 'concentric', which means that the muscle is getting shorter.

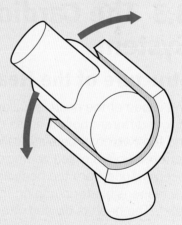

Figure 4.27 Hinge joint

Think of three other sporting examples for each type of muscle contraction.

Definition

Isometric 'iso' means 'the same', 'metric' means 'length'.

 Key learning points

- The major muscles of the body are: triceps, biceps, quadriceps, hamstrings, deltoids, gluteus maximus, gastrocnemius, abdominals, obliques, pectorals, trapezius, erector spinae.
- There are three different types of muscle: smooth, skeletal and cardiac.
- Muscles work in antagonistic pairs as muscles can only produce a 'pulling action'.
- There are three different types of muscle contraction – concentric, eccentric and isometric.

Quick Quiz 5–10 mins

Muscular system

1. Where would you find the biceps muscle?
2. Where would you find the quadriceps muscle?
3. What type of muscle is the heart muscle?
4. What type of contraction means that the muscle length remains the same?
5. Give a sporting example of an eccentric muscle contraction.
6. Where would you find skeletal muscle?
7. Explain what an antagonistic muscle pair is.
8. Give an example of an antagonistic muscle pair.
9. Where could you find smooth muscle in the body?
10. Where would you find the erector spinae muscle?

4.3 The Cardiovascular System

Structure of the Heart `P5`

The inside of the heart is hollow and is made up of four different hollow areas called chambers. The top two chambers are called atria and the bottom two are called ventricles. The atria receive blood from the body and the ventricles are responsible for pumping the blood out of the heart. The heart is divided into two sides, the right and the left side, by a wall of muscle called the septum.

Your heart is approximately the size of your fist, therefore the larger you are, the larger your heart.

Take a look at Figures 4.28 (a) and (b). The heart in (a) is from a sheep and is probably around the same size as yours; the heart in (b), however, is much bigger as it is from an ox, which is a much larger animal!

Function of the Heart `P5`

All of your body cells need a steady and constant supply of oxygen; this oxygen is supplied by blood. Blood is responsible for delivering oxygen to all the body's cells. In order for blood to get to these cells, the heart has to pump blood all around the body and the lungs. The left-hand side of your heart pumps the oxygenated blood to your body and head. The cells in your body then take the oxygen out of the blood and use it, and in so doing produce a waste product called carbon dioxide. This carbon dioxide is transported in the blood and continues on its journey back to the heart. The blood enters the right-hand side of the heart and is pumped out of the right ventricle to the lungs. At the lungs, the blood 'unloads' the carbon dioxide that it has picked up from our body cells and, instead, picks up the oxygen that we have breathed into our lungs. Carbon dioxide is then breathed out. You will find out more about this process when you

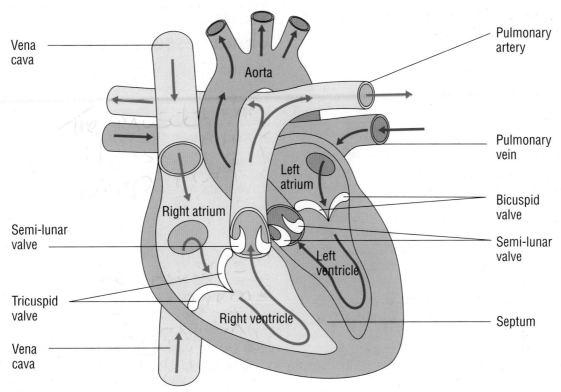

Figure 4.28 (a) Elements that make up the heart

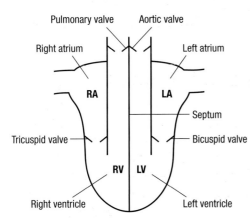

Figure 4.28 (b) The heart

come to explore the respiratory system later in this chapter.

Blood-flow through the Heart

Blood flows through the heart and around the body in one direction. This one-way 'street' is maintained by special valves placed within the heart.

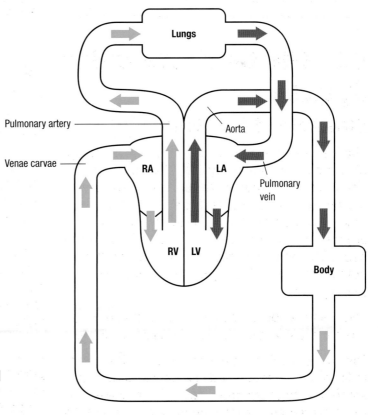

Figure 4.29 Blood flow through the heart

The heart is sometimes called a 'double pump' because the right-hand side of the heart pumps blood to the lungs and the left-hand side of the heart pumps blood to the body.

The Heart as a Double Pump

Right-hand Side

1. When the heart is relaxed, deoxygenated blood from the body enters the heart via the venae cavae.

2. Blood enters the right atria.

3. The right atria contracts (tightens) and pushes blood down through the tricuspid valve and into the right ventricle.

4. The right ventricle contracts, the tricuspid valve closes and blood is pushed up and out of the heart through the semilunar valve and into the pulmonary artery, which takes the blood to the lungs.

5. The heart relaxes and the semilunar valves close to prevent blood flowing back into the heart.

Left-hand side

1. When the heart is relaxed, oxygenated blood from the lungs enters via the pulmonary vein.

2. Blood enters the left atria.

3. The left atria contracts (tightens) and pushes blood down through the bicuspid valve and into the left ventricle.

4. The left ventricle contracts and the bicuspid valve closes. Blood is then pushed up and out of the heart through the semilunar valve and into the aorta, which takes blood to the rest of the body.

5. The heart relaxes and the semilunar valves close to prevent blood flowing back into the heart.

Structure of the Blood Vessels

In order to make this journey, blood is carried through five different types of blood vessels:

1. Arteries

2. Arterioles

3. Capillaries

4. Venules

5. Veins.

Arteries and Arterioles

These blood vessels are very similar; the only real difference is that arteries are larger than arterioles. They carry blood that has been pumped out of the heart and is therefore under high pressure. Consequently, these blood vessels need to be elastic in order to be able to expand, and have a thick wall to prevent them from bursting when blood under high pressure is pumped into them.

Capillaries

It is in these blood vessels that the action really happens! As already stated, the purpose of blood flowing around the body is to deliver oxygen and nutrients to all the body cells and take away waste products. It is in the capillaries that this exchange takes place; therefore capillaries are designed to allow maximum transfer of 'goods' to the body cells. They have extremely thin walls, only one cell thick, that allow the oxygen and nutrients to pass through to the body cells relatively easily. Capillaries also allow blood to pass through only in single file, one red or white blood cell at a time. This means that there is more time for the body cells to take out the oxygen and nutrients they need and 'unload' their waste products into the blood.

> **Definition**
>
> **Lumen** the 'hole in the middle' of a tube. (Think of a polo mint – the hole in the middle would be called the 'lumen'!)

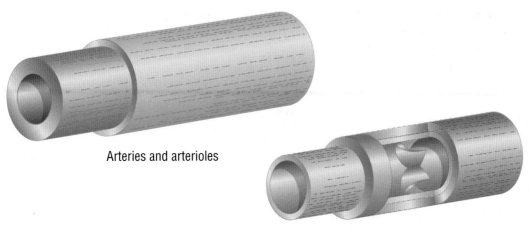

Arteries and arterioles

Veins and venules

Capillaries

Figure 4.30   Comparing the three blood vessels

Veins and Venules

These blood vessels carry blood under low pressure back to the heart. They have thin walls, are non-elastic and have large lumens. These are the holes in the middle which allow blood to pass through so that there is no resistance to blood flow. These blood vessels also contain one-way valves that prevent blood flowing in the wrong direction.

Function of the Cardiovascular System P5

The cardiovascular system is made up of the heart and all the blood vessels that take blood to and from all parts of the body. It is responsible for delivering oxygen and nutrients to every part of our body. It carries hormones to different parts of the body, and takes away waste products such as carbon dioxide and lactic acid. The cardiovascular system helps to maintain body temperature by redirecting blood to the surface of the skin when we are hot (that's why your face turns red when you are hot, because blood vessels close to the surface of the skin open up to try to cool the blood down).

 Key learning points

- The heart has four chambers: two atria and two ventricles.
- The ventricles pump blood to the body and lungs.
- Valves in the heart make sure blood flows in one direction.
- Blood travels through five different types of blood vessels: arteries, arterioles, capillaries, venules and veins.

 Activity **4.7**   30 mins   P5

Structure of the cardio-vascular system

Task 1

By hand, draw a diagram of the heart and label the following parts:

- left atria
- right atria
- left ventricle
- right ventricle
- septum
- bicuspid valve
- tricuspid valve
- semilunar valves.

Activity 4.7 continued

Task 2

Draw another diagram of the heart. This time label the blood vessels that lead into and out of the heart. These include:

- aorta
- pulmonary artery
- pulmonary vein
- vena cavae.

Task 3

Complete the table below.

Task 4

Write a paragraph to describe the structure and function of the cardiovascular system.

Name of blood vessel	Blood vessel structure	Function of vessel
Arteries		
Arterioles		
Capillaries		
Venules		
Veins		

Quick Quiz 10 mins

Cardiovascular system

Answer the following questions, then find your answers in the wordsearch below.

1. Name of the blood vessel leading out of the heart to the body.
2. Names of the top two chambers of the heart.
3. Process of blood vessels dilating for thermoregulation.
4. Name of the structure that separates the heart into the left- and the right-hand side.
5. Name of the type of blood vessel that takes blood away from the heart.
6. Names of the bottom two chambers of the heart.
7. Name of the smallest type of blood vessel.
8. This type of blood vessel has valves.

V	C	Y	A	D	U	U	F	A	S	E	V	I	R	A
A	A	R	W	I	A	I	R	T	A	S	N	T	A	H
S	P	A	S	S	R	S	S	H	T	E	O	Y	N	A
O	I	N	N	S	C	T	S	P	S	T	R	O	R	S
D	L	O	T	A	L	N	A	O	S	A	V	T	H	S
I	L	M	N	L	I	R	S	H	N	A	E	A	E	E
L	A	L	E	E	O	A	M	M	U	T	P	E	S	L
A	R	U	V	L	E	L	M	U	Y	R	L	N	G	C
T	I	P	Y	R	E	T	R	A	G	O	O	N	G	I
I	E	H	S	R	U	I	Y	S	I	A	H	X	S	R
O	S	T	S	P	E	P	R	S	E	P	T	U	M	T
N	O	Y	F	I	A	A	R	T	I	F	E	H	A	N
I	H	N	O	O	Y	C	U	O	N	T	N	A	H	E
S	T	C	N	E	R	I	A	D	T	E	R	S	T	V
T	E	T	N	I	N	I	E	D	P	N	V	L	E	T

4.4 The Respiratory System

The respiratory system is responsible for transporting the oxygen from the air we breathe into our body. Our body uses this oxygen in combination with the food we have eaten to produce energy. This energy is then used to keep us alive by supplying our heart with energy to keep beating and pumping blood around the body, and this in turn allows us to move and take part in sports and many other different types of activities.

Structure of the Respiratory System P6

The respiratory system is basically made up of a system of tubes and muscles that allows us to breathe in air from the surrounding atmosphere and take it down into our lungs.

1. Air enters the body through the mouth and nose.

2. Air passes over the epiglottis. The epiglottis closes over the trachea (also known as the windpipe) when we swallow food, to stop the food going down 'the wrong way' into our trachea and down into our lungs.

3. The air passes down into the trachea. If you reach up to the front of your neck, you will feel the trachea. The trachea is surrounded by horseshoe-shaped pieces of cartilage that keep it open.

4. The air passes down into two bronchi.

5. Air passes through the bronchi, which then divide into smaller tubes called bronchioles.

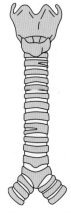

Figure 4.32 Trachae with horseshoe-shaped cartilage

6. At the end of the bronchioles, the air reaches the alveoli, which is where the 'action' happens: oxygen enters the blood whereas carbon dioxide is 'taken out' of the blood and enters the lungs. The alveoli are microscopic air sacs. They have very thin walls, and are surrounded by capillaries.

The respiratory system also includes two types of muscles that work to move air into and out of the lungs.

- The diaphragm is a sheet of muscle that runs along the bottom of the lungs.

- The intercostal muscles are found between the ribs (if you enjoy eating spare ribs you are actually eating intercostal muscles).

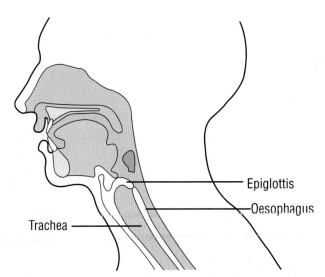

Figure 4.31 Epiglottis closing over trachea allowing food down the oesophagus

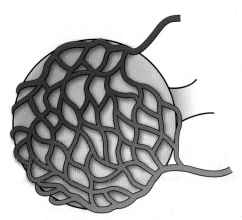

Figure 4.33 Alveoli

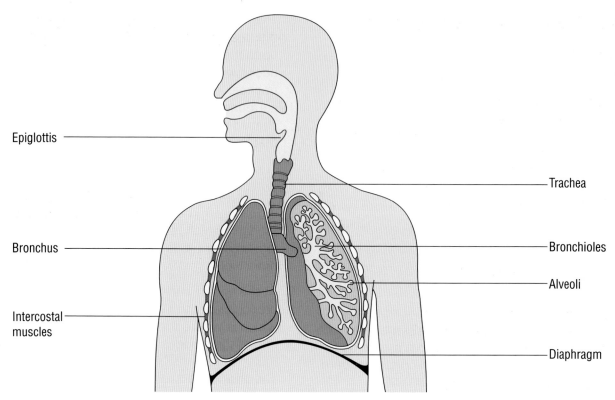

Epiglottis

Trachea

Bronchus

Bronchioles

Alveoli

Intercostal
muscles

Diaphragm

Figure 4.34   The respiratory system

Activity **4.8**   20 mins   P6

Structure of the respiratory system

Task 1

Draw a diagram to show the structure of the respiratory system. On your diagram, label the following structures:

- epiglottis
- trachea
- bronchus
- bronchioles
- alveoli
- diaphragm
- intercostal muscles.

If you need some help, take a look at Figure 4.34.

Task 2

Write a sentence about each part of the respiratory system that you have labelled to describe what happens at that point and a little bit about its structure.

For example, the air goes down the trachea, which is also known as the windpipe.

The trachea is kept in an open position by having ring-shaped pieces of cartilage along it.

Function of the Respiratory System

Mechanics of Breathing

Breathing is the term given to inhaling air into the lungs and then exhaling it. The process basically works on the principle of making the thoracic cavity (chest) larger, which decreases the pressure of air within the lungs. The surrounding air is then at a higher pressure, which means that air is forced into the lungs. Then the thoracic cavity is returned to its original size, which forces air out of the lungs.

Breathing in (inhalation)

At rest

The diaphragm contracts and moves downwards. This results in an increase in the size of the thoracic cavity and air is forced into the lungs.

Breathing out (exhalation)

At rest

The diaphragm relaxes and returns upwards to a domed position. The thoracic cavity gets smaller, which results in an increase in air pressure within the lungs so that air is breathed out of the lungs.

Gaseous exchange

> ### Definition
>
> **Gaseous exchange** in the lungs, oxygen is taken into the blood and carbon dioxide is breathed out.

The oxygen from the air we have breathed in passes through the walls of the alveoli through a process called diffusion.

> ### Definition
>
> **Diffusion** the process of gases moving from an area of high concentration to an area of low concentration. (This process is probably something you are familiar with in that if someone were to let off a stink bomb – or something similar! – in one area of a room, the smell would diffuse to other areas of the room.)

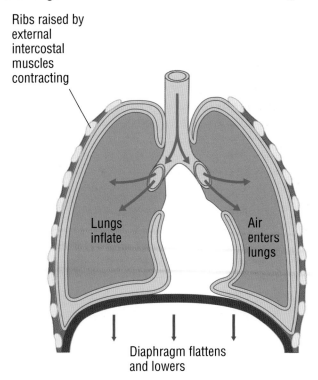

Figure 4.35 Inhalation, diaphragm and intercostal muscles

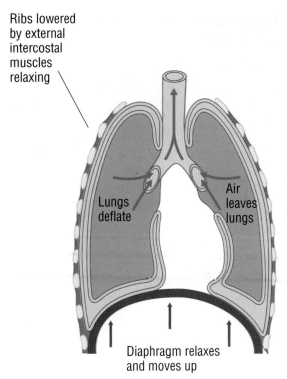

Figure 4.36 Exhalation, diaphragm and intercostal muscles

The oxygen has then passed through the walls of the alveoli and into the surrounding capillaries so that it then enters the bloodstream. In exchange for this oxygen, carbon dioxide passes out of the bloodstream through the capillaries and enters the alveoli. This carbon dioxide is then breathed out of the body.

Smoking

Figure 4.37 (a) and (b)   The lungs of (a) someone who smoked and (b) someone who has never smoked

If you smoke, the tar from your cigarette or cigar will start to block the alveoli in the lungs and eventually stop them functioning properly. The more you smoke, the more alveoli will be affected, which could also result in lung disease.

(k) Key learning points

- Air travels into the body through the mouth and nose, down the trachea and into the bronchus. It then passes into the bronchioles and down into the alveoli. In the alveoli gaseous exchange takes place, which takes oxygen into the body and passes carbon dioxide out of the body.
- The diaphragm and intercostal muscles contract to allow you to breathe in and out.

Activity 4.9   45–60 mins   M3 D2

The cardiovascular working together with the respiratory system

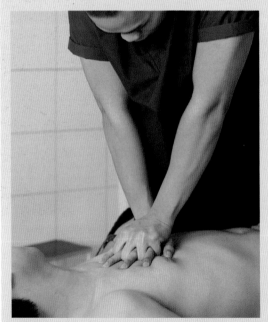

Figure 4.38   A paramedic performing CPR or 'the kiss of life'

Both the cardiovascular and respiratory systems work together to help to supply the body with oxygen and remove carbon dioxide. This process can clearly be seen when you consider the situation when a person becomes very ill or is injured and their heart stops beating and they stop breathing. When this happens, a first-aider needs to carry out a process called CPR – cardio pulmonary resuscitation – which basically means that they are breathing air into the casualty (kiss of life) and pressing down on their breast bone, which acts to push blood in and out of the heart and therefore helps to move the blood around the body.

Activity **4.9** continued

Task 1

Using hand-drawn diagrams to illustrate your answer, explain and evaluate how the cardiovascular and respiratory systems work together to supply the body with oxygen (M3) and remove carbon dioxide (D2).

To help you with your answer, consider the following points:

- Mechanics of breathing – explain how air gets into and out of the lungs.

- The heart acting as a double pump – explain how the right-hand side of the heart pumps blood to the lungs and the left hand side pumps blood around the body.
- Gaseous exchange – explain what diffusion is, then gaseous exchange, and exactly where it happens.
- Quotes from textbooks, internet sites or journals to 'back up' what you have said or explain a part of your answer.

Quick Quiz 5 mins ?

Respiratory system

Epiglottis	Diffusion	Trachea	Flattens	Inhalation
Carbon dioxide	Diaphragm	Oxygen	Gaseous exchange	Alveoli

Choose a word from the boxes above to answer the following questions.

1. **This gas passes out of the blood stream and into the lungs.**
2. **When a person swallows, this closes over the trachea to prevent food going into the lungs.**
3. **This has horseshoe-shaped cartilage to help to keep it open.**
4. **The diaphragm does this during breathing in.**
5. **This is the process where gases move from a high to a low concentration.**
6. **This is the area in the lungs where gaseous exchange takes place.**
7. **When exhaling, this muscle relaxes and moves upwards into a domed position.**
8. **This is the name of the process in the lungs where oxygen is taken into the blood and carbon dioxide is breathed out.**
9. **All of our body cells need this gas to survive.**
10. **This is the name for the process of breathing in.**

Useful websites

www.teachpe.com
Good source of images of sports physiology and anatomy.

www.bbc.co.uk/schools/gcsebitesize/pe/appliedanatomy
Interactive tests aimed at GCSE level, but which are still useful for revision of physiology and anatomy.

www.bbc.co.uk/science/humanbody/
Interactive tests and puzzles about how the human body works.

www.bhf.org.uk
Tips on how to keep your heart healthy.

www.getbodysmart.com
Free tutorials and quizzes from an American site that looks at human anatomy and physiology, helping you to see the structure of the different body systems.

www.innerbody.com
Free and informative diagrams of the different body systems, including respiratory, cardiovascular, skeletal and muscular.

www.instantanatomy.net
Free useful anatomy pictures and information, mainly from a medical viewpoint.

www.medtropolis.com/VBody.asp
A very good interactive website for anatomy with quizzes and tutorials for revision.

Further Reading

Beashel, P., Dibson, A. and Taylor, J., 2001, *The World of Sport Examined*. Cheltenham: Nelson Thornes.

References

Stafford-Brown, J., Rea, S. and Chance, J., 2003, *BTEC National in Sport and Exercise Science*. London: Hodder and Stoughton.

Chapter 5
Injury in Sport

Any person who undertakes a sporting activity will find that they are at risk of many different types of injuries. Therefore it is very important that people who take part in sports or wish to pursue a career in the sports industries have a good grasp of health and safety and are able to deal with a range of basic sports injuries.

This chapter will enable you to gain a good understanding of health and safety and how to take precautions in order to try to ensure that sport and exercise participants avoid injury. First the different types of injury and illnesses that can occur while taking part in sports are explored. Then the procedures that must be followed when dealing with an injury or illness for a range of people are covered. Basic definitions of risks and hazards are examined, followed by ways in which people, equipment and environmental factors may contribute towards injury. Rules and regulations put in place in order to help minimise the risk of injury will be discussed and, finally, to complete the chapter, you will learn why, how and when you should carry out a risk assessment and how to adapt it if necessary.

Learning Goals

By the end of this chapter you should:

- Know the different types of injuries and illness associated with sports participation.
- Be able to deal with injuries and illnesses associated with sports participation.
- Know the risks and hazards associated with sports participation.
- Be able to undertake a risk assessment relevant to sport.

To achieve a PASS grade the evidence must show that the learner is able to:	To achieve a MERIT grade the evidence must show that, in addition to the pass criteria, the learner is able to:	To achieve a DISTINCTION grade the evidence must show that, in addition to the pass and merit criteria, the learner is able to:
P1 describe four different types of injuries associated with sports participation and their underlying causes	**M1** explain why certain injuries and illnesses are associated with sports participation	
P2 describe two types and signs of illnesses related to sports participation		
P3 demonstrate how to deal with casualties suffering from three different injuries and/or illnesses, with tutor support	**M2** independently deal with casualties suffering from three different injuries and/or illnesses	
P4 describe six risks and hazards associated with sports participation	**M3** explain risks and hazards associated with sports participation	**D1** give a detailed account of why participants are at risk of injury while taking part in sport
P5 describe four rules, regulations and legislation relating to health, safety and injury in sports participation	**M4** explain four rules, regulations and legislation relating to health, safety and injury in sports participation	
P6 carry out and produce a risk assessment relevant to a selected sport	**M5** describe contingency plans that can be used in a risk assessment	**D2** justify the use of specialist equipment to minimise the risk of injury

5.1 Types of Injuries and Illnesses Associated with Sports Participation

Injury

Causes of Injury

Sports injuries are caused by either intrinsic or extrinsic factors.

Definition ⓓ

Intrinsic coming from the inside.

Intrinsic injuries result from stress inside an individual's body. Examples of intrinsic injuries are:

- an overuse injury such as shin splints
- knee-joint problems due to differences in leg length
- muscle strains due to imbalances in strength of muscle pairs
- limited flexibility can result in ligament sprains.

An extrinsic injury is caused by an outside force. Examples of an extrinsic injury are:

- a knee injury due to a bad tackle in football
- a head injury due to a collision with another player
- a black eye from being hit in the face by a squash ball.
- a cut knee from falling over on a dry ski slope.

Most injuries provide some signs and symptoms that can be used to diagnose the injury.

A sign of any injury is the physical evidence that we can see or detect by touch. This can include swelling, heat and discoloration.

Definition ⓓ

Extrinsic coming from the outside.

Symptoms are usually a list of problems associated with a particular injury, for example dizziness and nausea are both symptoms of concussion.

Definition ⓓ

Diagnose the act of identifying the type of injury (or illness).

Body Alignment

You should try to maintain good body alignment; this means you need to have good movement patterns and sustain a good body posture. A good body posture means that you maintain body alignment by keeping your back straight, shoulders back, stomach in and head looking forwards. Few of us are aware that we have poor body posture and poor body alignment until an injury occurs.

Effect of Levers

The effect of levers is a principle that primarily concerns the way in which we lift equipment. A lever consists of a rigid bar that rotates around a pivot point. Force is applied to the lever in order to lift a load. In a human, the rigid bars are the bones, the pivot point is the joint, and muscles apply the force in order to produce movement.

Think of your back as the lever; the fulcrum is at your waist and the muscles in the arms apply the force. If you are lifting a piece of equipment that weighs 4.5 kg (10 lb) and stoop to lift the equipment, the fulcrum will be in the centre and the stress on your back will be equal to the weight of the equipment plus your body weight.

However, if you stretch out further with your arms to pick up the piece of equipment, it will take more force to lift the piece of equipment, which will have the impact of placing even more stress on the back which may result in injury.

In order to reduce the length of the lever and therefore place less stress on the back, you should keep your back straight and bend your knees to lift equipment. If you place less strain on your back you are less likely to sustain a back injury.

Gravity

The effect of gravity means that if you lose your balance when playing sports, then you will more than likely fall over. You may then suffer from injuries as a result of this fall such as cuts, bruises or even fractured bones.

Types of Injury

Bruising (also known as a haematoma)

> Definition ⓓ
>
> **Haematoma** a mass of blood trapped in the body tissues, also known as bruises.

Haematoma, also known as bruises, are normally a result of an extrinsic force that squashes the muscle between the impact and the bone. This impact causes damage to the blood vessels, which leak blood into the tissue under the skin. This blood leakage is what causes the swelling and discoloration.

Strains

Strains are muscle injuries. A muscle strain is caused by muscle fibres becoming torn. The severity of the strain is linked to the percentage of muscle fibres that are torn (this also affects the recovery time). The more muscle fibres that are torn, the greater the severity of the injury.

Sprains

Sprains are injuries to your ligaments. Ligaments form a stringy structure that links bones together. Ligaments give stability to your joints. Ligament injuries often occur in sports that involve quick changes in direction. The most common ligament sprain is the ankle, for example from turning in football.

Tendonitis

Tendons join muscles to bones. Overuse from repetitive muscle contractions leads the tendon

to become inflamed and sore, making it difficult to perform the contraction without it hurting. Tendonitis is common in the achilles (the tendon connecting the heel to the calf muscle) and in the elbow joint (Tennis elbow).

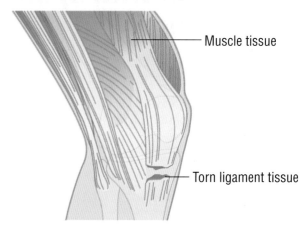

Figure 5.1 Knee ligament damage

Fractures

A fracture is a break in a bone. There is a range of different types of fractures. These include:

- A complete fracture, when the bone breaks into two pieces.

- A hairline fracture, a break in the bone. (A *complete* and a *hairline* are both known as closed fractures.)

- An open fracture, when the broken bone pierces the skin. This tends to be more serious as the open wound can easily become infected.

Figure 5.2 A complete fracture

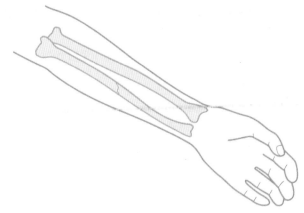

Figure 5.3   A hairline fracture

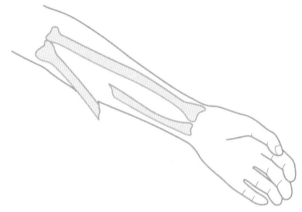

Figure 5.4   An open fracture

A bone that is broken in more than two places may have to be operated on and pinned together. A cast may be used to help immobilise the bone and help reset it, which will allow the broken ends to join together. After wearing a cast you will often lose strength in the area around the broken bone. Doctors will often prescribe strength and flexibility exercises to help regain the strength in the injured area.

Concussion

This is an injury to the brain, caused by a blow to the head. The blow to the head causes damage to the blood vessels in the brain. In some cases the injured person may become unconscious (pass out). Often the person will have headaches, feel dizzy, groggy and disorientated and possibly feel sick. Following concussion it is important to rest, as symptoms can last for weeks. Any person who gets a head injury should be referred to the hospital or a doctor to

be checked out. This is why it is important to wear a helmet when undertaking activities such as cycling, climbing and canoeing.

Spinal Injury

This is an injury to the spinal column. The spinal column includes bones (vertebrae), nerves and ligaments. Spinal injuries are often associated with head injuries and can occur in such sports as rugby and horse riding. It is important not to move a person with a back injury unless it is really necessary due to the possibility of further danger or injury to their spinal cord.

Activity **5.1**   30 mins   **P1**

Injuries in sport participation

Task 1

Choose and list four different types of injury that can occur through participation in sport.

Task 2

Write a sentence or two for each injury that you have chosen which describes how each injury could have occurred and also include whether it is an extrinsic or intrinsic sports injury.

Common Illnesses P2   M1

When taking part in any sports activity as a coach, player or leader it is important to be able to recognise the symptoms of different illnesses. A quick diagnosis can help ensure the health and safety of the group.

Asthma

This is an illness that affects a person's airways and their ability to breathe at ease. A person who has asthma normally has sensitive bronchial breathing tubes. Irritation or allergic reactions cause the tubes to become inflamed and then narrower, making it difficult to breathe. The muscles around the airway tighten, which causes the tubes to produce excess phlegm.

Symptoms include a tight chest, being short of breath and wheezing. Tablets and sprays can be taken that help to stop the tubes from being sensitive and becoming inflamed. Sprays and pumps can also be used during an asthma attack. These help relax the muscles around the airways, helping the person to breathe more easily.

Asthmatics should carry their medication with them at all times. It is important that a coach or sports leader is aware of any asthmatics in their group.

Hypoglycaemia

This is when the level of glucose (sugar level) in the blood drops below an individual's ideal level. This is common with people who suffer from Type 1 diabetes.

> ### Definition
> **Type 1 diabetes** occurs when a person's body is not producing any or enough insulin. Insulin is a hormone produced by the body to maintain blood sugar levels. A person with Type 1 diabetes requires regular insulin injections to maintain their blood sugar levels.

Hypoglycaemia occurs for a number of reasons, including not eating enough food, too much exercise, drinking too much alcohol and having too much insulin in the blood. This means that we do not have enough energy (glucose) going to the brain and the body. Symptoms of hypoglycaemia include confusion, shaking, paleness, hunger, irritability and temporary unconsciousness.

It is important for a person who has the above symptoms to eat straight away. Eating simple carbohydrates will help reverse the condition and a person will normally be fine within ten minutes.

Viral infections

The commonest forms of viral infections are colds and sore throats. These occur as a result of viruses (microscopic germs) that invade our cells and multiply. We can pass on these germs through sneezing, touching somebody and touching food.

Symptoms of viral infections include a high temperature, muscular aches and pains, a blocked nose, fever, sickness and diarrhoea. There is no medication available for viral infections, so the best advice is to stay at home, drink plenty of water to help flush the virus from your system, and take some paracetamol or ibuprofen to reduce the aches and pains and bring down your body temperature.

Heat Stroke and Exhaustion

Both of these problems are a result of dehydration (losing too much liquid and essential salts) and excess exposure to the sun and high temperatures. Heat exhaustion is caused from over-exerting yourself in hot weather. It can cause headaches, tiredness, thirst, excess sweating and muscle cramps. If you witness this happening you must ensure the person rests in a cool place and sips plenty of fluids.

Heat stroke can be far more severe and normally occurs when somebody with heat exhaustion continues to be exposed to high temperatures. The body loses the ability to cool itself down and its temperature will rise. This can cause the person to have fits and fall unconscious. Somebody with heat stroke should be admitted to hospital immediately as they may need to be put on a drip to rehydrate them and lower their body temperature.

Hypothermia

Hypothermia is when the body's core temperature drops below its normal temperature, which is anything below 36 degrees Celsius. Symptoms include loss of coordination, tiredness, slurred speech, loss of feeling and colour in hands and feet, and in extreme conditions loss of consciousness. Shivering is another key symptom. However, shivering can initially help increase heat production. This can work for only a little while as the body uses up vital energy and becomes tired.

Treatment should include getting the person into a warm, dry environment and providing them

Activity **5.2**   20 mins

Types and signs of illness

Case study 1

A 16-year-old girl called Chloe is taking part in a cross-school volleyball tournament. Her team are winning and they are all trying really hard to do their best. Towards the second half of the game, Chloe finds that she is beginning to feel quite out of breath and starts to wheeze. Her chest starts to hurt and feels tight. Chloe feels that she can't continue playing and signals to her teacher that she needs to stop playing.

Case study 2

Kevin lives in Australia, is 15 years old, and is running his first half marathon. It is a particularly hot sunny day with very little breeze. Kevin is keen to get the best time that he can and is running at a quicker pace than normal, with sweat dripping off him. After 10 miles he realises that he has not stopped to get any drinks from the drinks stands and is now feeling very thirsty. A mile or so later he starts to get a very bad headache and he is beginning to get cramp in his leg muscles.

Task 1

From the information given above:

- describe the signs of illness that Chloe is showing
- suggest which illness you think Chloe is suffering from
- explain how this illness can occur during sports participation.

Task 2

From the information given above:

- describe the signs of illness that Kevin is showing
- state what illness you think Kevin is suffering from
- explain how this illness can occur during sports participation.

with additional warm clothing and a hot drink or meal. Once the person is feeling better, try to get them to walk around, as this will increase their body temperature. If the person is wearing wet clothing they should take this off and put on dry clothes. Hypothermia is a major threat to participants of outdoor pursuits, especially those where the participants are exposed to extreme temperatures. It is important to consider the following factors:

- Wet and windy conditions will increase the risk of hypothermia.

- Try to stay dry – if you are wet your body temperature will fall rapidly.

- Ensure you use suitable clothing and equipment to keep yourself dry and warm.

Activity **5.3**   30 mins

Illnesses and injuries in sport

Task

You have now examined a range of different injuries and illnesses that are associated with sports participation.

Select:

- four different types of injury, and
- four different types of illness

and write a report that explains why each is associated with sports participation.

(k) Key learning points

- Different causes of injury are intrinsic factors, extrinsic factors, overuse, alignment, effect of levers, gravity.
- Different types of injury include overuse injuries, fractures, strains (ligaments), sprains (muscles), grazes, bruising, concussion, spinal injuries.
- Sign of an illness or injury is what you can see and feel, such as swelling and bruising.
- Symptom is what the casualty tells you, for example feeling sick.

5.2 Procedures and Treatment P3 M2

When treating a casualty you must first of all make sure that you are safe and not putting yourself at risk, for example if the casualty is lying just over the edge of a cliff it may well not be safe for you to go to them and treat them. However, it may be something that you can deal with, such as turning off an electricity switch. Your priority after checking your own safety is to ensure that you protect the casualty from further risk.

Dealing with an Emergency

When an emergency occurs it is important that you remain calm, so as to minimise the risk of injury to yourself and others. Your initial assessment could save somebody's life.

Upon finding a casualty or when a person is injured, it is important to summon assistance as soon as possible.

The following guidelines should be followed in an emergency:

1. Stay calm, as this will help you think more clearly.

2. Analyse the situation: is anybody hurt or in danger?

Quick Quiz 10 mins (?)

Injuries and illnesses

Extrinsic risk factor	Haematoma	Strain	Sign	Asthma
Intrinsic	Symptom	Sprain	Hypothermia	Concussion

Choose a word(s) from the boxes above to answer the following questions.

1. This is an injury to a ligament.
2. Shin splints is an example of an _____ risk factor.
3. This is the technical term for a bruise.
4. This is the name of an injury to a muscle.
5. This type of injury occurs from a blow to the head.
6. An example of this would be if a person said they were feeling sick.
7. An example of this would be if a person was sick.
8. A bad tackle in football is an example of an _____ risk factor.
9. A person suffering from this illness could have the following symptoms: a tight chest, being short of breath and wheezing.
10. This type of illness means that the person is extremely cold.

3. Ensure that you or anybody else is not at further risk of injury before proceeding.

4. Get help. This may mean contacting a first-aider or calling the emergency services.

5. Tell them where you are and what's happened, giving precise details.

6. Apply first aid (if required) until someone more experienced can take over.

Casualty a person injured or killed as a result of an incident.

Emergency a serious incident that happens suddenly or unexpectedly and is likely to require different forms of assistance.

Calling the Emergency Services

When calling the emergency services it is important to be as specific as possible. They will ask where you are, what has happened and if anyone is hurt. They will also ask for a contact phone number. If you send someone else to make the phone call, always ensure that they come back to you, so that you know the call has been made.

Often people who have been involved in an accident will suffer from shock. Shock usually makes it difficult for a person to focus on anything and both their heart rate and blood pressure may drop, which will make them feel faint. It is important that anyone who has been in an accident is looked after. By keeping the person warm and getting them to sit or lie down you will help reduce the risk of shock. It is also important to talk to the casualty and reassure them that everything will be fine and that help will be on its way soon.

Definition

Emergency services the organisations that deal with emergency incidents such as fire, crime, injuries and illnesses.

On-site qualified first-aiders

Most sports providers will have their own qualified first-aiders who will deal with any injuries or illnesses that can occur. Most minor injuries can often be dealt with on the spot, but major injuries often require further treatment. If the injured person is not admitted to hospital they should be referred to a doctor.

Reporting accidents

Accidents must be reported. Most sport facilities have their own documentation which has to be completed. If you witnessed an accident you would need to ensure that you completed the appropriate documentation and may also need to attend an interview with a site manager to discuss details of the accident.

Types of casualty

As a person working in the sports industry, you may encounter a range of casualties, for example those involving adults, children and/or people with particular needs. When dealing with each of these you should follow the same procedures, but if a child is the casualty try to find their parents to help, or contact them as soon as possible and make them aware of the situation. If you are dealing with a person with specific needs, such as a blind person, try to keep them informed of exactly what you are doing, or are about to do, for example 'I am going to take a look at your injury. Is that OK?'

5.3 Dealing with Different Types of Injury and Illness

Most minor injuries and illnesses can be dealt with on site – these could include muscle strains, ligament sprains, bruising, grazes, minor heat stroke, minor asthma attack etc.

The RICE Treatment Method

Virtually all minor sporting injuries can be treated using the RICE treatment method. Using this method helps reduce inflammation and pain, as it reduces the blood flow to the injured body part.

Rest – stop using the injured body part. This will help stop the pain and prevent further injury. Try to rest the injury for at least 24 hours.

Ice – this will help relieve the pain and has the effect of closing the damaged blood vessels from leaking blood to the injured area.

Compression – this will help reduce the swelling and protect the injured area. Be careful not to compress the injury too tightly, as this will stop the circulation to the injury.

Elevation – try to keep the injured body part elevated above the heart. If it is the leg, put some cushions or clothes underneath to elevate it. This reduces the swelling and drains the excess fluid away from the injured body part.

Major injuries such as fractures, concussion, spinal injuries and major illnesses such as a heart attack, uncontrollable asthma attack and heat stroke need to be treated by medical professionals.

Definition

Injury when referring to a sports injury this means physical damage to somebody's body caused by an incident.

Activity **5.4** 30 mins P3 M2

Dealing with injuries and illnesses associated with sports participation

Case study

A sports leader is running a 5-a-side football game with a group of 14–16 year olds. During the game a player slides in to tackle an opponent but makes contact with the opponent's shin rather than the ball. The sound of a cracking noise is clearly heard and the player that has been tackled falls to the ground in agony.

Task

The sports leader now has to deal with the casualty. If you were the sports leader, how would you deal with the following questions?

1. What sort of injury do you think the player has sustained?
2. How would you call for help?
3. Who would you call for help?
4. How would you protect the casualty?
5. How would you reassure and comfort the casualty?

Activity **5.5** 30–45 mins P3 M2

Role play dealing with casualties

You will need to work in pairs for this activity.

Task 1

Select a total of three injuries and/or illnesses associated with sports participation without telling your partner – try to ensure that one of your choices is minor and one is a major illness or injury.

For example: spinal injury, asthma attack and a sprained ankle.

Make a note of each injury and/or illness and research the signs and symptoms of each.

Task 2

Carry out a role-play exercise where one person acts as a casualty and the other acts as a person dealing with the casualty.

Points to consider:

- Follow the correct procedures to deal with your casualty.
- The casualty will need to describe their symptoms to you as they will not have the injury or illness. They could also help by giving you details of the signs of their illness or injury. For example, if their selected injury was a sprained ankle they could say 'my ankle has really swollen up' or 'my ankle feels really hot'.

Repeat this role play so that you both demonstrate how you would deal with three different injuries and/or illnesses.

Key learning points

- When approaching a casualty you should always make sure you will be safe.
- Protect the casualty from further injury.
- Get help as soon as possible either from on site first-aiders or call an ambulance.
- Ensure you are aware of what sorts of injuries require urgent medical assistance and which types can be treated on site.

Quick Quiz 10 mins

Dealing with injuries and illnesses associated with sports participation

Answer the following questions with either True or False.

1. A first-aid provider should always ensure they are safe prior to administering first aid.
2. If a person was thought to be having a heart attack you would call your local doctor out.
3. RICE treatment should always be used if a person has stomach cramps.
4. All accidents should be reported in an accident report.
5. If the casualty is a child you should always try to find their parents or guardians.
6. An emergency situation is when there is not enough equipment available for the planned activity.
7. A fractured bone can be treated and dealt with on site.
8. A casualty who suffers a grazed knee should be taken straight to hospital.
9. When calling the emergency services, you must tell the operator where you are and what sort of injury the casualty is suffering from.
10. Emergency services are the organisations that deal with emergency incidents such as fire, crime, injuries and illnesses.

5.4 Hazards and Risks Associated with Sports Participation P4 M3 D1

Definition

Hazard something that is dangerous, and therefore has the potential to affect someone's safety or cause an injury.

Most sport and outdoor pursuit activities contain many hazard factors that could affect a person's general health. Therefore the participants must ensure that they remain safe and avoid the possibility of injury or even death. This is normally the responsibility of the person leading the session.

Examples of hazards could include:

- broken glass on a football pitch
- a strong current in the sea, used for kayaking.

Definition

Risk the possibility of something bad happening.

A risk is linked to the chance of somebody being harmed by the potential hazard. Risks are often categorised into how likely they are to happen. Something that is a low risk means that the likelihood of it happening is low, whereas something that is high risk means that it is likely to happen.

Hazards

There are many potential hazards associated with participating in sporting and outdoor activities, many of which can result in the risk of injury. These can be categorised into three groups:

1. People factors
2. Equipment factors
3. Environment factors.

People Factors

These are hazards that are caused by people, such as yourself or another person. For example:

- Not warming up or cooling down correctly – this could lead to muscle strains.

- An opponent playing recklessly – a high tackle in rugby could cause a serious neck injury.

- Playing under the influence of alcohol or drugs.

- Playing your sport wearing jewellery.

- Playing your sport while chewing gum.

- Using the incorrect technique to lift weights.

- Overtraining and not allowing time for recovery can cause overuse injury.

- Not having enough experience to do the activity.

- Not being able to work as a team.

Equipment Factors

Many sport and outdoor activities require special equipment, and there are many equipment factors that can lead to a potential injury. These include the following:

- Not wearing the correct protective equipment.

- Using gym equipment without knowing how to use it correctly.

- Equipment not being set up correctly, for example climbing ropes and harnesses.

- Not having the correct clothing for the conditions.

It is important that all equipment is checked prior to being used to ensure that it is complete, in working order and not faulty or damaged.

Environment Factors

Environmental hazards are often uncontrollable; however, it is important to make a judgement on potential hazards prior to starting an activity. Where the environment could have a big impact on your sporting activity, for example mountain climbing or sailing, you should ensure you receive local weather forecasts for that day in order to determine if you should continue with the planned activity.

- The weather can cause sports fields to become a dangerous environment to play sport on. An icy or waterlogged field has the potential to cause many types of injury.

- Undertaking exercise in hot conditions can cause participants to become tired more quickly and can cause problems such as dehydration and heat exhaustion.

- If participants are unsure of the surroundings, this can lead to problems (for example getting lost in the mountains while walking).

- Extreme wet and cold weather can lead to hypothermia.

- High winds can cause a potential hazard to people undertaking water-based activities such as sailing.

5.5 Rules, Regulations and Legislation P6 M5 D2

There are many government initiatives that have been developed to ensure the health, safety and well-being of humans. The following are all linked to the sports industry.

The Health and Safety at Work Act (1974)

The Health and Safety at Work Act was introduced in 1974, due to thousands of accidents and near-misses in the work place. It obliges employers to take reasonable steps to ensure the health, safety and welfare of their employees while they are at work.

The following three factors can affect health and safety in the work place:

1. Occupational factors – people may be at risk from injuries or illnesses because of the work they do.

2. Environmental factors – the conditions in which people work may cause problems.

3. Human factors – poor attitudes and behaviour can contribute to accidents.

Statistics show that injuries at work are most commonly caused by:

- Lifting incorrectly
- Slipping, tripping, falling over
- Coming into contact with moving machinery
- Coming into contact with harmful substances
- Fire
- Being struck by a vehicle.

It is the responsibility of both employers and employees to ensure that Health and Safety are maintained (see Table 5.1).

Control of Substances Hazardous to Health Regulations COSHH (1994)

Hazardous substances are used in many working environments. These are classed as anything that can cause ill health such as asthma, skin irritation and poisoning.

COSHH covers substances that can:

- Be used directly in work, for example cleaning materials
- Arise from the work, for example dust or fumes
- Occur naturally.

For example, a swimming pool's plant room will have many chemicals that could cause illness or injury and they therefore fall under this Act. These regulations tell employees why they need to control hazardous substances and include:

- Labelling certain hazardous products
- Keeping certain substances in a suitable environment, for example a locked cabinet.

Health and Safety (First Aid) Act (1981)

This Act requires companies and organisations to have sufficient first-aid facilities and equipment in case of injury or illness affecting their employees. The number of qualified first-aiders will be related to the number of employees working in the organisation.

The Safety of Sports Grounds Act (1975)

After several severe disasters at football grounds, the Safety of Sports Grounds Act 1975 was introduced. The first part of the Act introduced licensing of sports grounds and ensures they adhere to certain guidelines. Sports grounds holding more than 10,000 must have set capacities and may be used for only a set purpose; if they satisfy this they are granted a safety certificate.

The certificate states:

- The number each section of the stadium holds.
- The situation of all exits including those to be used in an emergency.
- The number of crush barriers required.

The act also highlights problem areas that need to be dealt with efficiently. These include:

1. Potential hazards to individuals that could cause them to trip or fall at a sports ground.

2. Being able to evacuate the ground quickly in the event of an emergency.

This Act has been revisited since the Bradford and Hillsborough tragedies, which saw the introduction of the Taylor Report.

Fire Safety & Safety of Places of Sport Act (1987)

This Act was drawn up after the Bradford fire tragedy in1986. The Act requires that all sports arenas and stadiums have sufficient means of escape in the event of a fire. The venue must also provide adequate equipment for fighting fire.

The Children Act (1989)

This Act looks to ensure that there are consistent standards of care given to children. It requires organisations to provide training and ensure standards of care are maintained.

A sporting example of this would include a summer sports coaching camp requiring qualified, competent and police-checked staff who know how to work with young children.

Key learning points

- A hazard is something that is dangerous, and therefore has the potential to affect someone's safety or cause an injury. The different types of hazards can be:
  —People factors
  —Equipment factors
  —Environment factors
- A risk is the possibility of something bad happening.
- The Health and Safety at Work Act (1974) obliges employers to take reasonable steps to ensure the health, safety and welfare of their employees while they are at work.
- Control of Substances Hazardous to Health Regulations (COSHH) (1994) ensures any products that may cause ill health are used and stored correctly.
- Health and Safety (First Aid) Act (1981) requires companies and organisations to have sufficient first-aid facilities and equipment.
- The Safety of Sports Grounds Act (1975) aims to ensure that sports grounds are safe for spectators.
- Fire Safety & Safety of Places of Sport Act (1987) requires all sports arenas and stadiums to have sufficient means of escape in the event of a fire.
- The Children Act (1989) aims to ensure that there are consistent standards of care given to children.

Quick Quiz 10 mins

Health and Safety at Work Act	Hazard	Wet pitch	Health and Safety (First Aid) Act	High risk
Chewing gum while playing sport	Fire Safety & Safety of Places of Sport Act	Risk	The Children Act	Forgetting to wear a gum shield when playing rugby

Choose a word or words from the boxes above to answer the following questions.

1. This is the possibility of something bad happening.
2. This ensures that employers take reasonable steps to ensure the health, safety and welfare of their employees while they are at work.
3. This law requires companies and organisations to have sufficient first-aid facilities and equipment.
4. This is an example of an environmental hazard.
5. This law requires all sports arenas and stadiums to have sufficient means of escape in the event of a fire.
6. This law aims to ensure that there are consistent standards of care given to children.
7. This is an example of a people hazard.
8. This is something that is dangerous, and therefore has the potential to affect someone's safety or cause an injury.
9. This is an example of an equipment hazard.
10. Something that is this type of risk means that it is likely to happen.

Activity 5.6 30 mins   P5

Rules and regulations   M4

There are lots of rules and regulations relating to health and safety in the sports industry to try to ensure people who take part in sports are exposed to as few risks as possible so that they are less likely to suffer from an injury.

Have a think about where you work or where you would like to work in the sports industry. Investigate four rules, regulations and legislations that could apply to you when you go into your chosen career.

Task 1

Design a health and safety leaflet that describes and explains four rules, regulations and legislation that are related to health and safety for people who take part in sports.

5.6 Risk Assessment P6

Risk assessment is a technique for preventing any potential accidents, injury or ill health by helping people to consider what could go wrong either in the work place or on the sports field. A risk assessment looks at the possible hazards that may occur, the likelihood of them happening and how the hazards could be prevented.

In sporting activities and outdoor pursuits risk assessments are important and need to be undertaken by a range of people; a manager of a sports centre, a basketball coach and a mountain walker would all need to ensure that they had undertaken a risk assessment prior to starting their activity.

Risk assessments should be logged, stored and reviewed regularly to see if they are up to date and to check whether any of the details have changed. Britain's Health and Safety Commission (HSC) and the Health and Safety Executive (HSE) are responsible for the regulations of the risk to health and safety in the work places of Britain. All major organisations in sport will have a health and safety policy.

Undertaking a Risk Assessment

We have established that a risk assessment is about identifying hazards and assessing the risks associated with them. How do we undertake a risk assessment? This is something we do informally in everyday life. For example, a racing car driver wishing to overtake will look at factors such as the speed they are travelling, the layout of the track and the weather conditions, in order to overtake safely. By looking at these the driver is assessing the hazards so as to minimise the risk of an accident.

Risk Assessment

After you have highlighted a particular hazard you can use the following formula to assess the potential problems that may arise:

In the example shown on page 92, the likelihood of the risk happening multiplied by the severity results in a score of 4 which means that the risk is worth taking but with extreme caution. In order to minimise the risk, participants can wear specialist equipment or indeed something as simple as removing the broken glass off the football pitch will greatly reduce the risk of a person being injured by it.

Specialist Equipment D2

The use of specialist equipment, such as protective clothing and accessories, can help minimise the risk of sporting injuries or even help to reduce the likelihood of an accident happening. This could include having safety goggles, where a person is at risk of getting something in their eye such as a squash ball when playing squash or goggles when swimming to stop chlorinated water irritating the eye. Cyclists can wear helmets in case they fall off and bump their heads, while a batsman can wear protective equipment such as a box to prevent injury of sensitive body parts from the ball. Safety ropes are usually used in climbing and abseiling to minimise the risk of potential danger. In leisure centres, you will see warning signs of floors that are wet to make people aware of slippery floors. This is a control

LIKELIHOOD x SEVERITY

LIKELIHOOD – Is it likely to happen?

1. Unlikely

2. Quite likely

3. Very likely.

SEVERITY – How badly someone could be injured.

1. No injury/minor incident

2. Injury requiring medical assistance

3. Major injury or fatality.

Example: Broken glass on a park football pitch injuring a player

Likelihood of happening?   2 Quite likely

Severity?   2 Injury requiring medical assistance

By multiplying the likelihood against the severity you will be able to set a chart that looks at the potential problems and make a decision on whether you want to take the risk or whether it is too much of a hazard.

Likelihood x Severity	Is the risk worth taking?
1	Yes with caution
2	Yes possibly with caution
3	Yes possibly with extreme caution
4	Yes possibly with extreme caution
5	No
6	No

Example of a Risk Assessment Form

Location of Risk Assessment: SPORTS HALL

Risk Assessors name: O.Opsudaisy

Date: 28.09.10

Hazard observed	People at risk	Level of risk (liklehood x severity)	Use of Specialist Equipment	Risk rating with specialist equipment
Wet floor	5 a side footall players	2	Mop up water off the floor	1

measure to alert people that the floor may be wet and helps reduce the risk of injury by bringing attention to the hazard.

Reviewing the Risk Assessment

It is important that once a risk assessment has been undertaken, it is reviewed and updated regularly. As equipment gets older, it is more likely to go wrong and therefore become more hazardous. Undertaking an activity at a new venue or in a different environment also needs to be looked at even if you are undertaking an activity you are familiar with.

Contingency Plans

A contingency plan is set in case the original plan cannot be met. It is written on additional paper and kept with the risk assessment. It is an important tool that is used by a sports instructor or coach if they cannot stick to their original plan. There is a large range of external factors that may cause a sports instructor to have to use their contingency plan; poor weather, inadequate equipment, a change in the number of participants or a mixture of participants with different skill levels could mean that you will need to make new plans.

Reporting Procedures

Health and safety are the responsibility of everyone. In the work place, everyone should be responsible, but in sports activities it is often the responsibility of the instructor, coach or leader. If an accident happens or there is a near-miss, it needs to be reported and documented, so that it can be looked at, dealt with accordingly and, hopefully, stopped from happening again.

Activity **5.7** 60–90 mins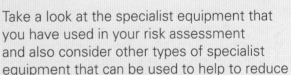

Carrying out a risk assessment

You have been asked to assist leading a sports session of your choice to a group of primary-aged children. Your sport can take place at a venue of your choice, for example outdoor football pitch, indoor sports hall, astro turf pitch.

Task 1

Think of and list the hazards that may be associated with your sports session and the sports participants.

Remember to consider: people factors, environmental factors and equipment factors.

Task 2

Produce a risk assessment for your selected sport that also includes risk control measures and whether further action should be required.

Task 3

Take a look at the specialist equipment that you have used in your risk assessment and also consider other types of specialist equipment that can be used to help to reduce the risk of injury to sports participants.

Write a report that justifies the use of this specialist equipment that explains:

● the purpose of the equipment
● why the equipment should be used
● what could happen if the equipment was not used
● any rules, regulations or legislation that relate to why the specialist equipment should be used.

Activity 5.8 45–60 mins M5

Contingency plans and specialist equipment

Task 1

Write a report that describes what a contingency plan is and how it can be used when in conjunction with a risk assessment.

Task 2

For the risk assessment that you have devised, include a contingency plan or plans to take into account any unforeseen circumstances that you might encounter, such as problems with the equipment, more children taking part than expected etc.

(k) Key learning points

- Risk assessments should be carried out before any practical activity.
- A risk assessment looks at the possible hazards and risks that may occur and how they can be prevented.
- Specialist equipment can be used to help minimise the risks and therefore make participants less likely to become seriously injured when taking part in activities.
- Contingency plans should always be made before activities so that activities can still take place despite unforeseen circumstances.
- Any accidents or near-misses should be reported and documented.

Quick Quiz 10 mins (?)

Find the following words in the wordsearch below:

CONTINGENCY
ASSESSMENT
REPORTING
SEVERITY
CAUTION
REVIEW
HSE
HSC

C	I	T	O	R	S	E	U	T	I	A	B
F	I	E	T	E	M	N	S	M	S	A	A
U	W	G	L	V	E	E	G	S	L	E	A
C	O	N	T	I	N	G	E	N	C	Y	G
A	H	H	N	E	K	S	H	R	D	N	B
U	P	S	P	W	S	L	S	S	I	T	A
T	I	O	E	M	R	G	I	T	C	S	S
I	E	M	E	E	C	Y	R	H	L	T	R
O	A	N	I	H	I	O	D	A	O	O	M
N	T	N	E	T	P	A	E	E	W	O	E
Y	T	I	R	E	V	E	S	F	E	A	D
O	S	B	R	E	L	K	E	T	N	E	A

Useful websites

www.safesport.co.uk

Invaluable tips related to specific sports to help making participating more safe.

http://health.kaboose.com/active-kids/Water_Safety.html

Safety tips on how to stay safe when active in and on the water.

Chapter 6
Sports Development

Sports have existed as a leisure activity in some shape or form since the birth of mankind. However, organised sports in the forms we would recognise have only been in existence for around 150 years. For example, football as we know it only set down its rules in 1863 and Rugby Union in 1872.

By the end of this chapter you will have a clear picture of how sport is provided for in twenty-first century Great Britain, how and why people participate, or even why they do not, who is responsible for the development of sport and the impact of sports development on society as a whole

Learning Goals

By the end of this chapter you should:

- Know the nature of sports provision.
- Know how and why people participate in sport.
- Know the role of local and national organisations responsible for sports development.
- Know the impact of different key issues on the sports industry.

To achieve a PASS grade the evidence must show that the learner is able to:	To achieve a MERIT grade the evidence must show that, in addition to the pass criteria, the learner is able to:	To achieve a DISTINCTION grade the evidence must show that, in addition to the pass and merit criteria, the learner is able to:
P1 describe local voluntary, public and private sector sports provision for three different sports	**M1** compare local and national sports provision, identifying areas for improvement	**D1** evaluate local and national sports provision, explaining ways in which provision could be improved
P2 describe three different types of national sports provision that support elite performance		
P3 describe ways in which people participate in sport and reasons for participation		
P4 describe factors that affect participation in sport		
P5 describe strategies used to encourage participation in a selected sport	**M2** explain strategies used to encourage participation in a selected sport	**D2** evaluate strategies to encourage participation in a selected sport, making recommendations for future strategies
P6 describe the role of one local and one national organisation responsible for the development of sport	**M3** explain the role of one local and one national organisation responsible for the development of sport	
P7 describe four key issues in sport and identify their impact on sport	**M4** explain the impact of four key issues on sport	

6.1 Definitions

Leisure, sport and physical recreation are often lumped together when referring to physical activity, but there are differences between the three terms.

Definition (d)

Leisure activities that take place in time off from work, usually done for purposes of enjoyment, relaxation and socialisation; may be active or passive and could involve any of the following: reading, watching television, playing sports, going to the cinema, playing bingo or going out for a meal with friends.

Sport a physical activity that is done with the aim of winning the event or competition. It will involve either physical skill or physical exertion and has to be played to rules that have been set down by a governing body. The governing body will also provide officials and some form of structured competition.

Physical recreaction the participation in physical activity for fun, which is central to physical recreation.

6.2 Local Provision for Sport P1 M1 D1

When we look at provision for sport in a particular area we look at three things:

1. Who provides the money to fund the sports?

2. Why do they provide this money?

3. What sports do they provide for?

Sport is provided by three very different sectors. What do these mean?

1. **Public sector** – this is money spent by the government on sport. 'Public' means money is raised by charging the general public tax, and then this money is invested in sport. In local provision this usually means the local council, which acts under guidance from central government but prioritises funding according to local needs. Public sector facilities might include swimming pools, parks and golf courses.

Compulsory Competitive Tendering (CCT)

In the early 1990s the national government decided that, in order to ensure that council-owned facilities were managed properly and gave good value for money, companies would be invited to manage these facilities on behalf of the local authority. The facility would still be owned by the local authority, but the local authority would no longer employ people to work in these facilities.

2. **Private sector** – this means that money is invested by private individuals to provide sports facilities. These individuals invest their own money with the hope of making a profit for themselves. In recent years several large fitness chains have emerged that have health and fitness clubs all around the country.

3. **Voluntary sector** – this means that sport is run and funded by volunteers to provide sporting opportunities for other people with the same interests. They do not want to make a profit; they just want to play sport. Local examples of this could be scout groups, local sports clubs, athletic clubs etc. If you stop to think about your local area and how many people are involved in sports that are unpaid, you will notice that it by far outnumbers those who have careers in sport and leisure.

Public Sector Provision

How to identify public sector facilities:

1. They are funded by money from the local council.

2. They are large in size.

3. They are usually named after the town, city or area.

4. They are priced to be available to everyone rather than to exclude people.

5. They offer facilities for team and individual sports.

6. Their facilities offer sports opportunities rather than comfort or luxury.

7. The people who work there are employed by the local council.

8. They often receive grants from Sport England or national governing bodies of sport.

Public sector facilities are provided by local authorities with the aim of offering people a positive activity to do in their leisure time. These facilities often lose money as they do not charge enough money for entrance or membership to make a profit. However, this is not important because they want to improve the quality of people's lives and offer them the benefits of taking part in sport.

Private Sector Provision

How to identify private sector facilities:

1. They are usually named after a person or given an attractive name.

2. They provide mainly for individual sports.

3. They offer often expensive memberships which are paid monthly or yearly.

4. They are often expensive to join.

5. They tend to be plush and luxurious.

6. They are aimed at certain groups of people rather than the general public.

Voluntary Sector Provision

The voluntary sector includes sports clubs which offer opportunities to play competitive sport.

How to identify voluntary sector clubs:

1. They provide for competitive sports.

2. They offer opportunities for only one sport.

3. They are funded by members on a yearly

membership basis and charge fees for individual matches as well.

4. They rarely own their own facilities and will hire facilities from the public sector.

5. They may receive sponsorship from local businesses.

6. They are managed by a committee that is voted for by the members.

7. They are usually named after their town or city.

8. They are not trying to make a profit.

9. They have to be affiliated through their national governing body.

In summary, voluntary sector clubs are funded and run by members for the benefit of all the members. The aim is to provide opportunities to be involved in sport on a competitive level. If you look at the sports you are involved in outside school or college, it is very likely that they will be through the voluntary sector.

Activity 6.1 45 mins   P1

Local sports provision

In groups of two or three, carry out research on the internet and using local papers complete a spider diagram that lists all the sports facilities which you have in your local area. Where possible, try to visit some of these facilities so that you can observe the facilities and the activities that they have to offer.

Task 1

Then using the sports facilities that you have researched, divide them into public, private or voluntary sector.

Task 2

Write a report that describes the provision in your local area for three different sports:

- the voluntary sector
- public sector
- private sector.

6.3 National Provision for Sport P2

National provision of sport is focused on supporting the pinnacle of the sports development continuum, the elite performers. This might include world and Olympic champions, world record holders, and the very best in national and international sports.

In recent years much government funding has been provided to support elite athletes.

In UK sport there are many levels of performance. If you imagine all of the sporting activity in the UK, you might start by thinking of Premier League football or rugby, Olympic and world class athletes in many sports, and professional tennis players and elite golfers.

It is easy to identify with these performers because they have a great deal of media exposure, that is to say, they are often on TV, in the newspapers, on the internet and so on.

It might be easy to forget all of the people who play sport for the first time, in parks, on lakes and at school, or those who might be somewhere in-between, perhaps part of a county team, a regional team or even semi-professional.

National Sports Centres

There are four national sports centres, which are all managed by Sport England and all provide national and international standard training and competition facilities to a number of national governing bodies of sport.

They are:

1. Bisham Abbey – which houses over 20 different sports including hockey, tennis and football.

2. Lilleshall – which specialises in gymnastics, the treatment of sporting injuries, archery and wheelchair basketball.

3. Plas y Brenin – in Wales, which caters for canoeing, mountain leader training and climbing, among other sports.

4. English Institute of Sport (EIS) – see the box below.

English Institute of Sport (EIS)

What is it?

While the key site is in Sheffield, Yorkshire, EIS is a nationwide network of sport science and sports medical support services, designed to develop athletic talent.
It offers excellent elite athlete support in: Sports Medicine, Physiotherapy, Strength & Conditioning, Physiology, Performance Nutrition, Sports Psychology, Biomechanics, Performance Analysis, Performance Lifestyle, Soft Tissue Therapy and Talent Identification.

Who is it for?

EIS supports summer and winter Olympic and Paralympic sports as well as English sports. The majority of the athletes it supports are those who are UK Sport Lottery funded.

The EIS is grant funded through the UK Sport Lottery Fund.

What facilities are there?

- Athletics arena (six-lane 200 m indoor tracks and indoor throws area)
- Badminton, netball, combat, boxing and table tennis halls
- World snooker academy
- Community health and fitness gym
- Sports science and sports medicine facility
- Elite heavy weights gym

Figure 6.1 EIS, Sheffield

The roles of governing bodies:

1. Setting rules for the sport.
2. Implementing the rules of the sport.
3. Changing rules of the sport.
4. Finding ways of improving the sport through technology.
5. Providing officials for matches.
6. Organising competitions.
7. Providing codes of conduct for players.
8. Disciplining players who break the rules or codes of conduct.
9. Fining or banning offending players.
10. Providing a system of drug testing.

Governing Bodies of Sport

To be recognised as a sport there must be a governing body to control the activities of the participants involved in that sport. Governing bodies are found at a local, national and international level. For example, Figure 6.4 shows the structure of governing bodies for football.

In this example, we have an international governing body (FIFA), a European governing body (UEFA), a national governing body (English FA) and county governing bodies (Herts FA), each of which has different responsibilities. You will find similar structures in all sports.

Activity **6.2** 50 mins   P2

Elite performance

Select three different types of national sport that you are interested in.

Task 1

Carry out research to find out how these sports and their elite participants are supported through national sports provision.

Activity **6.3** 45–60 mins   M1

Local and national sports provision   D1

Carry out research using newspapers, journals and the internet to find out about the national provision for three different types of sports.

Task 1

Draw out a table like the one shown below.

Write in your three selected sports. Then write a paragraph in each box to compare the local and national provision of each selected sport.

Task 2

Evaluate the local and national provision of your selected sports and then identify and explain ways in which you think this provision could be improved.

Sport	Local provision	National provision

11. Finding sponsorship for events and competitions.

12. Selling the rights to show the sport on television.

13. Raising money for the sport.

14. Managing and developing the sport.

Quick Quiz 1 10 mins

1. **Give a definition for sport.**
2. **What are the four levels of the sports development continuum?**
3. **Give a description of public sector leisure provision in your area.**
4. **Give a description of private sector leisure provision in your area.**
5. **Give a description of voluntary sector leisure provision in your area.**
6. **Name the four main national sports centres.**
7. **What is the EIS, where is it, and what does it do?**
8. **Find out three governing bodies, one from a racket sport, one from a team sport and one from a combat sport.**

(k) Key learning points

- Leisure can be defined as activities that take place in time off work and are usually done for purposes of enjoyment, relaxation and socialisation.
- Sport is a physical activity involving skill, which is done with the aim of winning the event or competition.
- Physical recreation involves activities that are physical in nature but are done for reasons other than winning.
- Public sector sport is provided by government and local authorities from money raised from the public.
- Private sector facilities are provided by private individuals to make a profit for themselves.
- Voluntary sector – this means that sport is run and funded by volunteers to provide sporting opportunities for other people with the same interests.

6.4 How and Why People Participate in Sport P3 P4 P5
M2 D2

Ways

There are many ways in which a person can be involved in sport, each of which gives different rewards and benefits.

Performer

Most people start off in the sports industry at the performance level. As they become more and more successful, their interest in sport grows and they start to become aware of other opportunities. Some people are lucky enough to go on and become professional sports people while others remain amateur and enjoy the rewards of participation.

Official

Some people will want to work as an official because it keeps them involved in the excitement of sport after their playing career has finished. It also gives them the chance to use the knowledge they have gained during their career.

Coach

Some people will use their expertise to assist in the development of other people involved in their sport. As the skills needed to become an effective coach are different from those needed to be an effective player, it can be that people find themselves more suited to coaching.

Administrator

An administrator is involved in running or managing a sport or team on behalf of the players involved. This involves the use of organisational skills.

Spectator

Many millions of people are involved in consuming sport through spectating, either in person or via the television. It is often the way in which people first become interested in sport. It is also a big source of income for the clubs that attract spectators.

Retailer

The retail industry in sport is a huge source of income. However, this money is not directly made available to sport, although sports retailers may sponsor teams to get their product known and recognised. This industry sells sports goods to make a profit for themselves.

Medical Staff

Physiotherapists, sports massage therapists, doctors and osteopaths are often involved in sport to provide support services to the athletes. Each top-level athlete will have their own support network around them.

Sports Development

Each local authority will have sports development workers to raise the profile of sport locally. The aim is to increase the participation levels in sport in their area, particularly within those groups which have low participation rates.

Reasons

As we have seen, people are involved in sport in different ways and for different reasons. The reasons we play sport will also change throughout life. For example, when we are young we may play sport because our friends do and we develop sporting role models from television. In our teens and twenties we are

involved in competitive sports, and as we get older we play sport for the enjoyment and to keep in shape.

People will be involved in sport for some of the following reasons:

- The thrill and excitement of competition.
- The desire to win and be good at something.
- The enjoyment of playing the sport and mastering new skills.
- To release built-up stresses and frustration.
- To improve self-image and self-confidence.
- To improve health and fitness levels and prevent disease.
- To socialise with people who have similar interests.
- To challenge the limits of what you are capable of achieving.

People may not always be aware of why they play sport until you ask them to think about it. However, usually it is to improve their life and well-being in some way.

Factors Affecting Participation

While we can see that sport benefits people and fulfils needs in their lives, it is important to point out that not all people have equal access to sporting opportunities.

These may be issues you take for granted, but in reality these differences exist because of the way our society is organised and how it has developed. There is a range of factors that will affect participation in sport and they include:

- Ability or disability
- Ethnic origin
- Age
- Location in the country
- Cost and income level.

Disability

Sport is an excellent way to make disabled people feel involved in life, good about themselves and able to achieve new skills. However, there are two barriers to participation: opportunity and accessibility. A law was passed in 2004 to make sure that all new buildings are accessible to disabled people. This means providing the following:

- Ramps for access
- Changing and toilet facilities
- Doors of an appropriate width
- Access to all facilities
- Adaptations to equipment for access
- Braille signs.

Public sector sports centres have become very sensitive to the needs of disabled people and most will offer access to a programme of sports activities.

Ethnic Origin

Recent statistics have shown a direct relationship between ethnic origin and participation in sport:

- White ethnic groups have the highest participation rates.
- People of Pakistani origin have the lowest participation rates.
- Women of Pakistani origin have particularly low rates of participation.
- Certain ethnic groups are well represented in some sports but very poorly represented in others.

Britain is now regarded as a multiracial society and we must work to meet the needs of all groups. Sports development officers are working hard to offer opportunities to people from all ethnic groups and meet their specific needs, for example offering women-only swimming sessions for Muslim women.

Age

As shown before, our needs change through the cycle of our lives, and the sports activities we play become less competitive and less physical as we get older. Football, rugby and cricket are all favoured sports of the younger age groups, while golf and walking are more popular in the 60+ age group.

Location in the Country

Statistics from the General Household Survey (2002) show that participation rates vary across regions. For example:

- In the south west of England 50 per cent of people participated in sport.
- In the south east of England 46 per cent of people participated in sport.
- In London 44 per cent of people participated in sport.
- In the West Midlands 39 per cent of people participated in sport.
- In the North East of England 37 per cent of people participated in sport.

So why the huge differences in participation rates?

1. Different availability of sports facilities.
2. Different amount of income available for sport.
3. Differing views on the importance of sport and physical activity.

It is not always clear why there are differences but the above three factors help to explain the reasons.

Cost and Income Level

The amount of money a person has to spend on their leisure activities is called disposable income. This depends upon their original income and the various costs and responsibilities they have. The more disposable income they have, then the greater choice of sports activities they will have. For example, to play sport in private sector facilities can be very expensive. Private health and fitness clubs will charge as much as £70 a month for membership. Sports such as golf, tennis, sailing and skiing are very expensive to be involved in. This is because the equipment is expensive, as is access to the facilities to play the sport.

However, some sports such as running or football are fairly cheap to participate in and are accessible to everyone.

Activity 6.4 1–2 hours P3

Participation in sport

Many different types of people enjoy taking part in sport and they have many different reasons as to why they choose to participate.

Task 1

Think about why you participate in sport and the reasons why you take part in sports.

Task 2

In a group of around four to five people, discuss why each person chooses to take part in sports and different types of factors that affect when they take part in them. In these groups try to answer the following questions:

(a) Is sport played by men and women in the same numbers?

(b) How many black British golfers do you see?

(c) Why are there lots of Asian cricketers but very few Asian rugby players?

(d) Why are participation rates for men in sport higher in the south of England (50 per cent) compared with the north of England (43 per cent)?

(e) How many disabled sports people can you name?

(f) Why do British tennis players tend to be from wealthy families?

Task 3

Carry out research by asking your family and friends why they take part in sports and the factors that affect their participation.

Task 4

Write a report from the information gathered in Tasks 1, 2 and 3, and describe the different factors that affect people's participation in sport.

6.5 Current Strategies to Develop Participation in Sport

Mass Participation

Current thinking in UK government policy-making is focused on mass participation, which means getting as many people in the UK as active as possible. Schemes that are involved in this process can attract more funding, receive government and lottery funding, additional staffing and even improved facilities for delivery.

The main plan includes:

- Making more use of existing facilities, such as schools outside of school times, for the whole community, in other words opening up the facilities for all to use.

- Having feeder primary schools linked with specialist sport schools.

- Setting up and supporting community clubs and arranging coaches and leaders for them.

School Sports Strategies and Sports Development Strategies

The government body known as the Department for Children, Schools and Families (DCSF) aims to increase the take up of sporting opportunities by 5 to 16 year olds.

They aim to do this by using programmes like:

- **Club Links** – in partnership with sports governing bodies like the Football Association (FA) and the Rugby Football Union (RFU) to improve and introduce these sports into all communities, for 22 different sports.

- **Step into Sport** – aimed at helping identify, train and recruit young sporting volunteers aged 14–19 years.

- **Sports Kitemarks** for schools, which aim to reward schools that can prove that they are helping to link their school with community sports provision.

- **UK School Games** – organised by the Youth Sports Trust (more about them later) and increasing competition in schools in the run up to the 2012 Olympics.

Sport Specific Schemes

Many sports in addition to the above government-led initiatives have their own plans to encourage participation. See the case study on England Athletics.

Strengths and Weaknesses of Strategies

The key strengths of all of these policies lie in what they set out to do, in other words to increase participation, and link schools with communities.

There are many examples of successful partnerships that exist across the country, and evidence points to a slow increase in participation.

However, in some areas there is little change. Critics of current policy for encouraging participation would point at the following as key areas for development:

- Some schools not having the facilities required to deliver, in other words poor sports facilities, or inadequate changing areas to meet the needs of the community

- Many schools reluctant to provide access for fear of vandalism and theft

- Poor take up of all schemes in the areas where participation is most needed.

Case Study: England Athletics

Athletics – exciting, diverse and vibrant

Hundreds of thousands of people across England are involved in athletics. In many different ways it really is the most exciting, diverse and vibrant sport there is. For many, athletics provides the ultimate challenge to their competitive abilities. The range of disciplines across the track, field, road and off-road provides an incredible diversity of events for different people with different skills and abilities, which means that it is impossible to stereotype what it means to be an athlete. For other people athletics is about fitness and participation but the range of age groups, events, competitions and clubs means that athletics really is a truly inclusive sport.

Alongside the athletes is an army of volunteers and staff who provide coaching, officiating and a range of support services to enable the athletes to do what they know and love the best.

England Athletics is therefore proud to be the national governing body for this great sport that also has a phenomenal heritage. We are working hard to develop and promote athletics across the whole of the country.

We sincerely hope you gain as much enjoyment and fulfilment from athletics as we do.

What we do

England Athletics has three core objectives:

1. To increase participation across a wider cross-section of the community.

2. To improve the quality of experience of every participant.

3. To support the development of the next generation of champions.

England Athletics delivers services, support and funding within the sport. Our role includes working with affiliated clubs, officials, schools, and coaches. We also provide national level competition and work on athlete development beneath world-class performance level. Our role is directly related to the work of the many volunteers whose efforts are fundamental to the success of athletics in England.

The work of England Athletics includes:

- **Clubs** – Clubs are vital to the provision of athletics in England. Schemes such as athletics networks are designed to deliver funding directly to where it can be used most effectively. Our aim is to raise standards and participation levels with minimum bureaucracy. The work done by England Athletics in other areas, such as coach and official development, is designed to help clubs thrive and achieve a high level of independence. England Athletics staff work with clubs to help in areas such as funding applications too.
- **Coach education** – Coaching is a major priority for England Athletics due to its deep-rooted, long-term and wide-spread benefits. We provide courses and assessments to enable people to qualify as coaches, and provide wider opportunities for coaches to increase their skills. These include coaching conferences, seminars and mentoring.
- **Officials** – we provide Level 1 and 2 courses (with Level 3 managed by UK Athletics) and oversee the tri-regional groups which manage senior officials in England.
- **Competitions** – we hold national championship events with the support of volunteers who are able to offer a high level of expertise. We commission and support other competition providers where their expertise and role make them the most effective provider of the appropriate competition.

Growth in Participation

Increased Leisure Time

Participation in sport has increased since the 1960s for the following reasons:

- Increasing car ownership.
- More available free time.
- Increase in sports facilities.
- Increase in promotional athletes by government agencies.
- Growth in knowledge of human and sport relationship.
- Increased coverage of sport on electronic media, mainly the internet and TV.

Fashion

Sport has become very fashionable in recent years. Sports retailers in the UK have been transformed from the kind of shop that sold sporting goods, to the place to buy sports goods that are not always used for sport, like replica football shirts and trainers.

Where the money goes

Income	1997	2007	Percentage difference
Gross Household income	£34, 796	£53, 835	+55%
Costs			
Income tax and N.I.	£8,506	£15,357	+81%
Council tax	£688	£1,321	+92%
House prices	£76,103	£252,056	+231%
Communication	£420	£743	+77%
Petrol	£657	£1,016	+546%
Insurance	£690	£1,047	+52%
Transport	£3,249	£4,824	+48.5%
Heating	£305	£446	+46.1%
Water	£201	£267	+32.7%
Food	£2,264	£2,771	+22.1%
Electricity	£336	£392	+17%

copyright www.Uswitch.com

Increased Disposable Income

As salaries have increased, so to has disposable income, which is the money that someone has left after all of their bills have been paid.

The growth in the population aged over 50 years, as a result of healthier lifestyles and improvement in modern medicine has meant that a greater number of people than ever, many of whom are retired, are in a position of having a large amount of money, which they may choose to spend on leisure. Recently though, following a recession, it is reported that disposable income in the UK is shrinking.

On page 106 there is a list that shows us what people spend their money on, and from that we can work out why there is less disposable income.

Activity **6.5** 35 mins   P5

Strategies to encourage participation in sport   M2

D2

Select a sport of your choice, then search the internet for your local sports development unit and find out the following information.

1. What opportunities are on offer to encourage participation in this sport?
2. What are the target age groups and gender for this sport?
3. How is the sport promoted?
4. Which organisations are used to help to promote this sport?

Task 1

From the information that you have gathered in your research, write a leaflet that describes, explains and evaluates a range of different strategies used to encourage participation in a selected sport.

Task 2

Towards the end of the information on your leaflet, make recommendations on strategies that can be used to increase participation of your selected sport in the future.

Key learning points

- People can become involved in sport in the following ways:
  - Performer at amateur or professional level.
  - Official to implement the rules of sport.
  - Coach to assist in the development of other people in their sport.
  - Administrator involved in running or managing a sport or team.
  - Spectator either in person or via the television.
  - Retailer to sell sports goods to make a profit.
  - Medical staff to provide support services to the athletes.
  - Sports development workers to raise the profile of sport locally.
- Participation in sport can be affected by the following:
  - Ability or disability – disabled people have lower activity levels.
  - Ethnic origin – certain ethnic groups, particularly Asians, have lower participation rates.
  - Age – younger people are significantly more active than older age groups.
  - Location in the country – people in the south of England seem to be more physically active than people in the north of England.
  - Cost and income level – certain sports are very expensive and this makes them less available to lower income groups.

Figure 6.2   Logo of School Sports Coordinator (SSCo)

At the centre is the **Partnership Development Manager (PDM),** who is responsible for the development of the programme, not just in their school but also in the partner schools. Each Sports College will have up to eight secondary school partners, all of whom have a **School Sport Coordinator (SSCo)**, usually a teacher who is given some extra time to develop school sport in their own school and family of primary/special schools.

Each of the secondary schools (and the Sports College) is linked to a number of primary or special schools. Each of these will have a **Primary Link Teacher (PLT)**, who is responsible for the development and delivery of high quality PE and sport in their own school.

6.6 The Role of Local and National Organisations Responsible for Sports Development

School Sports Partnerships

School Sports Partnerships are part of the wider School Sport Coordinator programme launched in September 2000 and funded by Sport England's Lottery Fund.

What Are They Like?

These partnerships are now in all areas of the country. Figure 6.3 demonstrates the structure of a typical partnership.

Further Education Sports Coordinator (FESCo)

The role of the FESCo (Further Education Sports coordinator) is to work within FE colleges to increase the participation of 16–19 year olds in sport and physical activity. FESCos are linked to the School Sports Partnerships and often work from the same office, but will spend most of their time at colleges and are looking to try to get more college learners active through sport and exercise.

Under its School Sport and Club Links (PESSCL) strategy, the government has ensured that SSCos are now an essential part of the development of sport through PE in schools.

These partnerships are meant to ensure that all children receive at least two hours of high quality PE in a week.

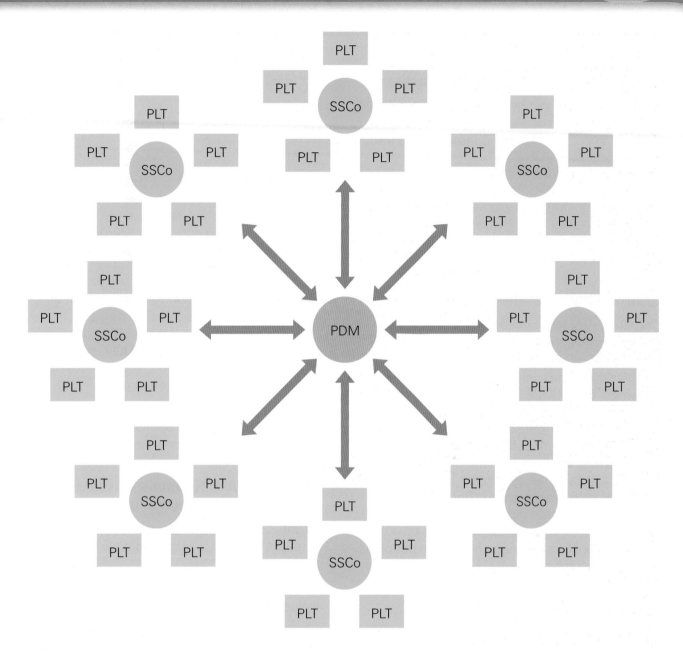

Figure 6.3 School Sports Partnership model
(Source: Teachernet.org)

National Governing Bodies

In order to find out more about who NGBs are and what they do, see if you can research the following information, and then present it to your group.

Task

Find the governing bodies for two team sports, two individual sports and two emerging (new sports) in the UK.

See if you can find out:

1. Where they are based

2. Where they get funding from

3. What are their main targets, for example national team development or grass roots development

4. How they go about developing the sport in your area.

County Sports Partnerships

County Sports Partnerships differ in their role, depending on the size of their county, the cultural mix of the people who live there, local facilities and existing organisations and schemes. County Sports Partnerships exist to perform a variety of functions, such as to help provide training and funding for elite athletes, to support the work of the School Sports Partnerships, to assist with the planning and operation of facilities, to support local sports clubs, to provide access and support for the disabled, to promote disabled sport and, perhaps more than anything else, to be a point of contact for all local queries and to help people to participate in sport in their county.

British Olympic Committee

The British Olympic Committee is made up of elected officers and paid staff. These elected British staff, one from each of the 35 Olympic sports, make up the National Olympic Committee, which meets four times a year to make all of the important decisions concerning Great Britain and the Olympics.

The role of the British Olympic Committee is varied. Its main tasks are:

- The **Performance unit** – supports Team GB with sports science and medicine, organises training camps, warm weather training and helps the coaches and team managers train and improve.

- **Games** services – responsible for the planning and delivery of the games themselves, whether here in Great Britain (GB) and Northern Ireland or overseas. They will organise and fund transport, accommodation and clothing among other things.

- **Marketing** – concerned with the promotion of Team GB, corporate sponsorship, licensing and the collection of donations via the British Olympic Appeal.

- **Press and Public Relations** – responsible for all communication concerning Team GB.

- **Legal** – looks after a range of issues including disputes related to drugs and doping.

- **Medical** – concerned with the welfare of the athletes both in training and at events, and includes doctors and physiotherapists.

Figure 6.4   Sir Steve Redgrave, a member of the British Olympic Committee

Figure 6.5   A basketball player

Youth Sports Trust (YST)

The Youth Sports Trust is a charity set up in 1994. Its principal aim is the improvement of physical education and sporting opportunity for young people.

Its main aims are to:

- Increase young people's participation and enjoyment of PE and school sport.

- Give young people the chance to experience and enjoy different types of activity at whatever level is right for them.

- Ensure youngsters receive the best teaching, coaching and resources possible and have the chance to progress if they show talent.

- Help our young people to live healthy and active lives and to be the best they can be.

The YST works hard with Specialist Sports Colleges to achieve these goals and support them with a variety of resources. In particular the YST supports the Gifted and Talented programme in schools, to help children to achieve their full potential and to develop life skills alongside sporting ones.

Sport England

Sport England is a government organisation responsible for developing clubs, coaches, facilities and volunteers.

Its staff work closely with schools, colleges and universities as well as local authorities (councils) to try to support and improve talent. Sport England recently revised its targets.

SPORT ENGLAND TARGETS 2008–11

Grow

- One million people taking part in more sport.

- More children and young people taking part in five hours of PE and sport a week.

Sustain

- More people satisfied with their sporting experience.

- 25 per cent fewer 16–18 year olds dropping out of at least nine sports.

Excel

- Improved talent development in at least 25 sports.

Figure 6.6   Young people are helped by the Youth Sports Trust

The Roles of Sports Development Organisations

Sports development organisations like Sport England, County Sports Partnerships, the Youth Sports Trust and others all play a role in delivering sport and exercise to the people of Great Britain.

Each of these has a role that is slightly different from the other, but broadly speaking, the overall objectives for all sporting organisations can be summarised under four main headings.

Supporting and Implementing the Sports Development Process

All organisations work to a strategy or plan that outlines what it is they plan to achieve, by when and how it will be possible. All of the organisations in this chapter have plans that are available for all to see, either on their website or as part of a publication.

If you were putting together a plan for swimming in your town, your plan might include the following:

- An introduction and overview of the current local facilities and participation rates.

- Current levels of swimming pool usage.

- How your town compares to others for providing sports facilities to people such as the disabled and for children.

- The aims of the project, for example to provide more access to schools, or to train more swimming coaches and teachers.

- An explanation of how you are going to do that, for example talent identification programmes, coaching courses, extending opening times, allowing certain groups free usage etc.

Community Sports Development

Every community in the UK is different. In fact, a community could be as little as three people but as large as thousands; it could be a school, a village, a faith-based group or even a sport.

A community development plan could include the following features:

- **Rural Schemes** – such as access to play and sports clubs and equipment for those who live a significant distance from the nearest town.

- **Club Development** – such as club accreditation and child protection initiatives, or sport groups.

- **Young People's Initiatives** – which may say how to get discounts for activities like swimming or archery, where to get swimming lessons, how to become a sports leader etc.

Sports Specific Development

Sports specific development is when a particular sport, for example basketball, produces a plan and develops this sport in a particular area. At any one time there are a number of sport specific development officers who have the task of improving their sport in their particular area. This could be by improving facilities or access to facilities like outdoor basketball goals, training coaches, leaders and officials so that local leagues and school leagues can

Figure 6.7 A young sports leader

Case Study: Basketball Development Officer

Have a look at this job description for a sport specific development officer. This one is for basketball. Discuss with your peers what you think are the key skills and qualities needed for this job, and who you might work with. You could also discuss how you would develop your sport in your area.

Basketball Development Officer

Organisation: Cheshire & Warrington Sports Partnership

Salary: Up to £19,000 per annum

Location: Based in Northwich, Cheshire

Type of contract: Full-time position (3 years subject to funding)

Job description:

Cheshire & Warrington Sports Partnership and England Basketball are seeking to recruit a dynamic basketball development officer.

You will develop basketball across Cheshire and Warrington, not only increasing the number of people participating in the game but also improving player satisfaction. This will involve working directly with affiliated basketball clubs as well as a range of colleagues in Local Authorities and School Sport Partnerships. You will have highly developed interpersonal skills, be IT literate and have experience of networking and supporting a range of partners. You must be well organised, self-motivated and be able to work on your own initiative.

This is a fantastic opportunity to lead on the development, implementation and coordination of basketball across Cheshire and Warrington.

thrive, developing local, county and regional squads for talent improvement or introducing the sport in primary schools.

Facility Development

Facility development is mostly about making sure sports people are able to participate at quality venues in appropriate locations.

Some organisations will help with advice on how to plan and fund facilities. County sports partnerships, for example, can help open up schools for community use in the evenings and at weekends. Most sporting organisations will be able to offer advice on how to secure funding where it is needed for facilities.

Figure 6.8   Wembley stadium – a footballing venue for the twenty-first century

(k) Key learning points

- School Sports Partnerships are part of the wider School Sport Coordinator programme.
- The Partnership Development Manager (PDM) is responsible for the development of the programme.
- County Sports Partnerships perform a variety of functions, such as training and funding for elite athletes, support of School Sports Partnerships, local sports clubs, providing access and support for the disabled, promoting disabled sport and helping people to participate in sport in their county.
- The Youth Sports Trust is a charity set up in 1994. Its main aim is the improvement of physical education and sporting opportunity for young people.
- The six main tasks of the British Olympic Committee are:
  - —Performance
  - —Games services
  - —Marketing
  - —Press and Public Relations
  - —Legal
  - —Medical.

Activity 6.7 45 mins   P6

Role of local and national organisations for the development of sport   M3

Both national and local organisations are responsible for helping to develop sports participation around the UK. These organisations include local authorities, sports development departments, school sports partnerships and national governing bodies.

Task 1

Carry out research into one local organisation that is responsible for the development of sport in your local area.

Task 2

Carry out research into one national organisation that is responsible for the development of sport in the UK.

Task 3

Design a poster with some text that describes and explains the role of one local organisation and one national organisation responsible for the development of sport.

6.7 Know the Impact of Different Key Issues in Sport P7 M4

In this section we will examine some issues that are current in the sports industry and the impact they have on people involved in sport. The issues are: ethnic origin, drug use, social influences and the effect of the media.

Issues

Race

Race, or ethnic origin, refers to the shared ancestry of a group of people. A member of an ethnic group could be prevented from joining a sporting group perhaps because they feel intimidated or unwelcome. The UK is very proud of its integration, compared with other nations, but there is still evidence of bigotry and race hate in sport that should not be tolerated by people today.

Activity 6.8 60 mins   P7

Current issues   M4

Task

In pairs, go to your learning centre. Find an article in a local or national paper involving the issue of ethnic origin, social influences or the influence of the media on sport.

Present your article to the rest of the group together with your thoughts about the issues.

Social Influences

In sport, participation in the UK has traditionally been divided by groups. Think about the kind of worker who would play football, and then the typical polo player, and you can perhaps see that sports have a social history and reflect the class systems.

Many sociologists claim that sport allows for social mobility – this means that sport allows people from a working-class background access to the kind of lifestyles previously enjoyed only by the very rich and upper classes.

Economic Influences

The amount of spare money that a person has will also dictate how they participate in sport and exercise. Think about what kind of person can afford to be a member at a private gym and compare them with gym users at the local sports centre.

Role of the Media

The media, traditionally considered to be newspapers and radio, is now widely expanded to include:

- Television
- Internet
- Films
- Books
- Magazines
- Mobile technology.

The internet has pages and pages devoted to sports fans, governing bodies that provide up-to-the-minute news and results services, all of which have the effect of increasing the profile of and interest in sport.

Sex Discrimination

Many people believe that sex discrimination is not a problem any more, but evidence would suggest otherwise:

- Women receive less than 5 per cent of men's media coverage in national newspapers.

> ### Definition
> **Discrimination the preventing of a group of people from doing something based simply as prejudice.**

- Sporting audiences are still mostly male.
- With some exceptions, presenters, journalists and editors are predominantly male.
- Women receive less money for sporting success.
- Female sports receive less sponsorship than male sports.

Until recently the prize money for women at major sporting events was less than for the men. Take a look at the table below, which shows the difference between the men's and women's prizes at the Wimbledon Tennis Championships.

Year	Men's Singles	Ladies' Singles
	£	£
1990	230,000	207,000
1991	240,000	216,000
1992	265,000	240,000
1993	305,000	275,000
1994	345,000	310,000
1995	365,000	328,000
1996	392,500	353,00
1997	415,000	373,000
1998	435,000	391,500
1999	455,000	409,500
2000	477,500	430,000
2001	500,000	462,500
2002	525,000	486,000
2003	575,000	535,000
2004	602,500	560,000
2005	630,000	600,000
2006	655,000	625,000
2007	700,000	700,00

(Source: http://aeltc.wimbledon.org/en_GB/about/history/prizemoney_history.html)

Healthy Lifestyles

In recent years in the UK, the government has made improved health a priority and it sees sport as one of the most important ways to improve the health of the nation.

The focus on elite provision, in other words money going to the highest level of performance, national teams, Olympic teams etc., has changed. The current focus for spending is nearly all related to what the government set out in a report called 'The Health of the Nation', published in 1992, in which it aims to improve the lifestyle of the entire nation, and to transform us from a nation of couch potatoes to one of mostly fit and healthy people.

Impact

Positive and Negative

The impact of these issues can be clearly seen in the following examples:

- **Performer** – the performer is perhaps under increasing pressure from all kinds of media, the internet and television particularly.
- **Providers** – providers of sport are in a position (at least, they were until recently) of increased disposable income.
- **Supporters** – the experience, for example, of a Premier League football supporter is mixed. On one hand, you could argue that the league is now one of the strongest in the world and that the quality of skilled play has increased. On the other hand, season ticket prices and merchandising are higher than ever.
- **Consumers** – the benefits for consumers and sport are also mixed; while the number of people spectating sport is at an all-time high, participation in physical activity for some groups, particularly 18–24 year olds, shows little sign of improvement.

Viewing and Media Scheduling

Sport is enjoyed by many people in their spare time, and many more enjoy watching sport on TV and the internet.

Increasingly powerful broadcasters change the start times of fixtures to fit the viewer at home. Not so long ago, all top-flight football in the UK was on Saturday at 3 p.m. Now football fixtures are moved to Sundays, earlier times on Saturdays, and even to Mondays to try to attract more viewers (customers).

Sporting Legacy (Olympics)

Legacy refers to just how useful the Olympics and Paralympics will prove to be to Great Britain during and, in particular, after the Games.
The Department for Culture, Media and Sport (DCMS) is responsible for delivering this legacy, and has set out five key commitments:

1. To make the UK a world-leading sporting nation.
2. To transform the heart of East London.
3. To inspire a new generation of young people to take part in local volunteering, cultural and physical activity.
4. To make the Olympic Park a blueprint for sustainable living.
5. To demonstrate that the UK is a creative, inclusive and welcoming place to live in, visit and for business.

Sporting Legacy and the Olympic Games

The London 2012 Olympics is set to change the face of modern Britain, and particularly London.

Most people involved in sport are excited at the prospect of the Games and the idea that the greatest athletes from all over the world will be in Great Britain competing, winning medals and producing an incredible spectacle.

The Olympic Games and Paralympic Games will have a far-ranging impact in a number of key areas:

1. **Tourism** – Thousands of athletes, spectators, coaches and support staff will boost all areas of tourism, including hotels, hospitality and catering.

2. **Transport** – the road, rail, underground and air networks left after the Games are set to improve the experience of travel in London.

3. **Housing** – Much of the accommodation for athletes and support staff will provide low-cost housing in deprived areas.

4. **Environment** – London 2012 is set to be the most environmentally sustainable global sporting event yet.

5. **Culture and sport** – There will be a range of facilities and resources available for sporting and cultural events in the future.

Quick Quiz 3 — 30 mins ?

1. What is a SSCo?
2. What is the name of the person in a primary school who is responsible for delivering sport as part of the partnership?
3. What is a PDM and what do they do?
4. Name seven functions of a national governing body of sport.
5. What are the six parts of the British Olympic Committee, and what do they do?
6. Which charity, set up in 1994, has as its main aim the improvement of physical education and sporting opportunity for young people?
7. Name four types of private sector funding.
8. What is TASS?
9. Give an example of stereotyping in sport.
10. Give three reasons why the media is so important to sport.

(k) Key learning points

- Certain ethnic groups such as Pakistanis and Indians have lower participation levels than white people. The issue of racism in sport covers the following areas:
  —Less opportunity for certain groups.
  —Stereotyping of the capabilities of Afro-Caribbean people and Asian people.
  —Fewer opportunities for ethnic groups to hold responsible positions in sport.
- Women have lower participation rates because they have less opportunity to play sport than men and are not always encouraged to do so by men.
- The media include newspapers, magazines, television coverage, radio and the internet. The media can influence sport in many ways by raising the profile of a sport or sports person. They can also influence the way that people will think about a sports event.

Activity **6.9** 60 mins   P7

Issues in sport and their impact on sport   M4

Think for a moment about the following:

1. How many television stations show sport and which sports do they cover?
2. How many radio stations cover sport and which sports do they cover?
3. What internet sites do you know that cover sports?
4. Name some sports magazines and any sports newspapers you know.

Task 1

Write a report that describes and explains the positive or negative impact of four key issues in sport. Examples of issues include:

- Olympics
- Race
- Social issues
- Economic influences
- Media
- Sex discrimination
- Healthy lifestyles.

Useful websites

www.culture.gov.uk

Online articles from the UK government that relate to current issues in sport, such as keeping children safe and effective ticketing at sporting events.

www.bbc.co.uk/sport

Constantly updated news and results board for a wide range of sports, including disabled and some minority sports; also offers links to tips from top sportsmen and women and individual sporting events and sports bodies.

References

Sir Norman Chester Centre for Football Research, 'British Football on Television', Fact Sheet 8, Leicester: University of Leicester, 2002.

Sport England, Research Briefing Note, 'Participation in Sport – Results from the General Household Survey 2002', London: Sport England.

Stafford-Brown, J., Rea, S. and Chance, J., 2003, *BTEC National in Sport and Exercise Science*. London: Hodder and Stoughton.

Wolsey, C. and Abrams, J. (eds), 2001, *Understanding the Sport and Leisure Industry*. Harlow: Longman.

Chapter 7
Planning & Leading Sports Activities

The increase in the number of people participating in regular sports activities has meant that more people are required to run a variety of different sports sessions such as after-school clubs and voluntary sports clubs. This chapter concentrates on the factors required to lead a range of sports activities and provide you with the basic skills that will help you to teach and coach participants in sport. Sports leaders play a vital role in developing skills, improving performance levels and providing motivation to sports performers.

Learning Goals

By the end of this chapter you should:

- Know the skills, qualities and responsibilities associated with successful sports leadership.
- Be able to plan and lead an activity session.
- Be able to review own planning and leadership of a sports activity.
- Be able to assist in the planning and leading of a sports event.
- Be able to review own planning and leadership of a sports event.

To achieve a PASS grade the evidence must show that the learner is able to:	To achieve a MERIT grade the evidence must show that, in addition to the pass criteria, the learner is able to:	To achieve a DISTINCTION grade the evidence must show that, in addition to the pass and merit criteria, the learner is able to:
P1 describe the skills, qualities and responsibilities associated with successful sports leadership, using two examples of successful sports leaders	**M1** explain the skills, qualities and responsibilities associated with successful sports leadership, comparing and contrasting two successful sports leaders	**D1** evaluate the skills and qualities of two contrasting leaders in sport, commenting on their effectiveness
P2 plan and lead a sports activity, with tutor support	**M2** independently plan and lead a sports activity	
P3 review the planning and leading of a sports activity, identifying strengths and areas for improvement	**M3** explain strengths and areas for improvement and development in the planning and leading of a sports activity	
P4 contribute to the planning and leading of a sports event		
P5 review own performance while assisting with the planning and leading of a sports event, identifying strengths and areas for improvement	**M4** explain strengths and areas for improvement in assisting with the planning and leading of a sports event, making suggestions relating to improvement	**D2** evaluate own performance in the planning and leading of a sports activity and event, commenting on strengths and areas for improvement and further development as a sports leader

7.1 Sports Leadership

> ### Definition
> **Leader a person who is in charge of a group.**

A range of skills is required to plan and lead sports sessions and events; many sports coaches and sports events organisers have excellent leadership skills.

Sports leadership can be very difficult. There are many skills and qualities that a leader will require to be successful. As well as having the correct skills and qualities, there are many responsibilities that fall upon the sports leader.

> ### Definition
> **Skill an action that is learned.**

A sports leader must develop many skills and they will become better with regular practice.

7.2 Skills and Qualities Associated with Successful Sports Leadership P1 M1 D1

Communication

Communication is successfully sharing information with other people, which is probably one of the most important skills for any sports leader to have. However, the art of good communication can be a difficult skill to learn. There are many ways of communicating within a sporting environment, but for communication to be successful you must know that the message sent has been understood.

A sports leader can communicate to a group in many ways. These include:

- verbal
- non-verbal
- by listening
- by demonstrating
- by assisting

1. **Verbal communication** is where you are speaking to a person or group – it is important to speak clearly to help the participants understand what it is you are telling them. Try to be concise and avoid any jargon that may confuse them. It is also important to be constructive and positive, as being negative or critical can upset the sports performers and affect motivation.

2. **Non-verbal communication** is where you communicate to a person or team without speaking. This is very useful in situations where it can be difficult to be heard, as in a range of different sporting environments. Examples of non-verbal communication can include the use of your body language, gestures, hand signals, facial expressions. Next time you are watching a sporting event, try to see if you can see the coach or manager on the side lines – throughout the game they will probably be making various gestures to their team to help them to play better or congratulate them on doing well.

3. **Listening** – listening is a vital part of the communication process; however, it is often forgotten. A good sports leader will listen to their group when appropriate and act on the information that they have received.

4. **Demonstrating** – demonstrations are a method of communication that helps participants learn new skills. It is important when showing people demonstrations that they are kept simple and they are done correctly, so that the participants do not pick up incorrect techniques.

5. **Assisting** – this is the part where the sports leader helps individuals who cannot perform a sports skill correctly. This method will include using a range of the mentioned techniques to help them understand what it is they should be doing.

Knowledge

A person leading a sports activity session will need to have a good knowledge of many areas. Taking part in lots of sports activities run by different people and showing a willingness to learn new things will give you a better understanding of delivering sports sessions. A sports leader will also need to have a good understanding of the many health and safety factors associated with sports. This will include having a good understanding of emergency procedures, awareness of the facilities being used, as well as having some basic first aid knowledge.

Target Setting

Setting targets and individual goals will help individuals improve their own sports performance. A sports leader will know what appropriate targets for each individual sports performer are and ensure that they set realistic and attainable goals. Setting goals will help motivate the sports performers to achieve these targets and therefore improve their performance.

Managing a Group

A sports leader may have to work with a large number of people in their group. There can often be conflict within a group of people, but a group leader must ensure that the group is able to work together. Effective management of the group will ensure that you get the best out of them.

Decision-making

A sports leader will have to make many different types of decisions when working with sports performers. What to do, and why, will need to be considered when making decisions. Knowing how to make the right decision will come through relevant experiences.

Evaluation

A good sports leader will take time to evaluate their own performance and that of their participants. Evaluating your own sessions will help you improve them in the future. Consider what worked well, what could be improved and how you can make your session more enjoyable, also what the feedback was from the participants.

Organisation of Sports Equipment and Facilities

It is important for sports leaders to be organised when arranging their sports sessions. It is important to consider what facilities are available when planning and organising your session. Once you know what facilities are available you can start to organise the sports equipment that you will need.

There are many equipment factors that a sports leader will need to consider before their session. These include what equipment is available to you and whether you have enough equipment for the group. It is important that any equipment to be used is in a safe, working condition, and that it is returned in the same condition in which it was lent out.

Time Management

Time management is an important skill to develop if you want to be successful. As a leader you are responsible for the sports sessions starting and finishing on time. Time management is therefore also linked to having good organisational skills. It is also important that a sports leader can prioritise items when required.

7.3 Personal Qualities Associated with Successful Sports Leadership `P1` `M1` `D1`

A sports leader also needs many personal qualities to be successful. These include:

- Using an appropriate leadership style
- Appropriate personal appearance
- Being positive
- Showing empathy

- Being motivated
- Being confident
- Having enthusiasm.

Leadership Styles

Leaders will vary in the styles and methods that they use with their groups. This includes the ways in which they deliver their outcomes and take responsibility for their groups.

The following leadership styles are commonly used in sports leadership:

The **autocratic style**, sometimes known as the command style, is where the person leading the group makes all of the decisions and imposes them on the group, who respond by doing what they are told. The leader concentrates more on the outcome, rather than the group. It is a method that is often used when dealing with large groups or in circumstances where there may be potential hazards.

The **democratic method** is different from the autocratic style as the leader involves the group and asks for their opinions when making the decisions. This enables the group to take more responsibility for their actions. The leader, however, will have the final say.

A **liberal leader** will look to use a combination of both autocratic and democratic methods.

The **laissez-faire** method of leadership allows the group to make all of the decisions required. This allows the group much freedom to do what they like. For this method to work the group needs to be highly motivated, as the leader does not provide any direction.

Activity **7.1**   30 mins   P1

Leadership in sport

Task

Consider the leadership methods used by a well-known sports leader. List and discuss the types of leadership styles and try to explain why each is used.

Personal Appearance

The personal appearance of a sports leader is very important. Sports leaders must remember that they are setting the standard. By dressing in the appropriate attire, you will gain the respect of the group, some of whom may see you as a role model. It is therefore very important to look smart. This can also make you feel more confident when delivering your session. What you wear can also differentiate you from the rest of the group so that you can be easily spotted.

Ambition

It is important that a sports leader is ambitious. A person who wants to succeed is more likely to become a good sports leader than somebody with little or no ambition. Sir Alex Ferguson, the Manchester United manager, is a great example of somebody with ambition, and he has gone on to be a very successful sports leader in the world of football.

Being Positive

Being positive in everything you do is another important quality that a sports leader must have. This approach will help keep the group motivated, as a group's outlook on things will often mirror that of its leader. The people within the group will also feel more comfortable and confident and are more likely to approach the leader if they are a positive person. When communicating or analysing performance, it is important that the leader maintains this positive approach. Any weaknesses need to be discussed constructively so that the group understands what it is they need to work on.

Being positive can be difficult at times; however, a good sports leader needs to be optimistic when things are looking gloomy. Look at Figure 7.1: is the glass half full or half empty?

An optimist would say it was half full.

Figure 7.1   Half full or half empty?

Empathy

> **Definition** (d)
>
> **Empathy** the ability to understand another person's feelings.

A good sports leader will need to be able to show empathy towards their sports participants.

Understanding the participants' needs and being able to relate to them will help a leader to motivate them.

Motivation

Motivation can be either intrinsic or extrinsic. A good sports leader will be self-motivated (intrinsic) and work for their personal satisfaction rather than for money and prizes (extrinsic).

7.4 Responsibilities Associated with Successful Sports Leadership

Sports leadership carries much responsibility and there are many factors and procedures that a sports leader must take into account, including:

- Professional conduct
- Health and safety
- Child protection
- Ethics and values.

Professional Conduct

Sports leaders must always conduct themselves in a professional manner. Professional conduct means demonstrating proper personal and professional behaviour at all times. As mentioned earlier in the chapter, many people will see the leader as a role model, and therefore the leader needs to behave appropriately at all times.

Health and Safety

The sports leader is also responsible for the health and safety of all participants. The leader needs to ensure that they provide a safe environment for people to undertake sport in, and that they minimise the risk of any potential injuries. Ensuring that rules and regulations are adhered to will also help reduce the risk of any potential injuries.

Child Protection

Society today requires sports leaders to have a good understanding of what child protection is. Over the past decade the number of children who have reported experiencing forms of abuse has risen drastically. It is important that the group leader does not put children at risk and knows how to spot any potential signs of abuse. The leader should also do their best to ensure that young people can have fun and enjoy their participation, while in a safe environment.

Ethics and Values

Ethics and values must also be considered by the sports leader. Ethics are actions that are fair, honest and responsible. It is important for a sports leader to promote these qualities. Values are thoughts that we believe are important. The sports leader should always ensure fair play in all sports and discourage any antisocial forms of behaviour.

> **(k) Key learning points**
>
> - Leader – the person in charge of a group.
> - Skills – actions that are learned and improved through practice.
> - Qualities – attributes that a person has.
> - Responsibilities – having authority and a duty to do something.

Activity **7.2** 45–60 mins   **P1**

Skills, qualities and responsibilities of sports leaders

M1

D1

You now have a good knowledge of all of the skills, qualities and responsibilities required to make a good sports leader.

Task 1

Draw a spider diagram to show all of the skills, qualities and responsibilities required by a sports leader.

Task 2

(a) Select two successful sports leaders. If possible try to select two contrasting leaders, for example one may have an autocratic style of leadership whereas the other may have a democratic style of leadership.

(b) Look at your spider diagram and pick out the skills and qualities that are associated with each leader, then write a report that describes, explains and evaluates the skills and qualities of each leader. Where possible, try to compare and contrast both leaders and comment on the effectiveness of each skill and quality.

Task 3

Now look at your spider diagram and examine the responsibilities required by each of your selected leaders. Write a report that describes and explains the responsibilities of each coach.

Quick Quiz 5–10 mins   ?

Insert the answers to these questions in the criss-cross puzzle above.

Across

5. This is a type of motivation.
6. This is important so that you look professional.
7. This should be done at the end of each sports session.

Down

1. This style of leadership is also known as the command style.
2. This can be verbal or non-verbal.
3. This method of leadership allows the group to make the decisions.
4. These are fair and honest actions.

7.5 Planning and Leading a Sports Activity Session P2 M2

Planning a Session

Planning a session means that you will need to look at every detail of the activity and consider every possible eventuality. Planning may be time-consuming, but it will help ensure that you get the best out of your sessions.

Remember: **Proper Planning Prevents Poor Performance!**

Aims and Objectives

There are many considerations when planning your activity session, but the first thing to consider is what you want to get out of the activity session. It is important to set aims and objectives – what you want the participants to be able to do at the end of the session. For example, the main aim of the session could be to try to ensure the participants are able to perform a lay up shot in basketball.

Participants

During your planning, you will need to consider a range of different aspects about the activity participants:

- the age of the participants that the session is being planned for
- the number of participants
- the ability of the participants
- the gender of the group
- specific needs of the group or individuals in the group
- medical concerns – for example, participants with asthma may need medication during the session.

The age of sports participants is a very important factor as a session that is appropriate for a group of 18 year olds would not be suitable for a group of 8 year olds. The younger the age group, the more simple the activity needs to be. You will also need to take into account the fact that you will need a higher number of helpers when working with younger children, whereas with older participants, such as teenagers or adults, you may find you don't need any helpers.

The number of participants will also help to dictate what sort of physical activity session you plan. You should always try to make sure that all the participants are actively involved in the session for the majority of the time – participants that have to sit and watch are more likely to become bored, which often leads to misbehaviour.

The ability of the participants will also need to be factored in to your planning. Leading an activity for a group of beginners is completely different from organising a session for more advanced performers. Also, when planning your sports activity session, you might consider what the group has done prior to your session or what is planned for the following sessions.

The gender of the group needs to be taken into account; some activities such as netball tend to be played only by females, whereas rugby tends to be a more male-dominated sport. If the participants are both male and female then it is usually better to choose an activity that can appeal to both and does not involve contact, such as volleyball or badminton.

It is important to know of any medical or special needs that any participants have prior to running a session. A good way for a leader to know the medical backgrounds of the participants is to get them to complete a Physical Activity Readiness Questionnaire (PAR-Q) before taking part in exercise. A PAR-Q looks at an individual's medical history and highlights any major factors that could stop them from participating.

Physical Activity Readiness Questionnaire (PAR-Q)

1. Has a doctor ever said you have a heart condition and recommended only medically supervised physical activity?

2. Do you have chest pain brought on by physical activity?

3. Have you developed chest pain in the past month?

4. Do you tend to lose consciousness or fall over as a result of dizziness?

5. Do you have a bone or joint problem that could be aggravated by the proposed physical activity?

6. Has a doctor ever recommended medication for your blood pressure or a heart condition?

7. Are you aware through your own experience, or a doctor's advice, of any other physical reason why you should not exercise without medical supervision?

8. Have you had any operations?

9. Have you suffered any injuries?

10. Do you suffer or have you suffered from back pain?

11. Are you pregnant?

12. Have you recently given birth?

If the person answers YES to one or more questions they should be instructed to talk with their doctor before beginning an exercise programme or taking part in fitness tests.

Resources

Planning and organising what equipment you will require for your activity should be done prior to the session. Time spent during the activity, putting up goals or pumping up balls etc., eats into the participant's time, so planning this in advance will help the session run more smoothly. You should also consider what facilities you will have to use for your session. These may well need to be booked in advance of the session and this is the responsibility of the activity leader. When planning your session you will need to ensure that you have enough material and activities to last the time allocated. It is a good idea to have a few more activities planned than you think you will need, then you will never run out of things to do during the session!

Activity **7.3**   30 mins   **P4**

Planning activities for different groups

You are planning to run a ball-based activity for a small group of 12 people. What sort of game would you plan if you had the following types of participants:

- a group of 15-year-old females
- a group of 8-year-old girls and boys
- a group of 12-year-old girls
- a group of teenagers who have hearing difficulties?

Try to explain how you have changed the activity to take into account the different types of participants.

7.6 Leading a Sports Activity Session

When delivering your session you will need to do many things to ensure that your participants understand what it is you are trying to cover.

First you will need to explain and demonstrate the skills that you require them to undertake. Demonstrations should be kept simple and it is important that they are carried out correctly. This will help ensure that the group understands what it is that you are trying to teach them. Some participants will need additional support when learning new skills, so it is important that you move around your group and look at the different individuals' needs.

It is also important to look to progress the session. This will help motivate the participants and prevent them from losing interest. Spending too much time on one activity can cause participants to switch off and start to do other things as they get bored. Progression also gives encouragement to performers as they can see their own achievements.

Sometimes you may need to adapt the session if things are not going to plan or if changes are necessary due to factors that are out of your

Activity 7.4 20 mins

P2

Case study: Jodie

As part of her sports leaders award, Jodie is due to run a rounders session for a group of 16 primary school children. Jodie is a little nervous but hopes the session will run well. The session is due to start at 10 a.m. and Jodie arrives there just on time. However, all of the children are already there and she hasn't had a chance to get the equipment out ready for the session. She has to leave the children sitting in the sports hall with their teacher while she gets the equipment from the store cupboard.

She manages to find most of the things she needs but cannot find a rounders ball and ends up spending a further 10 minutes looking around the store cupboard until she finds it.

When she returns to the sports hall the children are all messing around and chatting noisily. Jodie tries to calm them down but has forgotten her whistle which means she has trouble attracting their attention.

Task

(a) Describe what has gone wrong for Jodie.
(b) What should Jodie have done to avoid the problems she has encountered?
(c) Which skills does Jodie need to work on in order to improve her sports leadership?

Many sports leaders will use a session planner to highlight the requirements for the planned activity session. Figure 7.2 shows an example of a typical session planner.

---

control. For example, you may be leading a rugby activity session outside but the weather changes and there is a thunderstorm. If available, you may need to use indoor facilities in a sports hall with a hard floor so you would need to adapt the game to touch rugby rather than having players tackle each other as they would be more likely to injure themselves from falling on a hard sports hall floor surface compared with a grass rugby field.

What Components Should Go into Your Sports Activity Session?

The first thing to consider is: what is the activity session that you wish to carry out?

Sessions could include:

- a fitness session such as a circuit
- a practical coaching session
- a sports event such as a competition or race
- a competitive match.

A typical sports coaching session will progress through the following stages:

1. **Warm-up** – this will typically involve pulse-raising activities, mobility and flexibility work and some sports-specific skills that help prepare the performer for what they are about to do. It is important to consider what skills-related components of fitness will be used during the activity and how to integrate them into the warm-up, for example volleyball players require both power and hand–eye coordination in their sport, so both should be included in their warm-up.

2. **Fitness work** – if time allows, participants should undertake some fitness and training methods that are relevant to their sport, for example rugby players might incorporate aerobic conditioning and muscular endurance training into their sessions.

3. **Technical skills practice** – this is where you normally cover the main aims of your session. This will include your drill and routines that you have prepared. Remember

Date:	Venue:
Time:	Duration:
Group:	No. of participants:
Equipment required:	Aims of session:
Safety checks required:	

TIME	CONTENT
	Warm up:
	Fitness work:
	Main technical skills work:
	Game play/Tactical work:
	Cool down:
Injuries/Issues arisen:	
Evaluation of session:	

Figure 7.2   Session planner

to demonstrate the skills and give people the opportunity to practise them, while assisting those individuals who struggle.

4. **Tactical work** – once you have developed the skills, you should look at how and when you use them to gain an advantage over your opponents.

5. **Game play** – it is important to put the skills learned into a game context.

6. **Cool-down** – this is used to help reduce the build up of lactic acid and reduce the risk of DOMS (Delayed Onset of Muscle Soreness).

It is important that you record evidence of your sports activity session. You should use the feedback to help you evaluate the session. Evaluation is as important as the planning process since it can help you with future sessions as you will know what has worked well, any problems that arose and what should be changed.

Key learning points

- Planning an activity session is very important.
- Ensure you know the age, ability, special needs, medical needs and number of expected participants before planning your activity session.
- Ensure you know and have ready all of the equipment required for your activity session.
- A session plan should be completed prior to any activity session.
- Feedback should be obtained after an activity session.

Quick Quiz 2 5 mins

Warm-up	Young children	Demonstration	Aims	Cool-down
Medical needs	Females	Session plan	Game plan	Adapt

Choose a word(s) from the boxes above to answer the following questions.

1. These types of participants will need to have more helpers in an activity session.
2. This should take place at the end of an activity session.
3. This type of participant may prefer sports such as netball.
4. A PAR-Q can be completed to find this out about sports participants.
5. A sports leader should ensure this part of the activity is always delivered correctly and clearly.
6. This should be written out prior to any activity session.
7. This should take place at the start of an activity session.
8. This is the name for what the sports leader wants their participants to be able to do by the end of the session.
9. This is the part of the activity session where the participants get to put the skills learned into a game context.
10. A sports leader may have to do this to a session plan if things are not going as expected.

Activity **7.5** 60–90 mins   P2   M2

Planning and leading a sports activity

Task 1

Select a sports activity of your choice. Work out who is going to take part in the activity and their ability levels etc.

Task 2

Complete a session plan (see Figure 7.2 for help) for your sports activity, making sure you consider the following points:

- age of participants
- ability of participants
- aims of session
- equipment required
- warm-up
- fitness work (if applicable)
- technical skills work
- tactical work
- cool-down.

Task 3

With a group of appropriate participants, lead your planned sports session.

7.7 Reviewing Planning and Leadership of a Sports Activity P3 M3

It is always a good idea to review every activity session as soon after completion as possible. It is also a good idea to try to gain feedback from the participants to find out how they felt the session went. This feedback can be verbal where you simply ask them 'How was the activity session for you?', or it could be a more detailed questionnaire where the participant is asked to comment on the different aspects of the session content.

You can also gain feedback from a supervisor who may be able to give you tips on how to improve your skills. Another method of gaining feedback would be to have yourself video-taped while you lead a session. You can then view how you deliver the session, for example what sort of communication skills you use and how they are received by the participants etc.

Once you have reviewed your activity session, you should then aim to set targets to examine how you can improve your skills and qualities so that you can become a more effective leader. SMARTER targets are the sensible kind of target to set yourself.

Specific – your aim must be specific.

Measurable – how can you measure it?

Achievable – it must be possible to achieve the goal.

Realistic – be realistic with your aims; are they achievable?

Timed – set yourself a time period within which to achieve your goal.

Exciting – this will help motivate you to achieve your aims.

Recorded – record your aims; this will help you stick to them.

This method should be used when setting targets for how you can improve your planning, your skills and your qualities as a sports leader.

Activity 7.6 45 mins P3

Reviewing the planning and leading of a sports activity M3

After having planned and led an activity session, complete the following tasks.

Task 1

Design a feedback form that you could give to the participants in your activity session so that they can provide constructive feedback on how they thought your sports activity session went.

Task 2

Examine the feedback from the participants and speak to your supervisor or teacher to gain their opinion of your planning and leadership. Also, carry out a self-assessment on how you think you planned and led the activity session.

In a written report, carry out a review of your planning and leading of a sports activity. Identify and explain your strengths in the planning and leading of the activity.

Task 3

Identify and explain any areas for improvement and set yourself some SMARTER targets for how you can make these improvements.

7.8 Assisting in the Planning and Leading of a Sports Event

There are many different types of sports events. Some examples include:

- Sports day
- Tournament
- Competition
- Community event
- Indoor event
- Outdoor pursuit event.

Planning a sports event can be a major responsibility and there are many things that need to be undertaken for the event to run smoothly.

Facilities

Once you have decided what type of sports event you would like to run, it is important to book the facilities provisionally in advance. Provisionally booking a few dates will allow you to look at the potential interest in the event before making a decision. If you set the date first and then find that the facility is not available you could end up with a problem!

Any equipment required should be obtained in advance; if it is left until the last minute, the likelihood is that it will not be available.

Good administration skills are required as letters, invitations and other correspondence will need to be sent out to groups wishing to participate in the event.

Format and Rules

Once the venue and facilities have been decided and booked, rules need to be set. These may link to your aims and objectives. If it is a team sports event, you should consider the format of the competition. This could include a round robin or league process where everyone plays against each other, or a knockout tournament where the losing team is then eliminated from the event or competition.

Health and Safety

Health and safety considerations will need to be taken into account for an event to be successful. It is important that the event leaders are aware of the emergency procedures and are prepared for any potential incidents. Prior to the start of the event, the sports leaders should check that all equipment is in good, safe, working condition. Sufficient first-aid provision should be available. It is important that you consider whether you have enough first-aiders available and whether you have sufficient first-aid equipment. A large number of people undertaking a sports event increases the potential risk for some minor injuries. Organisations such as the St John's Ambulance may be willing to provide first-aid cover for a big event.

Risk Assessment

A thorough risk assessment should be developed prior to the event taking place. This should highlight all of the potential hazards, and the risk of them happening. It should also list the control measures used to reduce the risks.

Refreshments and Presentations

If many people are taking part in the sports event, it might be appropriate for refreshments to be provided. This may include food, but drinks should definitely be provided to all participants. At the end of the event a presentation should be held to award prizes to the successful participants. This needs much thought, including what to say and whom to thank for their hard work.

Assign Roles

A big sports event needs many people to help run it for it to be a success. You should consider what jobs need to be done and develop a list of positions that you can assign names to (see Figure 7.3). Highlight different people's strengths and weaknesses and then use this to find them a job that they will be good at.

Contingency Plans

A contingency plan is a back-up plan that is only used if something happens that means you cannot stick to your original plan; this is rarely used, but does mean that you could still put on an activity. When would you need a contingency plan?

- In adverse weather conditions.
- If you do not have the correct or any equipment.
- If you have an insufficient number of participants.
- When the facility/venue is not available or is closed due to staff illnesses or being double-booked.

Figure 7.3 Different roles involved in the running of a sports event

7.9 Reviewing the Planning and Leadership of Your Sports Event

Following your sports event, you should review your part in both the planning and the leading of the activity. You will need to consider your own effectiveness in the planning and leadership of the event, and what were the strengths and weaknesses. This will allow you to be able to make improvements for when you are involved in planning and running another sports event in the future.

How Can You Receive the Feedback Required to Review Your Event?

It is important that you receive feedback from a range of people. You should seek feedback from a range of people, for example observers, participants, your teacher. Ask them specifically what you did well or what needs improving. You could compile a questionnaire for them to fill in while watching you or at the end of the session. Self-assessment will help you get different perspectives on how the event went.

It is important to consider the following areas when writing your evaluation:

- Was enough planning undertaken prior to the event?
- Was the organisation on the day sufficient?
- Were there any health and safety concerns?
- What personal skills and qualities did you develop through running the event?
- Were the aims and objectives of the event met?

You should also include what considerations you would need to take into account if you were to organise another sports event.

You should always remember to use SMART targets when setting the aims and objectives of your event:

Specific – your aim must be specific.

Measurable – how can you measure it?

Achievable – it must be possible to achieve the goal.

Realistic – be realistic with your aims, are they achievable?

Timed – set yourself a time period within which to achieve your goal.

Key learning points

- All team members need to be assigned a role or roles.
- Planning should take into account health and safety, risk assessments and contingency plans.
- Record the planning stages so that they can be reviewed at a later date.
- Record the feedback from event participants so that it can be evaluated and can be used for self-improvement.

Useful websites

www.sports-council-wales.org.uk/ getactiveinthecommunity/organising-activities-in-your-community

Links that will help you to organise sports events in your local area or school.

www.staffsmoorlands.gov.uk/downloads/ No 14 - Organising an event.doc

Printable information sheet giving you plenty of ideas of how to organise your own event, whether sporting or otherwise.

www.runningsports.org

Tips and ideas for setting up sports events and review a sports development plan, with information on the different roles involved, details of practical training courses and a photo gallery.

Activity 7.7

P4
P5
M4
D2

Planning, leading and reviewing a sports event

Working in a team, think about what sort of sports event you could plan and lead between you.

Task 1

You will need to think about:

- what sort of event you would like to plan and lead
- when you plan to run the event
- who the event is for
- costs of the event
- roles for each member of your team.

Take this plan to your teacher/tutor to gain their feedback.

Task 2

Take minutes of the meetings you have with your team and make a note of the things that you need to do before each meeting. Keep a 'planning and event' diary to show what you need to do and when you need to do it by.

Task 3

On the day of the event, ensure you take a role in leading part of the event – and make a note afterwards of what you did and how you did it.

Task 4

(a) Think about how well you did in your role of planning and leading part of your sports event.
(b) Write a report that reviews your own performance and identifies, explains and evaluates your strengths and any areas for improvement.

Task 5

Investigate ways in which you can improve your performance, then write a report that provides some suggestions and your further development needs required for you to develop as a sports leader.

Quick Quiz 5 mins

R	T	D	S	E	M	R	E	T	F	E	F	E
E	C	O	N	T	F	S	S	E	Q	O	E	U
F	O	N	U	E	N	A	Q	U	E	T	E	T
R	M	I	E	R	H	U	I	I	D	M	D	E
E	P	H	O	M	N	P	H	N	B	R	B	A
S	E	N	T	P	M	A	T	R	O	M	A	H
H	T	L	M	E	U	S	M	L	C	I	C	A
M	I	E	N	U	A	A	E	E	K	T	K	S
E	T	T	R	A	M	S	S	R	N	R	T	N
N	I	N	H	E	Y	D	I	T	F	T	I	M
T	O	E	M	A	N	R	U	O	T	E	C	R
S	N	E	I	A	W	G	O	P	A	H	R	C
R	Y	O	H	I	S	T	E	E	T	C	T	B

Find the following words in the wordsearch:

REFRESHMENTS
COMPETITION
TOURNAMENT
EQUIPMENT
FEEDBACK
SMART
ROLES

Chapter 8
Technical Skills & Tactical Awareness for Sport

This chapter looks at techniques, tactics and ways in which to assess these skills. Training programmes will be explored and enable you to write a six-week training programme for an athlete which is designed to develop specific technical skills and tactical awareness.

Learning Goals

By the end of this chapter you should:

- Know the technical and tactical demands of a selected sport.
- Understand the technical skills and tactical awareness in a selected sport.
- Be able to plan and undertake a six-week programme to develop own technical skills and tactical awareness.
- Be able to review own technical and tactical development and set goals for further development.

To achieve a PASS grade the evidence must show that the learner is able to:	To achieve a MERIT grade the evidence must show that, in addition to the pass criteria, the learner is able to:	To achieve a DISTINCTION grade the evidence must show that, in addition to the pass and merit criteria, the learner is able to:
P1 describe the technical and tactical demands of a chosen sport	**M1** explain the technical and tactical demands of a chosen sport	
P2 assess the technical skills and tactical awareness of an elite performer, identifying strengths and areas for improvement	**M2** assess the technical skills and tactical awareness of an elite performer, explaining strengths and areas for improvement	
P3 assess own technical skills and tactical awareness in a chosen sport, identifying strengths and areas for improvement	**M3** assess own technical skills and tactical awareness in a chosen sport, explaining own strengths and areas for improvement	**D1** compare and contrast own technical skills and tactical awareness with those of an elite performer and the demands of a chosen sport
P4 produce a six-week training programme, with tutor support, to develop own technical skills and tactical awareness	**M4** independently produce a six-week training programme to develop own technical skills and tactical awareness, describing strengths and areas for improvement	**D2** evaluate the training programme, justifying suggestions made regarding improvement
P5 carry out a six-week training programme to develop own technical skills and tactical awareness		
P6 review own development, identifying goals for further technical and tactical development, with tutor support	**M5** independently describe own development, explaining goals for technical and tactical development	**D3** analyse own goals for technical and tactical development, suggesting how these goals could be achieved

8.1 The Technical and Tactical Demands of a Selected Sport P1 M1

Figure 8.1 A basketball player

Technical and Tactical Demands in Sport P1 M1

In order to perform sport well, it is necessary to have a good understanding and ability of the technical and tactical demands required from the sport.

Technical Demands

In all sports, the execution of skill is vital to the result of a performance or competition. It is important to understand the nature of skill, and the different types of skill that exist in sport.

Continuous Skills

Continuous skills are those which have a clear beginning or end and can be easily separated from the overall performance, like the leg action in running or cycling.

Discrete Skills

Discrete skills have a clear beginning or end and can be easily separated from the overall performance, such as in the case of a basketball free throw or a diver performing a dive.

Serial Skills

Serial Skills are composed of a number of discrete or continuous skills put together. These skills or techniques are put into a routine or pattern, such as an ice skating routine, a synchronised swimming routine or drop shot in tennis.

Activity 8.1   20 mins   P1

Types of skills   M1

Task

Look at the table of skills listed below and try to put them in the correct group, are they discrete, serial or continuous

Discrete	Serial	Continuous

- A long pass in football
- A gymnastics floor routine
- A penalty kick in football
- Race walking technique
- Rowing over 1500 metres
- A ten bounce trampoline routine
- A volleyball serve
- A cross country skiing competition
- A set of jumps in show jumping.

Tactical Demands

Strategy and tactics are key features in all sports. There are many examples of different kinds of tactics and how and when they might be employed. It is important to remember that tactics are only effective if the performer is able to execute them.

It is easy to think of tactics and strategies used in team games, for example full court pressure defence in basketball, chip and charge in rugby or playing the offside trap in football. In racket sports such as badminton an example of a tactic to use against a taller, less mobile player could be to make a lot of drop shots and push the shuttle to all the corners of the court.

Case Study: Tennis

In tennis it is just as important to understand your own game as that of your opponent. If you are constantly aware of your opponent's strengths and weaknesses then you can make a gameplan and adapt this throughout the course of the game. Here are some examples of tactics that you could use:

Figure 8.2   Andy Murray on the attack

Scenario	Tactic/Strategy
Opponent has good return of serve on forehand service	Plan to hit most of your serves to the backhand side
Opponent likes to charge at the net after a serve	Plan to hit a mixture of quick returns to their feet and lob shots
Opponent likes to argue about line calls and put off their opponent	Have a strategy for dealing with these unnecessary distractions, and remain focused
Opponent has a very good all round game, but struggles under match pressure	Try to show that you do not feel the pressure, and put them under more by breaking their rhythm, slowing down between services etc.

Defending and Attacking in Sport

 P1 **M1**

In many sports, tactics are absolutely vital. The right tactic at the right time can mean the difference between winning and losing. Often the difference between a good player and a great one can be how they tactically plan and constantly re-evaluate in a competition situation. Take a look at the case studies on Basketball and Tennis.

Stroke selection

Players of any sport will need to know when, and how to play a shot, and more importantly at what time. Practicing real game scenarios is important for coaches so that players can practise not just skills, but shot selection, and often decision-making under pressure

Variety

A good player will also have not just a range of good shots, but also the ability to know when to play them, all under pressure.

Case Study: Basketball

In all team sports, there is the added complication of having to consider not just your own positioning, decision-making and shot selection, but also that of your teammates and your opposition.

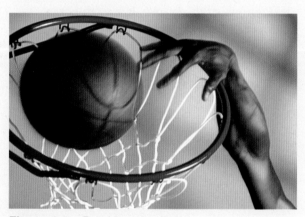

Figure 8.3   Dunking the ball

Scenario	Tactic/Strategy
Opponents have weak outside shooting but are very good at driving and scoring close up baskets	Consider a defensive formation that will block up the key area and help prevent this kind of scoring, such as a box and one or 2–1–2 zone defence
Opponents have a particularly tall, and agile centre who is very good at scoring close to the basket	Try 'fronting' the passes made to this player, in other words preventing them from getting the ball as much as possible
Opponents are slow at returning to their half having had their own offence	Build a structured and organised fast break to achieve an early shot opportunity
Opponents are strong and aggressive full court defenders who make it difficult to progress with the ball down the court	The coach will want to have a plan to beat this pressure that may involve a series of screens, but certainly one that has a series of movement patterns, known as a press break

Activity 8.2 40 mins   P1 M1

Tactics

Task

Using the grid below, identify either which sport the tactics come from, what they are or when would be a good time to use them. The example from football should help you with this activity. For some of the activity you may need to identify the tactic.

Tactic	Sport	What is it?	When you could use it?
Example: Offside trap	Football	A defensive strategy that has defenders push forwards at a critical time, so as to catch an attacking player in an offside position	To prevent a team from a repeated attack from a set piece, e.g. a corner
	Tennis	A shot played that usually goes high over your opponent's head	Usually played when the opponent is close to the net
Block	Volleyball		
	Cricket	Deliberately bowling a ball that looks fast to an unsuspecting batsman, but actually the delivery is much slower than it appears	To attempt to prevent the ball from being spiked/smashed over the net
Full court zone press		An attempt by the defending team to put extra pressure on the attacking team in order to force them into making a mistake	
Overhead clear	Badminton		To recover a rally and put the shuttle at the back of your opponent's court

Tactics can be:

- **Pre-event tactics** – a particular plan before the event; or

- **In-event tactics** – a plan implemented during the game such as switching from man-to-man to zone defence in basketball.

Tactics can be successful and unsuccessful. It is important to understand what determines the success of a tactic.

Tactics can fail if the opposition works them out too easily, if the tactics are employed too late or if the player or players are simply not able to understand or execute them.

If the conditions of the match are such that the player is losing, then that player might start to play defensive shots in an attempt to prevent them from falling further.

Figure 8.4 Tactics are a key element of playing team sports

Key learning points

- Technical demands are the kinds of specialised individual movements that are performed in a sport. Such as skills.
- Discrete skills have a beginning and an end and can be separated from the overall performance.
- Continuous skills have no obvious start or end and flow from one phase to the next with little or no change.
- A strategy is a play designed to meet a specific objective.
- Tactics are the actions that make the strategy work.

Activity **8.3**   45 mins   **P1**

Technical and tactical demands of sport   **M1**

Select a sport of your choice, preferably this sport will be one in which you take part in.

Task 1

Design a spider diagram that illustrates the technical and tactical demands of your selected sport.

Task 2

Prepare an information leaflet that:

(a) describes and explains the technical demands of your selected sport.

(b) describes and explains the tactical demands of your selected sport.

Definition

Tactics can be employed in order to make the strategy work. They can be used by individuals or teams, for example to beat an opponent.

 Quick Quiz 1   30 mins

1. Give a good description of a discrete skill and give a sporting example.
2. Give a definition for tactics and give an example from your sport.
3. What is a pre-event tactic and provide examples from athletics, table tennis and cricket?
4. What is a serial skill?
5. What is an in-event tactic and provide examples from basketball, tennis and triathlon?

8.2 The Technical Skills and Tactical Awareness in a Selected Sport

P2   **P3**   **M2**   **M3**   **D1**

Performance Analysis

The process of analysing sports performance will produce feedback for performers that will help to improve their performance. There are many different factors to consider when analysing a team's or individual's performance. Questions that an analyst may ask could include:

- Are they performing the required skills to the best of their ability?
- Are they using the correct techniques?
- Are they using appropriate tactics?
- Are they successful at employing these tactics?

It is important when analysing a sports team or individual that it is done in a competitive situation, so that you can get a true reflection of performance. Some athletes can look good in practice but do not have the big-match confidence and are unable to live up to expectations.

We can analyse sports performance in a number of different ways:

1. **Observation in real time** – involves the gathering of data; this could be the number of blocked shots in basketball, successful overhead smashes in badminton or the distance travelled from the cross in a trampoline routine. **Real time** means that it is carried out in action, or while the event is going on, so is best not done by the people taking part, but coaches or parents perhaps.

2. **Observation by video** – technology now allows us to record and save or upload our performance in a number of ways:

- With a camcorder and stored on our Hard Drive, CD, DVD, memory stick or USB device.

- With a mobile device, like a mobile phone, where with technology that usually comes with the phone, you could upload the clips to a computer using cables or Bluetooth technology.

3. **Notational analysis** – in its simplest form, this is the gathering of accurate data that might help you improve your performance. A basketball analyst might choose to record data that could help the coach at half time. A tennis coach may like some information on where an opponent has been most successful and with what kinds of shots.

Increasingly, technology such as Hawkeye and Prozone has had a huge impact on the way data is collected and presented.

The advantages of hand-notation systems are that they are inexpensive and if completed by a skilful recorder will produce information quickly, so that the coach or performer could have instant access to detailed information. The main disadvantages are that they are open to human error, can be difficult to interpret and can be difficult to carry out in certain conditions, for example bad weather.

The main advantages of computerised notation are that there is a better quality of data, more detail, less time spent presenting results and greater accuracy. The main disadvantages are that the software can be very expensive and that anyone who uses the system needs both sufficient training and practice.

Analysis Model

Figure 8.5 shows a sports observation analysis model. At any point you could be at each stage, but let us assume that you have not yet competed and you are preparing for a competition in a few weeks.

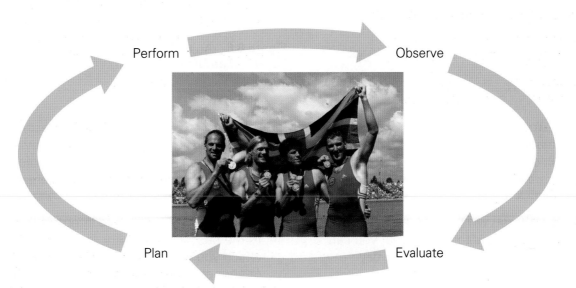

Figure 8.5   A sports observation model

Case Study: Chalkboard

Chalkboard is used by *The Guardian* newspaper to demonstrate a range of techniques and tactics, including types of passes. The clever feature about Chalkboard is that it allows people access to analyse their own matches and performances.

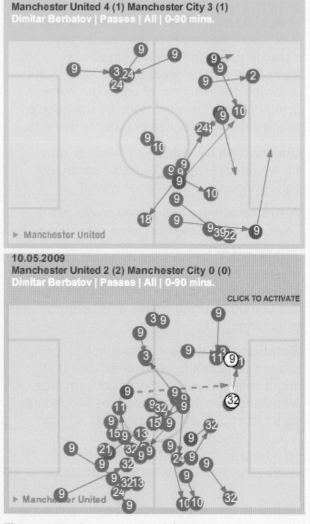

20.09.2009
Manchester United 4 (1) Manchester City 3 (1)
Dimitar Berbatov | Passes | All | 0-90 mins.

▶ Manchester United

10.05.2009
Manchester United 2 (2) Manchester City 0 (0)
Dimitar Berbatov | Passes | All | 0-90 mins.

CLICK TO ACTIVATE

▶ Manchester United

Figure 8.6   An example of Chalkboard
(© *Guardian* Newspaper Ltd)

1. **Plan** – Your plan will include as much information about the competition as possible, such as who your opposition is likely to be, travel arrangements, skills to practise and tactics to think about.

2. **Perform** – You will perform to the best of your ability and focus on what you can control, and do your best on the day.

3. **Observe** – This could be a video-recording or a notational analysis, completed by an observer or coach, but can also be informed by your personal reflections and comments from those that you respect.

4. **Evaluate** – This means to interpret the data to the best of your ability, identify areas on which you want to improve, and with the help of your coach, return to the planning stage for your next competition.

Strengths and Areas for Improvement

Perhaps the simplest form of observed assessment is a strengths and weaknesses assessment. This could be as simple as a list of a performer's strengths and weaknesses. This is an inexpensive and effective system provided that the observer has sufficient knowledge of what constitutes strong and weak performances and technique execution.

Performance Profiling

If a trampolinist is not performing a somersault correctly or is not coping with the physical demands of the sport, then the coach or trainer can design a suitable exercise or coaching programme. But what if the trampolinist has trouble with their nerves before the start of the competition or they have some kind of mental block that stops them from executing a skill?

Although not always obvious, psychological factors do affect sporting performances.

Definitions

Confidence belief in yourself and your abilities.

Concentration the ability to attend to relevant cues; not being distracted.

Control the extent to which you feel able to influence events.

Commitment the level to which you apply yourself.

Re-focusing after errors the ability to adjust to negative outcomes in a positive way.

Enjoyment the amount of fun that you can have.

Using Performance Profile

1. Talk with the performer and ask them to tell you how they feel about their sport. Do they ever feel anxious, and if so, when? Do they understand the terms above and, if so, how do they score them in terms of importance and relevance to themselves?

2. If you can, talk to their coach about how they rate these factors and if they would add any of their own.

In the performance profile above, it seems that the performer's main emphasis for any intervention should be focused on the areas that they identify as a weakness, in this case refocusing after errors and concentration.

Performance factors	Importance to performer	Self-assessment
Confidence	9	9
Concentration	9	6
Control	9	8
Commitment	10	10
Refocusing after errors	10	6
Enjoyment	7	9

The performer has been asked to rate, out of ten, the importance of each of the factors and then rate their own proficiency in that factor.

Activity 8.4 60 mins   P2

Assessing the technical and tactic awareness of an elite performer   M2

Select an elite sports performer of your choice.

Task 1

Decide on a method of analysing your selected player's performance, for example, observation of video footage, notational analysis.

Task 2

Carry out an assessment on your selected performer's:

1. technical skills and
2. tactical awareness.

Task 3

Write a report that identifies your selected performer's strengths and areas for improvement.

Technical and Tactical Skills awareness

The same process can be applied to technical skills and tactical awareness.

Technical Skills

The following is a performance profile for a boxer and is focused this time on skills as opposed to psychological attributes.

Performance profile	1	2	3	4	5	6	7	8	9	10
Breathing										
Bobbing/Weaving										
Balance										
Punching										
Blocking										
Parry										
Recovery										

The boxer would select the relevant score for each skill, and in doing so, identify what their action plan for improvement would be.

Tactical Skills

It is also possible to apply this principle to tactics. The table relates to the tactical profile of a midfield footballer

	1	2	3	4	5	6	7	8	9	10
Offside Awareness										
Recognising patterns of play										
Remembering the perceived weaknesses in the opponent's defence										
Coping tactically with substitutions										
The ability to read and respond to change in the opponent's tactics										

Elite Performance

Professional Sports Performers

These are performers who are paid to compete in their sport. Several sports such as rugby, cricket and football have professional teams and leagues. A performer who is paid for their performance and training but has another main source of income is called a semi-professional.

National Representatives

These are the sports people who have been selected by trial or observation, perhaps even through talent identification, to represent their country to perform.

National/World Record Holders

Anybody who records a time or distance in athletics can strive to be a national or world record holder. If your event is the 100 m sprint and you record a time that is recorded as faster than anyone in your country, then you become the national record holder. In the same way, if you jump higher than anyone else competing in the world, then you become world record holder.

National Champions

These people have competed and been successful in becoming the best in the country, either at a particular event, usually called a National Championships, or are part of a ranking, so they become number one in the nation, such as in tennis.

Olympians

About a year before an Olympic or Paralympic year, and sometimes nearer to that year, a single-event trial or a multi-event trial is held to decide who are the very best; the most successful will have the honour of competing for their country at the games. Many athletes value the Olympic Games, and the experience of taking part in them, as greater than world championships.

Methods of Assessment

Observation and Analysis

It is possible to be observed and analysed by your team- or club-mates, your coach and by yourself, particularly if you have access to a video of your performance.

Interviews

It is also possible to get a great deal of information from an interview. You could ask a performer about what they consider to be their strengths and weaknesses or you could ask them about what tactics they might use against a particular opponent. Remember that sometimes it is difficult to step away from yourself and analyse objectively, in other words, people partly removed from the action can sometimes get really good information from you that you may have been completely unaware about.

SWOT Analysis

A SWOT Analysis is an analysis that can be completed by a coach or the performer and would usually look something like the one below, which is for tennis.

Strengths	Weaknesses
Very effective at topspin backhand, particularly cross court. High percentage of successful first services.	Need to develop service wide to opponent's forehand from both sides. Concentration remains a problem after disputed line calls. Reluctant to move to net and apply server-volley tactic on good first serves.
Opportunities	**Threats**
Attend extra training. Free gym membership and use of courts. Invited to LTA coaching camp in Florida.	Distracted by group of friends/peers. Repeatedly late for training. Lacking in the desire to win and kill off rallies.

Activity 8.5 60 mins P3 M3 D1

Assessing own technical skills and tactical awareness

Task 1

Carry out an assessment of your own technical skills and tactical awareness. This can be carried out using the following technique:

- Take part in a sport of your choice and have two people observe your performance.
- The first observer will simply watch and record observation about the technique and record their information in a simple notation/collection sheet like the one below.
- The second helper should video your performance and then complete the same collection sheet.

Task 2

Write a report that shows how you have assessed yourself performing a selected sport, and the outcome of this assessment. Include in your report your assessment of your technical skills and tactical awareness.

Task 3

Identify and explain your strengths in your performance of your selected sport and also areas for improvement.

Task 4

Compare and contrast your own technical skills and tactical awareness with those of an elite performer who plays or takes part in the same sport.

Key learning points

- Observation involves watching sporting performances.
- Analysis is about deciding what has happened.
- Evaluation is the end product of observation and analysis. It is the final process where decisions are made and feedback is given to the performer.
- Qualitative analysis is largely subjective, meaning that it is open to personal interpretation and is therefore subject to bias or error. The more knowledge the observer has in this case, the more valid the observations.
- Quantitative analysis is more involved and scientific and involves the direct measurement of a performance or technique. Match statistics recorded while the game is in progress are called real-time. Match statistics recorded after the events are called lapsed-time.
- Notation is a way of collecting data and can be done by hand or with a computer:
  - Hand notation is a system of recording detailed analysis of a sport and noting the data on a paper sheet using a pre-defined set of symbols.
  - Computerised notation takes advantage of computer packages and can be used in real-time but is more commonly used in lapsed-time or afterwards.
- A SWOT analysis examines strengths, weaknesses, opportunities and threats.
- Performance profiles take into account the views of both the performer and the coach and make it possible to analyse technical, tactical and psychological factors that affect performance.
- An intervention is an interruption that brings about change, in this case a change in sporting performance.

Quick Quiz 2  45 mins ❓

1. **Name four factors that you should consider when analysing an individual's performance.**
2. **Explain what qualitative analysis is, and give an example of a TV pundit.**
3. **What is the main advantage of analysing video data of sporting performance after the event (post-competition)?**
4. **What is the principle advantage of analysing in real-time?**
5. **Give a definition for notation in sport.**
6. **Name six psychological factors that can make up a performance profile.**
7. **What is the foundation level in UK sport? Provide a local example.**
8. **What is the participation level in UK sport? Provide a local example.**
9. **What is the performance level in UK sport? Provide a local example.**

8.3 Planning a Six-week Programme to Develop Technical Skills and Tactical Awareness

Aims and Objectives

It is important when designing any programme that you consider exactly what it is that you need to improve, and then how you are going to achieve it.

First you need to identify the strengths and weaknesses of a performer. You can observe and assess these using the methods described earlier in this chapter, particularly the SWOT analysis, performance profiling and perhaps using a notation system.

An example of a technical weakness in a basketball player could be getting free from a defender to take a jump shot.

An example of a tactical weakness in a basketball player could be recognising the right time in an offence to take a shot.

Once you have decided what improvements you would like to make, you can start to plan your programme.

Your plan could include aspects of:

● Tactical development

● Technical skills development

● Physical development

● Psychological development.

An **aim** is what we set out to do, while an **objective** is what you want to achieve. For example, you may set an aim of being a better badminton player, while your objective may describe how you intend to achieve this, for example, by the end of the six-week programme I will be able to tactically read my opponent better, and improve my foot speed and recovery shots.

Targets

It is a good idea to use the SMART principle in designing your programme.

Specific

Measurable

Achievable

Realistic

Time-based

Specific

This means that the programme meets what the targets want it to meet. For example, instead of saying that attacking play is a technical weakness in football, you could say that running off the ball, part-completion and beating a defender are weaknesses.

Measurable

This is the way in which you measure your results. If you have identified that you want to improve a basketball player's jump shooting, then you might measure this by counting how many shots are successful in a training or game situation and then measure again after the training programme. For example:

- Before programme 50/100 jump shots successful (50 per cent)
- After programme 80/100 jump shots successful (80 per cent).

So the improvement would be measured as a 30/100 improvement, or better known as a 60 per cent improvement.

Achievable

What you set out to improve must be possible. It would not be fair to ask a beginner in trampolining to complete a complicated routine with multiple somersaults.

Realistic

It must be possible and realistic to achieve what you intend to achieve.

Time-based

There should be a reasonable amount of time to complete the programme, for example six weeks.

The Training Plan

A typical training plan should contain the following:

- A detailed, technique-specific warm-up.
- Details of the kind of drills and skills that you intend to use, including:
  - —What each drill/practice intends to achieve
  - —The resources and equipment needed
  - —Information about the participants
  - —A description of the activities/practices used.
- A planned and considered warm-down.

Figure 8.7   A trampolinist in flight

Example of a rugby warm-up:

Time	Activity	Organisation	Coaching points
0–15	1. Change, recap on last session	Players go out to the rugby grids or astro & line up on the edge of the pitch	Recap: Most: WALT: Develop the skills of passing while moving & continue to reinforce the rule regarding passing out of hand in rugby
15–25	2. Warm-up: Pulse raiser & static	Players find a space in the square of cones marked out on the field or the centre circle on the astro. Then react to the instructions called out by the teacher 4 balls are added into the warm-up & passed round within the area. Non-doers set up the working grids. Teacher's position Dots equate to the positioning of the cones for the grids. The orange grid is used for demonstrations.	Gear 1: Fast walk Gear 2: Jogging Gear 3: 3/4 pace Gear 4: Sprinting Calls: 1. Pass ball to each other (small pop of the ball) 2. Jogging on spot 3. Press up position 4. Targets up Stretches: a) Calf stretch b) Thigh stretch c) Hamstring stretch d) Side of the torso stretch e) Shoulder stretch f) Triceps stretch g) Neck manipulation

Technical Development

These are practices that would improve your technical skill execution, such as:

- Performing skills from complex routines in isolation, and slowly combining more and more skills until you form a 10-bounce routine in trampolining.

- Practising a set offence in basketball, memorising the pattern of movement for you and your team-mates and practising first with no opposition, then with passive defenders and finally at normal game speed/ intensity.

Tactical Development

These are the application and practising of skills and gaining knowledge to apply these tactics in situations that are realistic for your performance.

These can be divided into:

- Functional practices

- Phases of play

- Conditioned games.

Activity 8.6 30 mins P4

Fault correction   M4

Take a look at the technical weaknesses listed below:

Technical weaknesses

Sport	Fault
Trampolining	Full-time jump cannot get all the way around
Football	Poor at tackling
Basketball	Weak at rebounding
Tennis	Poor topspin on both sides

Task 1

Work out what drills or practices you can use to improve these techniques.

You can use coaching books or websites for the sports, or perhaps speak to a coach from that sport and find out what they would do.

Task 2

Try to come up with at least three practices and think about in which order you would use them.

Developing Tactics

Recording Documentation

It is important that both the coach and performer keep a record of what they are doing in training sessions.

Logbooks and training diaries

Logbooks are useful for recording all kinds of information:

Performer's logbook/diary

- Details of training sessions.
- Reflections/feelings about training sessions.
- Technical details, for example a trampolinist's routine details.
- Worksheets.
- A code of conduct.
- A food diary.
- Personal thoughts and feelings.
- Tactical and technical development points that they have worked out with their coach.
- Training and performance goals.

Coach's logbook/diary

- Details of their sessions (lesson plans).
- Schemes of work (for the whole session).
- Details of performers.
- Scouting reports.
- Health and safety information.
- Copies of development plans for each performer.
- Governing body information.

Figure 8.8   Reading a map is a vital skill on the mountainside

Activity 8.7 30 mins

Producing a six-week training programme to develop own technical skills and tactical awareness

In order to improve your own technical skills and tactical awareness in a selected sport, it is a good idea to design a training programme that will help you to achieve these goals.

Task 1

Design a six-week training programme that is designed to improve your technical skills and tactical awareness or a selected sport.

Include in your training programme:

- specific practices to work on identified technical weaknesses
- sessions where you will participate in your selected sport against differing levels of participants.

Task 2

Carry out your six-week training programme and record your progress in a logbook.

Task 3

Once you have completed the training programme, describe and evaluate its strengths, then describe and justify suggestions on how you could improve the training programme.

When a programme is in place it is necessary to monitor its progress, to assess its effectiveness and possibly to suggest some changes. Monitoring is a process that should happen during the programme. There are many ways of monitoring technical and tactical development programmes. These could include:

- Direct observation
- Video monitoring
- Feedback from the performer
- Feedback from the club/team-mates
- Interviews with the performer and coach
- Questionnaires for the performer and coach
- Skills tests
- Fitness tests.

It is important that monitoring of the development programme occurs throughout the six weeks so that you can be sure that it is effective.

Review   P6   M5   D3

Evaluating Performance against Targets

When the technical and tactical programmes are complete, and assuming that you have

monitored their effectiveness, it is now time to evaluate the programme.

First, you should take some measurements to show whether or not the programme has been successful (remember SMART).

In your conclusion or summary you must consider the factors that affect the success of the programme. These are many and could include:

- Performer's level of motivation for the programme
- Performer being injured
- The amount of help that their coach gives
- The weather
- The amount of time for practice
- The competitive level of the performer
- The kinds of tactics opponents use.

Factors Affecting Technical and Tactical Development

Many factors can influence the effectiveness of technical and tactical development:

- The weather can force cancelled fixtures, and interrupt training schedules.

- Availability of training and or competition areas.
- Illness and player injury.
- External factors such as peer pressure, family bereavement, even holidays.

It is normal for coaches who are organised to have plans in place for dealing with these kinds of issues; these are referred to as contingency plans.

Action Plans and Recommendations

From your findings it is possible to develop future development plans.

If you have carried out a detailed programme with a performer, the results should indicate the success of the programme and perhaps other issues will come to light. For example, if the programme is on a tennis player and aims to improve a technical aspect, say volleying technique, you might discover when you interview him or her that they have an issue with poor line calls. In other words, when they disagree with a line call they seem to lose 80 per cent of the shots that follow. In this case it might be appropriate to design a new programme that helps them with this kind of stress.

Establishing Goals

Goals should be established using the SMART principle and should be negotiated between the coach and the performer, and in the case of children should include parents or carers. This is because if a performer has an input into what they should be aiming to achieve, they are more likely to be motivated than if they are simply just given a list by their coach.

> Definition (d)
>
> **Goal what a performer is intending to achieve; the outcome they desire from their actions.**

Short-term Goals

Short-term goals are set over a short time-frame, perhaps one day to one month. These could include something that you want to change in the next training session.

Long-term Goals

Long-term goals are set over a longer period of time, technically a season, perhaps four years for an Olympic athlete, or possibly even an entire career for some performers.

Short-term goals	1 session to 1 month
Medium-term goals	1 month to 3 months
Long-terms goals	3 months to several years

These goals should form the basis of any future development plans.

Activity 8.8 60 mins **P6**

Reviewing own development **M5**

Task 1 **D3**

Write a report that reviews your own development in your selected sport.

Task 2

Try to come up with three short-term, medium-term and long-term goals that would help your development in a chosen sport. Remember that these goals should be on improving technical and tactical weaknesses and should be based on the SMART principles:

Specific   e.g. to be able to complete at least half of my first serves (tennis)

Measurable   e.g. to cut down on the number of times I make passing errors (rugby)

Achievable   e.g. to improve my somersault technique (trampoline)

Realistic   e.g. to watch and learn how to apply an offside trap (football)

Time-based   e.g. to contribute to the performance levels of a volleyball team

Explain and analyse these goals and provide suggestions on how you think you will be able to achieve them.

 Quick Quiz 3   30 mins   ?

1. **What is the difference between an aim and an objective?**
2. **Give two examples of technical weaknesses/areas for development.**
3. **Give two examples of tactical weaknesses/areas for development.**
4. **What does SMART stand for?**
5. **Name five things that you might want to include in a training logbook or training diary.**
6. **Name four ways of monitoring sports performances.**
7. **What is the difference between a short-term and a long-term goal?**

References

National Coaching Foundation, 1996. *Analysing and Observing Performance*, Leeds: National Coaching Foundation.

Lyons, K. and Hughes, M., 1994, *Analysing Performance Coach Resource Pack*. Leeds: National Coaching Foundation.

Key learning points

- The factors that affect the success of a programme could include:
  - Performer's level of motivation for the programme.
  - Performers being injured.
  - The amount of help that their coach gives.
  - The weather.
  - The amount of time for practice.
  - The competitive level of the performer.
  - The kinds of tactics opponents use.
- A goal is what a performer is intending to achieve. It is the outcome they desire from their actions.

Useful websites

www.bbc.co.uk/schools/gcsebitesize/pe/video/rugby/evasion_tacticsrev1.shtml

Video demonstration giving tips and tactics for successful evasion in rugby.

www.bbc.co.uk/schools/gcsebitesize/pe/video/badminton/griprev1.shtml

Video demonstration of how to grip a badminton racquet correctly.

www.bbc.co.uk/schools/bitesize/pe/video/tennis/shot_selectionrev1.shtml

Video demonstrating different tennis shots and suggesting when to use each shot most effectively during a match.

http://news.bbc.co.uk/sport1/hi/rugby_union/skills/7362451.stm

Video demonstration by Jeremy Guscott and Brian Moore showing effective tackling skills in rugby.

www.mastersport.co.uk/soccerskills/htm

Lots of videos demonstrating specific footballing shots and techniques.

Chapter 9
Psychology for Sports Performance

Sport psychology can be defined as:

> 'The scientific study of people and their behaviour in sport activities and the practical application of that knowledge.'

In simple terms sport psychology looks beyond the physical skill of the individual and asks why he or she behaves in certain ways. In reality, we are all 'amateur' psychologists because we are always asking why we performed so well on one day and not another. We are always discussing psychological topics and we often hear sports people discussing psychology. For example, we hear how team spirit and a desire to win helped England beat Australia to win the Ashes; how Wayne Rooney needs to control his anger if he is to become a better player; and we hear about the mind games of various football managers as they seek an advantage over their opponents.

Learning Goals

By the end of this chapter you should:

- Know the psychological demands of a selected sport.
- Know the impact motivation can have on sports performance.
- Know the effect of personality and aggression on sports performance.
- Be able to develop and review a psychological skills training programme to enhance own sports performance.

To achieve a PASS grade the evidence must show that the learner is able to:	To achieve a MERIT grade the evidence must show that, in addition to the pass criteria, the learner is able to:	To achieve a DISTINCTION grade the evidence must show that, in addition to the pass and merit criteria, the learner is able to:
P1 describe four psychological demands of a selected sport	M1 explain four psychological demands of a selected sport	
P2 describe the impact of motivation on sports performance	M2 explain the impact of motivation on sports performance and two strategies that can be used to maintain and increase motivation	D1 analyse the impact of motivation on sports performance and two strategies that can be used to maintain and increase motivation
P3 describe two strategies that can be used to influence motivation		
P4 describe personality and how it affects sports performance		
P5 describe aggression and two strategies that can be used to control it	M3 explain two strategies that can be used to control aggressive behaviour	D2 evaluate two strategies that can be used to control aggressive behaviour
P6 assess own attitudes and psychological skills in a selected sport, identifying strengths and areas for improvement		
P7 plan, carry out and record a six-week training programme to improve psychological skills for a selected sport, with tutor support	M4 independently plan, carry out and record a six-week training programme to improve psychological skills for a selected sport	
P8 review the psychological skills training programme, identifying strengths and areas for improvement	M5 review the psychological skills training programme, explaining strengths and areas for improvement	D3 review the psychological skills training programme, justifying strengths and areas for improvement

9.1 Psychological Demands of Sport P1 M1

Success in sport can be presented in the form of a pyramid (see Figure 9.1).

Clearly you need skills of technique as the basis for success and then knowledge of how to use these skills in terms of tactics and rules. However, these will work only if you have the correct attitude or psychological state.

> ## Definition ⓓ
>
> **Attitude** the thoughts and feelings we have at any time and how they influence our behaviour.

Attitude is the thoughts you are having, how these thoughts make you feel, and the result of these thoughts and feelings can be seen in the behaviour you produce. For example, if you have a big competition coming up you may get very nervous and this makes you seem quiet and scared. If you were able to have a more confident attitude you would appear to be relaxed and more sociable.

Attitudes can be changed through mental skills training and this can in turn change the performance you produce. This is the job of a sport psychologist – to improve performance by teaching a sports performer how to control their thoughts.

What Are the Psychological Skills Needed to Perform Well at Sport?

Sporting environments impose psychological demands on the performer and they have to use their psychological skills to overcome these demands. These psychological skills are shown in Figure 9.2.

Anxiety Control

Anxiety is the feelings of nervousness or apprehension you have in a situation. It can result in doubts about whether you will be successful. In order to be successful you need to be able to control your feelings of anxiety and stop them controlling whether you are successful or not.

Self-confidence

Confidence is the extent to which you feel you are going to be successful in a certain situation. The more confident you are, then the more likely you are to be successful; in turn success will lead you to expect more success next time.

Motivation

This is the desire or level of need that you have to be successful. Your motivation can be seen through the amount of effort you put into being successful, how long you stick at working towards the task and what you are willing to give up for success.

Control of Aggression

Aggression is any behaviour that has the aim of harming or hurting another human being. This could be done through physical actions or verbally. The consequences of aggression in sport are serious in terms of the penalties you may

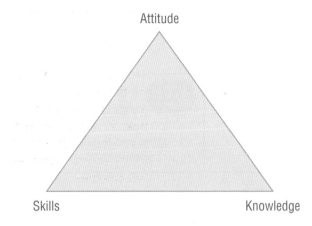

Figure 9.1   Success in sport

receive (bans, fines etc.) and of the damage you may cause another player. Aggressive actions are against the spirit of the game and can result in serious injuries. Therefore, it is vital to play sport in a controlled way and control any feelings of aggression you may have.

Competitiveness

Competitiveness is when you play a sport at a high tempo and with lots of energy. It is different from aggression because it is when you are playing within the rules of a sport. You can see competitiveness in players because they will never give up at their sport.

Concentration

In sport you are presented with a lot of information and you need to concentrate on the information that is relevant to your performance. Also during any sport you will need to concentrate on different things at different times. For example, if you are taking a free kick, you need to look at where the goalkeeper and opposition players are positioned, then think about what technique you will perform, think about relaxing yourself and then take the kick.

Decision-making

In any sport you play you will always be presented with many options about what you should do next; however, your success is based on choosing the right options out of the many available. For example, in golf you have the choice of many clubs to use, different shots to choose from, different places to land the ball, and you have to choose the right one to be successful.

Problem-solving

You could see all sports as problems to be solved; for example, in tennis the problem is to overcome your opponent and win the match but he or she will present you with lots of problems you need to overcome such as their strong serve, forehand smashes and spinning backhands. If you are to be successful you need to develop strategies to overcome these problems.

The sport psychologist will assess the psychological needs of each performer and then work with him or her to improve on their weaknesses.

Figure 9.2 The psychological demands of sport

Activity **9.1**   ⏱ 30 mins   **P1** **M1**

Assessing the psychological demands of sports

Task

To achieve a pass you need to describe what is meant by each term in a sporting context; to progress to a merit it is useful to give an example as this will help to show that you understand what is meant by your description. This example could be from your own experience or from something you have seen. To help you with

achieving **P1** and **M1**, fill in the following table:

Factor	Description of factor	Explanation of factor, using an example
Anxiety control		
Self-confidence		
Motivation		
Control of aggression		
Competitiveness		
Decision-making		
Problem-solving		

9.2 The Impact of Motivation on Sports Performance **P2** **P3** **M2** **D1**

'Motivation is the direction and intensity of effort'

(Source: Sage, 1977)

By direction, Sage means the activity that the motivation is aimed at and the intensity refers to how much effort is made towards the activity. Motivation can be looked at in different ways and we will examine the reasons sports people give for their motivation. These can be divided up into sources inside the body (intrinsic) and sources outside the body (extrinsic).

Before we get into the chapter, read the case study about Nush and Harry. We will refer to this as we go through the chapter.

Trait versus Situation Motivation

Trait motivation says that your behaviour is due to your personality and what is important to you. Put simply, your personality, needs and the goals you have will cause you to behave in certain ways. The most successful people say there is a driving

Quick Quiz 1   ⏱ 10 mins

What psychological factors affecting performance do you think each person is talking about in these following quotes.

1. **'When I play sport I start to think about other things after about 20 minutes.'**
2. **'I know I lost the game because I kept playing the same shot when I could have played other shots.'**
3. **'As I started to win the game I was thinking about how happy I would be to win and became really nervous.'**
4. **'It is really important for me to win at sport, which is why I train so hard.'**
5. **'I just kept saying to myself – you can do this!'**

Case study: Nush and Harry

Nush is a netballer player who has always been motivated to play as much sport as she can. She finds the competition exciting and loves to learn new skills and try them out during a match. She would play netball every day if she could and although winning is important she values the enjoyment and satisfaction above any trophies she wins. Her family are very encouraging and supportive of her but she has never felt any pressure from them to play or succeed.

Harry is a football player who has always been driven to succeed by his parents; they have always ensured that he has the best clothing and football boots. He gains most satisfaction from beating his opponents and the bigger the win, the happier he is. He is never much concerned about how they win as long as they do. He loves to look at his trophies and medals and remember the victories behind them. He likes the idea that his family and friends see him as a good player and a successful person.

force within them that causes them to do what they do. You could probably see that Nush in the case study shows trait motivation because she has always been motivated to play as much sport as she can.

Definition

Traits the particular characteristics or qualities that make each person different.

Situation motivation says that motivation level is due to the situation you find yourself in and how excited you are by it. Some people cannot pass by a football game without having to join it because this situation excites them. It also

depends how important or interesting you think the situation is. If you think a game and the result are important, you will try a lot harder than if you think the outcome does not matter. Likewise you work harder in certain lessons because you think they are important or find the subject interesting.

Intrinsic and Extrinsic Motivation

This work is based on a second definition by Sage (1977), who says that motivation is:

> 'the internal mechanisms and external stimuli which arouse and direct behaviour'

This carries on the theme of motivation coming from inside the individual (the internal mechanisms) and outside the individual (external mechanisms). We can call motivation from inside 'intrinsic motivation' and from outside 'extrinsic motivation'.

Intrinsic Motivation

Behaviour that is intrinsically motivated has the following features:

- Behaviour is chosen for the pleasure of participating.
- Behaviour provides its own satisfaction.
- There is no reward outside participating in the activity.

Extrinsic Motivation

Behaviour that is extrinsically motivated has the following features:

- Behaviour where the goal of participation is outside the activity.
- Behaviour in the activity is a means to an end rather than for the pleasure of being involved – this can be in the form of rewards such as a trophy, money or praise.
- Success is needed to ensure maximum results.

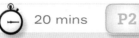

Activity 9.2   20 mins   P2

Intrinsic and extrinsic motivation   M2

Task

Read through the case study of Nush and Harry and decide whether you think they are mainly intrinsically or extrinsically motivated and then provide reasons why you think this. How does this impact on their sports performance?

Quick Quiz 2   15 mins   ?

Link the following motivation-related terms to the following statements.

Term	Definition
Trait motivation	I am motivated depending upon the environment I find myself in.
Situational motivation	I am motivated because it gives me great satisfaction to play sport.
Intrinsic motivation	The greater the reward on offer the greater my motivation.
Extrinsic motivation	Motivation is an important part of my personality.

9.3 How to Develop and Maintain Motivation   M2   D2

The main way that sport psychologists develop motivation is through the use of goal setting.

Definition   d

Goal what an individual is aiming to achieve. It is the outcome they desire from their actions.

Short-term and Long-term Goals

Short-term goals are set over a brief period of time, usually from one day to one month. A short-term goal may relate to what you want to achieve in one training session or where you want to be by the end of the month.

Long-term goals will run from three months to over several years. You may even set some lifetime goals that run until you retire from your sport. In sport we set long-term goals to cover a season or a sporting year. The period between one and three months would cover medium-term goals.

Usually short-term goals are set to help achieve the long-term goals. It is important to set both short-term and long-term goals – particularly short-term goals because they will give a person more motivation to act now.

Outcome and Process Goals

An outcome goal focuses on the outcome of an event or performance, such as winning a race or beating an opponent.

A process goal focuses on the process or actions that an individual must produce to perform well.

Both types of goal are important and we find that short-term goals are normally process goals while long-term goals are outcome goals.

When goals are set you need to use the SMART principle to make the goals workable. SMART stands for the following:

Specific

Measurable

Achievable

Realistic

Time-constrained.

Specific

The goal must be specific to what you want to achieve. This may be an aspect of performance or fitness. It is not enough to say 'I want to get fitter'; you need to say 'I want to improve strength, speed or stamina etc.'.

Measurable

Goals must be stated in a way that is measurable, that is, using figures. For example, 'I want to improve my first serve percentage' is not measurable. However, if you say 'I want to improve my first serve success by 20 per cent', it is measurable.

Achievable

It must be possible actually to achieve the goal.

Realistic

We need to be realistic in our goal setting and look at what factors may stop us achieving the goal.

Time-constrained

There must be a timescale or deadline on the goal. This means you can review your success. It is best to put a date you wish to achieve the goal by.

How to Set Goals

The best way to do this is to answer three questions:

1. What do I want to achieve? (Desired state)
2. Where am I now? (Present state)
3. What do I need to do to move from my present state to my desired state?

Then present this on a scale.

1. Write in your goal at point 5 and your present position at point 1.

2. Decide what would be halfway between points 1 and 5 and this is your goal for point 3.

3. Then decide what would be halfway between your present state and point 3; this is your short-term goal for point 2.

4. Then decide what would be halfway between point 3 and the desired state; this is the goal for point 4.

5. All these goals are outcome goals and must be set using the SMART principle.

6. Work out what needs to be done to move from point 1 to point 2. These are your process goals and must again use the SMART principle.

It is best to use a goal-setting diary to keep all your goal-setting information in the same place and to review the goals on a weekly basis.

Other Methods to Influence Motivation

Imagery

Imagery can be used alone or in conjunction with goal setting. When an individual develops pictures in their mind of seeing themselves achieving something, it can be very powerful as the brain cannot always tell the difference between something that is real and something that has been imagined. If you can imagine yourself achieving your goal it can help you to actually achieve it. Also if you remember and imagine times when you were very motivated in the past, it can help you to be motivated in the present.

Self-talk

This is a description for what we say to ourselves when we are thinking and it is generally positive or negative. You can motivate yourself by saying encouraging things to yourself such as 'it is important you play well today' or 'come on, you can do this'.

(k) Key learning points

- Mental skills required to be successful at sport include:
  - Motivation – the drive to be successful.
  - Arousal control – remaining relaxed under pressure.
  - Confidence – knowing you will succeed.
  - Concentration – focus on what is relevant.
  - Emotional control – control negative emotions and boost positive ones.

- Motivation is 'the internal mechanisms and external stimuli which arouse and direct behaviour' and can come from inside the individual (the internal mechanisms) and outside the individual (external mechanisms). We can call motivation from inside 'intrinsic motivation' and from outside 'extrinsic motivation':
  - Intrinsic motivation comes from involvement in the activity itself. This would be feelings such as pleasure, enjoyment, excitement, self-confidence and feelings of doing something well.
  - Extrinsic motivation comes from sources outside the activity and would include financial rewards or physical rewards such as medals or trophies.

- When goals are set you need to use the SMART principle:
  Specific
  Measurable
  Achievable
  Realistic
  Time-constrained

Activity 9.3 20 mins P3

Strategies to influence motivation

Task

Choose two strategies that can be used to influence motivation and describe how they will work.

Quick Quiz 3 10 mins

Which of these statements are True and which are False?

1. It is important to set short-term goals so that the person has the motivation to act immediately.
2. Process goals are concerned with the actual performance the individual achieves.
3. Long-term goals run for between three and nine months.
4. 'To improve my fitness' is a good example of a specific goal.
5. It is important to set a time-scale to your goal so that you know when to review its success or failure.
6. Self-talk involves you saying motivational phrases to yourself.

9.4 Personality and Sport P4

Personality in sport is an area that has been deeply researched and there are usually three areas examined:

1. Are certain personalities attracted to sport?

2. Are certain personalities more successful in sport?

3. Does sport change an individual's personality?

These are interesting questions and the answers would help us to understand sporting excellence better.

If you were ever asked to explain someone's personality you would probably use words such as happy, sociable, quiet, warm or confident. Personality is how you present yourself to the outside world. Each person is unique in this respect and while you may compare yourselves to others you are not really like anyone else.

Personality will cover a person's thoughts, emotions and behaviour and how you do what you do. There are several different theories of personality, which are examined here.

Are You a Type A or Type B Personality?

Instructions: Give yourself a score between 1 and 7 to show which of the two statements applies to you best.

> **Definition**
>
> **Personality** the sum of those characteristics that make a person unique.

Statement	Score	Statement
Don't mind leaving things temporarily unfinished	1 2 3 4 5 6 7	Must get things finished once started
Calm and unhurried about appointments	1 2 3 4 5 6 7	Often late for appointments
Not competitive	1 2 3 4 5 6 7	Highly competitive
Listen well, let others finish speaking first	1 2 3 4 5 6 7	Anticipate others in conversation, interrupt by finishing their sentences
Never in a hurry, even when pressured	1 2 3 4 5 6 7	Always in a hurry
Able to wait calmly	1 2 3 4 5 6 7	Uneasy when waiting
Easy-going	1 2 3 4 5 6 7	Always going at full speed
Take one thing at a time	1 2 3 4 5 6 7	Always trying to do more than one thing at once
Slow and deliberate in speech	1 2 3 4 5 6 7	Speak fast and forcefully using a lot of gestures
Concerned with satisfying	1 2 3 4 5 6 7	Want to get recognition from others for yourself and not others doing things well
Slow at doing things	1 2 3 4 5 6 7	Fast at doing things
Relaxed	1 2 3 4 5 6 7	Always active
Express feelings openly	1 2 3 4 5 6 7	Keep feelings to yourself
Have a large number of interests	1 2 3 4 5 6 7	Only have a few interests
Satisfied with life	1 2 3 4 5 6 7	Always want more from life
Never set own deadlines	1 2 3 4 5 6 7	Always work to deadlines
Feel limited responsibility	1 2 3 4 5 6 7	Always feel responsible
Never judge things in terms of quantity, only quality	1 2 3 4 5 6 7	Quantity is more important than quality
Casual about work	1 2 3 4 5 6 7	Take work very seriously
Not very precise	1 2 3 4 5 6 7	Very precise and careful about detail

Trait Approach

Traits are the basic units of personality and this theory says that personality is relatively unstable or unchanging. Your personality develops when you are young and it stays pretty much the same through life. It also says your behaviour is consistent across a range of situations because our traits make us behave in certain ways. The trait approach says that the environment is not so important and if you are a competitive person, then you will be competitive whatever situation you are in and no matter how important a competition may be.

The most basic trait approach looks at whether you are a type A or type B personality.

Scoreboard

20–59 means you have a type B personality. You are relaxed and contented and deal well with stress. You enjoy life and are happy with what you have.

60–79 means you have a type A/B personality. You have a mixture of both personality types. This is a happy balance.

80–109 means you have a type A personality. You are a very driven person who is competitive and has to succeed. You are also likely to experience stress and changes in mood. You may have a quick temper and get angry easily.

110–140 means you are an extreme type A personality. This means you are very likely to experience stress and it may affect your health.

Introverts versus Extroverts

You could say that the type A versus type B categories are too narrow an explanation of personality and you are right because they do not take into account the uniqueness of the individual. This was looked at by psychologists Eysenck and Eysenck (1964) who took two different aspects of personality and ranked them from 1–12 depending on how much of each you had.

These two aspects of personality are:

1. Introverted vs Extroverted
2. Stable vs Unstable

Definitions

Introvert a person who is shy, quiet and inward-looking; they are not so good in social situations and like to spend time on their own.

Extrovert someone who is outgoing, likes talking and mixing with people and is good in social situations; they do not like to spend too much time on their own and are easily bored.

Stable someone who is not easily affected by emotions and feelings. Their mood is stable and will not change easily and they tend not to worry about situations.

Unstable someone easily affected by emotions and feelings, who they will change their mood easily and often worry about everything.

Eysenck used a questionnaire to work out which category a person falls into and he would place you in one of four categories (see Figure 9.3).

Stable introvert	Unstable introvert
Stable extrovert	Unstable extrovert

Figure 9.3 Aspects of personality

Situational Approach

This theory disagrees with the trait theory because it says that behaviour is the result of the situation the person finds themselves in. It is based on the work of Albert Bandura (1977), who says that our behaviour is influenced by two factors:

1. **Modelling** – this is watching other people and copying what they do. This may be our parents, friends, family or people we admire.

2. **Feedback** – this means that if how we behave is rewarded in a positive way, we are more likely to repeat it. However, if it is punished, we will be less likely to repeat it.

This theory says you learn how to behave rather than behaviour being the result of the personality you are born with. It helps to explain how people change their behaviour in certain situations. For example, you may have a person who is very quiet normally but when they play sport they become competitive and aggressive.

The truth of whether behaviour is the result of the individual or the situation is not clear. It is probably somewhere in the middle. We can see how some people are affected by their situation, while other people will not be affected the same way in the same situation.

Activity **9.4**   30 mins   P4

Type A and Type B personalities

Task

In a group of four, pick two differing personalities in five sports and decide whether you think they fit into type A, B or A/B, based on how you have seen them behave. For example, you may compare Roger Federer to Andy Murray.

How do you think their personality affects their performance in their sport?

Quick Quiz 4   10 mins   **?**

Which of the following statements are True and which are False?

1. **Personality is the sum of a person's characteristics that make them unique.**
2. **Traits are unstable aspects of our personality that affect how we behave.**
3. **An introvert describes a person who is outgoing and likes mixing with people.**
4. **Team players tend to be extrovert in nature.**
5. **Modelling is watching other people's behaviour and copying what they do.**

9.5 Aggression in Sport

Aggression is used in different ways when talking about sport. Sometimes aggression is seen as good – when a player makes a hard tackle and gains an advantage. Or it could be seen as bad – when a blatant foul is committed or someone commits a shoulder barge in rugby.

> 'Aggression is defined as any behaviour directed toward intentionally harming or injuring another living being.'
>
> (*Source*: Baron and Richardson, 1994)

To be seen as an aggressive action it will need to fit four guidelines:

- There is a behaviour which can be seen.
- The result is harm or an injury.
- There must be an intention to harm.
- It is directed towards another living being.

(*Source*: Gill, 2000)

Types of Aggression

Aggressive behaviours can be divided into three types: assertion, hostile aggression and instrumental aggression.

Behaviour which people would call 'good' aggression can be called 'assertive behaviour'.

Definition

Assertive behaviour behaviour that involves playing within the rules with high intensity and emotion but without intention to do harm.

For example, a basketball player who marks his opponent in a very energetic way by getting close to them and crowding them is being assertive, not aggressive. This is also the case with rugby players making hard but fair tackles on their opponents.

For example, the aim of boxing is to cause damage to your opponent with the goal of winning the fight, not just for the sake of causing them damage.

Definitions

Hostile aggression when the aim of an action is to cause physical harm or psychological damage to an opponent.

Instrumental aggression occurs when you act in an aggressive way but the aim is to achieve a positive outcome or goal.

Methods of Controlling Aggression

Before you can work out how to control aggression you need to look at why aggressive behaviours occur. The main reasons are as follows:

1. **Frustration in a situation** – the player becomes frustrated because they believe they have been dealt with unfairly or they have been stopped from achieving their goal by unfair means. This can be regularly seen in the reactions of players during games.

2. **The person is aggressive by nature** – the person has aggressive behaviour as part of their personality.

 Key learning points

- Personality has been defined as 'the sum of those characteristics which make a person unique'.
- The trait theory says that personality is inherited and remains relatively stable, while social learning theory says that we learn our personality and it is always developing.
- Aggression is defined as 'any behaviour directed toward intentionally harming or injuring another living being'. (Baron and Richardson, 1994)
- There are three types of aggressive behaviour:
  - Assertion, which is playing in a very competitive and energetic manner but not intending any harm.
  - Hostile aggression is when the aim of an action is to cause physical harm or psychological damage to an opponent.
  - Instrumental aggression occurs when you act in an aggressive way but the aim is to achieve a positive outcome or goal

Anger Management Techniques

As a sport psychologist, you have no control over the situation your athletes will find themselves in but you can control how they respond to the situation. You can teach athletes to work out what triggers their aggressive behaviour and then you can teach them skills to control their emotions. The best way to do this is to teach them relaxation techniques that can be applied to a specific situation. Relaxation techniques include using relaxing imagery or focusing on and controlling your breathing.

Activity **9.5** 60 mins   `P5` `M3` **D2**

Controlling aggression

Task

Using either your own experiences or an internet search of newspapers to find real sporting examples, find two examples of how a coach/instructor/manager has dealt with an individual's aggressive behaviour. For the two examples, answer the following questions:

1. Does this aggressive act meet all four criteria that have been laid down to define aggression?
2. What strategies have been used to control the individual's aggression?
3. Explain what these strategies are and how they would work.
4. Evaluate each of the two strategies by looking at what you think about the strategy would make it help control aggression and what about the strategy may not work well.

Sports people often behave aggressively because of the high value placed on winning and the fear of losing. Also, some teams may target a certain player who they know can behave aggressively and use physical actions and verbal insults to get an aggressive response from them as they think it will give them an advantage.

The sports person should be taught that while it is important to win, it is important to do so within the rules, and that by acting aggressively they damage their chances of winning.

Quick Quiz 5 15 mins ❓

1. **How are assertion, instrumental aggression and hostile aggression different?**
2. **Give two ways an athlete can be taught to control their aggression.**

9.6 Assessing Mental Skills `P6`

An assessment of an individual's mental strengths and weaknesses can be made in different ways. We will look at the use of a questionnaire and then at performance profiling as ways of assessing psychological skills.

Using a Questionnaire

Questionnaires such as the one below can be used to assess mental strengths and weaknesses. There is no scoring system as such, but the questions are designed for you to establish areas of strength and areas of weakness.

Example Questionnaire

Name:

Sport played:

- Explain any past experience you have of psychological skills training.
- Explain your involvement in sport and any important competitions or events coming up.
- What do you consider to be your psychological strengths and weaknesses?

Below is a list of statements; circle the answer appropriate to your experience:

1. I always feel motivated to succeed, whatever activity I am doing.

   Don't know   *Never*   *Sometimes*   *Usually*   *Always*

2. I always work towards clear goals.

   Don't know   *Never*   *Sometimes*   *Usually*   *Always*

3. I set myself goals on a weekly basis.

   Don't know   *Never*   *Sometimes*   *Usually*   *Always*

4. I always make full use of my skills and abilities.

   Don't know   *Never*   *Sometimes*   *Usually*   *Always*

5. When I am involved in my physical activity, I often find my attention wavering.

   Don't know   *Never*   *Sometimes*   *Usually*   *Always*

6. I am easily distracted during whatever activity I am involved in.

   Don't know   *Never*   *Sometimes*   *Usually*   *Always*

7. I perform much better when I am under a lot of pressure.

   Don't know   *Never*   *Sometimes*   *Usually*   *Always*

8. I become very anxious when I am under pressure.

   Don't know   *Never*   *Sometimes*   *Usually*   *Always*

9. If I start to become tense, I can quickly relax myself and calm down.

   Don't know   *Never*   *Sometimes*   *Usually*   *Always*

10. I find it easy to control my emotions, whatever the situation.

    Don't know   *Never*   *Sometimes*   *Usually*   *Always*

11. I am always able to remain upbeat and positive, whatever the situation.

    Don't know   *Never*   *Sometimes*   *Usually*   *Always*

12. If I am criticised by a coach or trainer I tend to take it very badly.

    Don't know   *Never*   *Sometimes*   *Usually*   *Always*

13. I am easily able to deal with unforeseen situations.

    Don't know   *Never*   *Sometimes*   *Usually*   *Always*

14. I have my own set of strategies for dealing with difficult situations.

    Don't know   *Never*   *Sometimes*   *Usually*   *Always*

Performance Profiling

Performance profiling is a way of getting the athlete to analyse their own strengths and weaknesses. It is completed in the following way:

1. Ask the athlete to come up with ten categories of mental skills they think are important to them.

2. Ask the athlete to rate out of ten how high they need to be on each category.

3. Ask the athlete to rate where they are now.

You can then use this information in different ways:

1. Assess their strengths and weaknesses.

2. See what they feel is important in their sport.

3. As their coach you may have different ideas about what is important and their level of skill. This exercise will highlight any differences in your points of view.

You can present the information on a grid such as the one shown on the next page.

> ### Activity 9.6 30 mins P8
>
> **Psychological strengths and weaknesses**
>
> **Task**
>
> Complete the Psychological Skills questionnaire to identify your psychological strengths and weaknesses.

9.7 Planning a Psychological Skills Training Programme P7 M4

Once you have identified any weaknesses, you can then plan a training programme for the individual. This programme must have clear objectives that the individual is aiming to achieve. To demonstrate how this can be done, look at the following case study.

Case Study: Marlon

Marlon is an 18-year-old club level sprinter who trains six times a week. Marlon does not get the most out of his training because he tends to give up towards the end of each session. He finds that he enjoys talking to the other sprinters in his group at the expense of focusing on his training. He has no clear idea about what he is trying to achieve through training in either the short or long term. He also finds that he performs best when the pressure is off and that he often underperforms in the most important meetings.

Goals of psychological skills training

1. To improve 100 m time by 0.2 seconds by the end of the season

2. To improve 200 m time by 0.35 seconds

Objectives of psychological skills training

1. To address motivation during each session.

2. To improve his concentration skills during training sessions and competitions.

3. To address underperformance in important competitions.

Action plan

1. Goal setting to address motivation. This will involve setting clear long-term and short-term goals, including goals for daily training sessions.

2. Relaxation training to address the levels of arousal and poor performances at important competitions.

3. Self-talk training to address any confidence problems, which may also be causing underperformance.

4. Concentration training because low concentration skills might contribute to underperformance.

Training Plan

Week 1 – Goal setting
Establish the basis of psychological skills training and ensure motivation for physical and mental training.

Week 2 – Relaxation 1
Practise progressive muscular relaxation five times this week.

Week 3 – Relaxation 2
Practise mind-to-muscle relaxation five times this week.

Week 4 – Concentration
Practise concentration exercises each day.

Week 5 – Self-talk
To increase levels of confidence.

Week 6 – Mental rehearsal and sitting relaxation
Learn to relax sitting up, to make mental rehearsal for competition more practical. Mental rehearsal will bring all the skills of the training programme together.

Backing up the Training Programme

While the desired outcomes of the training programme are clear, it is important to back the training programme up with certain measures to ensure the programme is successful. This can be done with the following measures:

Activity **9.7** 30 mins **P7**

M4

Planning a psychological skills training programme
Task

Once you have completed the psychological skills questionnaire, prepare a six-week training plan. Once you have planned the programme, carry out the programme and make a record of all the sessions you completed and comment on how effective you found the session.

1. Set clear goals using the SMART principle as discussed before.

2. Use a psychological skills diary or logbook to record progress in each session and then in actual performances.

3. Ensure that the programme is regularly evaluated against its objectives to gauge its success.

9.8 Reviewing the Training Programme

Once the training programme has been completed, the success of the programme needs to be reviewed. The review can look at two main issues:

1. Has it addressed the objectives that have been set (has it improved their performances?)

2. What was the individual's experience of the techniques and were they effective?

Methods of Reviewing the Programme

The more methods that can be used to review the programme then the more information that will be gained and the following are some methods of gaining information you could use:

- Interviews
- Questionnaires
- Observations of other people
- Personal reflection
- Review of diaries/logbooks
- Reviewing performances
- Reviewing outcomes of performances.

By using these varied methods you can identify the strengths and weaknesses of the training programme that you have designed and from this you can look at what actions you need to take to improve performance even more and achieve the new goals that you have set.

Useful websites

The following websites will help you with your learning and for finding information for assignments.

www.bbc.co.uk/wales/raiseyourgame/sites/concentration/inthezone/pages/linda_papadopoulos2.shtml
Advice on how you can improve your focus by a celebrity psychologist.

www.bbc.co.uk/wales/raiseyourgame/sites/motivation/psychedup/pages/adrian_moorhouse/shtml
Olympic gold medallist Adrian Moorhouse and a sports psychologist pass on their tips for achieving mental toughness.

www.bbc.co.uk/wales/raiseyourgame/sites/motivation/psychedup/pages/linda_papadopoulos.shtml
Video of celebrity psychologist Linda Papadopoulos explaining how you can make your mind work *for* rather than *against* you during sport.

www.brianmac.co.uk/psych.htm
Tips for gaining the winning edge in sports.

Activity 9.8 60 mins   P8 M5 D3

Reviewing the psychological skills training programme

Task

Review your training programme by using the following template.

What are the strengths and weaknesses of the programme?	Explain why you have identified each of the strengths and areas of improvement	Justify why you have identified each of the strengths and areas of improvement

Hint: The training programme is designed to improve your physical performance by working on your mental skills. To say that something is a strength you need to have evidence about how you felt when you were performing or how it changed how well you performed.

Further Reading

Burton, D and Raedeke, T. D., 2008, *Sport Psychology for Coaches*. Leeds: Human Kinetics.

Cox, R.H., 2007, *Sport Psychology: Concepts and Applications*. New York: McGraw-Hill.

Weinberg, R.S. and Gould, D., 2007, *Foundations of Sport and Exercise Psychology*. Champaign, IL.: Human Kinetics.

References

Bandura, A., 1977, 'Self-efficacy: Toward a unifying theory of behavioural change', *Psychological Review*, 84. 191–215.

Baron, R.A. and Richardson, D.R., 1994, *Human Aggression*. New York: Plenum Press.

Eysenck, H. J. and Eysenck, S. B. G.,1964, *Manual of Eysenck Personality Inventory*. London: University of London Press.

Gill, D., 2000, *Psychological Dynamics of Sport and Exercise*. Champaign, IL: Human Kinetics.

Sage, G.,1977, *Introduction to Motor Behaviour: A neurophysiological approach* (2nd edition). Reading, MA: Addison-Wesley.

Chapter 10
Nutrition for Sports Performance

Good nutrition plays a key factor in a sports person's performance. It is necessary to consume the right foods and fluids and the right quantity of each, otherwise a sports person will not be able to perform to their maximal ability. Different sports also require different types of food in order to feed the body the nutrients it requires. There is a huge variety of foods to choose from, so it is necessary to learn which ones are appropriate for which sports.

Learning Goals

By the end of this chapter you should:

- Know the nutritional requirements of a selected sport.
- Be able to assess own diet.
- Be able to plan a personal nutritional strategy.
- Be able to implement and review a personal nutritional strategy.

To achieve a PASS grade the evidence must show that the learner is able to:	To achieve a MERIT grade the evidence must show that, in addition to the pass criteria, the learner is able to:	To achieve a DISTINCTION grade the evidence must show that, in addition to the pass and merit criteria, the learner is able to:
P1 describe the nutritional requirements of a selected sport	**M1** explain the nutritional requirements of a selected sport	**D1** evaluate the nutritional requirements of a selected sport describing suitable meal plans
P2 collect and collate information on own diet for two weeks		
P3 describe the strengths of own diet and identify areas for improvement	**M2** explain the strengths of their own diet and make recommendations as to how it could be improved	**D2** justify recommendations made regarding improving their own diet
P4 create a personal nutritional strategy, designed and agreed with an adviser	**M3** contribute own ideas to the design of a personal nutritional strategy	
P5 implement a personal nutritional strategy		
P6 describe the strengths of the personal nutritional strategy and identify areas for improvement	**M4** explain the strengths of the personal nutritional strategy and make recommendations as to how it could be improved	

10.1 Nutrients

Food can be broken down into three main groups:

- Carbohydrates
- Fats
- Proteins.

These are called macronutrients. This basically means that we need to eat each of these food groups in large quantities.

Within each of these food groups, you will also find one or both of the following:

- Vitamins
- Minerals.

These are referred to as micronutrients – nutrients we only need in small quantities.

Carbohydrates

We should consume mainly carbohydrates in our diet; in fact, around 50–60 per cent of our calorie intake should come from carbohydrates. The main purpose of carbohydrate is to give us energy for our bodies to move and take part in sports. Carbohydrate is broken down into glucose and carried around the body in the bloodstream. This glucose is transported in the blood to the working muscles and used to make the muscles produce movement. Any carbohydrates that are eaten and not used are stored in the muscle and liver as glycogen.

> **Definition**
>
> **Glycogen a polysaccharide consisting of glucose units; forms the body's store of carbohydrate.**

Once the muscle and liver stores of glycogen are full, excess carbohydrate is turned into fat and stored in fat cells.

There are two main types of carbohydrates: sugars and starches.

Sugars

These are also called simple carbohydrates because they can be broken down in the body quickly and easily. As a result, when we eat sugary foods they give the body a quick burst of energy that is sometimes referred to as a 'sugar high'. These carbohydrates taste sweet and can be found in a wide variety of foods such as fruits, sweets, jam, biscuits, fizzy drinks.

Milk also contains sugar but does not taste as sweet as the foods listed above.

Starches

These are also called complex carbohydrates because they take longer to break down in the body and give a slow and prolonged supply of energy to the body. These do not taste sweet and can be found in a wide variety of foods such as bread, pasta, potatoes, rice, cereals.

Fats

25–30 per cent of our calorie intake should come from fats, mainly unsaturated fats. Although fats are generally thought of as the bad food, and if we eat too many they will make us fat, they are necessary for a variety of reasons. Fat is used as an energy source but it produces energy at a much slower rate than carbohydrates; therefore fats supply the energy when we are taking part in low-intensity exercise.

There are two main types of fats: saturated and unsaturated fats.

Saturated Fats

Saturated fats are usually called the 'bad fats' because if you eat too many they will raise your cholesterol levels and thereby increase blood pressure. They are found mainly in animal produce; some examples include meat, cheese, cream, butter, lard and chocolate.

Unsaturated Fats

These are the 'good fats' and can actually help to reduce cholesterol levels, which will usually have the effect of decreasing blood pressure. They usually come from plant sources; examples include olive oil, rapeseed, nuts and oily fish.

Proteins

10–15 per cent of our calorie intake should come from protein. Our muscles, skin, organs, hair, nails, hormones and many more body parts contain protein. Protein in the diet is essential as it is used to make us grow and repair broken tissue; for example, after a work-out lifting weights, the muscle tissue will have been broken down and needs to be repaired. Protein can be found in a variety of foods including meat, poultry, fish, eggs, milk, beans and nuts.

Vitamins and Minerals

Vitamins and minerals are present in very small quantities in many of the foods that we eat. Our body cannot make vitamins or minerals, so it is essential that we eat a diet that contains all the vitamins and minerals that we need. There are many different types of vitamins and minerals and each serves their purpose in maintaining a healthy body and helping it to work effectively.

Vitamins

Vitamins can be divided into two main groups: fat-soluble and water-soluble.

Fat-soluble vitamins can be stored in fat within our bodies. This group contains vitamins A, D, E and K (see Table 10.1).

Key learning points

	Amount we should eat	Function	Examples of food sources
Carbohydrates	50–60%	Provide energy for sports performance.	
Sugars		Provide short bursts of energy	Jam, sweets, fruit, fizzy drinks, sports drinks.
Starch		Provides energy for longer periods.	Pasta, rice, bread, potatoes, breakfast cereals
Fat	25–30%	Provides energy for low-intensity exercise e.g. walking. Insulates the body against the cold.	
Saturated fats		Helps to protect internal organs.	Mainly animal sources: cream, lard, cheese, meat.
Unsaturated fats			Mainly plant sources: nuts, soya, tofu.
Protein	10–15%	For growth and repair.	Meat, eggs, nuts, fish, poultry.

Table 10.1 Fat-soluble vitamins

Vitamin	Food sources	Function
A	Carrots, liver, dark green vegetables, mackeral	Maintains good vision, skin and hair
D	Oily fish, sunlight, eggs	Helps build bones and teeth
E	Nuts, whole grains, dark green leafy vegetables	Antioxidant that prevents damage to cells
K	Leafy green vegetables, peas, milk, egg yolk	Helps to form blood clots

Water-soluble vitamins cannot be stored in our body; any excess we eat is excreted, so we have to be sure to eat their food sources on a regular basis (see Table 10.2).

Table 10.2 Water-soluble vitamins

Vitamin	Food sources	Function
B group	Cereals, liver, yeast, eggs, beef, beans	Helps to break down food to produce
C	Most fresh fruit and vegetables, expecially citrus fruits	Fighting infection, maintains healthy skin and gums, wound-healing

Minerals

Table 10.3 shows the minerals that are present in very small quantities in many of the foods that we eat.

Table 10.3 Minerals

Mineral	Food sources	Function
Iron	Liver, lean meats, eggs, dried fruits	Blood production
Calcium	Milk, fish bones, green leafy vegetables	Helps to build strong bones and teeth, helps to form blood clots
Sodium	Salt, sea food, processed foods, celery	Maintains fluid balance in cells, helps in muscle contraction
Potassium	Bananas	Works with sodium to maintain fluid balance, aids muscle contraction, maintains blood pressure
Zinc	Meats, fish	Tissue growth and repair

Fibre

This is not a nutrient but is necessary in our diet in order to keep us healthy. Fibre is found in fruit, vegetables, beans and grains. Fibre cannot be broken down by the body but is required to help move food through the digestive system and out the other end. Fibre works by absorbing water, which makes the stools softer and bulkier, which helps to prevent constipation and haemorrhoids.

Water

We could live for many days if we did not eat food; however, we would only be able to survive for around three days if we had no water to drink. Although water has no nutritional value in terms of energy, it is essential to life and plays many roles within the body. Water helps to maintain the body at a constant temperature through sweating, it transports nutrients around the body, and is used to get rid of waste products from the body in the form of urine and faeces. We take water into our body via drinks and the food we eat. For our body to work at its best, we need to consume around 2.5 litres of water per day; however, this figure needs to be increased if we are living in hot conditions or if we are exercising.

Key learning points

- Vitamins B group and C are water-soluble.
- Vitamins A, D, E and K are fat-soluble.
- Fibre is needed in the diet to help move food through the digestive system.

Quick Quiz   ⏱ 20 mins   ❓

Which food groups would you put the following foods in?

Food	Food group
Brussel sprouts	
Eggs	
Olive oil	
Bananas	
Milk	
Fish	
Beans	
Bread	
Potatoes	
Nuts	
Butter	

10.2 Healthy Diet P1 M1 D1

A healthy diet is a diet that contains all the nutrients we require in order to ensure our body can function to the best of its ability and also reduce the risk of a number of diseases such as cancer, heart disease and diabetes. The best way to ensure we are eating the right foods is to have a varied diet and eat plenty of the 'good foods', which will be highlighted later on, and only eat few of the 'bad foods', which are usually the very tasty foods that we crave and would like to eat more of! We also need to be sure we are eating the right quantities of food, which will give us enough energy to take part in sporting activities.

Food Groups

Foods can be divided into five different groups (see Figure 10.1).

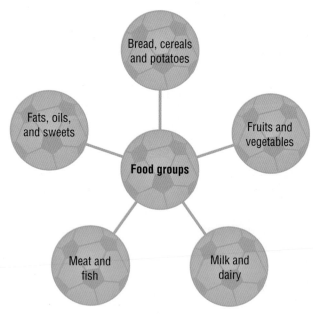

Figure 10.1   Food groups

Bread, Cereals and Potatoes

Our daily diet should consist mainly of foods from this food group. Every meal should include at least one food from this group. These foods are all starchy carbohydrates and include bread (wholemeal bread is better for you as it contains more fibre), potatoes, pasta, rice, oats, breakfast cereals (but try not to eat cereals with added sugar) and noodles. This group of foods supplies us with carbohydrates, fibre, iron and some of the B group of vitamins.

Fruits and Vegetables

You should aim to eat at least five portions of fruit and vegetables every day. One portion weighs around 80 g, which is roughly equal to one piece of fruit or one medium-sized carrot. You can eat fresh fruit and vegetables, frozen, canned or juiced. Beans (for example, butter beans and baked beans) and pulses (for example, lentils) are also included in this group. You should aim to eat a variety of fruit and vegetables rather than sticking to the same ones each day. This group of foods supplies us with a range of vitamins including vitamin C and vitamin A, carbohydrates and fibre.

Milk and Dairy Foods

You should aim to eat around two to three servings from this food group each day. This is roughly equivalent to a glass of milk or a matchbox-size of cheese. Foods in this group include milk, cheese and yogurt. You should try to choose the low-fat versions of these foods, such as skimmed milk and reduced-fat cheese in order to keep your fat intake low. This group of foods supplies us with calcium, protein and vitamin A and some B group vitamins.

Meat and Fish

You should eat moderate amounts from this food group; two portions a day are usually adequate. Foods in this group include all kinds of meat and meat products (for example, beefburgers, sausages etc.), poultry, eggs and fish. However, vegetarians can have alternative foods that contain the same benefits as this group but are not from animal sources, for example tofu, soya,

nuts, lentils. Foods from this group are high in protein, iron, B vitamins, vitamin D and zinc.

Fats, Oils and Sweets

We should eat only small quantities of foods from this group. Most people in the Western world eat too many foods from this group. Foods containing high quantities of fats and oils include butter, margarine, olive oil, cakes, biscuits, pastries, ice cream, cream and fried foods (for example chips, burgers etc.).

Foods containing high quantities of sugar include fizzy drinks (not the diet drinks), sweets, cakes, puddings, chocolate and jam.

Food Pyramid

In order to see how much of each food group we should consume, a food pyramid has been devised (see Figure 10.2).

The position of the food group in the pyramid is determined by the quantities we should eat. There are four layers in the pyramid. The bottom layer is the largest and contains foods that we should eat in the greatest quantity; the top layer represents foods that we should eat sparingly.

Key learning points

- Foods can be divided into five different groups:
  - Breads, cereals and potatoes – most of the food we eat should come from this group.
  - Fruits and vegetables – five portions per day.
  - Milk and dairy foods – two to three portions per day.
  - Meat, fish – two portions per day.
  - Fats, oils and sweets – we should aim to eat very few foods from this group.

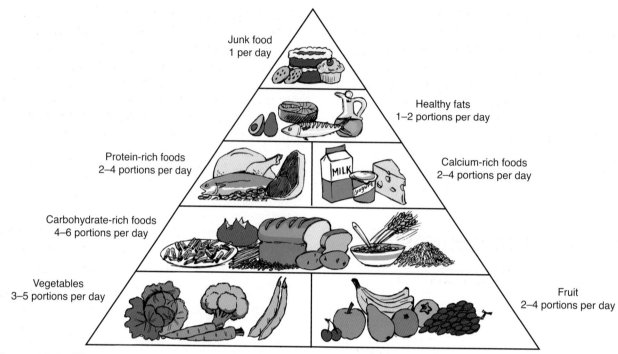

Figure 10.2   The nutrition pyramid

Salt

Salt is actually made up of the two minerals sodium and chlorine. We need sodium in the diet in order to maintain fluid balance and help our muscles function; however, most people today eat too much salt in their diet, which can lead to high blood pressure and heart disease. Salt is present in high quantities in processed foods, crisps and also added to salt-free foods during cooking. An adult should eat no more than 6 g per day and children should eat less (the amount depends on their age).

Preparation of Food

The way you prepare food has a huge impact on its nutritional value. For example, we should eat plenty of potatoes; however, if you fry the potatoes to make chips, the food then belongs in the fats and oils food group, as it now has such a high concentration of fat.

Fluid Intake

When we take part in sports, we sweat in order to cool our body down. This lost water must be replaced, otherwise our sports performance will suffer or if we become severely dehydrated we will become ill (see Table 10.4).

Table 10.4 Loss of fluid as a percentage of body weight

Loss of fluid % of body weight	Effect on the body
2%	Reduced ability for sports performance
4%	Reduced muscle function
5%	Heat exhaustion
7%	Hallucinations
10%	Heat stroke and potential death

If you feel thirsty it actually means you are already dehydrated, so you should consume non-alcoholic drinks regularly even when you do not feel thirsty. The amount of fluid we need varies from person to person – age, climate, diet and physical activity all have an influence. Intakes of 1.5 to 2 litres of fluids a day are recommended in typical British climates and this includes water and other drinks like squash, fruit juices, tea and coffee. Taking part in sports in hotter climates obviously means you will need to drink more fluids, as you will be sweating more in order to cool your body down. Some of our fluid requirement comes from the food we eat, especially foods such as fruit and vegetables. Water and isotonic sports drinks are the best drinks to consume before, during and after taking part in sports in order to ensure your body remains completely hydrated.

10.3 Sport-specific Requirements

  D1

People who take part in sports need to eat a diet that provides enough energy in the form of carbohydrates and fats, as well as essential protein, vitamins and minerals. Most sports people should aim to eat a diet that consists mainly of carbohydrates – around 55 per cent to 60 per cent (10 per cent to 15 per cent from sugars and the rest from starches). No more than 30 per cent of kilocalories should come from fat, and 10 per cent to 15 per cent from protein.

However, the type of sport that you play can have an effect on how much protein and carbohydrate you eat. An endurance athlete will need to eat more carbohydrate for energy and a strength- or speed-based athlete will need to eat a bit more protein to replace the damage that has been done to muscles during training.

The timing of food intake is also very important; when the right food is eaten at the right time it will ensure that your body has enough energy so that you can perform to the best of your ability.

Quick Quiz 2 ⏱ 15 mins ❓

Match the different food groups to the descriptions of the food groups.

Food groups	Descriptions
Bread, cereals & pasta	You should aim to eat around two to three servings from this food group each day. This group of foods supplies us with calcium, protein and some group B vitamins.
Fruits & vegetables	You should eat moderate amounts from this food group: two portions a day are usually adequate. Foods from this group are high in protein, iron, vitamin D and zinc.
Milk & dairy foods	You should aim to eat at least five portions a day. This group of foods supplies us with a range of vitamins, including vitamin C and vitamin A, as well as some carbohydrate and fibre.
Meat & fish	We should only eat small quantities of foods from this group. We must eat some of these foods as it is essential to have small quantities of fat in the diet. Sugars add to the flavour of food and do give us short bursts of energy. However, their consumption should be limited as too much could lead to tooth decay.
Fats, oils & sweets	Every meal should include at least one food from this group. This group of foods supplies us with carbohydrates, fibre, iron and some of the B group of vitamins

Activity 10.1 30 mins

Nutritional requirements of sports

Task

Part 1

To identify the nutritional requirements of your sport you need to answer the following questions:

(a) What are the endurance demands?
(b) What are the strength demands
(c) Do I use a lot of power?
(d) What are the demands for speed
(e) Will I lose a lot of fluid?

Part 2

Then you can look at the functions of the macro- and micro-nutrients and match them up by using the following table.

Demands	Carbohydrate	Protein	Fats	Vits/Mins	Water
Endurance	High – a match lasts at least 90 minutes so needed for energy		Needed for energy to complement energy from carbs	Needed to help in energy production	Will lose a lot of fluid through sweating so will need to increase water intake
Strength	Carbs are still vital in the production and replacement of energy for the production of strength	Yes – muscle will be broken down during strength aspects of the game		These are an important component of muscle and other structures so will be vital	
Power		Power is needed for jumping, shooting and throwing, so protein demands will rise			
Speed		Speed is a vital component of football, so protein demands will rise		Needed to help in energy production	

Timing of Food Intake

Before Sports

Eating before taking part in sports can be beneficial to performance. You should aim to eat one to four hours before taking part in sports, and choose a starchy carbohydrate food that is easily digested, such as a banana or bowl of cereal. The more you eat, the more time you need to give the body to digest the food before taking part in sports.

During Sports

While taking part in sports, most people will sweat in order to cool down, so it is important to drink plenty of water. If the sport you are taking part in lasts for 90 minutes or more (an endurance sport), or if you feel that you have low energy levels, drinking a sports drink will help to maintain your energy levels.

After Sports

If the sport you have taken part in was strenuous, the body's carbohydrate store will be low and will need to be filled up. Eating foods and drinks high in carbohydrates within the first two hours of stopping exercising will help to maximise the filling of these carbohydrate stores.

> **Definition**
>
> **Endurance sport** any sport that lasts 90 minutes or more.

Endurance sports include football, marathon running and distance swimming. People who take part in these sports would benefit from drinking a sports drink and eating sugary foods during the course of the event in order to maintain their energy levels.

Supplementation

> **Definition**
>
> **Supplementation** the process of adding nutrients to your diet.

A sports person may supplement their diet in order to ensure they are taking in the right quantities or excessive quantities of nutrients in the belief that it will help to maximise sports performance. However, if you are eating a healthy, varied diet, then you probably do not need to take supplements.

Vitamin and Mineral Supplementation

Supplementation may be appropriate if you are eating a low-calorie diet (1200 calories or less), if you are a vegetarian, are in a diseased state, or have a lack of food choices or availability. The supplement should not contain more

than 100 per cent of the Recommended Daily Allowance (RDA) for any vitamin or mineral. Sports performance will be improved only if you are deficient in that particular vitamin or mineral. If there is no deficiency, then they will provide no increase in sporting performance and can actually cause damage to the body.

Protein Powders/High-protein Diets

Taking part in sports, especially resistance-based sports such as weightlifting, increases protein breakdown, so people who take part in these sports may need to increase their intake of protein or may wish to consume protein powders that are made into drinks. This protein is used to help repair damaged muscle tissue and make the muscles grow bigger and stronger. However, excess protein that is eaten will be broken down and used to make energy or stored as fat. These supplements are quite expensive and often provide the same amount of protein as one pint of milk. However, this type of supplement would be useful for sports people who have a very high calorie requirement and would otherwise find it difficult to eat enough food.

Creatine Supplementation

At present, creatine is a legal supplement, which means any athlete or sports person may take this supplement and still compete in events. Athletes take creatine supplements as it is thought this will increase their sports performance in power events such as sprinting or the shot put.

> **Key learning points**
>
> - Protein powders/high-protein diets may be of use for weight trainers and body builders.
> - Creatine supplementation is legal and may improve power events.

Importance of a Healthy Diet

A healthy diet not only makes you look good and feel good, it will also keep you healthy and reduce the risk of you getting heart disease, cancer, diabetes and a range of other life-threatening diseases.

10.4 Assessing Your Own Diet

The best way to assess your own diet is to keep a record of everything that you eat over a period of time, usually two weeks, because that gives a truer picture of what you normally do. If you do keep a food diary it is vital that it covers week days and weekends because we tend to eat differently at these times. The food diary should contain as much detail as possible and should look like the one in Table 10.1.

Day/Time	6–10 a.m.	10 a.m.–2 p.m.	2–5 p.m.	5–9 p.m.	9–12 p.m.
Monday	Meals Snacks Drinks	Meals Snacks Drinks	Meals Snacks Drinks	Meals Snacks Drinks	Meals Snacks Drinks
Tuesday	Meals Snacks Drinks	Meals Snacks Drinks	Meals Snacks Drinks	Meals Snacks Drinks	Meals Snacks Drinks
Wednesday	Meals Snacks Drinks	Meals Snacks Drinks	Meals Snacks Drinks	Meals Snacks Drinks	Meals Snacks Drinks
Thursday	Meals Snacks Drinks	Meals Snacks Drinks	Meals Snacks Drinks	Meals Snacks Drinks	Meals Snacks Drinks
Friday	Meals Snacks Drinks	Meals Snacks Drinks	Meals Snacks Drinks	Meals Snacks Drinks	Meals Snacks Drinks
Saturday	Meals Snacks Drinks	Meals Snacks Drinks	Meals Snacks Drinks	Meals Snacks Drinks	Meals Snacks Drinks
Sunday	Meals Snacks Drinks	Meals Snacks Drinks	Meals Snacks Drinks	Meals Snacks Drinks	Meals Snacks Drinks

The more information you can put in about what you have eaten then it will make the analysis easier. It is also useful to put in the exact timing of your meal or snack.

Activity 10.2 45 mins   P2

Allow 45 minutes and two weeks to complete

Task

Prepare your own food diary using Table 10.1 as a template and then fill in the diary over a period of two weeks. Be honest and write as much detail as you can as this will make it easier to review the food diary later.

How to Assess the Diet

A qualified dietician would spend a long period of time looking at exact calorie intake and whether you got enough of each of the vitamins and minerals. That is unrealistic and time consuming at this stage so we need to make some general observation on the food diary. This can be done by answering the following questions:

1. How does your diet match with the healthy eating pyramid?

2. Are you eating enough carbohydrate and is it the right type?

3. Are you eating enough fibre?

4. Are you eating enough protein and is it from good sources?

5. Are you eating enough or too much fat?

6. Is the timing of meals appropriate?

7. Are you eating enough fresh fruit and vegetables?

8. Are you getting enough vitamins and minerals?

9. Are you eating fresh foods or are they processed?

10. Are you eating too much deep fat fried foods?

11. Are you eating too much salt?

12. Are you drinking enough water?

13. What is your tea and coffee consumption like?

14. Are you eating correctly before and after exercise?

Hint: look back to the section on the preparation of foods as it gives ideas about healthy eating.

There may be other questions or issues that come up when you look at the diet. Once you have gained the general information you can then organise the information by placing it into:

- Areas of strengths

- Areas that need improvement

- Recommendations for improvement.

Activity 10.3 60 mins   P3

Assessing your diet   M2

Task   D2

Using the information from your food diary assess the strengths and areas for improvement. Then decide upon what recommendations you can make to improve your nutrition.

10.5 Planning a Personal Nutritional Strategy P4 M3

These recommendations that you have made can then become an action plan that clearly shows the actions that need to be taken. It could look like the action plan on page 188.

Name:

Current situation

Nutritional goals:

Nutritional strategy:

Carbohydrates:

Protein:

Fats:

Vitamins:

Minerals:

Hydration:

Supplements

Foods to avoid:

Plans for meals:

Advisers (who will support me?):

Activity **10.4** ⏱ 60 mins   **P4**

Developing a personal nutritional strategy.   **M3**

Task

Prepare your personal nutritional strategy to cover all of the details above.

10.6 Reviewing a Personal Nutritional Strategy **P6** **M4**

Reviewing any change that has been made is a vital part of the process because not all of the recommendations may be successful.

It may be down to the inconvenience of preparing the foods, or the foods that have been recommended don't taste good to you. All changes need to fit the needs and likes of the individual they have been made for. A review could be included as a separate part of the food diary so that you can reflect on what you have been eating and how effective it has been in meeting the goals. The review would need to cover the following areas:

- How does the nutritional strategy meet your needs?
- How easy has it been to adopt the changes?
- What did you like about the new strategy
- What did you dislike about the new strategy?
- Was the cost of the food realistic for you?
- Did you get the results you wanted?

Again this information can be reviewed to come to a list of the strengths of the new strategy and then any areas where improvements need to be made.

Useful websites

www.ausport.gov.au/ais
Provides invaluable tips on nutrition for sports participants, including suitable recipes that can be downloaded easily.

www.netfit.co.uk/nutrition/nutrition/index.htm
Free useful food facts with the focus on health and fitness.

www.nutrition.org.uk/healthyliving/lifestyle/how-much-physical-activity-do-i-need
Nutrition tips relating to physical activity from the British Nutrition Foundation.

www.nutrition.org.uk/healthyliving/lifestyle/eating-for-sport-and-exercise
Information from the British Nutrition Foundation on the best types of food to eat with specific sports in mind.

http://sportsmedicine.about.com/od/sportsnutrition/a/SportsNutrition.htm
The basics of sports nutrition from training to competition.

Further Reading

Bean, A., 2009, *The Complete Guide to Sports Nutrition*. London: A&C Black.

Bean, A., 2009, *Food for Fitness*. London: A&C Black.

Burke, L., 2007, *Practical Sports Nutrition*. Champaign, IL: Human Kinetics.

Chapter 11
Development of Personal Fitness

To work with athletes and improve their chances of achieving excellence demands a detailed understanding of the term 'fitness'. Once we understand the various aspects of fitness we can then carry out some tests to assess fitness and prepare a training plan.

Learning Goals

By the end of this chapter you should:

- Be able to plan a personal fitness training programme
- Know personal exercise adherence factors and strategies
- Be able to implement and review a personal fitness training programme.

To achieve a PASS grade the evidence must show that the learner is able to:	To achieve a MERIT grade the evidence must show that, in addition to the pass criteria, the learner is able to:	To achieve a DISTINCTION grade the evidence must show that, in addition to the pass and merit criteria, the learner is able to:
P1 plan, design and agree a six-week personal fitness training programme with a coach	**M1** contribute own ideas to the design of a six-week personal fitness training programme	
P2 write aims and describe personal exercise adherence factors and strategies	**M2** explain personal exercise adherence factors and strategies	**D1** evaluate personal exercise adherence strategies for overcoming barriers to exercise
P3 implement a six-week personal fitness training programme, maintaining a training diary		
P4 describe the strengths of the personal fitness training programme, identifying areas for improvement	**M3** explain the strengths of the personal fitness training programme, making suggestions for improvement	**D2** justify suggestions related to identified areas for improvement in the personal fitness training programme

11.1 Planning a Fitness Training Programme P1 M1

Gaining Information

When designing a personal fitness programme it is important to make the programme as personal as possible. It must meet the needs of the individual it is written for or it will result in the person being unhappy or unsuccessful. The key to this is gathering as much information as possible on the individual. This is done through the use of a comprehensive questionnaire. This questionnaire will be part of an initial consultation with the individual and must cover at least the following: medical history; activity history; goals and outcomes required; lifestyle factors; nutritional status and other factors that will affect fitness.

SAMPLE QUESTIONNAIRE

Section 1 – Personal details

Name _____

Address _____

_____

_____

Telephone Home _____

Mobile _____

Email _____

Occupation _____

Date of birth _____

Doctor's name and address _____

_____

_____

_____

Emergency contact name and address _____

_____

_____

_____

Section 2 – Sporting goals

1 What are your long-term sporting goals over the next year or season?

_____

_____

_____

2 What are your medium-term goals over the next three months?

_____

_____

_____

3 What are your short-term goals over the next four weeks?

_____

_____

_____

Section 3 – Current training status

1 What are your main training requirements?

- Muscular strength
- Muscular endurance
- Speed
- Flexibility
- Aerobic fitness
- Power
- Weight loss or gain
- Skill-related fitness
- Other (please state).

2 How would you describe your current fitness status?

_____

_____

_____

3 How many times a week will you train?

_____

4 How long have you got for each training session?

_____

Section 4 – Your nutritional needs

1 On a scale of 1 to 10 (1 being very low quality and 10 being very high quality) how would you rate the quality of your diet? _____

2 Do you follow any particular diet?

- Vegetarian

- Vegan

- Vegetarian and fish

- Gluten free

- Dairy free.

3 Describe how often you eat and a typical day's intake.

_____

_____

_____

4 Do you take any supplements? If so, which ones?

_____

_____

_____

Section 5 – About your lifestyle

1 How many units of alcohol do you drink in a typical week? _____

2 Do you smoke? _____ If yes, how many a day? _____

3 Do you experience stress on a daily basis? _____

4 If yes, what causes you stress (if you know)? _____

_____

5 What techniques do you use to deal with your stress? _____

_____

_____

_____

Section 6 – About your physical health

1 Do you experience any of the following?

- Back pain or injury

- Knee pain or injury

- Ankle pain or injury

- Swollen joints
- Shoulder pain or injury
- Hip or pelvic pain or injury
- Nerve damage
- Head injuries.

2 If yes, please give details

_____

_____

_____

3 Are any of these injuries made worse by exercise? _____

4 If yes, what movements in particular will cause pain? _____

_____

_____

_____

5 Are you currently receiving any treatment for any injuries?_____

Section 7 – Medical history

1 Do you have, or have you had, any of the following medical conditions?

- Asthma
- Bronchitis
- Heart problems
- Chest pains
- Diabetes
- High blood pressure
- Epilepsy
- Other.

2 Are you taking any medication? (If yes, state what, how much and why)

_____

Name: _____

Signature: _____

Trainer's name: _____

Trainer's signature: _____

Date: _____

Activity **11.1**  60 mins   **P1**

Designing a questionnaire

Task

Design your own questionnaire, based on the above template, which you can use to gain the information you need to design your own personal fitness training programme.

Physical Fitness Training Programme

Once you have found out the goals of the individual and the information that is relevant to planning a programme, you need to assess what types of training are available to help the individual meet their goals. When you are designing a training programme you should initially consider a set of principles that you need to follow to ensure the programme will be effective. These are called the principles of training.

Principles of Training

In order to develop a safe and effective training programme you will need to consider the principles of training. These principles are a set of guidelines to help you understand the requirements of programme design. The principles of training are:

Frequency

Intensity

Time

Type

Overload

Reversibility

Specificity

1. **Frequency** – this means how often the athlete will train each week.

2. **Intensity** – this is how hard the athlete will work. It is usually expressed as a percentage of maximum intensity.

3. **Time** – this will indicate how long they will train for in each session.

4. **Type** – this shows the type of training they will perform, and needs to be individual to each person.

5. **Overload** – this principle shows that to make an improvement a muscle or system must work slightly harder than it is used to. This may be as simple as getting a sedentary person walking for ten minutes or getting an athlete to squat more weight than they have previously.

6. **Reversibility** – this says that if a fitness gain is not used regularly, then the body will reverse it and go back to its previous fitness level. The rule is commonly known as 'use it or lose it'.

7. **Specificity** – this principle states that any fitness gain will be specific to the muscles or system to which the overload is applied. Put simply, this says that different types of training will produce different results. To make a programme specific you need to look at the needs of the athletes in that sport and then train them accordingly. For example, a footballer would need to run at different speeds and have lots of changes of direction. A golfer would need to do rotational work but sprinting speed would not be so important.

Quick Quiz 1 15 mins

Match the principles of training to their correct description.

Description	Principle
The time length of each session	Type
Doing more than the body is used to	Frequency
The number of training sessions per week, month or year	Reversibility
The amount of effort expended in each training session	Specificity
Targeting the component of fitness you wish to improve	Time
If you do not use a fitness gain you will lose it	Intensity
Choosing muscular endurance, strength or flexibility	Overload

Types of Training

Flexibility

Flexibility is the 'range of motion available at a joint' and is needed in sports for two main reasons:

1. To enable the athlete to have the range of motion to perform the movements needed.
2. To prevent the athlete from becoming injured.

There are various methods of stretching muscles; we look here at static, PNF and ballistic stretching.

Definition

Flexibility the range of motion available at a joint.

Static Stretching

This is when a muscle is stretched in a steady, controlled manner and then held in a static or still position. It is taken to the point where the muscle contracts and a slight pain is felt. This is called 'the point of bind'. At this point the stretch is held until the muscle relaxes and the discomfort disappears.

A **static** stretch can be a maintenance stretch or a developmental stretch. A **maintenance** stretch is held until the discomfort disappears and then the stretch is stopped. A **developmental** stretch is different because, when the muscle relaxes and the discomfort disappears, the stretch is then applied further to a second point. It is taken to a point when the discomfort is felt again, held until the muscle relaxes and then applied again. It lasts for around 30 seconds, while a maintenance stretch lasts for around ten seconds.

PNF Stretching

Proprioceptive Neuromuscular Facilitation is an advanced type of stretching that develops the length of the muscle. It needs two people: one person to do the stretching and one to be stretched.

- The muscle is stretched by the trainer until the point of bind.

- At this point the trainer asks the athlete to contract the muscle and push against them at about 40–50 per cent effort.
- This contraction is held for ten seconds.
- When the muscle is relaxed, the trainer stretches the muscle further.
- Again a contraction is applied and then the muscle is re-stretched.
- This is done three times.

This is a more effective way of developing the length of the muscle as the contraction will actually cause the muscle to relax more quickly and more deeply.

Ballistic Stretching

This means a 'bouncing' stretch as the muscle is forced beyond its point of stretch by a bouncing movement. It is a high-risk method of stretching but it may be used in specific sports such as gymnastics. It must never be used on people training for health and fitness reasons rather than sports.

Resistance Training

Resistance training means using any form of resistance to place an increased load on a muscle or muscle group. Resistance can be applied through any of the following:

- Free weights
- Resistance machines
- Cable machines
- Gravity
- Medicine balls
- Air
- Water
- Resistance bands
- Manually.

The following are popular methods of resistance training: resistance machines, free weights, plyometrics and circuit training.

Resistance Machines

A range of machines has been developed to train muscle groups in isolation. They were originally developed for bodybuilders but their ease of use and safety factors make them a feature of every gym in the country.

Free Weights

Free weights involve barbells and dumbbells, and are seen to have advantages over resistance machines. Mainly they allow a person to work in their own range of movement rather than the way a machine wants them to work. Also, when a person does free weights they have to use many more muscles to stabilise the body before the force is applied. This is particularly so if the person performs the exercise standing up. They also have more 'functional crossover' in that they can replicate movements that will be used in sports and daily life. This is seen as a huge advantage.

Plyometrics

Plyometric training will develop power, which is producing strength at speed. It usually involves moving your body weight very quickly through jumping or bounding. Any sport that involves jumping in the air or moving the body forwards at pace will need power training. Examples of plyometric training include jumping onto benches while holding weights in your hand or across your back, and jumping on top of vaulting horses or benches and then off again.

It is a very strenuous type of training and an athlete must have well-developed strength before performing plyometrics.

Circuit Training

Circuits have been popular in this country since the 1950s, particularly in the army. They comprise a series of exercises arranged in a specific order and performed one after the other. There are normally eight to 12 stations set out and organised so that each muscle group is worked in rotation. Circuits can be performed for a range of fitness gains but are usually done to develop aerobic fitness or a general fitness base. They can be made specific to various sports by including exercises for the muscles used in that sport and some of the skills specific to that sport.

Aerobic Training

Continuous Training

This is also called 'steady-state' training and involves an individual maintaining a steady pace for a long period of time. To be effective it needs to be done for a period of over 20 minutes. It is useful for developing a strong base of aerobic fitness; however, it will not develop speed or strength.

Interval Training

This type of training is described as having the following features:

'. . . a structured period of work followed by a structured period of rest.'

In other words, an athlete runs quickly for a period of time and then rests at a much lower intensity before speeding up again. This type of training has the benefit of improving speed as well as aerobic fitness.

Definition

Interval training a structured period of work followed by a structured period of rest.

Examples of interval sessions

- Four sets of five minutes at 70 per cent effort with two minutes' rest in between.

- Six sets of 45 seconds at 90 per cent effort with 90 seconds' rest.

- Six sets of 50 metres at 100 per cent effort with one minutes' rest.

The intervals need to be designed so that they are specific to the demands of the sport.

Fartlek

Fartlek is a Swedish term for 'speed play' and it involves an athlete running at a range of different speeds for a period of 20 to 30 minutes. This type of training is excellent for replicating the demands of a sport such as football, rugby or hockey where different running speeds are required at different times. It can be used to develop aerobic or anaerobic fitness depending on the intensity of the running. It can also be done for cycling or rowing training.

Putting the Programme Together

The programme should use the following structure:

Warm up:

> Aerobic heart-rate raiser (5 minutes)
>
> 2–3 dynamic stretches.

Cardiovascular work (20 minutes):

> Choose from running, rowing, cycling or cross training.

Resistance work (30 minutes):

> 6–8 exercises: a mixture of free weights, cable machines, resistance machines or other resistance equipment.

Core work (5 minutes):

> 2–3 exercises for the stomach and back.

Cool down:

> Aerobic exercise to lower pulse
> 6–8 stretches to all the muscles worked in the main session; some will be development and some will be maintenance.

Cardiovascular and resistance work could be done in the other order depending on what the individual wants to focus on most.

To achieve M1 you need to contribute your own ideas to designing your training programme.

Ⓚ Key learning points

- Before designing a training programme, you need to produce a comprehensive questionnaire. It must cover the following: medical history; activity history; goals and outcomes required; lifestyle factors; nutritional status and other factors that will affect fitness.
- Principles of training:
  - Frequency means how often the athlete will train each week.
  - Intensity is how hard the athlete will work.
  - Time is how long they will train for in each session.
  - Type is the type of training they will perform, and needs to be individual to each person.
  - Overload is working a muscle or system slightly harder than it is used to.
  - Reversibility says that if a fitness gain is not used regularly, then the body will reverse it and go back to its previous fitness level.
  - Specificity states that any fitness gain will be specific to the muscles or system to which the overload is applied.
- Types of training:
  - Flexibility training is to develop the 'range of motion available at a joint'. There are various methods of stretching muscles: static stretching, ballistic stretching and PNF stretching.
  - Resistance training means using any form of resistance to place an increased load on a muscle or muscle group. Resistance can be applied through any of the following:
    - Free weights
    - Resistance machines
    - Gravity
    - Medicine balls
    - Air
    - Water
    - Resistance bands
    - Manually.
  - Aerobic training is to develop the efficiency of the heart, lungs and working muscles. It can be of three types: continuous training, interval training and fartlek training.

Activity 11.2 60 mins   P1 M1

Designing a personal fitness programme

Task

Using the principles of training, the types of training available and the guidelines for putting the programme together, design yourself a personal fitness training programme for a period of six weeks using the following template:

	Week 1	Week 2	Week 3	Week 4	Week 5	Week 6
Aims						
Components of fitness targeted						
Content of sessions	Warm up CV work Resistance work Core work Cool down					
Notes						

11.2 Personal Exercise Adherence Factors and Strategies   P2 M2

A big issue in physical activity is the number of people who start exercise programmes but then give them up after a short period of time. There are many reasons for this and we will look here at the barriers that may stop people from taking up exercise and then keeping going with their exercise programmes.

Research done by the Canadian Fitness and Lifestyle Research Institute (1992) in Weinberg and Gould (2007, p. 419) showed the main barriers stated by people who were not currently taking exercise:

Quick Quiz 2 20 mins ?

In the wordsearch below, find as many words as you can related to fitness training methods.

I	D	Y	J	E	J	U	C	H	W	A
N	K	T	S	J	D	M	E	C	W	E
T	W	H	R	E	V	M	O	I	W	C
E	B	Y	N	S	H	L	C	R	E	N
R	D	V	S	E	L	B	A	C	T	A
V	W	S	T	Y	K	S	L	U	H	R
A	A	G	B	S	T	A	T	I	C	U
L	X	H	N	T	E	S	Y	T	U	D
S	F	A	R	T	L	E	K	S	K	N
D	B	N	R	Y	R	U	W	P	L	E

Major barriers (and the % of people who stated them)

- Lack of time (69%)
- Lack of energy (59%)
- Lack of motivation (52%).

Moderate barriers (and the % of people who stated them)

- Excessive cost (37%)
- Illness or injury (36%)
- Lack of facilities (30%)
- Feeling uncomfortable (29%)
- Lack of skill (29%).

The main factors that will motivate people to exercise include:

- Improving and maintaining health
- Feeling a sense of achievement
- Improving self-esteem
- Weight management or changing appearance
- Managing or controlling stress
- Enjoyment and socialising.

Exercise Adherence Strategies P2 M2

Adherence means keeping to or sticking to the exercise sessions that you have started. For example, if you have committed to taking exercise three times a week then adherence is keeping to that promise.

Having a personal fitness training programme is important in maintaining adherence because the programme is designed for you to meet your needs and goals. It is more likely to help you improve and see these improvements happen – that is the greatest motivation an individual can have.

Goal Setting

Setting goals is an effective way of keeping an individual motivated and improves their chances of sticking to their exercise programme. To make sure the goals are effective you need to make sure that the goals are SMART. In summary SMART means:

Specific

Measurable

Achievable

Realistic

Time-constrained.

Specific – means that the goal relates to the types of fitness that need to improve. To get fit is a poor goal because it is not specific, while to improve muscle tone is a better goal.

Measurable – the goal must be stated in figures so you can measure whether it has been achieved. 'I want to reduce body fat' is a poor goal 'but, I want to reduce body fat by 3%' is much better because you can now measure it.

Achievable – the goal must be possible to achieve or it will not be motivational.

Realistic – the goal must be realistic for an individual and take into account factors that may prevent the goal being achieved.

Time-constrained – there must be a time-scale for when the goal is to be achieved because a deadline is needed to review whether the exercise programme has been successful.

Support and Reinforcement

It is beneficial to have a support group around an individual to keep them motivated. At a gym a trainer or instructor often supports the people who train there and may even ring them or send them a text if they miss any exercise sessions. Other people in the gym or doing the same activity can support you, as can your friends and family.

Rewards for Achieving Goals

It is common for gyms to offer rewards for people who attend frequently; this may be something as simple as a T-shirt or water bottle or maybe even a massage. People like to be recognised for the efforts they put in. You can even give yourself a reward of something special if you achieve your goals.

Activity 11.3 ⏱ 30 mins   D1

Evaluating methods to promote adherence

Task

Choose three strategies for ensuring that people stick to their exercise programmes. You could choose goal setting, support and reinforcement, and rewards. Evaluate each method by looking at what you think are the strengths and weaknesses of each method. You could use the following table.

Technique	Strengths	Weaknesses

11.3 Implementing the Personal Fitness Training Programme   P3

To achieve P3 you need to complete all the training sessions that you prescribed for yourself when you completed P1 and M1. It is important to make records of each training session and to review each training session. You might look at what exercises you found hard and which you found easy, and also what parts of the training you enjoyed. This will help you when you come to review your training programme.

11.4 Reviewing a Personal Fitness Training Programme   P4 M3 D2

Training Diaries

The programme is planned out in detail and implemented with great energy and enthusiasm, and likewise it must be reviewed in an organised manner. The individual must keep a training diary that covers every session, whether it is physical training, technical development or mental skills. Only then can the training be accurately and systematically reviewed.

A training diary should include the following details:

- A record of what was done in each session
- A record of the performances in training
- A record of achievements in competition
- How motivated the individual has been feeling.

This can then be used to demonstrate progress, keep the individual motivated and understand any improvements that have been made (or not).

Review

The individual will review the success and effectiveness of their training programme in three ways:

- Repeating their fitness tests
- Evaluating performances
- Reviewing their training diary.

By reviewing the outcomes of the training programme the strengths and weaknesses of the programme can be assessed. The review will come up with the following information:

- The strengths of the programme where goals have been met.

- Areas of improvement where goals have not been met.

- How the programme can be modified to meet the goals that have not been achieved.

Based on all this information, the next stage of the training programme can be developed.

Activity 11.4 ⏱ 3 hours P3

Allow three hours over a six-week period

Task

Maintain a training diary by recording details of each training session. You might use a template like the one below for each session:

Name:

Date:

Aims of session:

Warm-up:

CV work:

Resistance work:

Sets x Reps	Exercise	Resistance	Rest	Notes

Cool-down:

Review of training session:

Activity **11.5** 45 mins

Evaluating your training programme

Task

Once you have completed the six-week training programme it is time to review it. This can be done by answering the following question:

Has my programme achieved the aims that I wanted it to achieve?

If the aims have been achieved then the programme has strengths and, if not, it has areas for improvement.

You can review the programme by using the following table.

Strengths	Areas for improvement	Describe the strengths/ areas for improvement (P4)	Explain the strengths/ areas for improvement and make suggestions for improvement (M3)	Justify the suggestions related to areas for improvement (D2)

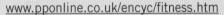

Useful websites

www.pponline.co.uk/encyc/fitness.htm
Video demonstrations of training techniques and free printouts of general articles on fitness and training (subscription necessary for full access).

www.expertfootball.com/training/fitness.php
Fitness and training tips specifically aimed at improving the fitness and technique of footballers.

Http://news.bbc.co.uk/sport1/hi/health_and_fitness/4270714.stm
Tips on fitness training to improve your performance with reference to specific sportsmen and women.

www.thefitmap.co.uk/quizzes/fitness/advanced
Provides self-assessed quizzes that cover a wide range of training and fitness areas; useful for revision.

Further Reading

Coulson, M., 2007, *The Fitness Instructor's Handbook*. London: A&C Black.
Dagleish, J. and Dollery, S., 2001, *The Health and Fitness Handbook*. Harlow: Pearson Education.
Sharkey, B.J. and Gaskill, S.E., 2006, *Fitness and Health*. Champaign, IL: Human Kinetics.

References

Weinberg, R.S., and Gould, D., 2007, *Foundations of Sport and Exercise Psychology*. Champaign, IL: Human Kinetics.

Chapter 12
Lifestyle and Sports Performance

This chapter looks at sports performance in a broad sense and shows how an athlete's lifestyle choices will influence their success or failure.

Learning Goals

By the end of this chapter you should:

- Be able to manage your own work commitments and leisure time.
- Know appropriate behaviour for an elite athlete.
- Know the factors that influence effective career planning.
- Be able to participate in a media interview.

To achieve a PASS grade the evidence must show that the learner is able to:	To achieve a MERIT grade the evidence must show that, in addition to the pass criteria, the learner is able to:	To achieve a DISTINCTION grade the evidence must show that, in addition to the pass and merit criteria, the learner is able to:
P1 produce a realistic plan for work commitments and leisure time, for one month	**M1** explain the way work commitments and leisure activities have been planned	
P2 describe three different pressures on elite athletes	**M2** explain three different pressures on elite athletes and suitable strategies that can be used to deal with these pressures	
P3 identify strategies that can be used to deal with pressures on elite athletes		
P4 describe appropriate behaviour for elite athletes in three different situations	**M3** explain appropriate behaviour for elite athletes in three different situations	**D1** evaluate the effects and consequences of the behaviour of elite athletes
P5 describe realistic goals in a personal athletic career plan, including second career choices	**M4** explain goals in a personal athletic career plan, and second career choices	**D2** justify goals in a personal athletic career plan, and second career choices
P6 describe three financial issues elite athletes need to consider		
P7 describe the skills needed to communicate and work effectively with others	**M5** explain the skills needed to communicate and work effectively with others	
P8 prepare, and be the subject of, a media interview, describing own strengths and areas for improvement	**M6** explain own strengths and areas for improvement when participating in a media interview	**D3** present recommendations on how to improve own media interview skills

12.1 Managing Work Commitments and Leisure Time P1 M1

Sports performers will increasingly find that they have many demands on their time. Their success is dependent upon their managing this time appropriately so that they have the right amount of time for training, eating, rest and recovery.

Any person's life could be divided into three general areas:

- Work commitments
- Survival activities
- Leisure time.

In the case of a sports performer their work commitments would include the following: training, competition, education and study, and any paid or unpaid employment.

Survival activities would include eating, sleeping and personal hygiene, such as cleaning and washing.

Leisure time is what remains after work and survival commitments have been met. Leisure time consists of activities that are freely chosen and done for pleasure. These are important because they may have a positive or negative impact on the athlete's sporting performance.

Time Management and Planning

It is important to point out that for a performer to give themselves the best chance of success there are three activities they need to do correctly, and these must be at the centre of their time-management plan. These activities are:

1. The correct type and amount of training.

2. An appropriate nutritional strategy giving them correct amounts of each nutrient.

3. Enough time for rest and recovery between training sessions.

It is worth saying that an athlete does not get fitter while training. Training provides the stimulus for the body to get fitter but it actually happens while the person is resting. We could say that while it looks like athletes are lazy, actually their laziness helps them get fitter!

If you examine Jessica Ennis's training schedule, you will see that she does little else except train, rest and eat. The results that her commitment to her regime have given her have been outstanding. It is this type of commitment which is the model for success.

The best way to plan a schedule is to look at the week as having seven blocks of 24 hours, which make up 168 hours. What is done in each of these 168 hours must increase an athlete's chances of success because, if it does not, it will increase their chances of failure. To plan the schedule you need to follow these steps:

1. Work out how much time will be spent with basic survival activities. For example, sleep will consist of eight hours a night, eating is around two hours a day if you include cooking, washing may take up to one hour. Already we have lost 11 of our available 24 hours.

2. Work out how much time will be spent training. This also needs to include any time spent travelling to venues and any other work related to training, such as time spent with coaches or advisers discussing performance. Periods of rest and recovery from performance will also be included here, as they are enforced rather than chosen. In this calculation you also need to look at time spent studying. All athletes are encouraged to study so that they have skills to rely on in later life.

3. Any time remaining will be allocated to leisure activities. It may be a lot less than you imagined. However, this time is vital for the athlete so that they can do activities they enjoy and not become bored and stale. Leisure-time activities should not conflict with the athlete's goals and desired outcomes, and can be separated into appropriate and inappropriate activities.

Activity **12.1** 30 mins   P1   M1

Managing your own time

Complete the questions in Part 1 to show how you use your time currently, and then complete the second task to show a plan for your work commitments and leisure time.

Part 1

(a) How long do you currently spend on each of these activities?

Sleeping
Eating and cooking
Personal hygiene
Other.

(b) How long do you currently spend on work-related activities?

Training
Travel
Recovery
Attending lectures
Travel to college
Studying
Paid work.

(c) How much time have you got left? How do you spend that?

Part 2

Take a typical 24-hour period and plan hour by hour how you will be spending your time.

7 a.m.	8 a.m.	9 a.m.	10 a.m.	11 a.m.	12 p.m.
1 p.m.	2 p.m.	3 p.m.	4 p.m.	5 p.m.	6 p.m.
7 p.m.	8 p.m.	9 p.m.	10 p.m.	11 p.m.	12 a.m.
1 a.m.	2 a.m.	3 a.m.	4 a.m.	5 a.m.	6 a.m.

Part 3

To achieve a merit, explain how the time plan, including work and leisure activities, has been planned.

Quick Quiz 1 30 mins

What three activities must an athlete consider when planning their time management?

Pressures on Athletes   P2   M2

The athlete does not live his or her life on paper, nor is the world organised around them. They have to live in an unpredictable world full of people who try to pull them one way or another. You can have the best time-management plan but it is difficult to plan for the vagaries of public transport or chance meetings with people. Pressures can be split into two categories:

- Pressure from other people
- Social pressures.

People

Everyone has a network of people they deal with on a weekly basis, and they will include the following:

- Friends
- Training partners
- Family
- Coaches
- Advisers
- Selectors
- Teachers
- Lecturers.

Social Pressures

Many social activities in British society centre on activities that are not compatible with athletic performance. For example, consumption of alcohol, smoking and recreational drug use will all have a negative effect on the athlete's performance. It is essential that they are not sidetracked by these activities and choose social activities that fit in with their goals. The athlete does have a choice, and the choice they make will directly impact on their chances of success.

How to Deal with These Pressures?

The athlete must make sure that they have resources that will help them to deal with the pressures they face.

Resources can come in many forms. They may be any of the following:

- Support network of supporters, for example coach or adviser

- Clear goals and strategy for how to achieve their goals

- Use of role models, for example people who have achieved their goal; also, studying how they achieved that goal

- Use of diaries or training logs to track progress accurately

- Development of psychological skills to influence their own behaviour

- Development of their own personal qualities.

The overall message is that success does not come by chance. It is the result of careful planning and preparation. Although unforeseen events will occur, planning will keep the athlete on the right lines. The athlete has a choice regarding how they spend their 168 hours every week and they must understand how their choices impact on their behaviour. The most successful athletes have made massive sacrifices in order to be successful.

 Key learning points

- Time can be divided into the completion of three activities:
  - Work commitments would include training, competition, education and study, and any paid or unpaid employment.
  - Survival activities would include eating, sleeping and personal hygiene, such as cleaning and washing.
  - Leisure time is what remains after work and survival commitments have been met.
- Pressures on athletes can be split into two categories:
  - Pressure from other people
  - Social pressures.
- People can place positive or negative pressure on an athlete and may include: friends, training partners, family, coaches, advisers, selectors, teachers and lecturers.

Quick Quiz 2   15 mins

1. **Where may pressure come from for athletes?**
2. **What is the difference between supporters and saboteurs?**
3. **Give four resources that can help athletes deal with these pressures**

Activity **12.2** 🕐 20 mins   P2 P3 M2

Pressures on athletes

Fill out the following table to show three pressures on athletes and how they can be dealt with. The first one is provided as an example.

Pressure	Description of pressure	Explanation of why this is a problem	Strategy to deal with the pressure
Spending late nights socialising with friends	It is easy to spend time going out with friends and staying out as late as them	The athlete needs to make sure they get the right amount of rest so they can recover and train properly	Make it clear that you will have to leave at a certain time before you go out for the evening. Educate your friends about why it is important that you rest.
Excess alcohol consumption			
Use of drugs			

12.2 Appropriate Behaviour for an Elite Athlete P4 M3 D1

Behaviour of athletes is an area of constant coverage by the media. Most of the time it focuses on the bad behaviour of athletes rather than on the positive aspects.

Why is the behaviour of athletes important?

There are many reasons why athletes' behaviour is important.

1. They are role models for future generations.
2. Their behaviour will affect their chances of success.
3. They must keep to the rules set.
4. They must abide by a code of ethics.

They Are Role Models for Future Generations

Whether athletes like it or not, they are role models who are copied by millions of young people. We can clearly see that people learn by copying the behaviour of people they respect, whether this behaviour is seen as being positive or negative.

Their Behaviour Will Affect Their Chances of Success

To produce excellent results, a person must operate from a 'position of excellence'. This means that everything they do should reflect excellence. It will include their conduct and behaviour, how they stand, how they dress and what they do on the sports field.

They Must Keep to the Rules Set

Any sport has a clear set of rules regarding how to play the sport, what behaviour is acceptable and how a person should behave in regard to the officials. Also outlined will be the penalties for not playing within the rules. These penalties will affect an athlete's chances of present and future success.

They Must Abide by a Code of Ethics

Ethics are a set of principles or values that are held and acted upon by people. Rather than being rules, they are an accepted way of behaving and are agreed by a group of people within the sport. Most professions will have a code of ethics to advise their members on how they should conduct themselves.

 Key learning points

There are many reasons why the behaviour of athletes is important:
- They are role models for future generations.
- Their behaviour will affect their chances of success.
- They must keep to the rules set.
- They must abide by a code of ethics.

12.3 Effective Career Planning

Goal Setting

Clearly, for success the athlete must have a clear plan of where they are going and how they are going to get there. There is a detailed discussion of how to set goals in Chapter 9 and those principles can be applied to any aspect of life.

Definition ⓓ

Goal what an individual is trying to achieve; the object or aim of an action.

Goals can also be split into short-term and long-term goals:

- **Short-term goals** – these are goals that are set over a period of time that might be between one day and one month. A short-term goal might relate to what you aim to achieve in one session, but will usually relate to a period of around one month.

Activity 12.3   60 mins

Appropriate behaviour

Part 1

Match the following appropriate behaviours to the correct category:

Showing politeness and good manners

Wearing the appropriate clothing

Going to bed at a reasonable hour

Avoiding excess alcohol consumption

Abiding by the rules

Accepting decisions of officials

Eating the right foods

Resting at appropriate times

During competition and training	At home	During social functions

Part 2

Explain why these are appropriate behaviours

Part 3

What are the positive effects of these behaviours and the negative consequences of the opposite behaviour?

- **Medium-term goals** – these fill the gap between short-term and long-term goals and would cover a period of between one to six months.

- **Long-term goals** – these goals relate to periods that might run from six months to several years. Some people set 'lifetime goals', which cannot be assessed until retirement. Most long-term goals are set for achievement over the course of either a year or a competitive season.

It is important to set long-term, medium-term and short-term goals. The fulfilment of short-term goals will contribute to the achievement of long-term goals.

Careers

The athlete is in a special situation because they have to focus on their primary career as an athlete but also keep an eye on the future. The life of an athlete is unpredictable as it may flourish or end at any time, so they have to be prepared for the future.

Additional Considerations for the Athlete's Career

While the athlete will have a network of people to ensure their success and their goals so that they know where they are headed, they must also make plans for things that may go wrong. These are called contingency plans and the following situations need to be considered:

- Illness

- Injury

- Accidents

- Falling out with their coaches

- Falling out with their club.

Second Careers

There is a full range of careers available to athletes and, with the introduction of internet-based courses, a wide range of courses is available. However, most people choose to study sport-related courses due to their interests and to the easy availability of information for research and case studies (see Figure 12.1).

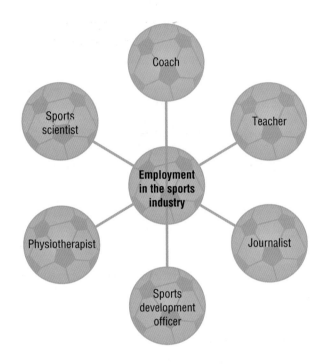

Figure 12.1   What careers may athletes choose?

Sports Coach

For a practitioner of a sport at a high level, it is a natural progression to want to share this knowledge. There are opportunities to coach at all levels of a sport and to all age groups. Each governing body will have a scheme to enable you to become qualified to coach at different levels.

Sports Teacher

Teaching or lecturing can be done at schools, colleges or universities, and you will notice that all sports teachers have a keen practical interest in their subject. Teaching may be in physical education or towards diplomas and degrees in sport or sport science. A teacher needs to develop their academic knowledge as well, and has to hold a degree in sport or teaching, as well as a certificate in education. Full-time study will take at least four years.

Journalist

Many former sports people work as sports journalists and write for newspapers and magazines. With the growth of online publications and specialist websites there are new areas where writing can be published. A journalist usually has to hold a degree and belong to the professional body.

Sports Development Officer

Local authorities employ sports development officers to increase participation in their local area. They usually target certain groups of people for specific reasons. There is often a large choice of schemes for children in particular, to help them become interested in sport. The local authority will be looking for people with sports qualifications and particularly with a range of coaching awards.

Activity **12.4** 60 mins

Career planning
Part 1

Using the following form, lay out your plans for your athletic career and your choice of second career (non-athletic).

Part 2

Explain the goals that you have chosen.

Part 3

Justify why you have chosen these goals over other goals.

Name:

Sport/s:

Goals (Athletic)

1. Long-term goals

....
....

2. Medium-term goals

....
....

3. Short-term goals

....
....

Goals (Non-Athletic)

1. Long-term goals

....
....

2. Medium-term goals

....
....

3. Short-term goals

....
....

Physiotherapist

General and sports physiotherapy is a popular choice for athletes to consider, owing to its practical nature. Physiotherapists need to hold a degree and, while there are many universities offering degrees, competition for places is fierce. Due to this competition you need to work towards the highest grades to get a place. The work itself is interesting and varied and is done in hospitals or at sports venues.

Sports Scientist

A sports scientist works to improve the performance of any athlete and such work may require a knowledge of physiology, biomechanics, nutrition and psychology. Fitness testing and evaluation are a key part of this work, to highlight areas of weakness. Sports scientists will need to hold a degree in their subject and are usually researching towards a higher degree.

Quick Quiz 3   15 mins

1. **Give four reasons why it is important for athletes to set goals.**
2. **What are the differences between short-, long- and medium-term goals?**

Financial Management

As an athlete starting out, you may be limited in your income (money coming in), and your expenditure (money going out) may be quite high, as you need to pay coaches, eat well and travel to training and competitions. It can be easy to get into financial trouble and this will cause worries and may affect your career. It is important to know how to manage your money and this is best done through the use of a budget.

Hopefully, expenditure will not exceed income. If your income is higher than your expenditure it means you will be able to save some money by putting it in a separate bank account. This type of investment is vital for any large future purchases or to fall back on if you have a period where you have unexpected spending. Savings accounts can be set up and managed online.

Taxation

You will always have to pay a certain amount of your income to the government in the form of income tax. If you are on a salary, the tax will automatically be deducted, but if you are self-employed you need to pay this twice a year. For any private work you need to put some of your income aside each month to pay this tax.

Example of a budget

Income

Start by considering all the ways money comes into your account. The following are sources of income:

Salary	£_____
Private work	£_____
State benefits	£_____
Grants	£_____
Support from parents	£_____
Other income	£_____
Total	£_____

Expenditure

Then consider all of your expenditure:

Home

Rent	£_____
Electricity	£_____
Gas	£_____
Water rates	£_____
Council tax	£_____

Transport

Car loan	£_____
Petrol	£_____
Bus fares	£_____
Taxis	£_____

Daily expenses

Food	£_____
Toiletries	£_____
Laundry	£_____

Bills

Telephone (home)	£_____
Mobile	£_____
Pension	£_____
Life insurance	£_____

Entertainment

Meals out	£_____
Pubs and bars	£_____
Internet connection	£_____
Books	£_____
Newspapers & magazines	£_____
CDs/music	£_____
Cinema	£_____
Sports	£_____

Sport-related

Clothing	£_____
Footwear	£_____
Equipment	£_____
Travel costs	£_____
Competition costs	£_____
Physiotherapy	£_____
Massage	£_____
Total	£_____

Pensions

When you plan your finances you need to consider the future and what will happen when you are 65 and retire from all work. It is advisable to have a private pension and to put a portion of your income into the pension each month. This accumulates interest and will pay you a monthly income when you retire.

Key learning points

- 'A goal is what an individual is trying to achieve. It is the object or aim of an action.'
  - Short-term goals are set over a period of time that might be between one day and one month.
  - Medium-term goals cover a period of between one to six months.
  - Long-term goals run from six months to several years but are usually set for a year or a competitive season.
- Having completed their sporting career, athletes have a choice of occupations they can enter: sports coach, sports teacher, journalist, sports development officer, physiotherapist, sports scientist.
- Financial management: athletes should save money, pay tax on money earned if self-employed and contribute regularly to a pension plan.

Activity 12.5   15 mins P6

Financial issues

Using the following table, describe three financial issues an athlete needs to consider.

Financial issue	Description
Income	E.g. The athlete needs to develop as many sources of income as he or she can. For example, from private work, sponsorship or grants
Expenditure	
Taxation	

12.4 Preparing for and Participating in a Media Interview

The huge increase in the amount of sport that has been covered by the media over the last 20 years has meant that sports performers are more likely to have a media profile and need to be prepared to act confidently when they are interviewed for television, the radio or newspapers. Communicating with media professionals is a skill that can be learnt and developed and is often a part of a sports performers' education. This section looks at a range of communication skills before specifically looking at how to deal with the media.

Communication is important for the following reasons:

- It is essential to the development of any relationship

- It is needed to convey our thoughts and knowledge to other people

- It is the basis of developing understanding and rapport

Forms of Communication

Communication is done in two ways:

1. Verbally – talking, giving commands, asking questions, explaining.

2. Non-verbally – body language, gestures, listening.

Verbal Communication

Communication is a two-way process and in any situation involving verbal communication we will have three components: a sender, a receiver and a message. The sender puts their thoughts and feelings into words and the receiver will interpret these words to find the meaning of the message. Communication is difficult because everyone gives different meanings to words and interprets messages in different ways. To understand someone we need to use questions.

Non-verbal communication

Body language is an important component of communication and helps to develop a relationship. People tend to like people who are like them and you will notice that people who get on will copy each other's body position. This is a good rule to follow – copy a person's body position in terms of whether they are sitting forward, back or to the side. Also, give them as much eye contact as they give you and, if they smile a lot, then you should smile a lot too. Gestures are important to people as well. If they use gestures, then use the same gestures back to them. They will not notice you are doing this and it will help to build rapport. Above all, it is important to listen to what someone is saying.

Asking Questions

Questions broadly come in two types: open and closed.

An open question is used to find out more information from someone and will begin with words such as:

Why   What
How   When
Where

Closed questions are used to make a situation clear and can be answered 'Yes' or 'No'.

Active listening

It is easy to pretend you are listening but much more difficult to really listen. To show that you are listening you can use the following skills:

1. Show you are giving undivided attention by maintaining eye contact. Look away occasionally and do not stare.

2. If you lean forward slightly it will encourage the other person to talk, as will smiling occasionally and nodding your head.

3. Ask open-ended questions to help them to talk.

4. If you are unclear about what is being said, then check your understanding.

5. Summarise occasionally to show you understand and this will help you to keep listening.

How not to listen

All of the following will show you are not listening and do not care:

1. Showing signs of boredom or impatience.

2. Being condescending or patronising.

3. Passing judgement or laughing inappropriately.

4. Talking too much.

5. Using distracting body gestures or fiddling with paper or pens.

6. Interrupting.

7. Not giving a person time to answer a question.

Extracting Key Points from Written Materials

Reading efficiently is a great skill to have, as it will save lots of time. We read for different purposes; for example, we may read a novel from cover to cover and let the story take us where it is going. Or we read to pick out relevant details and information.

There are the following different reading styles:

- Skimming
- Scanning
- Searching.

Skimming

This involves going through a text at two or three times normal reading speed and focusing on the introduction, conclusion, first line and first paragraph. This type of reading gives us a flavour of the text to see if we want to buy it or read it in full.

Scanning

This is done when you are looking for information such as an address or a topic from a glossary or index.

Searching

This is done when you know what you are looking for. It involves you picking out key words or phrases to find the relevant information.

Activity 12.6 30 mins   P7   P5

Communication skills

Consider the scenario that you are explaining to an athlete the skills they need communicate with other people and work effectively with others. Choose the four most important skills.

Skill	Description	Explanation
E.g. Body language	The amount of eye contact we use and posture we hold give messages to the person we are communicating with	Eye contact can show that we are interested in what the other person is saying and are concentrating on them. Our posture can be open to show we trust the other person or closed to show we are not really interested
Listening skills		
Verbal skills		
Asking questions		

Working effectively with others

An athlete does not operate alone and must be prepared to communicate with a network of people. These will include coaching staff, managers, advisers, fellow athletes and media professionals.

These different groups of people will require different things from the athlete and communication must be done in different ways.

Media

The term 'media' relates to all groups of people responsible for reporting action and events to the general public. Significantly, all events can be distorted to meet the ends of any group of people, as all events can be looked at in more than one way. Likewise, the words an individual uses can be interpreted in many different ways.

The media come in many different forms. Currently sporting events are reported through these different media:

● Newspapers

● Television

● Radio

● Internet

● Magazines

● Teletext services.

Planning for Media Interviews P8 M6 D3

A media interview can take many forms and may be seen on television, heard on radio or read in a newspaper. However, all interviews will have a common purpose, and that is:

● To gain information from a person to be shared with other people.

An interview is done to find out information at different times and it is important that the athlete is clear on what the purpose will be. It may be any of the following:

● To talk about success

● To talk about failure

● To talk about an issue or problem

● To talk about a forthcoming event.

Preparation

The athlete must prepare for the interview and they should consider the following:

● What questions may I be asked?

● How should I respond to these questions?

● How much should I give away and how much should I conceal?

● How would the public expect me to be dressed?

● Whose help or advice do I need?

Delivery of the Interview

Once in the interview it is important to consider all aspects of your presentation:

● **Body language** – although we present most of our body language without thinking, we can be aware of the way we look and what this says about us. To present a confident image, you need to sit in an upright posture with your shoulders pulled back but in a relaxed way. Your facial expressions should be relaxed and your hands should be held in front of you. Crossing your arms or legs suggests that you feel insecure or uncomfortable; as do fidgeting and moving around. If you are standing up, you should hold an upright and relaxed posture with your shoulders pulled back.

● **Answering questions** – when a question is being asked be sure to concentrate on the question and what is being asked. Once the question has been asked, then consider your reply before answering. If you are unclear about what the question is asking, then get clarification before carrying on. If you are thinking of your answer as you are being asked the question, you may miss important information. When you answer, make sure that you speak slowly and clearly, and that you choose your words well.

(k) Key learning points

- To develop a relationship with anyone we must be able to communicate accurately and clearly.
- Communication is done in two ways: verbally and non-verbally.
  - Verbal communication includes talking, giving commands, asking questions and explaining.
  - Non-verbal communication includes body language, gestures and listening.
- The term 'media' relates to all groups of people responsible for reporting action and events to the general public. The media come in many different forms including newspapers, television, radio, the Internet, magazines and teletext services.

Activity **12.7** 60 mins **P8**

Preparing for a media interview

Task

(a) Prepare a list of questions that you might be asked during a media interview.

(b) Describe the strengths and areas for improvement in your own communication skills.

(c) Present the recommendations you would make to improve your communication skills.

Activity **12.8** 30 mins **P1** **M1**

Managing your own time

Complete the following questions showing how you use your time currently and then complete the second part to show a plan for your work commitments and leisure time

Part 1

(a) How long do you currently spend on each of these activities?

Sleeping.................................. 8 hours

Eating and cooking................... 2 hours

Personal hygiene...................... 45 minutes

Other...

(b) How long do you currently spend on work-related activities?

Training............................... 2 hours

Travel................................. 1 hour

Recovery... 1 hour

Attending lectures......................... 5 hours

Travel to college............................ 1 hour

Studying.. 2 hours

Paid work..

(c) How much time have you got left? How do you going to spend that?

.... 1 hour and 15 minutes

.... Reading/watching TV/socialising

....

Part 2

Take a typical 24-hour period and plan hour by hour how you will be spending your time.

Activity 12.8 continued

Part 3

To achieve a merit explain how the time plan, including work and leisure activities, has been planned.

7 a.m.	8 a.m.	9 a.m.	10 a.m.	11 a.m.	12 p.m.	1 p.m.	2 p.m.	3 p.m.	4 p.m.	5 p.m.	6 p.m.
Sleep	Breakfast Travel to college	Lectures	Lectures	Lectures	Lunch	Lectures	Lectures	Travel	Rest	Training	Training

7 p.m.	8 p.m.	9 p.m.	10 p.m.	11 p.m.	12 a.m.	1 a.m.	2 a.m.	3 a.m.	4 a.m.	5 a.m.	6 a.m.
Dinner	Studying	Studying	Reading, watching TV Socialising	Washing	Sleep	Sleep	Sleep	Sleep	Sleep	Sleep	Sleep

Further Reading

Fyfe, L., 1998, *Careers in Sport*. London: Kogan Page.

Masters, J., 2007, *Working in Sport: How to Find a Sports Related Job in the UK or Abroad*. Oxford: How to Books Ltd.

Useful websites

www.isrm.co.uk/

National body for professionals involved in providing, managing, operating and developing sport and recreation services in the UK, offering up-to-date industry news, information on qualifications, careers advice and current vacancies.

www.skillsactive.com/sportrec

Provides video presentation about the importance of skills and training in the sport and recreation industry, and gives extensive links to a wide range of sports bodies that can offer training, qualifications or opportunities to work.

Chapter 13
Work Experience in the Sports Industry

The majority of people studying for the Level 2 BTEC in Sport plan to embark on a career in the sports industry. There is a huge variety of jobs in this sector, so it is vital for you to be aware of the range of occupations available and to gain first-hand experience of what your chosen job entails. Not only will this give you a better picture of what is expected from you in your career of choice, it will also demonstrate your commitment to future employers.

This chapter gives you information that will allow you to plan and carry out a practical work-based project within the sports industry.

Learning Goals

By the end of this chapter you should:

- Know the range and scope of organisations and occupations within the sports industry.
- Be able to use relevant documents and skills relating to sport-based work experience.
- Be able to plan and carry out a project during sport-based work experience.
- Be able to present and review the project.

To achieve a PASS grade the evidence must show that the learner is able to:	To achieve a MERIT grade the evidence must show that, in addition to the pass criteria, the learner is able to:	To achieve a DISTINCTION grade the evidence must show that, in addition to the pass and merit criteria, the learner is able to:
P1 describe three different types of organisation within the sports industry, giving examples		
P2 describe three different occupations within the sports industry and the skills that each require	**M1** explain the skills required for three different occupations within the sports industry	
P3 locate three advertisements for jobs from different sources available within the sports industry	**M2** use advertisements for jobs available in sport to identify appropriate work experience in the sports industry	
P4 produce an application for work experience in sport	**M3** explain own personal skills and qualities in relation to those required for an occupation in sport	**D1** evaluate own personal skills and qualities in relation to those required for an occupation in sport
P5 prepare for an interview for work experience in sport		
P6 undertake an interview for work experience in sport		
P7 plan a project, related to a theme, for work experience in sport		
P8 undertake a project during work-based experience in sport		
P9 present the project, describing the benefits and identifying areas for improvement	**M4** present the project, explaining the benefits and making recommendations for improvement	**D2** present the project, evaluating the benefits and justifying recommendations relating to identified areas for improvement

13.1 Organisations within the Sports Industry P1

There is a range of organisations that provide places for sports participation; these can be broken down into three different sectors (see Figure 13.1).

Figure 13.1   Sports provision

The Public Sector

The public sector is defined as institutions funded by money collected from the public in the form of direct taxes and indirect taxes, and also the national lottery.

The public sector is made up of national government and local government (or local authorities). Public-sector facilities are provided for by local authorities with the aim of offering people a positive activity to do in their leisure time. These facilities often do not make a profit as they charge minimal prices to encourage participation. The public sector has a role as an 'enabler', and the main recipient is Sport England.

The Private Sector

Private-sector sport is provided by individuals or groups of individuals (companies) who invest their own money in facilities. As a result these facilities are usually named after people, such as the David Lloyd clubs, although some have a brand name, such as Virgin Active or Cannons.

The private sector provides sports facilities for two main reasons:

1. To make a return on their investment for themselves and their shareholders.

2. To make a profit out of sport.

The private sector provides for sports that are increasing in demand. The areas the private sector is involved in are:

- Active sports – tennis, golf, health and fitness suites, snooker and pool, water sports and tenpin bowling.

- Spectator sport – stadiums for football, rugby, cricket, tennis, golf; football is by far the most popular spectator sport.

- Sponsorship – sponsoring well-known sports personalities so that they wear and advertise branded products and sports goods.

The Voluntary Sector

The voluntary sector is made up of clubs that operate as non-profit-making organisations, and which are essentially managed by and for amateur sportsmen and women.

Most amateur clubs are run on a voluntary basis. Some voluntary clubs own facilities, but the majority hire facilities, usually provided by the public sector.

Most clubs, such as football and athletics clubs that people join to enable them to participate in competitive sport, are in the voluntary sector. Voluntary-sector clubs often work in partnership with the private or public sector; for example they use public-sector facilities or gain sponsorship from the private sector (for example in the evening you may find the swimming pool at your leisure centre being used for swimming club or kayaking club training sessions).

Funding of Voluntary Clubs

The voluntary sector is funded primarily by its members in the form of subscriptions. Every club will have an annual subscription fee and match fees. These are to cover the costs of playing, travel and equipment. Money can be raised from sponsorship, applying for national lottery grants, applying for a grant from the government or local authority, or running fund-raising events.

Partnerships

Partnerships occur when two or more of the sectors come together to provide opportunities for sport. We have already seen how the public sector often rents out its facilities to the voluntary sector to give them an opportunity to play sports. Sponsorship, which is primarily provided by the private sector, is also given to the public and voluntary sectors.

Sports facilities are also built as partnerships. For example the new English National Stadium at Wembley is a private-sector initiative by Wembley plc; however, they have received a national lottery grant from the public sector. They will also go into partnership with other private-sector organisations to raise finance and gain sponsorship.

Dual use is where two organisations use the facility. An example of this would be where a school has use of a leisure centre's sports facilities in the daytime and then local clubs and fitness classes use it when the school is closed in the evenings, weekends and school holidays.

Joint use is where a school has purpose-built sports provision that is used by both the school and the local community.

Activity **13.1** 30 mins P1

Organisations within the sports industry

Task 1

Using the internet and other suitable reference materials, for example local papers, Yellow Pages etc., select three different organisations within the sports industry, each from a different sector:

- Public
- Private
- Voluntary.

Name each organisation and provide a description about how it is used, who uses it and how the organisation is funded.

13.2 Occupations within the Sports Industry P2

There is a huge range of jobs available in the sports industry, from sports massage therapist to mountain leader. In order to gain the skills and qualifications you require, you may need to continue your studies to a higher level or complete a part-time course. The following list gives a range of different jobs available in the sports industry, but is by no means exhaustive:

- Fitness instructor
- Leisure attendant
- Sports centre manager
- Kayak instructor
- Sports coach
- Sports development officer
- Sports/PE teacher
- Professional sports performer
- Sports massage therapist
- Sports nutritionist
- Sport psychologist
- Sports retailer.

Fitness Instructor

This job involves assessing people's fitness levels, designing their exercise programmes and instructing these programmes in the gym. Fitness instructors may also teach aerobics classes and circuit classes, and supervise people in the gym.

Skills and Qualifications

Instructors need sound anatomy and physiology knowledge gained from a sport science course, and also a recognised fitness instructor's award from a training organisation such as Premier Training International, YMCA or Focus. To teach specific skills such as aerobics, circuits or stability ball work, extra qualifications are required. First aid and cardio-pulmonary resuscitation (CPR) qualifications are also essential. Instructors must have good communication skills, be friendly and be able to remain calm under pressure.

Leisure Attendant

Leisure attendants are responsible for preparing and supervising the sports hall, swimming pool and changing rooms in a leisure facility. Most leisure attendants will also be involved in coaching or supervising sports sessions in their sports hall.

Skills and Qualifications

A sports qualification is desirable but not essential; however, the National Pool Lifeguard Qualification is compulsory in order to work poolside. In order to coach sports, leisure attendants need specific national governing body coaching awards. Leisure attendants need to be outgoing and people-oriented. Communication skills are important, as you may have to deal with a range of people.

Sports Centre Manager

Managing a sports centre involves some of the following activities: managing and motivating staff; programming facilities and organising activities; establishing systems and procedures; preparing and managing budgets; monitoring sales and usage; marketing and promoting the centre; dealing with members and any complaints or incidents.

Skills and Qualifications

Managers may have been promoted into this position having qualified with a BTEC First or National Diploma or GNVQ. Most managers will hold higher-level qualifications such as a degree or HND in leisure management or business studies. To be an effective manager you need the following personal qualities:

confidence, enthusiasm, assertiveness, communication skills, self-motivation, presence and professionalism.

Kayak Instructor

A kayak instructor will usually be qualified in a range of outdoor pursuits and work at an outdoor pursuits centre. The role involves checking equipment, ensuring weather conditions are appropriate and then teaching a range of abilities on to how to kayak safely and effectively.

Skills and Qualifications

You will have to have a high level of personal proficiency (3-star minimum) and then attend an instructor training course. You will also need to be qualified in rescue skills and first aid. You must have good communication skills, be able to withstand cold and wet working conditions and also have very good safety awareness.

Sports Coach

Sports coaches are usually former or current competitors in their sport. They are responsible for developing the physical fitness and skills of their athletes. They need to be able to evaluate their athletes' performances and offer feedback to improve their performances. As a result they will require knowledge of many aspects of sport science, such as anatomy and physiology, biomechanics, nutrition, psychology and sports injury.

Skills and Qualifications

Every sport will have its own system for awarding coaching qualifications, and coaches must hold the relevant award. Many coaches also hold qualifications in sport or sport science.

Coaches need to be able to motivate athletes and gain their trust. They need to be good communicators and listeners, and be able to show patience and empathy towards their athletes.

Sports Development Officer

A sports development officer works to increase participation rates in sport and provide opportunities for people to play sport in a local area. They work for local authorities and may have responsibility for specific groups of people, such as ethnic minorities, women or disabled people.

Skills and Qualifications

Most sports development officers have at least a BTEC National in sport or sports science and usually also hold a degree or HND in sport, sport science or leisure management, along with a range of coaching qualifications. You need an interest in and knowledge of a range of sports and the needs of a community. You have to be able to communicate with people from different backgrounds and be sensitive to their needs. Good leadership, motivational skills and an organised approach to work are also necessary.

PE Teacher or Lecturer

You can teach PE in schools to children from the age of five to 18 years; if you choose the younger children you will also usually have to teach a range of other subjects from the National Curriculum. If you teach PE in a secondary school, this will usually be the only subject you will be required to teach. A lecturer teaches in a college or university and usually specialises in a few subject areas such as physiology or psychology.

Skills and Qualifications

A teacher needs to be educated to degree level and to be qualified as a teacher. There are two ways to do this: first, to take a four-year teaching degree such as a Bachelor of Education (BEd) or a Bachelor of Arts with Qualified Teaching Status (BA (QTS)); or to take a three-year degree in sport science or sport studies and then complete a one-year Postgraduate Certificate in Education (PGCE). It is important to note that in order to be a teacher you must have passed English, maths and a science at GCSE grade C or above and have passed at least two A levels.

Teaching is a very demanding profession and you need to be patient and able to deal with young people and their various needs. Teachers need to be organised, maintain discipline and be able to adapt their communication skills to the group they are teaching. You should also have a good level of personal fitness and enjoy working with young people.

Professional Sports Performer

Ultimately the goal of every sports performer would be to play their sport full time at a professional level. However, it is only the most talented who get this opportunity and there is only a limited number of sports where you can play professionally. Football, cricket, rugby league, rugby union and golf have the largest number of professional players. However, most professional players have to have a second job to ensure their income.

Skills and Qualifications

No formal qualifications are needed, although you need to investigate the best route into a sport, as every sport will be slightly different in terms of the way it recruits young players.

Technical efficiency at the chosen sport, along with physical fitness, are the most important assets; however, self-motivation, commitment and determination will also be needed.

Sport Psychologist

A sport psychologist is involved in mentally preparing athletes for competition. It is a varied job that will differ depending on the individual needs of performers. A psychologist will be involved in helping teams and individuals set goals for the short and long term, learn strategies to control arousal levels and stay relaxed in stressful situations. They are also often involved in lecturing and conducting research, as well as actually practising their skills.

Skills and Qualifications

A sport psychologist will usually be a graduate or sport scientist who has then completed post-graduate training. This would involve a Master's degree or a PhD in sport psychology.

Psychologists need to have good listening and interviewing skills in order to assess the needs of their athletes and to develop strategies to help them. A psychologist should be able to build up a relationship of trust and be seen as someone whom the athlete can talk to confidentially.

Sports Retailer

Sports retail involves working in a sports shop, selling sports goods. This can involve using your knowledge of sport and matching a client's needs to specific products. For example different types of runners will require different types of running shoes and you will need to be able to identify which shoes they need.

Skills and Qualifications

A knowledge of sport is needed, but many people working in retail will need business skills and customer care skills. A BTEC in business studies or leisure studies would be appropriate. If you have aspirations to run a sports shop, it may be necessary to hold an HND or degree in a management-based subject.

This work will require an ability to deal with members of the public and be willing to meet their needs as necessary. You must be good at communicating and be able to stay calm under pressure.

Key learning points

- The three different sectors that provide sports facilities are public, private and voluntary.
- Dual and joint use is where organisations share the facilities.
- There are many different occupations in the sports industry – it is important to find out the skills required for each job to find out if it would be suitable for you.

Activity 13.2 60 mins   P2

Occupations within the sports industry   M1

Task 1

Have a think about three different occupations in the sports industry that you would be interested in pursuing. Make a note of all three.

Task 2

Using the internet, textbooks or other suitable reference materials, carry out research to find out more about your three selected occupations.

Task 3

Produce a leaflet that describes and explains the three different occupations that you have researched and include details on the skills required for each.

13.3 Sources of Information on Jobs in the Sports Industry P3 M2

The following are good sources of job advertisements:

- Local newspapers
- Regional newspapers
- National newspapers
- Job and careers centres
- Trade publications
- Recruitment agencies
- Direct contact with employers
- Word of mouth
- The internet
- Skills Active.

Quick Quiz 1   ⏱ 10 mins   ❓

| David Lloyd | Public sector | Pool lifeguard | Private sector |
| PE teacher | Youth football club | Dual use |

Choose a word(s) from the boxes above to answer the following questions.

1. **This type of sector tries to make a profit out of sport.**
2. **A public swimming pool is an example of a facility from this sector.**
3. **This sort of job requires shift work.**
4. **This is an example of a sports centre in the private sector.**
5. **This is an example of a voluntary organisation.**
6. **You would need a degree to go into this profession.**
7. **An example of this would be where a school has use of a leisure centre's sports facilities in the daytime, and then local clubs and fitness classes use it when the school is closed in the evenings.**
8. **A person entering this job would need to have a lot of hiking experience and appropriate qualifications.**

Useful websites   Ⓦ

www.ispal.org.uk/info_hub.cfm

Provides information sheets, career advice, self-development and other training courses invaluable for people working in the sports, leisure and recreation industries in the UK (subscription membership required for full access).

www.leisurejobs.com/

Provides an extensive job search facility for vacancies in the sports, fitness and leisure industries, together with practical advice on the most effective way of putting together your job application.

The internet is an excellent source of jobs in sport and the websites are regularly updated. Some useful websites are given here.

Trade publications are also an excellent source and they should be available in your college library. The following are particularly worth looking at:

- *Leisure Management and Leisure Opportunities*
- *Leisure News and Jobs*
- *All Sport and Leisure Monthly*
- *Health and Fitness*
- *Institute of Leisure and Amenity Management (ILAM).*

Activity 13.3   ⏱ 45–60 mins   P3   M2

Finding and using job advertisements in the sports industry

Task 1

Using a range of different sources, local papers, internet sites etc., complete the table below by finding three different adverts, each from different sources, for different jobs that are available in the sports industry that you are interested in.

Name of job	Source

Task 2

Take a photocopy or a print out of each advert.

Task 3

Write a paragraph for each job advert to show how it would be an appropriate place for you to carry out work experience.

13.4 Applying for a Job (P3) (M3) (D1)

To apply for work you need to use a suitable method to approach a prospective employer. Most job advertisements will specify which method you should use. There are three main methods that you may be asked to use:

1. **Curriculum vitae (CV)** – a concise, written document that summarises your skills, qualifications and experience to date for a prospective employer. It needs to be accompanied by a covering letter.

2. **Application form** – some jobs will not accept a CV and will ask you to complete a pre-designed application form asking you to show why you are suitable for the job. This also needs to be accompanied by a covering letter.

3. **Letter of application** – some jobs will require you to apply in writing. The information will be similar to that of a CV, but presented in a different format.

Curriculum Vitae (CV)

A CV is used for a range of reasons:

● To demonstrate your value to the employer

● As a marketing tool to get an interview

● To sell yourself to the employer.

There are three main styles of CV:

1. **Chronological** – this is the most common format and involves you presenting your experiences of education and work in date order.

2. **Functional** – this type of CV highlights your skills and is directed towards a certain career. For example you may be qualified in more than one subject, but you would only highlight the skills that are relevant for the type of work you are trying to gain.

3. **Targeted** – this type of CV emphasises skills and abilities relevant to a specific job or company. It is tailor-made for one job. You would examine the job specification and then adapt your CV to show how you meet the desired criteria for the job.

A CV needs to be prepared very carefully and should be wordprocessed.

Content of a CV

1. **Personal details** – full name and address, home telephone number and mobile number, email address and date of birth.

2. **Current position and current employment** – if you are employed, state your position and your main responsibilities.

3. **Key personal skills** – highlight your main personal skills, attributes and abilities.

4. **Education and qualifications** – state the names and dates of all academic qualifications received, with the most recent first.

5. **Training or work-related qualifications/ courses** – include all coaching awards, first aid certificates etc. and any additional vocational or on-the-job training you have received.

6. **Previous employment** – state all the past employment including work placements, voluntary work and part-time work you have had, with the following information: name of employer, job title and a brief summary of responsibilities.

7. **Leisure interests** – here is an opportunity to show the interests you have outside the academic environment. State the sports you play and at what level (it may be appropriate to list some of your achievements in sport), and other hobbies and activities in which you are involved. It is particularly good to state any positions of responsibility you have held, such as club captain, scout leader or cadet force rank.

8. **Other relevant information** – anything else you feel may be of value to the employer, such as an ability to drive.

9. **References** – give the names, addresses and phone numbers of two people who can vouch for you. If you have a current employer, they should be the first; if not, a past employer or someone else in a position of responsibility, such as a teacher, would be appropriate. It is important that you ask them before using them as a referee in case they are not willing to write you a reference.

Activity 13.4   30–60 mins   P4

Preparing your own CV

Task 1

Make a list of all your:

- qualifications
- key personnal skills
- work experience
- leisure interests /hobbies.

Task 2

Using the information in task 1 and the details in the list under 'Content of a CV', use a computer to wordprocess your own CV.

Filling in an Application Form P4

Many employers will produce their own application form, which you need to fill in when applying for a position. They will use this form to select the candidates they wish to interview. Forms that are completed incorrectly or untidily will probably be discarded without being read.

Here are some useful tips on completing the form:

- Photocopy the form first and use the copy to practise on.

- Read the instructions on the form carefully and follow them exactly, for example it may ask you to use black ink or block capitals.

- Even if some of the information on the form is given in the covering letter, you must still include it on the form. Never write 'refer to CV', as the reader may not bother.

- Check that your referees are willing to provide a reference for you before putting in their details.

- Take a photocopy of your completed form so that you can remind yourself what you have written.

- Make sure you do not miss the closing date, and post the form well in advance.

- Include a covering letter with your application form.

Letter of Application

A letter of application relates your experience to a specific company or job vacancy; it should always be sent with a CV and perhaps an application form. It should be businesslike and complement the information in your CV. If you are writing in response to an advertisement, refer to the job title and where you saw the vacancy advertised, and ensure the letter is addressed to the correct person. Indicate why you are attracted to the position advertised, and highlight why you think you are suitable and what key personal skills and experiences you have that are relevant to the vacancy. Finish the letter by stating that you look forward to hearing from them soon and would be delighted to attend an interview at their convenience.

Activity 13.5   40–60 mins   P4   M3   D1

Producing an application for a work experience placement

When you have found an organisation or company in sport where you would like to go for your work placement, you will need to prepare and produce an application.

Task 1

Using a computer, produce an application for a work placement of your choice.

Task 2

In your application, explain and evaluate your own personal skills and qualities – for example communication skills, time management, ability to work as a member of a team, ability to lead a team etc. – and then relate each to the job that you are applying for. For example if you were applying for the job of leisure centre assistant, good teamwork skills will be useful because the job role requires you to work as member of a team – putting up and taking down sports equipment, cleaning the premises etc.

Activity 13.6 60 mins

P4 M3 D3

What is an employer looking for from a job application?

Case Study

Name: David Oldham
Age: 38
Position: Leisure Centre Manager

What annoys you the most from job applications and interviews?

I don't like it when you interview people who haven't bothered to find out anything about the organisation. I also get very annoyed by interviewees who arrive late without a good reason. How people dress is very important too. If I have an interviewee turn up in jeans it shows that they are not too bothered about making a good first impression – the whole aim of an interview is so that the interviewee can try to show me that they want the job!

What is your top tip for people who are applying for a job?

Make sure your CV is up to date and not too long – two sides of A4 is usually the maximum that I would expect. If a person does have an invitation to an interview then it is a good idea to try to learn around four to five things about the organisation and job role, and dress smartly.

What is your favourite interview question?

I've interviewed many people for this role, why should I choose you?

What sort of things do you want your interviewee to discuss in an interview?

I want to hear about their personal skills and qualities and then evidence to show how they have put these skills and qualities to good use! There's not much point telling me that they are good communicators or good at working as a member of a team if they have no way of showing me that they have done this in the past and done well at it.

Task 1

From reading the case study above, list five ways in which you could prepare yourself for an interview.

Task 2

Think of an organisation where you might like to work. Research and list five things about that organisation that you could use to discuss in an interview.

Task 3

How would you answer the interview question: 'I've interviewed many people for this role, why should I choose you?'

Task 4

Make a list of four of your skills and five of your qualities. Now write a sentence for each to describe where each skill or quality has been used in a real-life situation.

Task 5

What would you plan to wear for an interview?

Preparation for Interview P5

One of the most important aspects of an interview is the preparation that takes place beforehand. Learn all you can about the company and the job role. This can be done via the internet; it is even better if you actually visit the workplace. During this visit, not only will you have worked out how to get there, you will also see how people dress, exactly what facilities are available and even ask some of the staff questions.

Questions

You should think about which questions you are likely to be asked, for example 'Why are you interested in this job? What are your strengths? What are your weaknesses? What do you think this job entails? Why do you think you will be good at this job?' Once you have worked out suitable answers, practise delivering them out loud, either with a friend or in front of a mirror. You may wish to record yourself with a camcorder and then see or hear yourself 'in action' and make improvements where necessary. You should also study your body language, which includes your facial expressions, mannerisms and gestures. If you smile and look enthusiastic, this will portray the right image. However, you may find that you slouch or have a blank facial expression without even being aware of it while answering questions.

Be prepared to discuss anything you have written on your CV or letter of application. For example you may be asked why you decided to study for a First Diploma in sport or to explain your choice of work placement etc.

You should also prepare questions to ask the interviewers, as this will show the interviewer that you are interested and want to know more about the company or job role – however, be sure not to ask questions that have already been answered within the job role specifications or during the course of the interview.

Dress

You will need to decide what you are going to wear well in advance of the interview. If you are not sure what to wear, it is best to choose smart dark-coloured clothes such as a suit or smart trousers or skirt and a shirt/blouse. Clothing that is too tight or revealing is rarely acceptable attire for an interview. Ensure that your clothes are clean and ironed and also comfortable. Ensure that your hair is clean and you have a suitable haircut or style for the interview. If you have lots of visible body piercings, you may wish to take some out in order to portray the image you think the company is looking for.

Location

If possible, visit the place you are going to for interview beforehand. Travel at the same time of day at which you will be leaving for your interview so that you can see if there are any issues with rush hour traffic etc. You should always plan to arrive at your interview location at least ten minutes in advance in order to allow time to compose yourself.

Interview Skills

Body Language

Body language can say an awful lot about how we feel, how confident we are and how enthusiastic we are, and people will often form a first impression about someone based upon their body language alone. Therefore, it is important to convey the right message by using appropriate body language:

- Greet your interviewer with a firm handshake.

- Maintain eye contact – this shows that you are interested in what the person has to say; however, you should not overdo the eye contact as this can sometimes look threatening.

- When answering questions, emphasise key points by leaning forward and using expressive gestures.

- Speak with an expressive voice to convey your enthusiasm and interest rather than a monotone voice that suggests a lack of interest and boredom.

- You should sit with your back straight, as this communicates self-assurance and eagerness; do not slouch, as this gives the impression that you are not interested or are lacking in confidence.

- Do not fidget or twiddle your fingers while the interviewer is talking, as this suggests you are not paying attention.

- When the interviewer is talking, nod your head and smile in relevant places to demonstrate your interest in what they are saying.

Answering Questions

You will have rehearsed many of the answers that you give during the interview and therefore know what you need to say and how to say it. However, you will undoubtedly be faced with a few questions that you have not prepared for. Give yourself a few seconds to sit and think about your answer and then respond honestly and as positively as possible. If you do not understand the question, ask the interviewer to repeat it. If you still do not understand the question, you can respond in a variety of ways; here are two examples:

1. Say 'Do you mean…?' This shows that you understand some of what they said but need clarity.

2. Ask them to explain their question in more detail.

Activity 13.8   30–60 mins   P6

Undertake an interview for work experience

This activity could be carried out for 'real' with your potential work placement supervisor or simulated with your teacher.

Task 1

(a) Ensure your CV and job application form (if required) are ready and that you are dressed appropriately.
(b) Greet your interviewer appropriately.
(c) Answer questions from the interviewer as fully as you can.
(d) Ensure you are portraying the right image with your body language and the way in which you speak.

Your teacher or work placement supervisor will then complete an observation record to assess your interview performance.

Activity 13.7   45–60 mins   P5

Preparing for an interview

Imagine you are having an interview for a job of your choice.

Task 1

With a partner, carry out a role-play interview.

Before the interview, try to ensure you are:

- dressed appropriately
- have completed a CV and application for the job of your choice.

During the interview, remember to:

- ensure you are giving the right signals from your body language
- speak clearly
- make eye contact with the interviewer.

The interviewer will need a copy of your CV and will ask appropriate questions relating to your CV and the job role.

After the interview, the interviewer should then give you feedback as to what they thought was good and which areas need to be improved.

Task 2

Carry out research to find out where your real interview will take place. Work out which method of transport you are going to use to get there that will get you there with time to spare. Remember, if you are travelling in rush hour, a journey that usually only takes ten minutes outside of rush hour can take a lot longer in the rush hour.

Key learning points

- Use a range of different sources to find out about jobs such as the internet, journals and local newspapers.
- Ensure your CV is well presented and is no more than two pages long.
- Ensure you fully prepare yourself for an interview, taking into account how you will get there, what sort of questions you may be asked and ensuring you speak clearly and use appropriate body language.

Quick Quiz 2 10 mins ❓

Answer the following statements with either True or False.

1. A CV is a concise, written document that summarises your skills, qualifications and experience to date.
2. You can wear whatever you want to an interview.
3. A letter of application is similar to a CV, but presented in a different format.
4. In an interview it is OK to slouch or rock back on your chair while answering questions.
5. You should always plan your route to get to where you are having your interview.
6. You should think about which questions you are likely to be asked before your interview.
7. The following are good sources of job advertisements: *Heat* magazine, *Cosmopolitan* and *Match*.
8. Greet your interviewer with a firm handshake.
9. Most CVs are written by hand rather than typed up.
10. It's a good idea to try to find out something about the company that you are going to go to for an interview.

Planning Your Work-Placement Project P7

The hardest part of the project is getting started. Thinking of a good idea takes time and effort. On the first day, or before you start your placement, you should discuss your thoughts for your project with your employer, because they may have a project with which they need help, and this may be beneficial to both of you. Here are some ideas:

- Conduct a study into gym or club usage – when is it heaviest and why?
- Conduct a study into the local competitors in the area.
- Take an area of the outdoor pursuits centre that is underachieving and develop a proposal for how to improve its performance.
- Survey members' attitudes to certain aspects of the club, such as the equipment in the gym.
- Help to organise a social event or a competition in your work placement.

The main things you need to take into consideration are:

1. What do I find interesting and would like to research?
2. What does my employer want me to investigate?
3. Do I have access to the right people or tools to carry out my research?

Aims and Objectives

The aim or objective of the research is vital – without a clear aim the research has no guidance.

Definition

Aim something that a person is expected to do in order to learn from it.

Objective what a person is expected to know and be able to do after having completed an activity/project.

This is an area that people undertaking research projects regularly have difficulty with. They often have a general idea for a project, for example assessing how the sports facility could be improved, but not a specific objective. Using this example, what exactly would you find out? Whom would you get the information from? The topic is too general; it needs to be focused on one particular aspect of the leisure facility; for example do the exercise classes cater for all the local population? Does the gym equipment work out all the major muscle groups? Are there enough swimming classes for all ages and abilities within the local population?

These projects are much clearer; you know exactly what you are trying to measure and the group of people or resources you will need to examine in order to answer your questions.

Sources of Information

Once you have decided on your project's aims and objectives, you then need to explore how you are going to find out the required information.

There are many methods of obtaining information. Here are a few ideas:

- Libraries
- The internet
- Local council
- Questioning the people who attend the sports facility
- Questioning the other staff in the sports facility.

Arrangements

While deciding where you would like to carry out your project, you should also include in your decision-making the locality of the placement. If the sports facility is not within walking distance how are you going to get there? You will need to investigate methods of public transport and look at the cost and travel times. If the facility is too far away from home for you to travel to every day then you will have to see if the facility provides staff accommodation and if it would be available to you. Alternatively, you may have family living near to your chosen facility and be able to stay with them for the duration of the placement.

Placement Requirements

You will need to speak to your supervisor before the placement in order to see if you need to provide your own clothing and, if so, what is required. Most leisure centres provide their staff with a uniform; however outdoor pursuits centre staff usually provide their own clothing. This could be quite expensive if you do not have any of your own already. It may be worth asking your supervisor if they have any kit you could borrow for the duration of the placement.

Any equipment you require will usually be provided, for example a whistle for a lifeguard, but again, it is worth asking your supervisor if you will need to buy anything and check that you can afford it prior to your placement.

Information on Your Placement Provider

Find out which sector your placement provider belongs to; it may be public, private, voluntary, a partnership, joint usage or dual usage. You may need to speak to your supervisor or other members of staff to find out. This information may then have an impact on the project you decide to investigate. For example most private-sector facilities aim to make money, therefore if you are working in a private-sector sports facility you may choose to research a project that looks at a method of increasing the number of members, which would have the effect of increasing profit.

You should also determine the target market of your sports facility as this will influence your project choice. For example, if the majority of the clientele are senior citizens then you should plan your project to cater for this market.

Examine the amenities the sports facility has to offer then factor this into your decision-making process. For example, if the facility has an aerobics studio but only has three classes a

Activity 13.9 45 mins

Planning a work placement project

Think about what sort of project you could investigate that is appropriate to where you are carrying out your work placement.

Task 1

On a 'planning page(s)' write out the aims and objectives for your project. Remember an aim is something that you plan to do and an objective is something that you plan to find out.

Also include what you think will happen.

Task 2

Find out how you are going to travel to and from your work placement – look into public transport options, cycle paths etc.

Write a paragraph about this on your planning page(s).

Task 3

Find out and make a list on your planning page(s) of what you will need to wear at your placement and if you are required to bring any equipment, for example a whistle or a stopwatch.

week, you could carry out research to determine if there is enough interest for more classes and, if so, which type of class.

Occupation Information

The purpose of a work placement is to help you determine if the job you have chosen to undertake or observe is suitable for you. Therefore, once you have thought of a job you would like to perform you will need to find out if you have or are going to have the right qualifications to be accepted for this job. For example, if you would like to work in outdoor pursuits, you will need to have a good level of personal proficiency and/or be working towards water-based or land-based outdoor pursuits qualifications, such as mountain leader or kayak instructor.

On top of the qualifications required, every job has a different set of roles and responsibilities that you must examine to see that you are capable of carrying them out. Working in the sports industry often entails working unsociable hours so, if you only want to work in the daytime, you may have to consider a different job.

13.5 Regulations

There are a number of regulations in place to help protect employees, employers and customers while at work. The Health and Safety at Work Act

(1974), The Control of Substances Hazardous to Health Regulations (COSHH) (1994), The Health and Safety (First Aid) Regulations (1981), The Safety at Sports Grounds Act (1975), The Fire Safety & Safety of Places of Sport Act (1987) and The Children Act (1989) can be found in Chapter 2. You should also be aware of the following regulations as they may apply to you and in your work placement.

The Health and Safety (Young Persons) Regulations (1997)

This lists four requirements employers must meet if they are employing young people under the age of 18:

- Assess risks to young people under 18 years old before they start work

- Address specific factors in the risk assessment

- Take into account their inexperience, lack of awareness of existing or potential risks and immaturity

- Provide information to parents or guardians of children about risks, and determine whether the young person should be prohibited from certain duties.

The Offices, Shops and Railway Premises Act (OSRPA) (1963)

This Act aims to secure the health, safety and welfare of people employed to work in offices, shops and certain railway premises.

An employer must notify the appropriate enforcing authority before they employ the person and provide specific details as laid down in the Notification of Employment of Persons Order (1964).

The Working Time Regulations (1998)

The Working Time Regulations state that working time is when someone is 'working, at his employer's disposal and carrying out his activity or duties'.

Young workers (someone who is above the minimum school-leaving age but under 18) may not ordinarily work more than eight hours a day and 40 hours a week. They may work longer hours where necessary to either maintain continuity of service or production, or respond to a surge in demand for a service or product.

If a worker is required to work for more than six hours at a stretch, he or she is entitled to a rest break of 20 minutes. The break should be taken during the six-hour period and not at the beginning or end of it. The exact time the breaks are taken is up to the employer.

13.6 Skills P8

During your work placement you will probably realise that you already have a number of skills that are appropriate to your placement. For example, you may realise that you have good interpersonal skills and find it easy to deal with customers' questions and/or complaints. However, while on the placement you will no doubt also find that you do have some skills that need to be developed. For example, you may find it difficult to meet deadlines or that you

are always rushing to get to work on time – in which case you will need to improve your time management skills.

You will also be taught a number of new practical skills such as putting up and taking down equipment. You will no doubt have some knowledge of this from practical units you have covered and find that you just need to adapt these skills to meet the requirements of the new apparatus.

Activity **13.10** 60 mins   P8

Undertaking a work-based experience in sport

Task 1

While you are on work experience, keep a daily diary which details:

- your hours of work
- your duties
- highlights of the day
- what you did well
- areas for improvement.

13.7 Presenting and Reviewing the Project P9 M4 D2

Monitor and Review

In order to be able to assess your work-placement project you should review your work periodically in order to ensure it is all going to plan. Try to evaluate what the strengths of the project are. For example, are you working well with the team in order to gain the information you require? Then assess which areas you need to improve in. For example, if your project involves obtaining information from customers through completion of a questionnaire and you do not have enough complete questionnaires, you may wish to change the way in which they are distributed.

Always stay vigilant to see if any opportunities arise that may improve your project. This could be something as simple as asking to sit in on a staff meeting, which may give you additional information for your project.

Make a note of the skills you have acquired and developed during the placement as you may wish to record this evidence on your CV. They will probably be transferable skills and therefore relevant for future employment.

From your time on the work placement you should have a good idea of what you need to do in order to develop your career in the sports industry. You may find that some organisations will pay for you to carry out any further training you require, while others will expect you to fund the training yourself.

You should also try to gain feedback from a variety of sources including your supervisor, colleagues and possibly a customer or two that you have had regular contact with. Through interviews or questionnaires try to gauge their assessment of your performance. You can then use this information to determine the areas in which you excel and the areas in which you need to improve.

Presentation of the Project

Try to work out the best way of presenting your project. You will need to consider the equipment you have available for your presentation and the audience to which you will deliver the presentation.

Here are a few ideas:

- Poster presentation: this is basically a range of pictures, illustrations or tables with descriptions of what each picture means.

- Oral presentation: this is where you present your work by speaking to an audience. This sort of presentation usually includes visual aids such as overhead transparencies or PowerPoint slides.

- Diary/logbook: this is where you keep a daily record of everything that you have done that is related to the project.

- Written assignment: this is where you produce a written piece of work with pictures and tables where appropriate.

- Video presentation: this is where you video relevant work for your project. You may also choose to video an oral presentation and show this to the audience.

You may decide to choose a combination of these different presentations to deliver your project – for example a poster presentation and an oral presentation.

Benefits of the Project

The project that you undertake should provide a number of benefits to both you and the centre in which you have worked.

You should develop new skills and have a much greater knowledge of the sports industry. You should have a better idea of what you need to do in order to be eligible for your chosen career. The experience that you have had demonstrates to future employers that you are committed to a career in the sports industry. You may also ask your placement provider for a reference that, again, could be very advantageous when you are seeking work.

Your project should have given your centre useful information that they can use in order to make improvements. This will encourage the experience provider to give further work placements to young people studying in schools and colleges.

Activity **13.11** 60–90 mins

Presenting your project

Once you have completed your project you will need to present your findings to your school and possibly your work-placement supervisor too.

Task 1

Prepare a five-to-ten minute illustrated presentation about your project.

Task 2

Deliver your presentation, ensuring that you describe, explain and evaluate the benefits that you have found for both yourself and for the centre in which you have worked.

Task 3

Conclude your presentation by identifying areas for improvements and making recommendations that can be justified on how these improvements can be made.

Quick Quiz 3 5 mins

Transferable	Aim	Health and Safety (Young Persons) Regulations	COSHH	SWOT
The Working Time Regulations	Logbook	Objective	The Offices, Shops and Railway Premises Act	Poster presentation

Choose a word or words from the boxes above to answer the following questions.
1. **This should be decided at the start of your project.**
2. **This lists four requirements employers must carry out if they are employing young people under the age of 18.**
3. **This is something that a person is expected to know and be able to do after having completed an activity/project.**
4. **This Act aims to secure the health, safety and welfare of people employed to work in offices, shops and certain railway premises.**
5. **This Act states how long people should work for per day and per week.**
6. **This type of analysis will determine your strengths and areas for improvement.**
7. **This is an example of how you can present the results from your project.**
8. **This is where you keep a daily record of everything that you have done.**
9. **These are the types of skills that you will probably learn while on placement.**
10. **You may need to be aware of this law if you are handling substances that may be hazardous to health.**

Key learning points

- Ensure you have specific aims and objectives for your project.
- Make sure your aims and objectives are linked to a specific area.
- Ensure you have an understanding of the rules and regulations in your work placement.
- Carry out a SWOT analysis of your project to determine its strengths and weaknesses (see Figure 3.2).
- Ensure in your presentation you are able to discuss the benefits of taking part in the work placement to:
  - yourself
  - the centre in which you are working and
  - the work-experience provider.

Useful websites

www.uksport.gov.uk/vacancies/

Jobs bulletin board that is regularly updated with details of vacancies from grassroots to elite level sport in the UK.

www.isrm.co.uk/jobs/career_intro.html

Useful advice on how to make the most of your opportunities to start a career in sport and recreation management.

http://www.media-awareness.ca/english/special_initiatives/toolkit/being_interviewed/index.cfm

Invaluable advice to bear in mind when being interviewed by journalists; includes what to do before and during the interview, and how to focus on what *you* want to say.

www.thefa.com/GetintoFootball/FALearning/FALearningPages/FrequentlyAskedQuestions.aspx

Invaluable advice on how to get started in football coaching and medicine with frequently asked questions answered authoritatively by experts at the Football Association.

http://careersadvice.direct.gov.uk/helpwithyourcareer/jobprofiles/

Specific careers advice for anyone thinking of becoming a fitness instructor, sports coach, sport psychologist, or sport scientist, with quick links to job descriptions, person specifications, and advice on how to get started.

References

Beashel, P., Dibson, A. and Taylor, J., 2001, *The World of Sport Examined*. Cheltenham: Nelson Thornes.

Stafford-Brown, J., Rea, S. and Chance, J., 2003, BTEC *National in Sport and Exercise Science*. London: Hodder and Stoughton.

Chapter 14
Exercise and Fitness Instruction

Ensuring that sports performers have appropriate training programmes is central to their success. However, it is also vital that these programmes are taught in a professional manner. In the growing health and fitness industry the standard of instruction is rising rapidly, as is the standard of training. People paying for these services have become more aware of what they want (see Figure 14.1) and what makes a good instructor. This chapter looks at the skills behind designing effective training programmes and how to instruct people in a safe and effective manner.

Learning Goals

By the end of this chapter you should:

- Know the principles of exercise-session design and exercise programming.
- Be able to plan an exercise programme.
- Be able to assist in instructing exercise sessions.
- Be able to undertake a review of exercise sessions.

To achieve a PASS grade the evidence must show that the learner is able to:	To achieve a MERIT grade the evidence must show that, in addition to the pass criteria, the learner is able to:	To achieve a DISTINCTION grade the evidence must show that, in addition to the pass and merit criteria, the learner is able to:
P1 describe the principles of fitness training	**M1** explain the principles of fitness training	**D1** relate the principles of fitness training to a range of clients with different needs
P2 describe the health and safety issues an exercise instructor needs to consider for their clients		
P3 produce exercise programmes for three different types of client	**M2** produce detailed exercise programmes for three different types of client	**D2** produce exercise programmes, justifying the range of activities suggested for three different types of client
P4 assist in instructing induction, resistance training, cardiovascular training and circuit training sessions for selected clients	**M3** demonstrate effective communication with selected clients	**D3** demonstrate competence in monitoring and adapting exercises to suit different client ability levels
P5 review three different exercise sessions identifying strengths, areas for improvement and personal development needs	**M4** justify identified personal development needs	

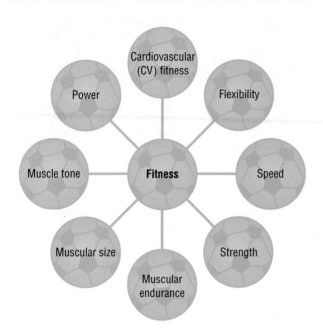

Figure 14.1 Different aspects of fitness that people may want to improve

14.1 Principles of Training P1 M1 D1

When designing an effective training programme you must take into account a range of factors to make sure that the training programme will be effective; these are called the principles of training and it is essential that you learn and use these:

Frequency – means how often the person will train. This may be three times a week.

Intensity – means how hard training will be and is usually stated in terms of what percentage of their maximum heart rate the person will work at.

Time – means how long each session will last.

Type – refers to the type of training they will be performing, for example cardiovascular fitness (CV) or resistance training.

Overload – means that to improve a person's fitness they need to work slightly harder than they are used to working. We can tell when a person has been overloaded because they may feel slightly stiff or sore for the next day or two.

Reversibility – means that just as a fitness can improve with training, it can also be lost if the

training stops. It is commonly known as the 'use it or lose it' principle, because if you don't use the fitness gain you will quickly lose it.

Specificity – means that the training they perform must be specific to the goals the person has. For example, if they want to improve their golf, then the training programme must achieve this aim.

Progression – this means we must build up our exercise intensity gradually so that we give our body time to adapt and cope with the stress placed upon it.

Overtraining occurs when a person does not take enough rest between training sessions and they cause themselves damage. They will eventually become injured or suffer from tiredness.

Health and Safety for Exercise Sessions P2

If you briefly think about what factors may make an exercise session unsafe, you should come up with a list such as the following:

- Poor technique
- Poor equipment
- Poor clothing and footwear
- Injuries
- Medical conditions
- Poor instruction
- Client unprepared for their session.

Therefore we need to minimise these kinds of risk by doing several things before training the client:

1. Fill out a detailed medical questionnaire and lifestyle form. These are called PAR-Q or participation questionnaires and are designed to discover what type of exercises the client can and cannot perform.

2. Fill out an informed consent form, in which the client is made to understand the risks of exercise and sign that they are willing to accept these risks.

Activity 14.1 40 mins

P1   M1   D1

Principles of training

Task

Using the following table, briefly summarise each of the principles of training, give an example of each, and then show what they would mean for each of the four types of client. Some of the boxes are filled in to give you an example.

	Frequency	Intensity	Time	Type	Overload	Reversibility	Specificity	Progression
Summary	How often		45 minutes per session		Working harder than you are used to			
Example	3 times a week							
Low fitness level	3 times a week	60–70% of max heart rate	30 minutes	CV resistance	Weights heavier than they are used to	If they don't keep training they will become less fit	Specific to their low level of fitness	Once the exercises are too easy
Moderate fitness level								
High fitness level								
Sport specific								

3. Check the training environment before every session to ensure all equipment is working properly and that there are no injury risks.

4. Ensure the trainer is appropriately qualified and insured against personal injury.

5. Carry out an induction with the client. This entails showing the client how each piece of equipment works and observing the client use the piece and offering advice when needed.

6. Check the client before every session to ensure they have no injuries and are dressed properly.

7. Conduct a full warm-up and cool-down with the client.

The Exercise and Fitness Code of Ethics is a document produced by an organisation called the Register of Exercise Professionals to ensure that we deal with our clients in an appropriate manner and that their safety is our priority.

Activity 14.2 30 mins

P2

Health and safety talk

Task

Prepare a two-minute health and safety talk you would give to a person that you were taking into the gym for a training session to describe the importance of health and safety.

Warm-up

A warm-up is performed to make sure that the heart, lungs, muscles and joints are prepared for the activities that will follow. Therefore, the warm-up needs to be specific to the training session that is being performed.

Objectives of a Warm-up

A warm-up can be summarised as having three main objectives. They are:

1. To raise the heart rate.

2. To increase the temperature of the body.

3. To mobilise the major joints of the body.

The aim of the warm-up is slowly to raise the body temperature by moving all the major muscle groups in a steady, rhythmical way. The effect of this is that there will be more blood flowing to the muscles, bringing with it oxygen to produce energy. Also, the muscles will become more elastic and less likely to become injured. In addition, the warm-up should involve some of the movements that the person will perform in their main session. This gives the warm-up 'specificity' and acts as a rehearsal.

How to Warm up

A typical warm-up will involve the following components:

- A pulse raiser
- Joint mobility
- Dynamic stretching for muscles.

The pulse raiser involves rhythmical movements of the large muscle groups in a CV-type activity, such as running, rowing or cycling. The pulse raiser should gradually increase in intensity as time goes on. A pulse raiser would typically last for around five minutes but may go on for ten minutes. At the end of the warm-up the heart rate should be just below the heart rate that will be achieved during the main session.

A warm-up for a run may involve one minute walking, one minute brisk walking, one minute jogging, one minute running and then one minute fast running.

Joint mobility is used to enable the joints to become lubricated by releasing more synovial fluid onto the joints and then warming it up so that it becomes more efficient. This means moving joints through their full range of movement. The movements will start off small, and slowly become larger until a full range of movement is achieved. The joints that need to be mobilised are shoulders, elbows, spine, hips, knees and ankles. If a trainer is clever they can use the pulse-raising movements to mobilise the joints as well. For example, rowing will have the effect of raising the pulse and mobilising all these joints.

Dynamic stretching is a relatively recent introduction and it means stretching the muscles through their full range of movement in a controlled manner (see Figure 14.2). Static stretching, where a muscle is stretched and held, is now a thing of the past. This is because it causes a fall in heart rate and tends to relax the muscles. Dynamic stretching keeps the heart rate high and fires up the muscles.

Squat with arm swing

Dynamic chest stretch

Spine rotation

Figure 14.2 **Three dynamic stretches**

To perform dynamic stretching, the client needs to copy the movements in the session they will perform and repeat the movements in a steady and controlled fashion.

Cool-down

A cool-down is performed to bring the body back to its pre-exercise state following exercise.

Objectives of the Cool-down

The cool-down has three main objectives:

1. To return the heart rate to normal.

2. To get rid of any waste products built up during exercise.

3. To return muscles to their original pre-exercise length.

The aim of the cool-down is the opposite to the aim of the warm-up in that the pulse will lower slowly and waste products such as carbon dioxide and lactic acid are washed out of the muscles. Also, as the muscles work during the main session, they will continually shorten to produce force and they end up in a shortened position. Therefore, they need to be stretched out so that they do not remain shortened.

How to Cool down

The cool-down consists of the following activities:

- Lowering the heart rate

- Maintenance stretching on muscles worked

- Developmental stretching on short muscles.

To lower the heart rate you need to choose a CV-type exercise involving rhythmical movements and large muscle groups. This time the intensity starts high and slowly falls to cause a drop in heart rate. This part should last around five minutes; an exercise bike is a good choice because it enables the client to sit down and relax as well.

Maintenance stretching, where the muscle is stretched and then held for around ten seconds, should be used. This will allow the muscles that have been shortened to be returned to their original working length. All the muscles that have been worked in the main session need a maintenance stretch.

Developmental stretching is used on muscles that are short and tight. The aim is to lengthen these muscles as they can cause problems and lead to injury. Developmental stretching involves stretching a muscle and then holding it for around ten seconds until it relaxes; once it has relaxed, the stretch is increased and held for ten seconds, and this is repeated three times.

Key learning points

- Frequency means how often the person will train. This may be three times a week.
- Intensity means how hard training will be and is usually stated in terms of what percentage of their maximum heart rate the person will work at.
- Time means how long each session will last.
- Type refers to the type of training they will be performing, for example CV or resistance training.
- Overload means that to improve a person's fitness they need to work slightly harder than they are used to working.
- Reversibility means that just as a fitness can improve with training, it can also be lost if the training stops.
- Specificity means that the training a person performs must be specific to the goals they have.
- Overtraining occurs when a person does not take enough rest between training sessions.
- A typical warm-up will involve the following components:
  - A pulse raiser
  - Joint mobility
  - Dynamic stretching for muscles.
- The cool-down consists of the following activities:
  - Lowering the heart rate
  - Maintenance stretching on muscles worked
  - Developmental stretching on short muscles.

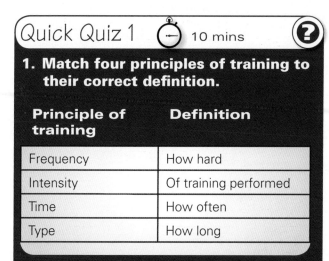

Quick Quiz 1 ⏱ 10 mins ?

1. **Match four principles of training to their correct definition.**

Principle of training	Definition
Frequency	How hard
Intensity	Of training performed
Time	How often
Type	How long

2. **Define the following components of fitness: overload; specificity; reversibility.**
3. **Give five factors that may make a session unsafe.**

14.2 Planning an Exercise Programme P3

To be an effective trainer it is important to be able to write an appropriate training programme. This section looks at the process you need to go through in order to write an effective training session for a client.

Stage 1 – Gathering Information

The first step is to gain relevant information about the client so that you can plan a personalised training programme. The key is to build up a picture of the individual and what their life is like. Then you can look at what exercises you will plan for them. This is done through the use of a questionnaire, which the client will fill out on your first meeting.

Factors to Consider

What a person does or does not do in their life will have an effect on their health and fitness levels as well as on their chances of being able to keep the training programme going.

All the following factors need to be taken into consideration:

1. **Occupation** – hours worked and whether work is manual or office-based.
2. **Activity levels** – amount of movement they do on a daily basis.
3. **Leisure-time activities** – whether these are active or inactive.
4. **Diet** – what, how much and when they eat.
5. **Stress levels** – either through work or their home life and how they deal with it.
6. **Alcohol intake** – how much they consume and how often.
7. **Smoking** – whether they are a smoker or ex-smoker and the amount they smoke.
8. **Time available** – the client needs to fit the training into their schedule, and the trainer needs to be realistic when planning the programme.
9. **Current and previous training history** – this will give an idea about the current fitness level of the client and also their skill level.
10. **Equipment available** – not all training will be gym-based, so the trainer needs to be realistic about what they can ask the client to do.

Activity 14.3 ⏱ 30 mins   P3

Preparing a questionnaire

Task

Prepare a questionnaire of ten questions to enable you to gather the relevant information you need to design a training programme.

Stage 2 – Establishing Objectives

To ensure success, the programme needs to be specific to the desired outcome. Therefore, it is important to find out exactly what the client wants. If you ask them what they want to achieve they will say that they want to get fit. You need to question them further and find out what this means to them. You may need to make suggestions as they may not know themselves. Their objectives could be any of the following:

- Cardiovascular fitness
- Flexibility
- Fat loss
- Improved health
- Muscular strength
- Muscular size
- Muscle tone
- Power.

Once you have established the objectives, it is time to plan the programme.

Stage 3 – Planning the Programme

Programme design is an area of controversy and different trainers have different ideas about what is right and what is wrong. Table 14.1 shows the type of structure the programme will normally use.

Table 14.1 A typical exercise programme

Programme component	Activity	Time
Warm-up	Raise pulse Mobilise joints Dynamic stretches	5–10 minutes
Resistance component	6–10 free weights or resistance machine exercises	30–45 minutes
CV component	Walking, running, cycling or rowing	20–60 minutes
Abdominal training	Abdominals and lower back	5 minutes
Cool-down	Lowering the pulse Developmental stretches Maintenance stretches	5–15 minutes

The training programme will usually last for one hour. The length of each component will depend on the objectives of the client and the importance they place on each (see Table 14.2).

Table 14.2 Meeting the objectives

Objective	Strength	Muscle size	Endurance	CV
Repetitions or duration	1–5	6–12	12–20	20 mins +
Recovery period	3–5 mins	1–2 mins	30–60 secs	N/A
Sets per	2–6	3–6 (large muscles) 2–3 (small muscles)	1 exercise	
Frequency per week	1–2 on each muscle group	1–2 on each muscle group	2–3 on each muscle group	3 sessions a week

(Source: Adapted from Baechle and Earle, 2008)

Client Groups

Clients are the central focus of the fitness industry and it is essential that we understand the individual needs and goals of a client. Each person needs to be treated as an individual to ensure they remain on their training programme. Clients will come from a range of backgrounds, ages, fitness levels, shapes and sizes.

For example, you may see the following groups of people as clients:

- Elderly
- Juniors
- Unfit
- Athletes
- People with specific goals
- Pregnant women
- People with medical conditions such as asthma or diabetes.

When you meet a new client it is important that you consider what this person is feeling and thinking. You need to place yourself in their shoes to consider what it is they need.

Activity to Suit Your Client

It is important to consider that not everyone will want to go to a gym to improve their fitness. You will need to be flexible in finding ways to make them more active in their daily lives. The Health Education Authority (HEA) have offered guidelines concerning health and fitness:

1. To improve cardiovascular fitness – a person needs to train three times a week for 20–60 minutes at 60–90 per cent of their maximum heart rate. This could be jogging, running, swimming, cycling or rowing.

2. To improve health – a person needs to be involved in an activity which makes them slightly warmer and slightly out of breath for 30 minutes for five to seven times a week.

This can involve activities such as brisk walking, gardening, mowing the lawn or recreational swimming. Also you can look at extra ways to increase activity levels such as walking rather than taking the car, taking the stairs instead of the lift, getting off the bus at an earlier stop or parking the car in the furthest parking spot!

Other Factors

As well as ensuring that the activity fits in with the client's lifestyle you also have to be aware of the cost to the individual and what they can afford, how they will travel to the venue if they have to, and its availability. It is becoming increasingly popular to train people in outdoor spaces such as parks. However, in our country with its unpredictable weather, you need to be flexible and have a range of venues available for training.

Quick Quiz 2 30 mins

1. **Which of the following are the correct aims of a warm-up?**
   - **To raise the heart rate**
   - **To lower the breathing rate**
   - **To mobilise joints**
   - **To increase the temperature of the body**
   - **To move blood away from the muscles.**
2. **Is the following statement about dynamic stretching true or false?**

   Dynamic stretching is stretching muscles through their full range of movement in a controlled manner to replicate the movements to follow.
3. **What is the difference between a maintenance and a developmental stretch?**
4. **Explain these four rules of programme design.**
   - **Work muscles in pairs to keep the muscles balanced.**
   - **Large muscles must be trained first.**
   - **Do the difficult exercises first.**
   - **Work the abdominal muscles at the end of the session.**
5. **What are the HEA guidelines for improving health and improving aerobic fitness?**

Activity **14.4**   2 hours   P3   M2   D1

Planning exercise programmes

Plan three exercise programmes for three different types of client. You need to follow the four rules stated above and make the programme specific to the needs of the client. To achieve M2 you need to provide as much detail as you can on the exercise and

to achieve D1 you need to justify why you have chosen the exercises you have. You can use the following template for your exercise programmes:

Name:
Dates:
Aims:
Exercises:

Name of exercise	Purpose of exercise	Time or sets and reps	Resistance	Rest

(k) Key learning points

- There is a range of factors that will affect fitness levels. They include: occupation, activity levels, leisure-time activities, diet, stress levels, alcohol intake, smoking, time available, current and previous training history, and equipment available.
- An exercise programme will have the following components:
  - Warm-up
  - Resistance component
  - CV component
  - Abdominal training
  - Cool-down.
- According to the HEA recommendations, to improve cardiovascular fitness a person needs to:
  - Train three times a week for 20-60 minutes at 60-90 per cent of their maximum heart rate.
- To improve health a person needs to:
  - Be involved in an activity which makes them slightly warmer and slightly out of breath for 30 minutes five to seven times a week.

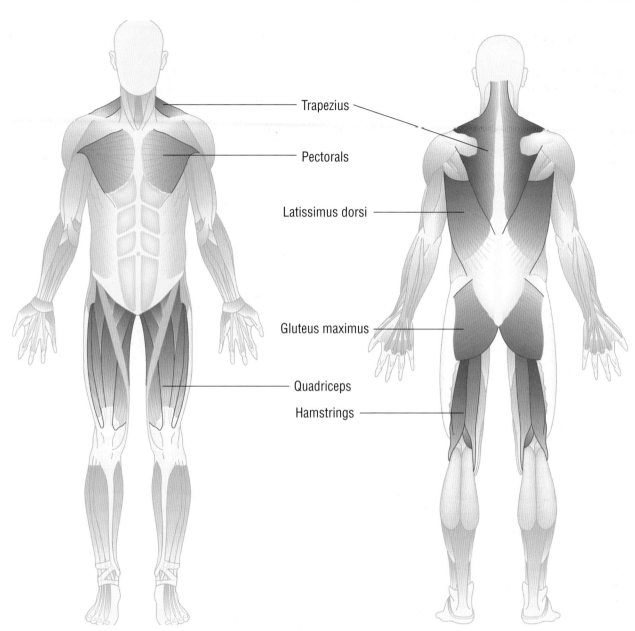

Trapezius

Pectorals

Latissimus dorsi

Gluteus maximus

Quadriceps

Hamstrings

Figure 14.3   The large muscle groups of the human body

14.3 Conducting an Exercise Session P4 M3 D3

Start of the Session

When you take a client through their exercise programme you need to follow a clear structure to ensure the training session is safe and that good client care is applied.

Before the session starts you need to check the equipment and the environment. For example, check the following:

- Availability of equipment
- Equipment is in working order
- All cables are strong
- Floor is clear of equipment and cables
- Temperature
- Ventilation.

The session will start when you meet the client. At this point you need to explain some safety issues and procedures. The following questions are appropriate:

- Have you any illnesses or injuries I need to be aware of?
- Have you eaten today?
- Is your clothing appropriate and have you taken off your jewellery?

Then you need to explain some procedures:

- Fire exits and fire drill
- First-aid kit, first-aider and nearest telephone
- Availability of water.

Finally, explain:

- The training programme
- The process of instruction.

Once this has all been covered, it is time to start the session.

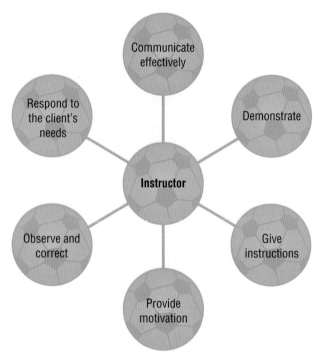

Figure 14.4 Roles performed by an instructor

During the Session

The aim of the exercise session is to get the client working for as much time as possible in a safe and effective manner. It is important that the client is supported and pushed to work as hard as they can within their limits.

The instructor will perform a number of different roles (see Figure 14.4).

Communicate Effectively

It is important that the client is able to understand you and respond in the way you would like them to. We communicate mainly through the words we use and also how we deliver these words and the body language we use. It is good practice to listen to your client and assess their level of knowledge before deciding how you will deliver your instructions. If a person is new to the gym you should keep things simple and use less technical language. The more experienced client will be able to communicate using more technical language.

Give Instructions

An instruction is providing information on how to perform a technique. When providing instructions, say what you want the client to do rather than what not to do. If you use the word 'Don't', for example 'Don't lock your knees,' it may increase the chances that they will actually do it!

Demonstrate

The instructor needs to give a demonstration to show the client how to perform the technique. Once a demonstration has been given, the instructor can explain the technique to the client and then let them practise to get the feel of the movement.

Provide Motivation

The reason most people do not achieve the results they want is because their motivation is too low: they give up when the going gets tough. You will motivate them with what you say, how you say it and by using positive body language. This will push them to work as hard as they can within the limits of their fitness.

Observe and Correct

The instructor will need to observe the client's technique from a variety of positions by moving around the client. Once they have observed for a short period, feedback should be given about what they are doing right and then what parts need to be corrected.

Respond to the Client's Needs

If a client has a problem with an exercise, then the instructor needs to correct it first by explaining and then by redemonstrating the technique. If they are still unable to perform the technique correctly, then the exercise needs to be changed.

Ending the Session

Once the session is complete, after the cool-down, it is a good opportunity to ask the client how they felt the session went. Also, you can tell them how you thought they did. Once the client has left, you need to put any equipment away and report any damage to equipment or advise of any problems you encountered.

Ⓚ Key learning points

- Before a session starts, you need to check the environment, the client and tell them about the safety procedures.
- During the session you need to be supporting the client in the following ways:
  - Communicate effectively
  - Give instructions
  - Demonstrate
  - Provide motivation
  - Observe and correct
  - Respond to the client's needs.
- At the end of the session ask your client for feedback about the session.

Activity 14.5 ⏱ 30 mins   P4   M3   D3

Review of my training session

Fill in the following log for each client to show how you have achieved P4, M3 and D3.

> What did I do to assist instructing an induction, resistance training, cardiovascular training and circuit training?
>
> How did I communicate effectively with my client?
>
> How did I monitor and adapt exercises to suit the different needs of my client?

14.4 Undertake a Review of the Exercise Session and Exercise Programme P5 M4

The Purpose of Reviewing Sessions

To improve as a trainer it is vital to review your performance regularly and identify any changes that need to be made. We can receive feedback from a range of sources and it is all useful.

Definition

Feedback information about performance; it is neither good nor bad, it is just information.

All clients are different and we need to see how effective we have been with each client. What works well for one person may not necessarily work with another. We need to keep reviewing how well motivated our client is and how their fitness levels are progressing.

Conducting a Review

When you conduct a review of your performance you could ask yourself some questions to focus your thoughts, for example:

1. Did you think the programme was effective in meeting your aims?

2. What did you enjoy and not enjoy about the training session?

3. To what extent did you feel safe?

4. Could the session be improved in any way?

The ideal time to conduct a review is as soon as you can after a session, while the issues are still fresh in your head and your client's head. You may even be able to ask the client some questions during the cool-down period, as the work is less intense and the client is starting to relax. You need to ask them specific questions regarding the session and its outcomes.

You could use a form as below and cover the following detail.

Self-evaluation

The client may not pick up things you see or feel yourself and therefore you must ask yourself the same questions and answer them in an honest manner. Particularly you must yourself assess in terms of the safety of the session and whether it was effective. Did it really meet the aims that you set for your session?

There are many benefits of self-evaluation:

1. You can plan future sessions to ensure they are enjoyable and effective.

2. Good evaluation is likely to increase the chances of the client sticking to their training programme.

3. The client will stay interested and motivated.

4. The client will keep progressing.

5. You will be able to identify any training needs you may have.

6. You can set yourself goals for personal development and any training needs you may have.

Regular evaluation can lead to improvements in performance. If you set yourself specific goals, then you can monitor your actual performance. Achieving goals relies on effective goal setting using the SMART principle. This is well covered in Chapter 9 but the acronym stands for:

Specific

Measurable

Achievable

Realistic

Time-constrained.

As you continue to evaluate yourself and improve your training skills, communication skills and motivational skills, you will see yourself become a more professional and effective trainer.

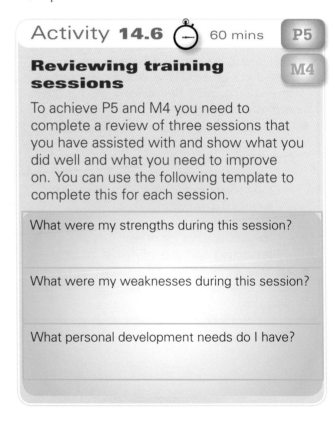

Activity 14.6   60 mins   P5

Reviewing training sessions   M4

To achieve P5 and M4 you need to complete a review of three sessions that you have assisted with and show what you did well and what you need to improve on. You can use the following template to complete this for each session.

What were my strengths during this session?

What were my weaknesses during this session?

What personal development needs do I have?

Useful websites

www.netfit.co.uk/training/trainingadvice/pregnant-training-exercise.htm

Training tips aimed at mothers-to-be, with the emphasis on keeping safe and well.

www.netfit.co.uk/previous.htm

Extensive range of exercise and training techniques, some sports specific, others more general.

www.elitesoccerconditioning.com/FitnessTraining/FitnessTraining.htm

Drills, tips and ideas to help you maximise your footballing fitness and techniques.

www.sport-fitness-advisor.com/resistance-training.html

Excellent advice on how to design a resistance training programme for any sport in seven steps.

Further Reading

Coulson, M., 2008, *The Fitness Instructor's Handbook: A Complete Guide to Health and Fitness – Fitness Professionals*. London: A&C Black.

Dagleish, J. and Dollery, S., 2001, *Health and Fitness Handbook.* Harlow: Pearson Education.

Franks, B.D. and Howley, E.T., 1998, *Fitness Leader's Handbook*. Champaign, IL: Human Kinetics.

References

Baechle, T.R. and Earle, R.W., 2008, *Essentials of Strength Training and Conditioning*. Champaign, IL: Human Kinetics.

Chapter 15
Sport & Leisure Facility Operations

Many of you studying this course will be planning to or already do work in a sport leisure facility. This chapter will give you information about the responsibilities that may be placed on you and how to deal with them while working in such a facility. Customer service is also covered in this chapter as it plays a key role in this industry and you must learn the most appropriate ways of dealing with your customers if you are to be successful in this field. This chapter will also cover practical elements of your job such as setting up, taking down and storing sports equipment. Finally, this chapter will also help you to monitor your performance while working in this industry and give you the skills to determine the areas in which you can improve.

Learning Goals

By the end of this chapter you should:

- Know about organisational structures and responsibilities within a sport and leisure facility.
- Know the importance of providing a safe and secure environment.
- Know about customer service in sport and leisure facilities.
- Be able to check, take down and store equipment for sports activities

To achieve a PASS grade the evidence must show that the learner is able to:	To achieve a MERIT grade the evidence must show that, in addition to the pass criteria, the learner is able to:	To achieve a DISTINCTION grade the evidence must show that, in addition to the pass and merit criteria, the learner is able to:
P1 describe the organisational structure of a selected sport and leisure facility	**M1** explain the responsibilities of four different staff teams in a selected sport and leisure facility	**D1** evaluate their responsibilities of four different staff teams in a selected sport and leisure facility
P2 describe the responsibilities of four different staff teams from a selected sport and leisure facility	**M2** explain how procedures help to provide safe and secure sport and leisure facilities	**D2** review own performance in the setting up, checking, taking down and storage of equipment for three different sports activities, justifying suggestions relating to own development
P3 describe why it is important to provide a safe and secure environment	**M3** explain the importance of effective customer service, and procedures used to achieve it, in a selected sport and leisure facility	
P4 describe procedures used to ensure a safe and secure environment in areas within a selected sport and leisure facility	**M4** independently set up check, take down and store equipment for three different sports activities	
P5 identify procedures used to provide effective customer service in a selected sport and leisure facility	**M5** review own performance in the setting up, checking, taking down and storage of equipment for three different sports activities, making suggestions for own development	
P6 describe the importance of providing effective customer service in a selected sport and leisure facility		
P7 set up, check, take down and store equipment for three different sports activities, with tutor support		
P8 review own performance in the setting up, checking, taking down and storage of equipment for three different sports activities		

15.1 Organisational Structures and Responsibilities within a Sport and Leisure Facility P1 P2 M1 D1

Organisational Structure

Every organisation has a structure with various levels, which is often depicted as a staffing structure or organisational structure. The person at the top of the chart is in charge and ultimately responsible for the success of the sports facility and the welfare of the staff and customers.

A typical hierarchical structure (this is an example of a local authority (council) facility) is shown in Figure 15.1.

This is not the only structure for the operation of a sports or leisure centre, but is a typical one. It could be that your local centre has a similar structure.

There are several roles that are common to most leisure facilities, but it is worth remembering that the roles and responsibilities of a position in one centre could be very different to that in other centres.

Figure 15.1   An example of an organisational structure within a sport & leisure facility

Recruitment of Staff

Recruitment of staff in sport and leisure, like in any area, requires a range of skills and qualities, which are enhanced by experience. Consider the following as a typical process for recruiting a casual recreation assistant:

1. Identify a need to the senior management and agree that a post is needed and can be advertised.

2. Prepare an advert and invite applicants.

3. Place the advert in the right place – local newspaper, the centre itself, online, by word of mouth to existing staff – and set a deadline date for application.

4. Sort the applicants and shortlist them for interview.

5. Arrange a panel for interviewing each short listed applicant.

6. Have the panel meet and agree the format of the interview and the role of each panel member. For example, if there were three interviewers, one may ask about the specifics of the job, another may be there to answer questions about the organisations and another to test the applicant's suitability for the job.

Facilities

Activity **15.1**   45 mins   **P1**

Organisation of a sport and leisure facility

Task 1

Visit a local sport or leisure facility and see if you can find out about its organisational structure – you may see a diagram with photos of each person or there may be details in a leaflet – ask the receptionist if you are having difficulty finding out this information.

Task 2

Design a leaflet that could be used at your local sport and leisure facility that describes the organisational structure of the facility.

Figure 15.2 Some of the facilities available at Guildford Spectrum Leisure Complex

Sport and leisure facilities are many and vary from area to area.

Leisure Centres

Leisure centres vary in size and what is contained within, some having perhaps a small sports hall, and a gym and nothing else, others with impressive state-of-the-art facilities.

Swimming Pools

Swimming pools are generally either publicly owned by the local council or privately owned and attached to health clubs in large organisations such as David Lloyd Leisure.

Figure 15.3 A swimming pool in a privately owned leisure facility

Gyms and Health Clubs

In recent years in the UK, there has been a growth in popularity in privately run sports clubs.

Organisations such as Fitness First, Esporta, Virgin Active, Bannatynes and Next Generation open up and compete for customers that tend not to use local authority facilities, who would rather pay more money and receive what they consider better facilities and customer service.

Many hotels have their own health and fitness facilities, which are open to both their guests and to paying members of the public.

Staff Teams

Leisure Centre Manager

Roles and responsibilities could include:

- Running the centre on a day-to-day basis
- Devising activity programmes
- Marketing the centre
- Making sure the building is clean and in a good state of repair
- Making sure health and safety regulations are followed
- Agreeing staff shifts
- Recruiting, supervising and training staff.

- Maximising income generation and managing budgets
- Attending regular meetings with management teams and/or the centre's owners
- Visiting local schools and other organisations to promote the facilities
- Attracting new members
- Dealing with complaints

Duty Manager

Roles and responsibilities could include:

- To work as an effective team member with all other duty managers
- To ensure that all plant and machinery is serviced regularly.
- To oversee and organise routine site and equipment maintenance
- To analyse the results from the pool water tests taken by staff
- To assist in the recruitment and selection of all staff
- To produce and monitor all rotas, including the authorisation of annual leave and absence cover
- To deputise for the manager in their absence.

Recreation Supervisor

Roles and responsibilities could include:

- Leading a small team of recreation assistants
- Deputising for the duty manager in their absence
- Covering recreation assistant duties at busy times or to cover staff leave or sickness.

Recreation Assistant

Roles and responsibilities could include:

- Monitoring the use of equipment and activities
- Ensuring the safety of users, staff and equipment

- Maintaining the cleanliness of facilities
- Setting up, maintaining and dismantling equipment according to the schedule of activities
- Dealing with customer enquiries and, on occasion, with emergencies requiring first aid
- Assisting in the organisation of sporting or leisure events
- Providing advice and supervision for the centre's activities.

Responsibilities of All Staff

There are certain expectations and responsibilities that all staff should adhere to regardless of their job specification and position within the organisation.

Case Study: Swimming Pool Lifeguard

Role of a Swimming Pool Lifeguard

A lifeguard must balance the welfare and well-being of those using a pool and keeping up with the latest techniques, to remain alert in warm and potentially repetitive situations, and to deliver customer care throughout. Many people perceive the role as a glamorous job for people who do not have to work very hard.

Qualifications

In the UK, lifeguards must train to the standards of the Royal Life Saving Society (RLSS) and complete a course called the National Pool Lifeguard Qualification (NPLQ), which they must renew every two years, and in addition log hours of training in between those assessments. The course is made up of practical, both wet and dry, and theory sessions and is usually delivered over 33 hours.

Working as a Lifeguard

Responsibilities

It is important that a lifeguard has the right attitude, that is to say that they have the following qualities as essential:

- A caring, customer-friendly attitude
- A high level of personal fitness
- Updated first-aid knowledge and practical experience of dealing with common injuries
- The ability to deal with stress, such as bad behaviour, and remain calm.

Qualities of a Lifeguard

A lifeguard must have, or be prepared to learn how to:

- Spot and prevent potential accidents
- Be decisive and communicate effectively
- Remain alert in warm and humid conditions.

Figure 15.4 A lifeguard on duty

Personal Presentation

You should always wear clothing that is appropriate to your working environment; most people working in a sport or leisure facility will be issued with a uniform so that members of the public can clearly identify members of staff. You should ensure your uniform is clean and ironed so that you portray a professional image. You should pay attention to your personal grooming and personal hygiene.

Time-management Skills

Every member of staff is expected to turn up ready for work on time or before their shift is due to start. If a member of staff is late they may face disciplinary action, which could lead to losing their job. Staff are usually given allocated break periods and must adhere to the times given. Unless given permission to do otherwise, staff are expected to work right up until the end of their shift period.

Attendance at Work

If you are unable to attend work you must telephone your line manager before your shift is due to start so that a member of staff can be called in to cover for you. A procedure for reporting your absence is always in place, and it is important that you notify the correct person as early as possible so that cover can be arranged

Performance at Work

All staff are expected to follow the rules and regulations laid out in the staff manuals and/or normal and emergency operational procedures documents (see p. 263 and 264). They are expected to carry out the duties detailed in their job specifications to a high level of proficiency.

Activity 15.2 25 mins

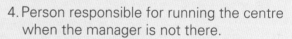

Responsibilities of staff in a sport and leisure facility

Task 1

Centre Manager	Recreation Assistant
Duty Officer	Lifeguard
Maintenance Officer	Receptionist
Cleaner	Administrative Assistant

Match the job descriptions below to the jobs listed in the box above to identify the job roles.

1. Person responsible for the presentation of the building and making sure that it stays tidy.

2. Person responsible for making sure that all of the pool plant machinery and major equipment stays in good working order.

3. Person responsible for dealing with paperwork, sending letters etc.

4. Person responsible for running the centre when the manager is not there.

5. Person responsible for ensuring that people are safe while they are swimming.

6. Person responsible for making sure that equipment gets set up and taken down at the right time.

7. Person responsible for dealing with phone calls and customers on the day.

8. Person responsible for everything in the centre.

Task 2

Select four different staff teams – for example management, maintenance, instructors, lifeguards, reception, grounds staff, security, cleaning etc., then design a poster with writing to describe, explain and evaluate the responsibilities of each staff team.

15.2 The Importance of Providing a Safe and Secure [P3] [P4] [M2] Environment

Safe Environment

The general manager and their team of managers of a sport or leisure facility are responsible for running a safe and secure environment. They will ensure every member of staff receives training on how the facility operates, together with two manuals that provide information on how every part of the facility should operate under normal conditions and what to do in an emergency situation – these are usually referred to as 'Normal Operating Procedures' (NOP) and 'Emergency Operating Procedures' (EOP).

The NOP gives instructions on how to deal with everyday situations, whereas the EOP gives instructions on how to deal with minor and major emergency situations such as disorderly behaviour from customers or dealing with a drowning incident.

Example of a Normal Operating Procedures (NOP) manual

This manual normally details the following:

- The services the leisure facility provides, for example swimming pool dimensions, squash courts and their dimensions etc., and information specific to that individual facility.
- Any potential risk factors and hazards that staff should be aware of, some of which may include:
  - Known hazards – unruly behaviour by the customer, customers with prior health problems, misuse of equipment etc.
  - Pool hazards – slippery poolside, diving in shallow water, blind spots in the pool etc.
  - Customers at risk – weak swimmers, elderly customers, customers under the influence of alcohol or drugs etc.
- Instructions on how to carry out risk assessments so that these hazards and risks can be minimised. (Carrying out risk assessments is discussed in detail in Chapter 2.)
- Methods of dealing with the public, incorporating forms of communication and rules and regulations the customers must adhere to; an example of this is the poolside rules – no running on the poolside, no pushing, no ducking etc.
- Staff duties and responsibilities. This will include information about what is expected from staff; for example they should wear the uniform provided, lifeguards must always carry a whistle, they must never leave a pool area unattended. There are usually details of staff training requirements too; for example a lifeguard will usually attend training sessions at least once a month so that their skills are up to date and have been practised recently.
- Details of staffing requirements for a range of situations, such as the number of lifeguards required poolside in relation to the number of swimmers, supervision of diving etc.
- Pool, sports hall and changing room hygiene, with instructions on how to carry out everyday cleaning duties.
- Details of first-aid supplies and how to locate a first-aider.
- Details of where alarms are located and how to use them. (All leisure facilities will have some form of alarm system to summon help or warn people of a fire.)

Checking Facilities

There should be regular inspections to ensure the facility is functioning as it should do; these checks may be required on a regular basis throughout the day or some may need to be performed at the start and end of the day. For example, examining the changing facilities to ensure they are clean and tidy, and testing the swimming pool water to assess the chlorine levels, should be carried out once every few hours, but checking all the lights are working inside and outside the building only really needs to be carried out once or twice a day.

Some checks will be carried out by external agencies or contractors; these include the fire department who will check such things as the number and functioning of fire extinguishers and that the fire exits are easily accessible. Contractors may have service agreements to ensure plant and equipment such as air-conditioning units are maintained to a safe standard.

Example of an Emergency Operating Procedures (EOP) manual

This manual details how staff should respond to a range of emergency situations. It will give details on how staff should respond if they were to encounter any of the situations listed below:

- Fire
- Customer suffering from a minor injury (for example grazed knee)
- Customer suffering from a major injury (for example knocked unconscious with a head injury)
- A drowning incident
- Bomb threat
- Emission of a toxic gas
- Structural failure
- Spinal injury
- How to deal with blood, vomit and faeces.

Legislation and Regulations

Health and Safety at Work Act 1974

The Health and Safety at Work Act 1974, and all of its subsidiary regulations, will apply to a sports centre in the same way that it would for any other facility. Basically, the centre must be maintained and operated to a standard so that nobody is exposed to risks to their health and safety.

Risk assessments of all activities undertaken by employees must be completed, with an assessment of any activity that could affect the safety of people using the centre.

RIDDOR

The Reporting of Injuries, Diseases and Dangerous Occurrences Regulations 1995 (RIDDOR), covers a whole range of incidents and requires that employees report on:

- Deaths
- Major injuries
- 'Over three days' injuries – where an employee or self-employed person is away from work or unable to perform their normal work duties for more than three consecutive days
- Injuries to members of the public or people not at work where they are taken from the scene of an accident to hospital
- Some work-related diseases
- Dangerous occurrences – where something happens that does not result in an injury, but could have done.

This would normally be completed by form and then via a clear process to the person in charge, perhaps the leisure centre manager.

First Aid

In most large sports facilities, the staff are encouraged to qualify in first aid, since the chances of an accident or injury while participating in sport or exercise is quite high. Qualified lifeguards will have learnt and practised most aspects of first aid as part of their lifeguard training.

Emergency procedures should be in place to evacuate a sports centre, including procedures to deal with fire, chemical release, explosion, terrorist threats etc. Accidents must be investigated and reported.

Manual Handling

More than one third of all reportable 'over three days' injuries and nearly ten per cent of 'major injuries' are associated with manual handling.

Many injuries are the result of repeatedly lifting, or pushing in the wrong way. Sprains, strains and fractures can occur if, for example, a trampoline is not folded away properly.

Legal Requirements

The Manual Handling Operations (MHO) Regulations 1992 (revised 1998) apply to manual handling operations, defined as 'any transporting or supporting of a load (including the lifting, putting down, pushing, pulling, carrying or moving thereof) by hand or by bodily force'.

This could cover any heavy or forceful job that, without care, could result in injury, for example:

- Lifting barge boards that separate sports hall courts
- Pulling and leaning over a swimming pool to put in lane ropes
- Putting tension in a volleyball net, which requires considerable force
- Lifting sports hall divider nets into their bags.

All sports hall equipment and facilities should come with guidance on how to erect/move/dismantle them safely

Working Time Regulations

Regulations covering working hours apply to almost every business. Working time regulations aim to improve health and safety by controlling the hours that employees work.

A Normal Operating Procedure for a sports centre should show:

- The rules governing working hours and shift patterns
- Rest periods, and change of work area, such as being moved from a lifeguarding position
- Annual leave.

Secure Environment

Leisure facilities are open to the public so, in theory, any person is able to enter the building. It is the duty of the staff within the leisure facility to ensure the facility is secure so that the customers are protected from abusive and violent behaviour. Arrangements should also be made to provide a secure environment for the customer to store his or her belongings.

Preventing Violence

The reception area should always be staffed. Any person who exhibits antisocial behaviour or appears to be under the influence of alcohol or drugs can then be refused entry to the facility.

Customers taking part in activities or competitions may become violent towards staff. Training on how to deal with people who are exhibiting unacceptable behaviour should also be given.

Preventing Theft

All customer and staff belongings should be stored safely and securely in lockers. In some instances CCTV may be provided in locker areas. This will give additional security to people's belongings. CCTV should also be placed in car parks together with signs telling people not to leave valuables in their cars. Equipment should be kept in an area that can be locked.

Theft of information is also something a leisure facility should take precautions to prevent. Most facilities have a database that contains all their customer information, which they use when sending promotional material etc. This information could be very useful to other leisure providers as it would give them the opportunity to advertise directly to your customers, which may make them change their leisure provider. Not only this, each facility must adhere to the Data Protection Act (1998), which means that it is illegal to use the information gained from individuals for anything other than its original intention. If the information is stolen, it is highly likely that the data will be used for something other than its original purpose.

Preventing Fraud

Fraud is the process of obtaining some form of benefit by intentional deception. In the sport and leisure industry, you may be involved in taking payment from customers, and this is where you may experience fraud. People may steal credit cards and try to use them to pay for goods or activities; you should ensure you check the card and signature carefully or, where chip-and-pin facilities are provided, ensure that authorisation is granted. People may also try to pay for goods with forged bank notes. You should always examine the bank notes carefully and check them against the training and information you have received. Fraud by staff is also something you should be vigilant against. Staff may try to steal something of value from the facility, be it money from the till or food while stocking vending machines. The guilty person may be dismissed from their job and probably face legal action too.

Preventing Vandalism

Vandalism is defined as intentional damage to property. Examples of vandalism include graffiti on walls, kicking lockers, damaging flowerbeds etc. Vandalism usually occurs in areas that are already damaged; so if you spot some writing on a wall, for example, you should report it immediately or attempt to remove the graffiti yourself in order to prevent further bouts of vandalism. Other methods of preventing vandalism include having better lighting outside so that vandals can be seen and stopped (or, better still, deterred in the first place), CCTV and regular patrols of problem areas.

Procedures

Fire and Evacuation Procedures

It is very important that in the event of a fire, or a terrorist threat, customers and staff are evacuated as quickly and safely as possible. All sports centres should have a policy that shows, for customers, what to do and where to go, and for staff, what everyone's role is in evacuating a building, including muster points and a policy for readmission to the building.

Many centres have coded messages designed to let the staff know what is going on, without alarming the customers. For example, a receptionist making the announcement 'Fred French to the swimming pool' could be a coded message indicating a reported fire in the swimming pool area.

Safety Signage

Signs in sports centres need to conform to the law, as with any other public place. So you would expect to see signs that show you:

Figure 15.5
A safety sign in a sports centre

- The location of fire exits

- First-aid stations

- Command signs, such as 'No eating area'

- Specialist signs such as swimming pool rules

- Guidance on first-aid procedures like CPR.

Many of these signs are required by law, while others are simply good practice. Signs are usually made of high-visibility acrylic and often luminous, so that they light up if there is no power for lighting.

Security

Security and procedures for common occurrences are essential in sports centres. Any public place will need to be aware of the threat to customers of physical or verbal abuse, crime including theft, and the general value that a customer needs to feel in terms of their personal safety while, for example, swimming, using a gym or playing badminton.

CCTV

Closed-circuit television or CCTV involves the use of cameras to help protect customers and staff from threats to security and crime.

Typically a number of cameras are placed all around a facility and viewed from a central monitor or monitors. This allows the person monitoring the cameras to identify any potential security hazards or track suspicious behaviour.

Some people say that this makes them feel more secure, but others complain that they feel as though they are being watched a little too much.

Staff Identification

Many sports staff are required to wear staff identity badges or labels that are designed to allow customers to know who you are, and potentially to make them feel more at ease about communicating with you. From a security point of view, it will also allow staff to know whether a person is actually a member of staff, in other words, if they have no badge, whether they should even be there.

Safety and Security in All Areas

Car Parks

Car parks are potential areas for crime and should be a priority for security patrols and CCTV as they will hardly ever have large numbers of people. For example, ten minutes after the start of an exercise class the car park could be full of cars but deserted, and potentially a good opportunity for a criminal. A solution you could offer:

- CCTV
- Regular patrols
- Good, bright lighting.

Reception

Reception areas also contain several potential security problems, such as:

- Pickpockets
- Large amounts of cash kept at reception
- Open for anyone to enter.

You could think about how your local sport centre manages reception security; perhaps they have turnstiles, high-sided and deep reception desks, and possibly buttons that link them to the police or fire service.

Changing Rooms

Once again, changing rooms need to be secure. The most common crime in changing room is theft. Criminals rarely steal from secure lockers, but will gladly take valuables from those who leave them, even for a minute, to have a shower.

Activity **15.3** 30 mins

Safe and secure sport and leisure facilities

Leisure facilities are open to the public so, in theory, any person is able to enter the building.

Task 1

Write a report that describes the importance of sport and leisure facilities to provide a safe and secure environment for both its customers and its staff.

Task 2

Go into one of your local sports or leisure centres and look for the following:

1. Is the reception area always staffed?
2. Are the staff all wearing uniforms?
3. Is there access for the public to use the centre's computers?
4. Is there CCTV in the locker rooms or car park?
5. How often are the toilets and changing areas cleaned or inspected?

From these observations, write a report that describes and explains the procedures used by this facility to ensure that they are providing a safe and secure environment for their customers and staff.

Regular same-sex patrols are particularly useful, since it would be inappropriate to have cameras in an area where people change.

Sports Areas

On occasion people become over competitive and aggressive and have been known to fight over sporting disputes, and it is worth having a plan for what action you would take in these situations.

 Key learning points

- All staff have a job specification to work to and must follow normal procedures and emergency procedures as documented in their work handbook.
- People working in a leisure or sport facility must maintain a safe and secure environment for their customers and staff.
- Staff should know the risks involved in sport and exercise.

Quick Quiz 1 45 mins (?)

1. **What is a Normal Operating Procedure?**
2. **Describe the key features of an Emergency Action Plan**
3. **Describe what you might check, in terms of security, for the following areas in leisure:**
   - **Swimming pool changing room**
   - **Football pitches**
   - **A bowling alley**
   - **A canoe club storeroom**
   - **A leisure centre crèche.**

Customer Service

Working in the leisure industry means you will be dealing with customers and you will therefore need to be able to learn skills in dealing with the public. These skills are very important as you need to be sure you are giving the customers the treatment they expect to ensure they keep coming back to your leisure facility. You will need to learn what the customers' needs are and how you can meet these requirements or even exceed them.

Definition

Customer service refers to the level of assistance and courtesy given to those who use the facility.

Importance of Customer Service

The leisure industry is very competitive and customer service plays an important role in ensuring the facility you work in keeps its customers (after all, with no customers there will be no leisure facility). If customers are happy with the services you provide, the facility in which you work will experience a number of benefits, including:

1. **Customer loyalty** – customers will return to a facility if they feel they have been treated well. If, however, they feel that they have been treated poorly, such as waiting too long for service or not having complaints dealt with effectively, then they are much less likely to return to the facility.

2. **New customers** – new customers can be generated through word of mouth from existing customers. If someone is happy with a facility, they are more than likely to recommend it to other people.

3. **Increased sales and profits** – if customers are happy, they will continue to use the facility, which, in turn, increases the amount of money an organisation makes.

4. **A good image** – most leisure and recreational facilities want to portray a good image to the public and this can be done through providing good customer care.

5. **Employee satisfaction** – can be gained through ensuring the employees are given thorough training in customer care. This training will help to ensure the employees can handle complaints rather than becoming upset.

6. **A competitive edge over other facilities that provide the same service** – a competitive edge is very important in the leisure industry as there are usually a number of facilities that provide the same services in one area. If one facility provides better customer service than another one, they are likely to have more customers than the other.

Customer Types

There are many different types of customers who use leisure facilities and you should have a basic understanding of how to deal with every person you meet. Here are some examples of customers you may meet, together with some suggestions on how you should deal with them.

Individuals

Many people using the fitness facilities will come there by themselves. You should try to establish a relationship with the customer so that they feel valued and are more likely to return. If you are involved in training the individual, you should be able to monitor and comment on their progress so that they feel you are interested and keen to help them reach their fitness goals. If you are working on the administration side, then simply saying 'Hello' and 'Goodbye' to people helps them to feel welcome, especially if you can remember their name!

Groups

Dealing with groups means that you rarely get the chance to find out the needs of every customer in the group. You may deal with groups if you are teaching a swimming class, for example, or instructing a step aerobics class. In these cases you will need to communicate clearly to the whole group through speech and demonstrations. You should always ensure you offer the group time to speak to you on a one-to-one basis, either at the start or at the end of the session. You can also communicate to groups through the use of posters, letters and signs etc.

Different Age Groups

In the leisure industry you can expect to deal with people of all ages, from babies and toddlers right through to the over-60s. Therefore, you should be able to have an understanding of their needs, for example be aware of where the baby-changing facilities are, ensure you know about reduced prices for the over-60s, be aware of special swimming sessions for the over-60s etc.

Different Cultural Backgrounds

You need to be aware of different cultural needs and be able to cater for them accordingly. For example, some cultures will not allow males to see females in their swimsuits. Therefore, you must be able to give these females details of when there are female-only swimming sessions. These sessions would also have to have only female lifeguards on duty. You should be aware of people who use the facility who do not have English as their first language, and ensure there are signs and promotional materials that they can understand.

Specific Needs

A good leisure facility is able to cater for every person in its local area, including people who have specific needs. An example of a person with a specific need is someone with restricted mobility; these people may require the use of a walking stick or wheelchair, for example. In these cases the facility should have appropriate access so that people can enter the building unaided. If the building is on two stories, there must be a lift or ramps to allow the person to move up to the next floor. If the facility has a swimming pool, there must be some form of access available for people with disabilities, such as a chair hoist.

Customer Service Procedures

The different procedures required to ensure customer service is of a high standard are shown in Figure 15.6.

Figure 15.6   Customer service

Making the Customer Feel Welcome

This is the first opportunity you have to demonstrate your customer care. A simple greeting with a smile as the customer arrives through the door gives the impression you are pleased to see that person, which makes them feel welcome. This service should be in place in both the reception area, as the customer enters the building, and in the area in which their activity is to take place, for example in the gym, where the gym instructors should make a point of acknowledging the customer's arrival.

Making the Customer Feel Valued

This service can be provided by ensuring the customer's needs are being met. In order to find out what the customer's needs are, there are a number of methods you could employ. Here are some examples:

- You could simply ask them for their thoughts on the facility and its services

- Produce a questionnaire about the facility or a particular aspect of that facility, for example an aerobics class questionnaire asking about the times and the types of classes available

- The facility could have a customer 'comments box'.

Answering Customers' Questions

If you work in a leisure facility, you should be able to answer questions about the basic operations of this facility, such as opening hours and the services the facility has to offer. If, however, you do not know the answer, you must be able to direct the customer to someone who does – never tell a customer that you do not know the answer to their question and then walk away.

Dealing Effectively with Complaints

How you deal with a customer's complaint is very important. You should always ensure you respect the customer and listen carefully to the complaint. Ensure you give an apology,

---

Activity **15.4** 40 mins   P5 P6 M3

Customer service skills in sport and leisure

Sport and leisure facilities rely on customers coming to their centre and using their facilities; it is therefore very important that these customers are kept happy so that they continue to use the facility.

Task 1

Design a leaflet that could be handed out to members of staff working in a selected sport and leisure facility that describes and explains the importance of providing effective customer service.

Task 2

Carry out research to find out about the different procedures used in your selected sport and leisure facility – for example, leaflets, customer charter, website etc., then write a report that describes and explains these procedures.

even when it is not your fault, and try to find a solution to the problem. You should be sure to keep calm and not argue with the customer. If a solution cannot be agreed on, you should bring your manager into the discussion. Once a solution has been agreed, ensure that what you have promised does happen.

Personal Presentation

Customers will form an impression about the facility within a few seconds of arrival. This impression is based on what they see, hear and smell, so the presentation of staff does make a significant impact upon this first impression. If you look smart, your uniform is clean and ironed, and you have taken care over your personal grooming and hygiene, the customers will adopt a positive attitude towards you and the rest of the facility.

 Quick Quiz 2   40 mins

1. See if you can give a definition for customer service.
2. Name six effects that good customer service can have on a sport or leisure business.
3. Describe how you could make a customer feel welcome on their first visit to your sports centre.
4. Sometimes, like when it is very busy, customer service should come second place. True or False?
5. Design a quick four-step procedure for dealing with a customer complaint.
6. Write down a telephone-answering script that is an improvement on this one: 'Alright mate, you OK, what do you want then?'
7. Name three ways in which a customer can be made to feel valued.

 Key learning points

- You must be able to deliver a high level of customer service if you work in the sport or leisure industry. Good customer service produces customer loyalty, new customers, increased sales and profits, a good image, employee satisfaction and a competitive edge over other facility providers.
- Every sport or leisure facility should be able to provide a service for all members in its local community, including people with a different cultural background, people with specific needs and people of all ages.

15.3 Checking, Taking down and Storing Equipment for Sports Activities

If you are working in a sports facility, you will probably be involved in setting up, checking, taking down and storing sporting equipment. This section will guide you through basic procedures that you will need to follow to ensure you are performing these duties safely.

Setting up Equipment

Different Types of Equipment

Equipment in a sport or leisure facility is varied and consideration needs to be given to its storage, how it is put up and how it is taken down safely. Examples include:

- Complex, heavy equipment like a trampoline
- Simple equipment like a badminton net
- Powered equipment, like some kinds of basketball goal, or a running machine

- Items that require a team to set up – like gymnastics equipment or large floor mats.

Obviously, the more complex the equipment, the more training is required to set it up and bring it down.

Set up, Check and Take down

While the equipment in sports centres can be very different, the approach to setting up, checking and taking down is the same.

1. Identify and locate the equipment required; it could be in a store room or a secure area.

2. Follow the standard operating procedures for safe erection, including the required number of staff.

3. Follow the correct procedures in the NOP for handling, putting up and even safe moving of the equipment.

4. Check the equipment for safety and, importantly, know what you should check for.

5. Report any faulty parts or poor functioning to the correct member of staff.

6. Follow the same procedure for dismantling the equipment.

Before setting up any equipment, you must check the area or room to ensure it is free from any new hazards; these may include water from a leaking roof or drinks spilt on the floor, rubbish, inadequate lighting due to bulb failure, an uneven floor surface etc.

Activities

Indoor Football

When setting up the goalposts, make sure the goal frame is in the correct position and stable. An unsteady goal frame may fall on someone, which could result in a serious injury. If the goalpost you use is moveable, then it will probably have some form of weighting system to keep it upright. Some goalposts have sockets to secure them to the floor. You will

receive training on your facility's type of goalpost and learn the procedures for putting them up properly. You should also check to see that the net is secured to the frame properly. Some facilities also place mats around the goalposts so that the goalie can have a soft landing if they need to dive for the ball.

Badminton

There is not a huge variation in designs of badminton posts, so the setting up procedures will generally follow these guidelines. Pull the post towards you so that the post is resting on its wheels. You can then push the post to its position at the side and in the middle of the badminton court (this is usually marked on the court). Place the post so that its 'foot' is pointing in towards the court; repeat for the second post. Attach a net to the outside of one post, then unwind the net across to the other post. Anchor the net onto the outside of the second post. Secure both sides of the bottom part of the net to the inside of the posts.

Basketball

The basket is usually pushed back against the sports hall wall. You will need to use a reaching implement that can hook onto the basket and lever it forwards. The basket is in place when it is out as far as it can go. Place your reaching implement in a safe area away from and off the court. Baskets that drop down from the ceiling may be operated automatically by pushing a button or by using a winding mechanism.

Volleyball

Volleyball posts can usually be moved in the same way as badminton posts. Once the post has been put into position, there is usually a socket in the floor to lock it into position and ensure that it remains stable and upright. You will then need to secure the net to the posts. Each set of posts has different methods of raising the net to the playing height, so you will receive appropriate training in how to do this.

During and After Play

Once you have set up the apparatus, you should continue to be vigilant and ensure that the apparatus remains in the correct position. You should also check the environment to ensure it is safe. For example, the surface may become wet through sweat or a drink spill, in which case you should take action and stop play in order to dry the surface.

Review

In order to ensure that you are performing your job well, and in order to be even better at your job, you must first of all assess your progress. This can be carried out through obtaining feedback from your colleagues and/or your customers and/or your manager. The larger the range of people you use, the better idea you will have of your performance.

The feedback that you receive could be formative or summative:

- **Formative feedback** – aims to help the person to improve as part of the assessment process.
- **Summative feedback** is usually at the end of training and is generally considered more formal.

Feedback can come from the following sources:

Colleagues
Your colleagues will be able to give you information on how well you work as a member of a team, your communication skills, your health and safety awareness.

Manager
Your manager will be able to give you their views on how well they feel you are carrying out your job specification. They will examine a number of things, some of which may include your timekeeping skills, your appearance, your ability to carry out your various job roles and your manner of addressing people in authority.

Customer
You may wish to ask for feedback from a number of customers, some that you see regularly and some that you have met only once or twice. This will give you an idea of what level of customer service you are providing. The customers you have met only once or twice will be able to give you feedback on the first impression you make; for example, did you appear welcoming by saying 'Hello' and smiling? Customers that are well known to you will be able to give more detailed feedback on the level of customer service you are providing; for example, are you always helpful, are you interested in their fitness progress?

Self-evaluation
You should be able to give yourself an honest analysis of how you have performed. If you put in 100 per cent effort, then you should be pleased with yourself, as you have done the best you can. If, however, you have not performed as well as you could have, due to lack of effort, you will need to assess why you did not put in as much effort as you were capable of. Every person benefits from some sort of training so that they can continually improve and develop themselves. You should look at training courses that are available to help you reach your goals, for example if you would like to do more coaching, you should take some national governing body coaching awards.

Strengths and Areas for Development

As part of any review, it is possible to produce a list of what we are good at, and what we need to improve upon. Of course we can do this ourselves, but it is probably best done with our line manager, so that we can reflect on what to develop for the future and how to best make use of our strengths

Key learning points

- All sports facilities have their own procedures for setting up equipment, as the types of equipment can vary significantly.
- You will be shown how to carry out these duties effectively and safely, and must adhere to these guidelines at all times.
- You must be vigilant to ensure that the environment is safe for your customers before, during and after their activity has taken place.

References

Roberts, I., 2001, *Leisure and Recreation*, London: Heinemann.

Wolsey, C. and Abrams, J. (eds), 2001, *Understanding the Sport and Leisure Industry*. Harlow: Longman.

Quick Quiz 3 30 mins ?

safety	trampoline	gymnastics	standard
hazards	formative	badminton net	summative

Choose a word(s) from the table above to answer the following questions or fill in the blanks.

1. **This is an example of complex, heavy equipment.**
2. **This is an example of simple equipment.**
3. **When setting up equipment it is important follow the _____ operating procedures for safe erection, including the required number of staff.**
4. **Check the equipment for_____ and, importantly, know what you should check for.**
5. **This type of feedback aims to help the person to improve as part of the assessment process.**
6. **This type of feedback is usually at the end of training and is generally considered more formal**
7. **Before setting up any equipment, you must check the area or room to ensure it is free from any new _____.**
8. **A team is usually required to set up equipment for this type of sport.**

Chapter 16
Leading Outdoor & Adventurous Activities

There has been a large increase in participation in outdoor and adventure activities in recent years. As well as the traditional school groups there are other newer markets such as corporate training events and stag and hen groups.

An increase in demand for this kind of activity brings an increase in demand for key staff such as leaders and instructors.

This chapter will help provide you with the knowledge that will support your participation in these activities. It will focus on leadership skills in a variety of disciplines, with safety forming the basis for all of them.

Learning Goals

By the end of this chapter you should:

- Know the skills, qualities and responsibilities associated with successful outdoor and adventurous activity leadership
- Be able to plan and lead, under supervision, outdoor and adventurous activities
- Be able to review own planning and leadership of outdoor and adventurous activities.

To achieve a PASS grade the evidence must show that the learner is able to:	To achieve a MERIT grade the evidence must show that, in addition to the pass criteria, the learner is able to:	To achieve a DISTINCTION grade the evidence must show that, in addition to the pass and merit criteria, the learner is able to:
P1 outline the skills, qualities and responsibilities associated with successful leadership of three different outdoor and adventurous activities	**M1** explain the skills, qualities and responsibilities associated with successful leadership of three different outdoor and adventurous activities	
P2 produce a plan for leading two different outdoor and adventurous activities, with tutor support	**M2** independently produce a plan for leading, and lead under supervision, two different outdoor and adventurous activities	
P3 lead, with tutor support and under supervision, two different outdoor and adventurous activities		
P4 review own performance in planning and leading outdoor and adventurous activities, identifying strengths and areas for improvement	**M3** explain own strengths and areas for improvement in leading outdoor and adventurous activities, making suggestions relating to improvement	**D1** evaluate own performance in leading outdoor and adventurous activities, commenting on own leadership effectiveness, strengths and areas for improvement and development

16.1 Skills, Qualities and Responsibilities Associated with Successful Outdoor and Adventurous Activity Leadership

Skills of a Leader

Being a leader in outdoor or adventure activities is more than being at the front or back of a group of canoeists, being first on the rope on a climb or choosing a route for a mountain biking expedition. Perhaps the most important skill in this setting is the ability to make a team from a group of individuals.

Communication

Leaders must communicate effectively with their group or with individuals, remembering that effective communication is a complex process involving listening, observing, use of body language and signals and speech.

A good leader will be an expert in their discipline and have knowledge of how people learn. During an activity the leader must:

1. Let the group know what the aims of the activity are.

2. Observe the group and evaluate their ability to cope.

3. Keep instructions simple and not use jargon.

4. Stop an activity if it is not safe or the group cannot cope.

5. Demonstrate technical skills effectively and check the learning of the group, for example a kayak coach can demonstrate a slap for support stroke and then watch the group execute the skill.

Activity 16.1 ⏱ 60 mins

Communication skills

Task

Read the two scenarios and for each decide what action and decisions you would take as a leader. You should justify your actions.

1. **Scenario one** – you are a kayak instructor who is leading a group of six kayaks including yourself on a river journey of 18 miles. You have two miles to go when one of the group complains of severe stomach pains and cannot continue. There is no way of contacting help because nobody has a signal on their mobile phone. The weather is getting worse, there is a distinct drop in temperature and there is nowhere to get out at the sides. What action(s) and decisions would you take?

2. **Scenario two** – you are mountain biking through a wood with a group of beginner mountain bikers. Without warning, two of the group start to fight over an accident for which each blames the other. Another member of the group brings the fight to your attention and also points out that more than half of the group are unaware that this has happened and have gone on ahead. Again, what actions do you take as leader?

You must always know the best way to get the attention of a group, a whistle or command perhaps, how and where they should come together as a group and consider your position as a leader for providing feedback.

You must also consider the way that leaders communicate:

- **Verbal communication** – what we say and how we say it, providing guidance, asking open questions and checking understanding.

- **Non-verbal communication** – using your body to communicate, particularly in remote, windy or noisy environments; think about what your expressions say about you, and what effect your eye contact has on your group members.

Use of Language

It is important that leaders use the right kind of language. It is easy to use terms that are unique to a sport and forget that others may not understand these terms; for example, would you tell a novice canoeist to 'Put in a reverse J, pry to recover using the gunwale for leverage'?

It is also possible to use analogies to help explain complex techniques; for example, one way of explaining how to get out of a capsized kayak could be to describe pushing off at the back of the cockpit with both hands 'like taking off a pair of trousers'. In this way a complex sequence of events can be simplified by using an example with which everyone is familiar.

> **Definition** ⓓ
>
> **Analogy** a comparison between two different things, in order to highlight some form of similarity.

Supervision and Support

Perhaps the most important skill of a leader is that of supervision. Once a session is up and running, a leader will need to constantly re-evaluate many things, including:

- The safety of the session

- The progress both of the group and the individuals that make up that group

- Whether the drills/practices or techniques are working.

Since different people learn at different speeds, and in different ways, it is important that a variety of methods of leadership are observed.

Decision-making

A leader must take responsibility for the safety and needs of a group. There will be times when the leader must decide on a course of action that will influence the safety and enjoyment of the group. An effective leader will make decisions based on what is best for that group at any given moment and using the best information available.

Equipment

A leader must consider not only what equipment is needed for an activity but also the condition and suitability of that equipment.

An orienteering leader, for example, should consider making available and checking the safety and suitability of the following equipment:

- A map – which must be up to date, accurate and weatherproofed

- Compasses – one for each of the group, and checked to see if they work properly

- Whistles – for emergency purposes

- Watches – so that individuals are aware of the time and can meet safety-check times

- First-aid kit – at a point near to the course

- Clothing – appropriate to the weather and conditions

- Control markers – clearly recognisable.

Improvisation

A leader must be able to improvise in certain situations:

- This could be improvising a motivational message or singing songs to raise the morale of a group

- It could also be improvising equipment – for example, a group on an expedition walk may get caught in a sudden downpour. If the group is carrying groundsheets, then these could be adapted to use as a temporary rain shelter or bivouac

- A climbing rope could be tied between two trees to form a drying area for wet clothing

- A leader can also take advantage of what the environment offers. Shelter can be offered by trees or bridges in remote areas

- Using fixed transit points like trees or a lighthouse for directional bearings will reduce the need to study maps.

Knowledge

One of the most vital skills of a leader is that they have a sound understanding of their discipline. Knowledge of their own activity should be extensive. A leader should know:

- What action to take in an emergency

- How to plan and prepare themselves for the activity

- How individuals learn and develop

- How groups form and perform, and how to involve the whole group

- What makes an activity enjoyable

- The safety guidelines and rules of the activity

- The principles of how to construct a session

- How to assess environmental conditions

- Basic and advanced skills in their sport.

Specific Skills

Leadership is more than observing and organising a group activity. The role of the leader has a great deal of responsibility. A leader must consider a number of factors even before embarking on an activity.

In addition to the skills of leadership, is the ability to perform and demonstrate those skills as and when appropriate.

1. **Aim** – the aim of the activity could be to lead a group on a six-mile sea journey by kayak

2. **Individual skills** – the leader must have a good idea of the level of performance of the individuals that form a group, and be aware of any special or additional needs, for example whether any of the group have a learning difficulty or medical condition that may prevent them from taking part in certain activities.

3. **Planning** – a leader must have a formalised plan of an activity. This plan should include details such as:

   - Group details

   - Start and finish points if different

   - A list of equipment taken

   - Expected duration of the session

   - Weather forecast.

4. **Organisation** – for an orienteering leader, for example, this would include preparing maps; marking a course; packing compasses, whistles and a first-aid kit.

Figure 16.1 A good leader plans ahead for the good of his or her team

Qualities of a Leader

The qualities required to be a successful outdoor and adventurous activity leader are shown in Figure 16.2.

Figure 16.2   Qualities of a leader

1. **Confidence** – in a leader may be the single most important quality. A leader who projects confidence is one whom a group or individuals can put their trust and faith in, often in potentially dangerous environments and situations.

2. **Authority** – is not necessarily just bossing someone about. It is possible to allow enjoyable and safe activity and fair play. In certain situations it may be necessary for a leader to show their authority:

   ● If a participant jeopardises their own safety or the safety of their group

   ● When it is important to represent the interests of their group to others in the best way, for example coastguards or customs officials.

3. **Humour** – laughing or directing sarcasm towards participants is not acceptable; however, there is no reason not to use humour in certain situations:

   ● To raise the morale of the group

   ● To help participants learn in a relaxed environment

   ● To help defuse tension in a group.

4. **Organisation** – this is more than just making sure that everyone starts off safely. A good leader will have considered all aspects of their preparation. They will have details of their participants, have checked and if necessary double-checked all equipment, made others aware of the details of any remote activity and thought through the whole process of an activity and all possible eventualities.

5. **Initiative** – this is the ability to work with your wits, in other words, to come up with a solution to a challenge or problem that fits the moment. A leader with good initiative will repeatedly come up with solutions to problems that occur.

6. **Patience** – the ability to accept that everybody is different and that people learn and perform at different rates. It is also important to deal with impatience within a group. For example, a climbing group is frustrated that it is being held up by a slow climber who also demands a great deal of the instructor's time. A leadership strategy in this situation might be to put the group in the mindset of the slower individual by asking the members how they would feel in that situation. Once they have reflected, each could be asked to offer some kind of support to the slower climber based on their experience and what they have to offer.

7. **Adaptability** – no activity or expedition is without some kind of difficulty, many of which cannot really be planned for – a sudden change in the weather, sea conditions, an individual being injured, or equipment failure. The important factor is how the leader responds in this situation. While you cannot be prepared for every eventuality, it is possible to change or revise plans and/or activity objectives.

Style of Leadership

No one leader is the same, and no one group, activity or expedition is the same. There are a number of ways in which a leader can lead. All styles of leadership can be put on a continuum that shows the focus of the leader's delivery technique (see Figure 16.3).

Figure 16.3   Leadership continuum

A leader who scores a 1 on this scale is often referred to as an authoritarian or as having a command-style approach. This kind of leader usually issues instructions and has very much a 'do it my way' approach to leadership.

A leader at the other end of the scale is often described as having a democratic style of leadership. In other words, for this leader it is important that the majority of decisions are made by the group. Leadership is a complex subject and many leaders use a mixture of styles depending upon:

- The situation
- The group.

For example, a trekking group caught in a snow blizzard are less likely to respond to a discussion as to what course of action to take. In this instance it is probably better that the leader uses a simple and authoritarian approach, in the best interest of the group.

Responsibilities of a Leader

Conduct

A leader is responsible for the conduct of the group or individuals under their charge. For everyone who takes part in an outdoor or adventurous activity there is an expectation that people behave in a mature way, and stick to the rules laid out by the governing body, for example the British Canoe Union, and also by the activity provider, all designed mostly with the safety of the group concerned, and the impact on others and the environment.

In addition to this, there is an added expectation on the leader concerning their conduct that, for all activities, will be based on a professional working code and should include:

- Safe working practice
- Fairness (sometimes called equity) to all
- To keep up to date with their sport or discipline
- To only have a professional relationship with their group
- To take part in training updates for both their sport and for important issues, for example child protection, as and when required.

Health and Safety

Emergency Procedures

An efficient and robust system should be in place in the event of an emergency. Details of all participants, including the leader/s, should be left in a safe and dry place where it can be easily accessed.

A leader must be able to:

1. Produce information about the group if needed.

2. Execute correct procedures that apply to their activity, for example the correct search techniques for climbers or orienteers, should someone be lost.

3. Treat minor injuries and report the details.

4. Contact the relevant authorities, for example police, ambulance or coastguard.

5. Demonstrate to a group the importance of safety in their activity by teaching safe practice and never taking unnecessary risks.

6. Produce evidence of insurance that covers both themselves and the group.

Activity 16.2 30 mins P1

Skills, qualities and responsibilities of a outdoor and adventurous activities leader

Task

In pairs produce a poster, a whiteboard or an interactive whiteboard display that outlines and explains the following:

Poster 1 **The Skills of an Outdoor Leader**

For example, communication, use of language, decision-making

Poster 2 **The Qualities of an Outdoor Leader**

For example, confidence, leadership style, humour

Poster 3 **The Responsibilities of an Outdoor Leader**

For example, health and safety, transport and travel, contingency plans

The posters should be as large as possible, and you should present both of your ideas on the poster.

The poster could have a central theme, like a picture of a leader or a name, or perhaps look like a spidergram or mind shower.

Under each of the headings, and as many as you can add of your own, you should add your interpretations of what they mean and, where possible, examples from your experience or an imaginary situation.

Figure 16.4   Preparation for your expedition is vital for safety's sake

Contingency Plans

Contingency plans are about expecting the unexpected. This means planning for any event that might happen.

To understand how to design a contingency plan, when planning an activity you could ask yourself a series of 'What would I do if . . .' type questions:

1. What would I do if someone is seriously injured?
2. What would I do if the minibus breaks down?
3. What would I do if the weather becomes really bad?
4. What would I do if a participant gets lost?
5. What would I do if we run out of food and drink?
6. What would I do if the leader is unable to continue?

In this way it is possible to imagine and then calculate what you would do in any given situation.

Transport and Travel Arrangements

Organising transport and travel is a complicated and time-consuming activity. Consider the needs of a group that intends to complete a 30-mile mountain biking trip.

Nutrition

When talking part in any activity it is important to try and estimate the energy requirements of that activity and, where necessary, replace the fuels that are being used.

While it is a good idea to stock up on carbohydrates one to two days before a long trip or expedition, there will be a need to carry some replacement foods, particularly for longer journeys in remote areas.

Figure 16.5 Carbohydrates provide your body with essential energy for physical activity

Fluid Intake and Replacement

As soon as we start any physical activity there will be some fluid loss; of course the amount of fluid loss will depend largely on the intensity of the activity and our body temperature. It is important that leaders ensure that the whole group has plenty of fluids or easy access to plenty of fluids.

How Much Fluid Do I Need?

You can assess your fluid requirements by weighing yourself before and after exercise:

1 kg lost = 1 litre of fluid deficit

2 kg lost = 2 litres of fluid deficit.

Your drink-up routine should be as follows:

- Avoid starting exercise dehydrated. Drink plenty of fluids for several hours prior to exercise.

- If you are well hydrated you should be able to pass a good volume of clear urine in the hour before exercise.

- Drink at least 500 ml (two to three glasses) 30 minutes to one hour before exercise.

- Drink at least 200 ml (one glass) every ten to 15 minutes during exercise.

- During exercise take advantage of all breaks in play to drink up.

- After exercise drink liberally to ensure you are fully rehydrated.

As already pointed out, it is absolutely vital that any kind of activity is properly planned. This planning must first take into account the participants who are going to be involved in the activity.

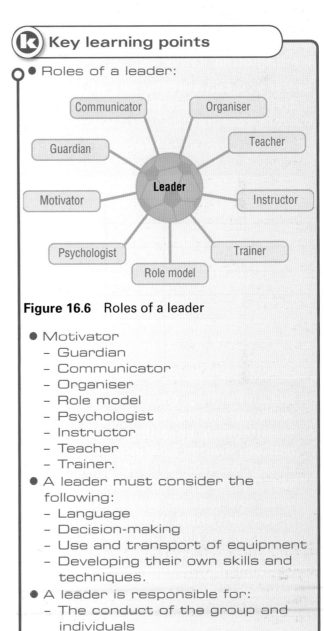

Figure 16.6 Roles of a leader

- Motivator
  - Guardian
  - Communicator
  - Organiser
  - Role model
  - Psychologist
  - Instructor
  - Teacher
  - Trainer.
- A leader must consider the following:
  - Language
  - Decision-making
  - Use and transport of equipment
  - Developing their own skills and techniques.
- A leader is responsible for:
  - The conduct of the group and individuals
  - Health and safety
  - Travel arrangements
  - Contingency plans.

Quick Quiz 1   10 mins

Knowing the range and type of activities that are considered outdoor and adventure activities is important. If you are thinking about a career in this industry, perhaps as an instructor or as an assistant instructor, the chances of you getting a job will rely on you not only being an expert in one discipline but also able to understand and potentially to lead or assist in leading other activities.

See if you can sort the mix of activities and place them into the correct category.

Caving	Climbing	Water sports	Trekking

Rock climbing, canoeing, hill-walking, caving, kayaking, orienteering, abseiling, improvised rafting, dragon boating, off-piste skiing, off-road cycling, white water rafting, ghyll scrambling, mine exploration, wave skiing, mountaineering, potholing, fell running, ice climbing, gorge walking, sea level traversing, sailboarding, sailing, pony trekking, windsurfing.

16.2 Planning and Leading Outdoor and Adventurous Activities P2 P3 M2

Participants

It is important to consider the following:

- **Age** – working with children requires a different set of skills compared with working with adults. You have to consider such issues as: immature behaviour, additional emotional needs and differing attention spans. The effects of physical activity on a child are very different to an adult.

- **Gender** – for ethical and legal reasons, when dealing with groups that contain a mixture of male and female participants, there should be an equal balance of male and female leaders or responsible adults.

- **Ability** – only plan to do what is within the capability of all the individuals in a group.

- **Numbers** – a leader should only work with a safe group size. This is determined by the nature of the activity and the skill level of the participants. Information on the correct leader-to-participant ratio is usually determined by the governing body, for example the British Canoe Union.

Medical Information

As well as gaining the consent of parents or carers for any activity, it is important that participants complete a medical details form similar to the one opposite.

Medical information and consent form (Under 18)

(Please complete in block capitals)

Activity/Event and date _____

Name _____

Address _____

Name and address of next of kin: Name and contact address of doctor:

_____   _____

_____   _____

_____   _____

Telephone _____   Telephone _____

Any medical disabilities, treatment, regular medication or allergies to declare (e.g. asthma, hay fever or diabetes etc.)

_____

_____

Special dietary requirements? _____

_____

I acknowledge receipt of and understand the details of all of the information about the activity/event and consent to the participation of: _____

I will make sure that my son/daughter understands the information given about his/her safety and the safety of the group, and that any rules and instructions given by staff are adhered to.

I will inform the leader of any changes to my son's/daughter's health or fitness before the start of the activity.

I am in agreement that those in charge may give permission for the participant mentioned above to receive medical/dental treatment in an emergency.

Signed (parent/guardian): _____   Date _____

Give relationship to participant if not parent _____

I understand that for my own safety, and the safety of the group, I will undertake to obey the rules and instructions of members of staff.

Signed (Under 18): _____   Date _____

Resources

Resources are a vital part of any outdoor and adventurous activity. Leaders need to think through every stage of a trip carefully and work out exactly what is required in terms of equipment.

A checklist like the one below for a mountain biking expedition is always a good idea.

Mountain Biking Expedition: Major Equipment Checklist

Name	Packed ✓
Bike	
Spares/Wheels/Tyres/ Hubs/Tubes	
Handlebars	
Chains	
Brakes	
Mudguards	
Toe clips	
Bottle cages and bottles	
Pumps	
Racks and panniers	
Clothing	
Tents	
Sleeping bags	
Stove	
Tool kit	
First-aid kit	
Camera	
Medicine	
Locks	
Gloves	
Shoes	

Packing and Storing

It is important that time is put aside when planning a trip to think about where everything will be packed. Will it be necessary to carry everything or can some things be transported in another way, or possibly even 'dumped' in advance at a location at which you intend to arrive as part of the activity?

Maps and Guides

It is necessary when planning a trip to become familiar with the layout and details of the course or route. Many walkers stick to pre-defined routes that are tried and tested, which have the advantage of being easier to follow and require less effort in mapping.

For some kayaking trips it is possible to cycle the route on a towpath or river-bank path, in this way scouting potential problems and possibly places to rest or shelter.

Travel and Transport

As well as working out the best way of being transported to and from an activity or event, some consideration should be given to cost. In other words, who will pay and how much?

The Environment

All of the governing bodies for outdoor activities have guidelines and codes of conduct relating to conservation and how best to respect the environment and prevent any unnecessary damage.

It is worth a leader of an activity also considering having a specific policy or agreement on exactly how they might minimise any adverse effects on the environment. This could range from making sure that you take home all of your rubbish, to using nylon brushes and not wire ones to clean footholds when climbing.

Figure 16.7   An ability to read a map is a useful skill

Activity 16.3 50 mins

P2 M2

Planning for leading outdoor and adventurous activities

You are to help a leader with the delivery of a session in a school, and part of that role is to produce a plan that you should present to the instructor, which shows what you would like to achieve in that session.

Task

Complete the plan for an outdoor or adventure session on the form below, showing what you would do for a specific session of year 8 school children in an activity of your choice.

SESSION PLANNER	
Leader's name:	Outdoor or Adventurous Activity:
Date:	Location:
No. of participants:	
Age/Ability:	
Specialist equipment needed:	
Venue:	
Equipment:	
Where are the following located:	
Fire exits and assembly points:	Telephone:
Toilets:	First-aid box:

16.3 Leading an Outdoor and Adventurous Activity P3

Demonstration of Appropriate Skills

As we have already said in the planning stage, it is essential that a leader is able to demonstrate the skills for a session both competently and safely. Think of the importance of the demonstration of a new technique or of belaying in climbing. In demonstrating a technique you could apply the well-used principle IDEA.

I = Introduce, here you would name the technique, and perhaps check what your group already knows. You could then explain the need or relevance of the technique.

D = Demonstrate, meaning show how the technique is performed, at full speed, and in smaller parts if necessary.

E = Explain, and give examples of the importance of the technique, and the overall importance of its use to the activity, for example a capsize drill in canoeing.

A = Activity, this is where you allow your group to practise the technique, under your supervision, and with you providing the group with feedback throughout.

Effective Organisation

Though organisation is important in the planning stage, it is equally important to remain organised throughout the duration of a session. As a leader you will need to constantly make sure that the situation remains safe and that learning and enjoyment remain balanced throughout.

Flexibility in your approach is vital here, so that if something is not going so well you have the ability to recognise it, and the experience and sense to approach the situation another way.

Group Management

To get the best from your sessions you must make sure that you follow the basic principles of organisation:

- Making sure that everything is ready for you (never assume anything!)
- Make sure that all of your group know the ground rules
- Be well prepared
- Know as much about your group as you can
- Start on time
- Be prepared for the unexpected; think about what you might do if, say, someone does not behave properly or someone gets injured
- Always check equipment and, better still, have someone else check it as well
- Let someone know the details of any trip and how long you should be.

It is also an important skill to recognise how a group reacts in all situations.

Know when to stop the group to make a point, and also the best way to bring them together, say a huddle in a safe area for climbers or the forming of a raft in kayaking.

Figure 16.8   Knowing what to do if your kayak turns over could save your life

Recording the Information

Session Planning

Leaders should be in the habit of producing a session plan for every activity. This plan should include the following:

- Group details
- Date and time
- Nearest telephone and hospital
- A full list of equipment required
- The aims and objectives of the session
- Details of the briefing and warm-up activities
- Details of the main part of the activity, including timings
- Details of the cool-down and debrief
- An area for evaluation and reflection

- A check-off list to ensure that all paperwork for all participants has been completed, for example medical consents.

Diaries and Logbooks

Diaries and logbooks are useful for a number of purposes, including:

1. Forming the basis for assessment.
2. A record of events, including personal developments.
3. Recording details of achievements in competition and training.
4. Recording personal feelings and reflections.
5. Detailing other scientific training data, such as nutrition plans, mental rehearsal routines, or exercise training programmes.
6. A starting point for negotiating performance goals with a leader.

Ⓚ Key learning points

- Planning – a leader must:
  - Be able to produce plans for all sessions
  - Be responsible for ensuring that all equipment is available
  - Be respectful to the environment
  - Adhere to governing body guidelines
  - Be prepared for problems.
- Leading – when leading the session, a leader must consider the following:
  - Supervision
  - Safety
  - Giving good-quality demonstrations and feedback.
- Activities – the session should contain:
  - A warm-up and briefing
  - A main activity phase
  - A cool-down and debriefing session.
- Recording – leaders should be in the habit of keeping accurate and up-to-date information in the following forms:
  - Diaries
  - Logbooks
  - Portfolios
    Videos
  - Observation records
  - Witness testimonies.

Portfolios

These are much larger than diaries or logbooks – usually folders or electronic files. They contain the evidence and information collected over a period of sessions or time. They can contain details of expeditions and trips, maps, charts and details of participants.

A portfolio may also contain session plans, staff details and records of incidents or near-incidents and risk assessments.

Camcorders and Digital Cameras

The use of camcorders and digital still cameras has increased as the price of this technology continues to drop. Leaders can use this technology:

- To make a video diary of a trip
- To analyse performance and behaviour
- To record course or route information
- As a teaching tool.

Observation Records/Witness Testimonies

Keeping a record of what you do or see can have a number of purposes:

- It can provide evidence for assessment
- It can help gather information in the case of a serious incident
- It can act as a permanent record of feelings and emotions.

Feedback Sheets

These can be used from participant to leader or from leader to participant and are usually issued at the end of an activity. Feedback could be technical, in other words relating to a skill, or simply focused on how to improve current practices.

Activity 16.4 50 mins **P3**

Leadership practice

In pairs, and in an outdoor setting, select two different outdoor and adventurous activities.

Task 1

For each outdoor and adventurous activity that you have chosen, plan a five-minute demonstration, taking into account the following:

(a) How well you communicated your technique.

(b) Your personal level of knowledge.

(c) Correct use of terminology.

(d) The overall quality of your demonstration.

Task 2

When you have completed your demonstrations, ask your partner for some feedback along with any comments on how to improve.

Task 3

Lastly switch roles, so that the other partner becomes the instructor and simply repeat the procedure.

16.4 Reviewing the Planning and Leadership of Outdoor and Adventurous Activities **P4** **M3** **D1**

Review

Feedback

Having completed an activity, it is important to gain some feedback on how to improve performance.

Quick Quiz 2 ⏱ 30 mins ?

IDEA	Log book	Children	Observation records	Safe
De-briefing	Main activity	Session plan	Checklist	Learning

Choose a word(s) from the boxes above to answer the following questions.

1. **Working with children requires a different set of skills compared with adults.**
2. **This can be used to help ensure you have packed all the equipment you need.**
3. **In demonstrating a technique this principal can be applied.**
4. **These can be used to check how well a person is demonstrating or leading a session.**
5. **This can be used to track a leader's own progress.**
6. **An activity session should include a warm-up, a _____ , a cool-down and a _____ session.**
7. **Leaders should be produce one of these for every activity.**
8. **As a leader you will need to constantly make sure that the activity remains _____ and that _____ enjoyment remain balanced throughout.**

Feedback can come from a number of sources:

- Yourself
- Your peers
- An assessor
- A supervisor
- An observer.

Strengths and Areas for Development

Whatever the nature and style of your leadership, and whatever the nature of your activity, no two leaders are identical. Information about strengths and weaknesses provides us with a template for improvement. A leader should learn something new from every session.

Examples of development feedback could be:

- Poor or ineffective stroke demonstration
- Unsafe activity
- Ineffective/unsafe knots used (climbing)
- Ineffective communication with the group
- Lack of confidence and experience.

All of the above can be improved. Leaders must review and develop their own self-assessment techniques, paying particular attention to what needs to be improved and in what order.

You could use a set of questions, such as those below, to help you identify what you may need to do to improve.

Leader Activity Evaluation

1. Aims and objectives – were they achieved?
2. Participants' performance – did it improve?
3. Were there any behaviour issues?
4. Health and safety issues – anything to report?
5. Organisation – were the skills taught and the techniques used appropriate?
6. What was my leadership like? (Communication, adaptations, style etc.)
7. Actions for the next session.

Setting Targets for Improvement

When you have identified areas for development, it is good practice to apply the SMART principle:

Specific – for example, has your belaying demonstration taken into account the learning needs of all of your group, in this case to a group of beginners.

Measurable – for example, test the effectiveness of your teaching; see if you can learn the skill well enough to produce an effective demonstration.

Achievable – in other words, know that you are capable of executing the skill well enough to demonstrate it to a group of beginners.

Realistic – is it possible?

Time-constrained – for example, review the situation in one month.

Development Plans and Opportunities

Once you have identified what the key areas for development are, you can then go about the process of how this could happen. What comes at the end of this process can be called an action plan or a development plan. The development plan is a set of targets that will help you achieve the ultimate aim of improving as a leader.

The kind of action points that you might find on a development plan could include:

● Planning to meet the needs of all; training that will improve my understanding of how people learn differently

● Working on NVC (non-verbal communication) by practising a set of skills in a small group and using your voice as little as possible; this could also include the observation of a leader or coach who is excellent at NVC

● Improving up-to-date knowledge by attending a course in your activity

● Producing a short report or blog on a forum on an identified issue, such as improving the range of practices used in demonstrating caving techniques.

Activity 16.5 40 mins   P4   M3   D1

Review and improve planning and leadership of outdoor and adventurous activities

In this activity you should think back to a previous activity that you were part of or perhaps even were the leader. It may be helpful to imagine that this is an interview task for an instructor's job.

Task 1

Complete the table below, and rate yourself from 1–10, where 10 means excellent and 1 means very poor.

Review point	1–10
Was my planning and progression OK?	
Did I communicate well and use the correct technique	
Was it safe?	
Was the warm-up and cool-down good enough?	
Did I use the best practices?	

Task 2

Having completed this chart you should then explain what you thought was good about the session, and what needed improvement, giving at least two points for each.

When you have done this you should complete the following table.

Action point	How can I improve this?
E.g. Poor communication	

Task 3

Finally, review your own performance in a brief report to the centre manager about the session. Make sure that your report includes the following details:

● Your leadership effectiveness
● Your planning ability
● What you could do to improve for next time
● Any training that you think may be helpful.

Quick Quiz 3 20 mins

1. **Name four factors about participants to consider when planning a trip.**
2. **Name three ways of planning a route for a walking trip.**
3. **Describe four ways in which you could help to protect the environment on an outdoor expedition.**
4. **In risk assessments, what is a hazard and what is a risk?**
5. **Name eight details that should be on any activity session plan.**
6. **How could a video camera be useful on an outdoor expedition?**

 Key learning points

After a session a leader can record, review and make use of:

- Feedback from participants, peers and observers
- A list of strengths and areas for development
- Targets that will help improve future sessions.

Further Reading

Martin B., Cashel C., Wagstaff M., Breunig, M., 2006, *Outdoor Leadership: Theory and Practice*. London: Human Kinetics.

Priest, S., Gass, M., 2005, *Effective Leadership in Adventure Programming*. London: Human Kinetics.

Useful websites

www.reviewing.co.uk/outdoors/links.htm
Portal to an extensive range of outdoor and adventure activity sites.

www.hse.gov.uk/aala/faq.htm
Frequently asked questions (with answers) on the scope of the present health and safety regulations, with details of voluntary schemes and general information.

www.opsi.gov.uk/si/si2004/20041309.htm
The full, printable text of the Adventure Activities Licensing Regulations 2004.

www.hse.gov.uk/aala/public-information.htm
Information about the Adventure Activities Licensing, covering what the licence is and is not required for.

www.mltuk.org/docs/mlts-winter-guidance.html
Detailed guidance notes for participants of the Winter Mountain Leader award, outlining the leadership, snowcraft and expeditionary skills required.

References

Ferrero, F. (ed.), 2002, *Canoe and Kayak Handbook: Handbook of the British Canoe Union*. Caernarfon: Pesda Press.

Stafford-Brown, J., Rea, S. and Chance, J., 2003, BTEC *National in Sport and Exercise Science*. London: Hodder and Stoughton.

Tannenbaum, R. and Schmidt, W., 1968, *How to Choose a Leadership Pattern*, Boston, USA: Harvard Business Review.

Vickers, P., 1990, *Bicycle Expeditions: Planning, Equipping and Undertaking Long-Distance Expeditions by Bicycle*. London: Expedition Advisory Centre.

Chapter 17
Expedition Experience

More and more people are enjoying taking part in expeditions to explore the countryside. Fresh air, exercise, exploring nature and peace and quiet are some of the reasons why people are choosing to go out on these excursions. However, in order to carry out such outings safely there are a number of skills that must be learnt and practised beforehand. Good navigation skills are essential together with route planning, risk assessing and awareness of the effects on the environment. You will also have to have knowledge of the equipment required and how to maintain it.

Learning Goals

By the end of this chapter you should:

● Know the safety and environmental considerations for a multi-day expedition.
● Be able to use skills and techniques required for a multi-day expedition.
● Be able to plan for a multi-day expedition.
● Be able to carry out and review a multi-day expedition.

To achieve a PASS grade the evidence must show that the learner is able to:	To achieve a MERIT grade the evidence must show that, in addition to the pass criteria, the learner is able to:	To achieve a DISTINCTION grade the evidence must show that, in addition to the pass and merit criteria, the learner is able to:
P1 describe the safety and environmental considerations for a multi-day expedition	**M1** explain safety and environmental considerations for a multi-day expedition	
P2 demonstrate the skills and techniques required for a multi-day expedition	**M2** explain the skills and techniques required for a multi-day expedition	**D1** justify use of skills and techniques in the undertaking of a multi-day expedition
P3 describe the equipment required for a multi-day expedition		
P4 produce a plan, with tutor support, for a multi-day expedition	**M3** independently produce a plan for a multi-day expedition	**D2** justify decisions made in the planning of a multi-day expedition
P5 carry out, with tutor support, a multi-day expedition, demonstrating the use of relevant skills and required equipment	**M4** independently undertake a multi-day expedition demonstrating the use of relevant skills and required equipment	
P6 review own performance in the planning and undertaking of a multi-day expedition, identifying strengths and areas for improvement	**M5** explain identified strengths and areas for improvement, suggesting strategies to improve future performance	**D3** evaluate performance in the planning and undertaking of a multi-day expedition, suggesting strategies to improve future performance and justifying suggestions

17.1 Safety and environmental considerations for a multi-day expedition P1 M1

Safety Considerations

Going on an expedition is great fun; you can often find yourself miles away from the roads, shops and other people. However, this isolation can prove to be very dangerous if you do not have good safety awareness.

Risk Assessments

Before embarking on your expedition you should have carried out a risk assessment in order to examine the hazards and risks that you may face. The process of carrying out such an assessment has already been explored in Chapter 5 and you will find all the details you need there in order to help you carry out your own risk assessment.

Emergency Procedures

If you or a member of your team needs urgent medical attention (for example, someone has broken their leg), you will need to find some way of contacting the emergency services.

Whether from a landline or a mobile phone you should dial 999 and ask for the police and mountain rescue team:

- Give them the casualty's name and a description of their injuries
- Give them the exact location of the injured person; this should include grid references and the map sheet number
- Give them the time and nature of the accident
- Give them details of the weather conditions.

You should then stay on the phone until you are met by a police officer or member of the mountain rescue team.

If the injury is life-threatening a rescue helicopter may have to be brought in. If this is the case, there are a few precautions that you will need to follow before and during their arrival:

- Secure all loose equipment; this can be done with stones or rucksacks
- Raise your arms in a V shape as the helicopter approaches; this will signal to the helicopter that you are the casualty group. Do not wave to the helicopter as this is the signal for everything is OK
- Shelter the injured person from the rotor downdraught
- Do not approach the helicopter unless directed.

If there is no landline or you do not have a mobile phone or there is no signal, you should instead be able to send a distress signal.

Distress Signals

You should signal using sound. You should have a whistle with you – give a series of six loud blasts followed by one minute's silence, and continue this process until you receive a response. However, if you are in an area where it may be difficult for other people to hear this sound, you should use a visual signal. Smoke from a fire gives a good visual signal. If you hear or see an aircraft, you should try to attract their attention with a mirror, glass or any other shiny object. You should also try to spread out any bright clothing you have on the ground, which will help to draw attention to you.

At night you should use a torch to signal the code SOS. This is done by giving three short flashes, three long flashes, followed by three more short flashes.

Activity **17.1** 45 mins **P1**

Role play: Injury on a mountain **M1**

Task

In groups of four, imagine one of you has injured yourself on a mountain.

Two people in the group will then carry out a role-play exercise to determine how they will get help for the injured person.

The fourth person in the group should observe and give feedback to the group on what they thought they did well and areas for improvement.

Safety Equipment

You should always carry a basic first-aid kit with you on any walk. The Rambler's Association recommends that the following items should be included in this kit:

- Ten plasters in various sizes
- Two large sterile dressings for management of severe bleeding
- One medium sterile dressing for care of larger wounds
- Four triangular bandages to support suspected broken bones, dislocations or sprains
- One eye-pad in case of a cut to the eye
- Four safety-pins to secure dressings
- Disposable gloves.

You should also have the following:

1. **A survival bag** – this is basically a large, heavy-duty bag that you can climb into to keep you insulated against the cold.

2. **A torch and spare batteries** – these should be in your rucksack so that you can see where you are going and also to give distress signals if required.

3. **A whistle** – this should be in your pocket or on a string around your neck so that it can be used to give distress signals.

4. **Food** – you should have more than enough food for your journey and also carry 'emergency rations' with you just in case you find yourself in a situation where you are trapped or have to spend longer on the walk than you intended. Your emergency rations should be energy-dense foods, such as Kendal mint cake or Mars Bars, which will give you a lot of energy.

Escape Routes

When planning your expedition you should have factored in an escape route that you can take if you are faced with a problem. The escape route should take you to lower ground and to some form of shelter. It is vital to have planned this in advance so that you have to be concerned only with the problem at hand and do not have to sit and take time considering the best route back to safety.

Environmental Considerations

When enjoying walking in the outdoors it is essential that you respect the environment in order to preserve its beauty. Some of the areas you choose to explore may have special protection such as Areas of Outstanding Natural Beauty (AONBs). An area of natural beauty is an area with a greatly valued landscape that should be preserved. There are 41 AONBs in England and Wales, and they include coastlines, meadows and moors. Wherever you walk in the countryside you should always adhere to the Countryside Code:

- Always close and secure gates after yourself
- Leave property as you find it
- Protect plants and animals – do not damage or move plants, trees or rocks from their natural habitat
- Do not leave litter of any type; take it home with you and dispose of it properly
- Keep dogs under close control
- Consider other people – do not make too much noise, do not block entrances and driveways with your vehicle

Key learning points

- Distress signals: six loud blasts on the whistle followed by one minute's silence, to be repeated until help arrives. Torch-light flashes: three short flashes, three long flashes, three short flashes, break, repeat.
- Always carry a first-aid kit, plenty of food and a survival bag with you on expeditions.
- Check the weather forecast before setting off on an expedition.

Quick Quiz 1 10 mins

Escape route	Whistle	Risk assessment	Country-side Code	Coastline
Glass	SOS	V shape	10	6

Chose a word(s) from the boxes above to answer the following questions.

1. This is an example of an area of outstanding natural beauty.
2. This is the number of plasters you should have in your first-aid kit.
3. This helps people to know what to do and how to behave in the countryside.
4. If you are in distress, this is the number of blows you should make on a whistle followed by one minute's silence.
5. This is the shape you should make with your arms when signalling to a helicopter that you are the group with a casualty.
6. With a torch this is three short flashes followed by three long flashes then three short flashes.
7. This can be used to attract the attention of an aircraft.
8. This should be carried out prior to an expedition.
9. This can be used to call for help.
10. This is used to take a group of people to lower ground and to shelter.

17.2 Skills and Techniques Required for a Multi-day Expedition P2 M2 D1

You will need a range of skills and have to practise many techniques before you are ready to take part in a multi-day expedition.

Using Maps

A map is an essential piece of equipment when out walking. It will show you where you are and where you want to go to as long as you are able to navigate properly. Maps give an accurate representation of the ground as seen from above. They are then scaled down to different sizes – most maps you will use are Ordnance Survey (OS) maps, with a scale of 1:25,000. This means one unit of length represents 25,000 units on the ground. So, if one unit is 1 cm, 1 cm would cover 250 m on the ground. Maps also contain different symbols to show different landmarks on the ground. Further useful information given on maps includes:

- Map title – this tells you the area of ground that the map covers
- Key to the symbols
- The year the map was made
- The sheet number – the whole of the UK is covered by 403 of these sheets
- Adjoining sheet numbers
- Grid numbers
- A scale line to measure distances.

Measuring the Distance of Your Route

There are two main methods you could use in order to measure the distance of your route. The cheapest method uses only a piece of string. Take a piece of string and place it along the exact route on the map. Place the string on the scale line and measure the distance it covers. This should give you an idea of the route you are planning. You could also use a commercially made map measurer, which you run along your route, and it will tell you the distance to be covered.

Activity **17.2**   20 mins   P2   M2

Using the scale on a map

Task

Look at an OS map and plan a route from an area that contains water or forest to another area that contains a building of some sort.

Work out the distance with a piece of string and the scale line on your map.

Navigation

Definition   d

Navigation the process of plotting and following a route from one place to another.

There are a number of different methods you could use to navigate your journey; the best will be determined by the lay of the land, the weather and the time of day or night. However, no matter what type of navigation you use, you will always need a map.

Grid Referencing

Across an OS map you will see a series of lines going up and across the map dividing it into 1 km block squares. These lines are blue and are known as eastings – these run *across* the map (and northings – these run *up and down* the map – see Figure 17.1). The lines are numbered and allow you to pinpoint your exact location on a map. When giving grid references you should always give the eastings first. A good way to

remember this is to think 'go along the corridor and then up the stairs'.

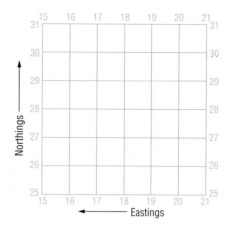

Figure 17.1   A grid showing eastings and northings

Activity **17.3**   10 mins   P2   M2

Using the grid references on a map

Task

Look at a map and choose three features.

Give the grid references of these three different features.

Contours

Definition   d

Contours lines on a map that show you the height of the land.

Most areas that you plan to walk will not be totally flat. Contour lines are drawn onto maps to show you the height and shape of the land (see Figure 17.2). The height between contour lines on OS maps is 10 m. The height is written into some of these lines, which gives you the height of the land above sea level. The numbers are written with the top of the number facing uphill.

Figure 17.2 A contour line

Contour lines will also give you a good impression of the shape of the land. Areas of the map that contain lots of closely packed contour lines show that the land has a steep slope. Valleys and ridges can also be shown by these lines (see Figure 17.3).

Figure 17.3 Contours showing valleys and ridges

Setting the Map

Setting the map is a method of placing the map in a position so that all the features are lined up and your location is at the central point. So, if you were to look to your left, you would see the same features on the ground as you would on the map, and the same would be true for looking ahead or to your right. You may find the writing on the map is upside down when you have set it.

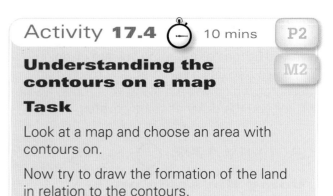

Activity 17.4 10 mins P2 M2

Understanding the contours on a map

Task

Look at a map and choose an area with contours on.

Now try to draw the formation of the land in relation to the contours.

This process can be carried out without any problems if there is good visibility. Look for a prominent feature on the map, such as a church, a hill or a village, then turn the map so that the features on the ground are in line with you at the central point.

If visibility is poor, as in foggy weather conditions or at night-time, you will have to use your compass to set the map. The compass will show you where magnetic north is. Then you will need to line up north on the map with north on the compass. While you are walking, ensure that you keep the map set (i.e. change its position) as you change direction, so, if you turn right, turn the map in the same direction so that it remains set.

Using a Compass

You need to carry your compass in such a way that it is accessible at all times and you are able to move it in any direction (see Figure 17.4). You must also be able to let it go without losing it; therefore the best method of carrying a compass is to attach a long cord to the compass and then carry it over one shoulder.

Figure 17.4 A compass

Taking a Bearing

When you are walking in poor visibility, such as on a foggy day or at night, you will need to take bearings from your map and walk on a bearing.

> **Definition** (d)
>
> **Bearing a direction of travel, between 0 to 360° from north in a clockwise direction.**

Place the compass on the map so that the arrow is pointing in the direction you wish to travel. Then line up the base plate with where you want to travel to. Next, turn the compass housing so that the north arrow is pointing to the north on the map. Ensure the lines within the compass housing are running parallel to the grid lines running northwards.

Now you need to convert the bearing to a magnetic bearing by adding magnetic variation, which is 5 degrees.

Hold the compass horizontally in front of you. Change your direction until the red end of the compass needle is over the orienteering arrow and parallel to the lines in the bottom of the housing. Look in the direction of the travel arrow to see if you can see a feature on the landscape that it lines up with. You can then walk towards this feature. When you have reached the feature, stop and repeat the process until you have reached your desired location. If you do not see a feature to walk towards, hold the compass in front of you and keep walking in the direction of the travel arrow.

Measuring Distance Travelled

There are two methods of estimating the distance you have covered: timing and pacing.

Timing

This process works on the principle of estimating your walking speed and knowing how long you have been walking for. The speed that you walk at will vary depending on whether you are walking uphill or on flat terrain. Most fit people walk at a speed of around 5 km per hour on flat ground. You will then need to add ten minutes for every 100 m of height gained or one minute for every 10 m gained (Naismith's rule). Walking down steep hills will take longer than walking on the flat, so you should add one minute for every 30 m descent.

Pacing

This process uses the principle of counting the number of steps you have taken and estimating the distance covered from these steps. It takes an average-sized male around 60 double steps to cover 100 m. From this you can then work out how far you have travelled. However, you do need to be aware that the size of your pace will vary when you are travelling up or down hill.

> **Activity 17.5** 20 mins   P2
>
> **Working out pacing**   M2
>
> **Task**
>
> Work out your own paces by counting how many double steps you take when walking along a 100-m athletics track.

Planning Your Route

This process should be thought through carefully and planned properly; if you do not give it full attention you may find yourself walking up some very steep mountains or having to walk through boggy ground when you really just wanted to have a fairly easy walk. Think about what you want to accomplish on your expedition and the features you would like to see, for example lakes or forests. Think about how far you would like to walk and the time it will take you or, if you are in a group, how long it will take your slowest walker. You will also need to factor in meal breaks and may wish to aim to eat lunch at a certain place, such as by a river or in a local cafe. If you are planning an overnight expedition, make sure you have given yourself enough

Team Leader: R. Ambler
Date: 26.10.05

Starting Point: GR 328800
Finishing Point: GR 337621

ETD: 0800
ETA: 1800

Leg	From	From	To	To	Bearing	Bearing	Distance	Remarks, hazards etc
	Location	GR	Location	GR	Grid	Mag		
1	River	327645	Style	337644	342	347	500m	Cairns
2	Style	337644	Xroads	341044	54	59	1700m	Steep slope

Figure 17.5 An example of a route card

time to reach your campsite and have chosen an appropriate place to pitch your tent for the night. You should then prepare a route card and make sure you leave a copy of it with someone, preferably a police officer at the nearest station to your route or a person at the nearest mountain centre (see Figure 17.5). This is very important as it will not only aid your navigation, but also, if you get into difficulty, this route card can be used to locate and rescue you.

Choosing Your Camp

Where you plan to camp should be flat and near a ready source of water such as a river or lake. Your campsite should also be able to offer some shelter such as in a hollow. You should also check to see if the land you intend to camp on is private; if so, you must ask permission beforehand.

Activity 17.6 1–4 weeks   P2   M2   **D1**

Skills and Techniques Required for a Multi-day Expedition

In order to carry out a multi-day expedition it is necessary to have a number of navigation skills as well as having a good understanding of how to select an appropriate campsite and of setting up camp.

Task 1

Devise a route plan for a six-mile hike that also plans for a suitable place to camp.

Task 2

Now use your route plan and take part in this six-mile hike. Demonstrate your skills and techniques so that you can:

- Navigate using a compass
- Navigate at night-time or in poor visibility
- Determine which direction to travel in without a compass
- Provide grid references for a range of natural features

Task 3

Demonstrate the ability to set up camp.

Task 4

Once you have set up camp, talk with your supervisor to explain and justify the use of the skills and techniques that you demonstrated on the six-mile hike and why they are required on a multi-day expedition.

Key learning points

- Know how to read and set a map.
- Ensure you are able to read and give grid references.
- Know how to use a compass.
- Know how to take and follow bearings.
- Know how to write a route card.

Quick Quiz 2 5 mins ?

Answer the following questions.

1. **This type of map has a scale of 1:25,000.**
2. **What sort of things should a good campsite have?**
3. **What is the normal walking speed for a fit person?**
4. **What is a bearing?**
5. **What is the name given to map lines running across the page from left to right?**
6. **Who should you leave your route card with?**
7. **Describe what 'setting a map' is.**
8. **What is the name given to describe the steepness of a hill?**
9. **What is the distance between contour lines?**
10. **Describe pacing.**

17.3 Equipment Required for a Multi-day Expedition P3

There is a huge range of equipment available for hikers; it is up to you to choose what you think is appropriate for your needs and what you can afford.

Footwear

One of the most important pieces of equipment you will buy is your footwear. If you choose the wrong type or it does not fit you properly, this could mean your expedition has to be ended prematurely because of blisters or injury. Hiking boots and shoes are available. Boots give ankle support, which helps prevent twisting ankles on uneven ground. The top of the boot or shoe should be waterproof or water-repellent. The soles should be able to give good grip on all walking surfaces you may face. The soles should also provide some cushioning from the impact of walking.

Taking Care of Your Boots

Every pair of boots you buy should come with a list of instructions from the company that made them. The main aim in caring for your boots is to keep them waterproof and supple. You should always clean off any dirt or mud from your boots after a walk and make sure they are dried inside and out. If your boots do get wet on the inside, place some crumpled-up newspaper inside them and let them dry naturally. If you have leather boots, you should also regularly apply Dubbin, Nikwax or some specialist leather oil or wax, which will help to keep your boots supple and waterproof.

Activity 17.7 40 mins   P3

The right walking boots

Task

(a) Look through hiking catalogues or internet sites. Read through the information on the hiking footwear they have to offer, then decide which footwear you would buy for:

- A hike on a summer day on low land in Britain
- A hike in winter in the Lake District.

(b) Explain why you have chosen each particular pair.

Basic Walking Clothing

Going on expeditions usually means you will face a range of weather conditions, especially if you are walking on high ground and if you are staying out overnight. You should dress in layers. This means that you wear several thin layers rather than just one heavy jumper, for example. This principle relies on the fact that you trap warm air between each layer, which will help to keep you warm (it will also allow you to remove a layer or more if you get too hot). The layer next to your skin should be made of a material that takes sweat away from the body. On top of this you could then wear a layer that is designed to keep you warm, such as a fleece with a windproof jacket on top. Obviously, the cooler it is, the more layers you may choose to wear.

Walking trousers, often referred to as 'tracksters', are comfortable to wear as they are lightweight and loose-fitting. If it is cold, you may choose to wear 'long johns' underneath your tracksters, as these will help to keep you warm.

You lose a lot of heat through your head, so a hat is an essential piece of clothing if you are walking in cold conditions. Alternatively, if it is a hot day, you should wear a sun hat to protect yourself against the heat.

Gloves are also an important piece of clothing in cold weather and there are many different types available. If you have circulation problems and suffer from cold hands, you may like to invest in some gloves that have heating systems in them.

The socks you wear are also important. You can buy walking socks that have extra padding on the heels and toes. There are also waterproof socks available and ones made from material that draws the sweat out and away from the skin of the feet. The main thing with socks is that they provide cushioning to the feet and help to prevent your boots rubbing and causing blisters. Many walkers choose to wear two pairs of socks, one thin pair next to the skin and one thick pair on top.

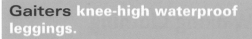

Definition ⓓ

Gaiters knee-high waterproof leggings.

Waterproof Clothing

You should invest in a good waterproof jacket at the very least if you plan to walk around Britain; waterproof trousers and gaiters are also a good buy.

The features you should look for in a waterproof jacket are:

- It is actually fully waterproof and not just shower-proof
- It is made from 'breathable material', which means it lets moisture out but prevents water entering
- It should have a hood or provision for a hood to be attached, preferably one with drawstrings so that it will stay on your head and not get blown off.

Rucksack

A rucksack is an essential item if you are planning an overnight or multi-day expedition. You will need to choose a rucksack that is the right size to carry the equipment you will require. Some rucksacks are rather small and these are referred to as daysacks, as they are the right size to carry everything you would require for a day out walking. The larger, multi-day rucksack usually has a lightweight frame with a hip belt, which helps to take the weight off the back and onto the hips.

Packing Your Rucksack

How you pack your rucksack will have an impact on how comfortable it is to carry and how easy it is to use:

- Place heavier items towards the top of the rucksack; this will place less strain on the back
- Place the items you will need during the day on the top, for example waterproof clothing, food etc.
- Wrap items in strong plastic bags, especially your spare clothing, as rucksacks are not completely waterproof
- Do not carry more items than you need.

Sleeping Bags and Tents

There are a number of different types of sleeping bag available. Choose one that is designed for the weather conditions you are likely to face, for example if you are walking in summer you will need a relatively lightweight sleeping bag. You will also need to buy a sleeping pad to go under your sleeping bag. This is to provide insulation against the cold from the ground and also give some cushioning.

Tents are made from poles that make a frame over which the tent material sits. There is a range of different types of tents.

Avian Tent

This type of tent has two poles and the tent fabric sits over these poles to form a Toblerone shape (see Figure 17.6). These tents are used in light weather conditions.

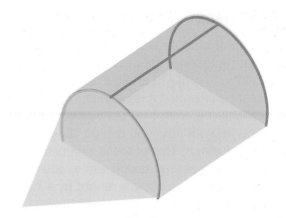

Figure 17.7   A hoop tent

Figure 17.8   A wedge tent

Dome Tent

These tents can be used in very heavy weather conditions but are quite difficult to erect (see Figure 17.9). They consist of three or more intersecting hoops, with the tent fabric sitting over them and forming a dome shape.

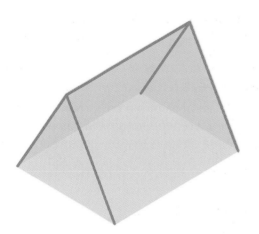

Figure 17.6   An avian tent

Hoop Tent

This type of tent has from one to three hoops over which the tent fabric lies to form a tube (see Figure 17.7). They are quite strong tents and can be used in heavy weather conditions.

Wedge Tent

A wedge tent uses two intersecting hoops, with the tent fabric sitting over the top to form a square shape (see Figure 17.8). These tents can also be used in heavy weather conditions.

Figure 17.9   A dome tent

Guidelines

Every type of outdoor activity has a governing body that represents the interests of its participants. In order to attain a personal or instructor qualification it is necessary to make contact with the governing body of your chosen sport and find out how you can go about achieving this aim. This process is in place to ensure that any person taking part in courses run by the governing body is taught by a fully qualified person who can ensure that every safety precaution is carried out before, during and after the teaching period.

Every outdoor pursuits centre has its own guidelines that staff must follow. For example most centre guidelines expect a designated member of staff to place up-to-date weather reports on the notice board so that other staff and customers can determine whether they should avoid high mountain walks due to adverse weather conditions.

Cooking Equipment

There is quite a variety of cooking equipment available and you will need to determine which are best for you and the expedition you are planning.

You will need to take equipment to cook the food in, such as a saucepan or a frying pan. Alternatively, if you are only planning to eat dehydrated food, a camping kettle could be taken and mess tins used to prepare the food and eat from.

Some hiking areas and some campsites will allow you to light a camp fire over which you can cook your food. However, there are some areas that do not allow open fires, so if you want to cook your food or boil water you must use a stove.

A very popular stove for hikers is the Trangia, which is lightweight and portable. It has a burner that uses alcohol as its fuel. It can be used in windy conditions and usually comes with its own cooking utensils.

Food Storage

Be sure to store your food in your rucksack above and away from your fuel stove (if you are taking one). Although the stove may not leak, fumes from the stove fuel can get through to your food and ruin its taste.

Make sure your food is in sealed containers. You may wish to discard any excess packaging but be sure to keep any cooking instructions next to the relevant food. Make sure that any snacks that you plan to eat during your walk are accessible and that your lunch is towards the top of your rucksack.

Activity **17.8** 90 mins   P3

Equipment required for a multi-day expedition

Task 1

Try to visit an outdoor pursuits shop and see for yourself the different types of equipment that are available for a multi-day expedition.

Task 2

Make a list of all of the equipment that you think you will need for a multi-day expedition, then write a report that describes each piece of equipment and why it is required.

17.4 Planning a Multi-day Expedition

Once you have decided where you plan to set up camp for the night, you may need to gain permission from the landowner. If you are planning to camp in a campsite, you should book ahead to be sure there is room for you and your team. You may decide to stay overnight in a youth hostel prior to the start of your expedition. If so, make sure you book ahead and are aware of the costs. Some youth hostels provide meals as part of the cost; check this out beforehand so that you know whether you need to provide your own food. You may need to provide your own bedding or towels; again, make sure you ask the person who takes your booking.

Ensure that you have completed detailed route cards and have a spare copy to leave with a responsible person who is available to monitor your progress. You should plan to have daily checkpoints in your route where you can meet the person monitoring your progress. If for some reason you do not make it to the daily checkpoint, the responsible person can then alert the authorities that something is wrong and get search parties to look for you. You should also leave your contingency plans with this person so that they are aware of any alternative routes you may take. For example, if the weather becomes foggy and you are high up in the mountains, you may have included in your contingency plan an alternative lower-level route where visibility may be better. Also consider emergency routes that you can take in case of bad weather conditions or injury. These routes should take you down safely and preferably lead you to a place where you can contact help.

In your plan you will need to work out how you are going to travel to the start of your expedition route and how you are going to travel back home. Is there a person who has access to a vehicle that can take you, the rest of the team and your equipment, or do you need more than one vehicle and one driver? Is there public transport that can take you there? If so, make sure you have an up-to-date timetable. You will also need to find out the cost of the journey and be aware, if you plan to travel before 9 am on a week day, that the cost may be higher than if you travel later in the day.

Food

The food you take for your expedition is very important. A full day of hiking uses a lot of calories, so you should be aiming to take enough food to enable you to consume around 3200–4500 calories per day. This may be twice as much as you usually eat. Make sure that you have food for three meals a day plus snacks.

The food you choose should be cooked easily and preferably non-perishable, especially if you are hiking in warm conditions. There is quite a large range of dehydrated foods that hikers take on expeditions. They are light and you just need to add hot water to them to eat. Most people tend to eat these foods for their evening meal and have sandwiches for lunch. For breakfast, something that can be eaten hot is usually a popular choice, like porridge. Snacks should provide lots of energy. Chocolate and energy bars are good choices.

Ensure that you have plenty to drink; your water bottle should be full at the start of each day. If you are walking in cold conditions, taking a flask and making tea, coffee or soup to drink during a rest period on your walk is a good idea.

You should also pack emergency rations in case you encounter any adverse conditions or a member of your party gets injured, which means you have to stay out on your expedition for longer than planned for. The emergency rations should be high-energy foods. Kendal mint cake is a popular choice as are chocolate bars and high-energy bars.

Weather

Weather conditions can have a huge impact on the safety of your expedition. For example if snow is forecast then you should avoid walking on high ground, or if the weather is going to be very hot and humid you must ensure you are prepared for these conditions with lots of water, appropriate clothing, head wear, sunglasses and sun screen. Make sure you obtain weather forecasts for the day you set off on your expedition and, if possible, try to find out the forecast for the day ahead. Use your mobile phone to ring a weather information provider in the morning before you start your hike, or you could take a radio and listen to local weather forecasts for your region.

(k) Key learning points

- Choose correct footwear for your expedition.
- Make sure your rucksack is the right size for the length of your journey.
- Make sure you have waterproof clothing on or packed in your rucksack.
- Ensure you have enough food for your journey and emergency rations.
- Take a tent that is the right size and appropriate for the weather conditions you may face.
- Make sure you dress in layers.
- Take a sleeping bag that is appropriate for the weather conditions you may face.
- Make sure you pack a first-aid kit, survival bag, torch and whistle.

Quick Quiz 3 5 mins (?)

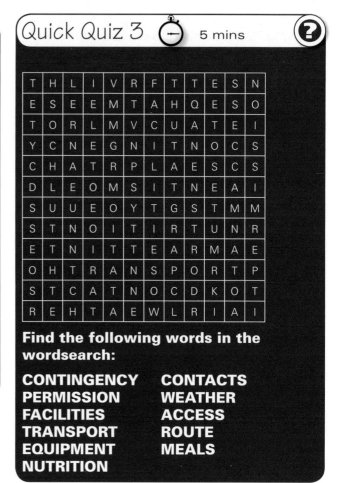

T	H	L	I	V	R	F	T	T	E	S	N
E	S	E	E	M	T	A	H	Q	E	S	O
T	O	R	L	M	V	C	U	A	T	E	I
Y	C	N	E	G	N	I	T	N	O	C	S
C	H	A	T	R	P	L	A	E	S	C	S
D	L	E	O	M	S	I	T	N	E	A	I
S	U	U	E	O	Y	T	G	S	T	M	M
S	T	N	O	I	T	I	R	T	U	N	R
E	T	N	I	T	T	E	A	R	M	A	E
O	H	T	R	A	N	S	P	O	R	T	P
S	T	C	A	T	N	O	C	D	K	O	T
R	E	H	T	A	E	W	L	R	I	A	I

Find the following words in the wordsearch:

CONTINGENCY	**CONTACTS**
PERMISSION	**WEATHER**
FACILITIES	**ACCESS**
TRANSPORT	**ROUTE**
EQUIPMENT	**MEALS**
NUTRITION	

Activity **17.9** 1–2 hours   P4 M3 D2

Planning a multi-day expedition

You are planning to carry out a multi-day expedition but will need to take some time to think about the planning of the event so that it can run as smoothly as possible.

Task 1

Prepare an appropriate route card for your multi-day expedition that also includes contingency plans and escape routes.

Task 2

Find out and get permission (if required) to camp in your selected campsite area.

Task 3

Write meal plans for what you plan to eat while on your expedition.

Task 4

Make a list of all of the equipment that you require to go on the multi-day expedition.

Task 5

Write a report that shows how you plan to find out the weather conditions for your expedition.

17.5 Carrying out a Multi-day Expedition P5 M4

Once you have completed the planning stages of your multi-day expedition, it is then time to carry it out and find out how well you have actually planned your expedition!

Route Choice

You may find that the weather conditions are worse than you had expected for the time of year, for example it could be extremely windy, which means you may have to change your route so that you are safer on lower ground.

Travelling Skills

When you are walking for long periods of time it is a good idea to try to conserve energy wherever possible. Energy conservation can be carried out through a number of different methods.

Camp Craft Skills

Once you have set up camp you will need to get used to living in the outdoors. If you are not staying on a campsite, you will probably not have access to any toilets. Your group will need to decide upon a private area that can be designated as the 'toilet' area. You will need to take a trowel or small spade to the 'toilet area' and dig yourself a small hole in which you can go to the toilet; the hole will then need to be covered over. If toilet paper is biodegradable, it can be buried in the hole; if it is not, however, it will need to be put in a 'toilet paper' bag and disposed of later in a bin or flushed down a toilet.

Your campsite should have a source of clean water running nearby. If you have a 'green' soap, this can be used to wash with. If you are unsure of the cleanliness of the water, water purification tablets should be used before drinking the water, or alternatively the water can be boiled for three minutes and is then safe to drink (once it has cooled down a little).

17.6 Review of a Multi-day Expedition P6 M5 D3

In order to gain a good understanding of your ability to carry out an expedition, you should aim to obtain feedback from a range of people who were involved in the process. Gather this feedback from the participants on the walk, your peers, your supervisor and any observers who may have watched you plan the expedition and carry it out. You may gain this feedback by just having a chat with each of these people, ensuring that you ask the same questions, so that you can determine how each person felt about each aspect of the expedition and your conduct.

Here are a few examples of questions you could ask your feedback group:

- What do they think you did well?
- Which areas can you improve in?
- How well did the expedition match the plan?
- How well did the expedition meet with governing body guidelines?

Set Targets

Once you have this information you can process it in order to set targets, so that you can improve your ability in planning and carrying out a multi-day expedition.

When targets are set you need to use the SMART principle to make the targets workable. SMART stands for the following:

Specific

Measurable

Achievable

Realistic

Time-constrained.

Specific

The target must be specific to what you want to achieve. This may be an aspect of navigation skills. It is not enough to say that you want to 'be a better navigator', you need to say 'I want to improve my map-reading skills.'

Measurable

A target must be stated in a way that is measurable, so it needs to have figures. For example, 'I want to be able to walk a further five miles per day on my next expedition.'

Achievable

It must be possible to actually achieve the target; for example there is no point having a target of climbing Mount Everest if you have only been on one multi-day expedition!

Realistic

We need to be realistic in our setting and look at what factors may stop us achieving the target.

Time-constrained

There must be a time-scale or deadline on the target. This means you can review your success. It is best to set a date you wish to achieve the target by.s

Development Opportunities

In order to help you improve your skills and knowledge in planning and carrying out a multi-day expedition, you should explore the range of training courses that are available. Look on governing body websites or in relevant publications as these will probably list the training courses available.

You could also look to see if there are any Venture Scout groups in your area that you may like to join as part of the Duke of Edinburgh's Award Scheme. Venture Scouts plan and carry out a multi-day expeditions.

Useful websites

www.ramblers.org.uk
Family-friendly advice on walking safely in the UK countryside, with ideas for routes suited for all levels.

www.thebmc.co.uk
Invaluable advice for beginners to elite mountaineers, from getting started to avoiding frostbite, from choosing the right equipment to deciding whether or not to buy second-hand.

www.mcofs.org.uk/mountain-safety.asp
Useful advice to avoid trouble on the mountain and life-saving tips such as appropriate first aid if the worst does happen to you.

References

Langmuir, E., 1995, *Mountain Craft and Leadership*, Glasgow: Scottish Sports Council.

Activity 17.10 2–3 days   P5 P6 M4 M5 D3

Carrying out a multi-day expedition

Using your skills & knowledge gained from Chapter 8 carrying out student activities complete the following two tasks:

Task 1

Carry out a multi-day expedition somewhere in the UK.

Task 2

Write a review of your own performance in both planning & implementing your multi-day expedition.

In your review, identify, explain & evaluate strengths & areas for improvement. Where possible try to suggest strategies to improve your future performance.

Chapter 18
Effects of Exercise on the Body Systems

This chapter explores the effects of both short- and long-term exercise on the body. The short-term effects of exercise on the musculoskeletal, cardiovascular and respiratory systems will be explored followed by the long-term effects of exercise and how the various body systems adapt to training.

The different energy systems are also explored together with the different sports that use each of these systems to supply energy. Lastly, the impact of drugs on sport and sports performance and the effect of drugs on society will be examined.

Learning Goals

By the end of this chapter you should:

- Be able to investigate the short-term effects of exercise on the body systems.
- Know the long-term effects of exercise on the body systems.
- Be able to investigate the fundamentals of the energy systems.
- Know the impact of drugs on sports performance.

To achieve a PASS grade the evidence must show that the learner is able to:	To achieve a MERIT grade the evidence must show that, in addition to the pass criteria, the learner is able to:	To achieve a DISTINCTION grade the evidence must show that, in addition to the pass and merit criteria, the learner is able to:
P1 describe the short-term effects of exercise on the musculoskeletal, cardiovascular and respiratory systems	**M1** explain the short-term effects of exercise on the musculoskeletal, cardiovascular and respiratory systems	
P2 investigate the short-term effects of exercise on the musculoskeletal, cardiovascular and respiratory systems, with tutor support	**M2** independently investigate the short-term effects of exercise on the musculoskeletal, cardiovascular and respiratory systems	
P3 describe the long-term effects of exercise on the musculoskeletal system	**M3** explain the long-term effects of exercise on the musculoskeletal, cardiovascular and respiratory systems	**D1** analyse the short- and long-term effects of exercise on the musculoskeletal, cardiovascular and respiratory systems
P4 describe the long-term effects of exercise on the cardio-respiratory system		
P5 describe two types of physical activity that use the aerobic energy system and two that use the anaerobic energy systems	**M4** explain the energy requirements of four different types of physical activity	
P6 investigate different physical activities that use the aerobic and anaerobic energy systems, with tutor support		
P7 describe four different types of drugs used to enhance sports performance and their effects		
P8 describe the negative impact of drugs	**M5** explain the negative impact of drugs	

18.1 The Short-term Effects of Exercise on the Body Systems

  part

Musculoskeletal System

The musculoskeletal system consists of the skeletal system and the muscular system.

Before taking part in exercise, we all know that we should warm our body up to prepare it for the different types of movements and activities that we are about to take part in. This process of warming up helps our musculoskeletal system to get ready for exercise and also makes us less likely to injure this system.

During a warm-up we usually increase the heart rate and carry out mobilisation activities. By increasing our heart rate, we are pumping our blood around our body at a faster rate, which then has the effect of warming up our muscles. When muscles become warmer they become more pliable.

> ### Definition
>
> **pliable** able to change shape more easily.

If you imagine a piece of plasticine when it is cold and you pull the piece of plasticine apart, it is likely to break and split into two pieces. However, if you warm the plasticine up in your hands and then pull it apart, it will start to stretch rather than break – this is because it has become more *pliable*. This same principle applies to muscles: if a muscle is cold and then suddenly stretched, it is more likely to tear, whereas if it is warmed up, it is more likely to stretch and not tear.

The process of mobilisation is used to increase joint mobility. Joint mobility enables the joints to become lubricated by releasing more synovial fluid onto the joints and then warming them up so they become more efficient. This means moving joints through their full range of movement. The movements will start off small and slowly become larger until a full range of movement is achieved. The joints that need to be mobilised are shoulders, elbows, spine, hips, knees and ankles.

When taking part in resistance exercises such as lifting weights, the process is actually designed to break some muscle fibres. These 'breaks' are called 'micro tears' as the damage is usually very minimal. However, this 'damage' has to occur in order for the muscle to have the stimulation to rebuild itself so that, over time, it will become bigger and stronger (see Long-term Effects of Exercise on the Muscular System further on in this chapter for more details).

Short-term Effects of Exercise on the Cardiovascular System

The cardiovascular system consists of the heart and the blood vessels through which the heart pumps blood around the body. During exercise, a number of changes take place to the cardiovascular system to ensure that the muscles receive the required amounts of oxygen and nutrients. The structure of the cardiovascular system is discussed in more detail in Chapter 4 Anatomy and Physiology for Sport.

If you take part in one exercise session, for example a game of basketball, the cardiovascular system responds in a variety of ways, some of which you may be well aware of:

- increased heart rate

- increased blood pressure

- redirection of blood flow:

  - blood vessels close to the skin surface become enlarged

  - more blood is pumped to working skeletal muscle

  - less blood is pumped to organs that are not in need of oxygen, for example the digestive system.

Heart Rate: Anticipatory Increase and Activity Response

During exercise the heart rate needs to be increased in order to ensure that the working muscles receive enough nutrients and oxygen, and that waste products are removed. Before you even start exercising there is an increase in your heart rate, called the anticipatory rise. The anticipatory rise occurs because when you think about exercising your body releases adrenaline, which makes your heart beat faster.

> ## Definition ⓓ
>
> **Adrenalin (also known as epinephrine) a hormone released during times of stress that gets the body ready for action, for example by increasing blood pressure, increasing heart rate etc.**

Once you start exercising, your body releases more adrenaline, which further increases your heart rate. In a trained athlete, heart rate can increase by up to three times within one minute of starting exercise.

Blood Pressure

Blood pressure is necessary in order for blood to flow around the body. Blood is pumped around the body under pressure because the heart contracts and forces blood into the blood vessels. Two values are given when a person has their blood pressure taken; a typical blood pressure for the average adult male is 120/80. The two values correspond to the systolic value (when the heart is contracting) and the diastolic value (when the heart is relaxing). The higher value is the systolic value and the lower is the diastolic value. Blood pressure is measured in milligrams of mercury, mmHg.

As discussed previously, exercise has the affect of increasing heart rate, which then has the effect of increasing a person's blood pressure.

A typical blood-pressure reading for a person at the onset of exercise would be around 140/85.

Redirection of Blood Flow

Blood flows through the body through arteries, arterioles, capillaries, veins and venules. However, not every one of these blood vessels is in use at the same time though. Blood is directed to where it is needed so, for example, after we have eaten some food, more blood is directed to the stomach to help us to digest it. When a person is exercising or taking part in a sport, blood is directed to the muscles that are working. For example, if a person is running, more blood will be directed to flow around the leg muscles so that oxygen and nutrients can be delivered to these muscles to enable them to function; if a person is playing tennis, more blood will be directed to the arm that is holding the racket compared with the other arm as the racket arm is doing more work.

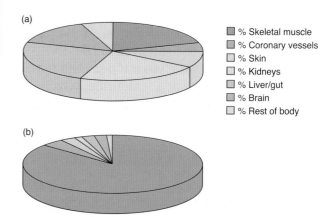

Figure 18.1 (a) Distribution of cardiac output at rest **(b)** Distribution of cardiac output during exercise

During exercise or sports participation, blood is also directed to flow through blood vessels that are close to the skin surface to help to cool the body down.

Short-term Effects of Exercise on the Respiratory System

The respiratory system is responsible for getting oxygen into the body and getting carbon dioxide out of the body; it is described in detail in Chapter 4 (Anatomy and Physiology). Oxygen is utilised to help produce energy so that we can take part in sporting activities. The process of creating energy also produces a waste product called carbon dioxide that needs to be removed from the body and is breathed out by the lungs.

Pulmonary Ventilation and Breathing Rate

The amount of air we breath in and out per minute is called pulmonary ventilation and is given the symbol V_E.

Pulmonary ventilation can be worked out using the following equation:

V_E = Frequency x Tidal volume

Frequency is the number of breaths per minute.

Tidal volume is the volume of air breathed in and out during one breath.

At rest, an average breathing rate is around 12 breaths per minute. The average tidal volume is 0.5 L (this will vary depending on age, gender and size of a person).

Therefore, the average pulmonary ventilation at rest is:

V_E = 12 x 0.5

   = 6 litres.

When you start to exercise, you need to take more oxygen into your body in order for it to be used to help produce energy. At the start of exercise, this increased oxygen demand occurs by breathing at a faster rate and breathing in more air and breathing out more air during each breath (that is, tidal volume increases)

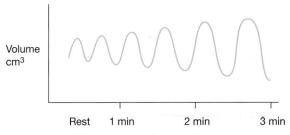

Figure 18.2   Tidal volume increasing

The intercostal muscles are used to aid breathing during exercise.

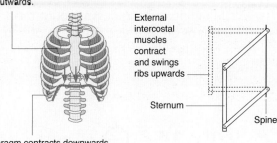

a) Inspiration

External intercostal muscles cause the rib cage to pivot on the thoracic vertebrae and move upwards and outwards.

External intercostal muscles contract and swings ribs upwards

Sternum

Spine

Diaphragm contracts downwards, increasing the 'depth' of the thoracic cavity.

b) Expiration at rest

Relaxation of respiratory muscles cause the rib cage to move downwards and inwards.

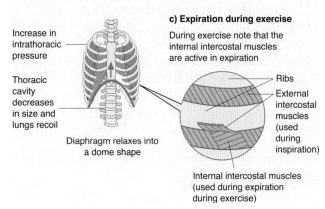

Increase in intrathoracic pressure

Thoracic cavity decreases in size and lungs recoil

Diaphragm relaxes into a dome shape

c) Expiration during exercise

During exercise note that the internal intercostal muscles are active in expiration

Ribs

External intercostal muscles (used during inspiration)

Internal intercostal muscles (used during expiration during exercise)

Figure 18.3 (a)   Inspiration **(b)**   Expiration

Definition   (d)

Intercostal muscles muscles located between the ribs. There are two kinds: internal and external. They help with inspiration and expiration during exercise.

The external intercostal muscles help with inspiration and the internal intercostal muscles help with expiration. As exercise becomes more strenuous, the abdominal muscles will also help aid expiration.

Activity **18.1** 20 mins

Measuring breathing rate

Task

(a) While sitting or lying down, count the number of breaths you breath in during one minute – try to breath as normally as possible.

(b) Write this number down and then work out your pulmonary ventilation using the equation given above.

(c) Compare your pulmonary ventilation with the rest of the class.

Activity **18.2** 45 mins

P1   M1   D1

Short-term effects of exercise on the body systems

When a person is taking part in sport or exercise, the musculoskeletal, cardiovascular and respiratory body systems all respond very quickly to help to get the body ready for this activity and to enable us to continue with the activity.

Task 1

Design a leaflet or a poster that describes, explains and analyses the short-term effects of exercise on:

- The musculoskeletal system – this means the muscular and skeletal systems.
- The cardiovascular system – the heart and the blood vessels through which the blood travels.
- The respiratory system – this will include breathing patterns and muscles required for breathing in and out.

Activity **18.3** 20 mins

P2   M2

Short-term effects of exercise on the respiratory system

Task

(a) While sitting or lying down, count the number of breaths you breathe in during one minute – try to breathe as normally as possible.

(b) Using a spirometer, work out how much air you breathe in and out (your tidal volume) at rest.

(c) Write this number down and then work out your pulmonary ventilation using the equation given above.

(d) Compare your pulmonary ventilation with the rest of the class.

(e) Take part in some form of physical activity or sport and then record:
- Your breathing rate for one minute
- Your tidal volume.

Activity **18.4** 15 mins P2 M2

Short-term effects of exercise on the cardiovascular system

Task 1

If you have a heart-rate monitor, place it around your chest. If not, find your pulse point either on your neck or at your wrist.

Sit quietly for five minutes, then take your resting heart rate. If you have a heart-rate monitor, write down the heart rate that appears on the monitor. If not, feel for your pulse point, then count your heart rate for 30 seconds. Double this figure and write it down.

Think about what exercise you are about to perform for one minute.

Record your heart rate after having thought about your exercise.

Perform step-ups onto a bench for two minutes or skip for two minutes with a skipping rope.

Immediately after you have finished your exercise, record your heart rate.

Task 2

Complete the table below.

Task 3

Try to answer the following questions:

1. What happened to your heart rate immediately before you started exercising?
2. What caused this change in your heart rate and why was it necessary?
3. Try to explain why there is a difference between your resting heart rate and your post-exercise heart rate.

Resting heart (bpm)	Pre-exercise heart rate (bpm)	Post-exercise heart rate (bpm)

Activity **18.5** 30 mins P2 M2

Short-term effects of exercise on the musculosketal system

For these activities you will need to compare the range of movement of your joints before and after exercise. It is important that you remember that your body will not be warmed up before exercise participation and therefore during any testing you must be very careful not to over stretch and risk the possibility of injuring your body.

Task 1

Take part in a range of different flexibility tests – these could include:

- sit and reach
- calf stretch
- shoulder stretch.

Make a note of the readings for each test.

Alternatively you could use a goniometer to examine the range of movement at different joints.

Task 2

Take part in a full warm-up as part of a sport or exercise session.

Task 3

Repeat the flexibility tests or retest the range of movement at different joints using a goniometer.

Task 4

Compare the readings between the pre- and post-exercise test measurements.

Key learning points

The short-term effects of exercise on the body systems are:

- Musculoskeletal
  - Increased joint range of Movement
  - Micro tears in muscle fibres from resistance exercises
- Cardiovascular
  - Increase in heart rate
  - Increase in blood pressure
  - Redirection of blood flow to working skeletal muscles and skin surface
- Respiratory system
  - Increase in breathing rate
  - Increase in tidal volume.

18.2 The Long-term Effects of Exercise on the Body Systems

 P3 P4 M3 D1

Chronic exercise means that a person has been participating in regular exercise for long periods of time (a minimum of eight weeks). This regular participation effects the body in a number of ways that make it more able to cope with the stresses of the exercise. This results in the person being able to exercise at higher intensities and/or for longer periods of time – this process is called adaptation.

The Effects of Long-term Exercise on the Musculoskeletal System P3 M3 D1

Definition (d)

Weight-bearing exercise an exercise where we are using our body weight as a form of resistance, for example walking, running etc.

Our skeleton responds to weight-bearing exercise or resistance exercise by becoming stronger and more able to withstand impact. This means we are less likely to injure ourselves, such as breaking a bone, if we fall over. This occurs because the stimulation of exercise means we increase the mineral content within our bones, which makes the bones harder and stronger. Exercise also has an effect on our joints by increasing the thickness of cartilage at the ends of the bones and increasing the production of synovial fluid. This will have the effect of making our joints stronger and we are therefore less likely to suffer from a joint injury.

If you exercise with some sort of resistance, for example weights, dyna band, body weight as in press-ups, it will stress the skeletal muscle. This actually results in parts of the muscle breaking. The more you stress the muscle with heavier weights, the more the muscle breaks down. After having rested and eaten the right foods, the body then starts to repair itself and will actually mend the muscle tissue and make it bigger and better than before. If you continue this process, the muscle tissue will keep getting bigger, which will result in an increase in your muscle size – this is called hypertrophy.

> **Definition**
>
> **Hypertrophy an increase in the size of skeletal muscle.**

Figure 18.4   Muscles get larger through resistance training

Resistance exercise will also result in increasing the strength of muscle tendons.

The Effects of Long-term Exercise on the Cardio-Respiratory System

Respiratory System

Taking part in aerobic exercise will increase your breathing rate so that you can take more oxygen into the body and get rid of the excess carbon dioxide. If you take part in regular aerobic exercise it will train the lungs by increasing the lung capacity.

> **Definition**
>
> **Lung capacity the total amount of air your lungs can hold.**

Cardiovascular System

The main changes that occur to the cardiovascular system through taking part in endurance exercises or sports are concerned with increasing the delivery of oxygen to the working muscles. If you were to dissect the heart of a top endurance athlete, you would find that the walls of the left ventricle are markedly thicker than those in the heart of a person who did not perform endurance exercise. This is called cardiac hypertrophy.

(a) 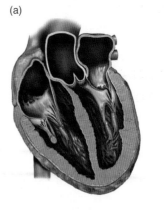   (b)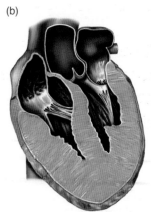

Figure 18.5   The heart of (a) a non-athletic person and (b) an endurance-trained athlete

Definition

Cardiac hypertrophy when the heart wall becomes thicker and stronger.

It occurs in the same way that we increase the size of our skeletal muscles – the more we exercise our muscles, the larger or more toned they become. In the same way, the more we exercise our heart through aerobic training, the larger it will become. This will then have the affect of increasing the stroke volume, which is the amount of blood that the heart can pump out per beat. As the heart wall becomes thicker, it can pump more blood per beat as the thicker wall can contract more forcibly. As the stroke volume is increased, the heart no longer needs to beat as often to get the same amount of blood around the body. This results in a decrease in resting heart rate.

An average male adult's heart rate is 70 bpm. However Lance Armstrong, who was a Tour de France cyclist, had a resting heart rate of 30 bpm!

Quick Quiz 2 5 mins

Answer the following questions with True or False.

1. Long-term exercise makes the heart muscle smaller.
2. Long-term exercise makes vital capacity of the lungs increase.
3. Long-term exercise increases a person's resting heart rate.
4. Long-term exercise results in a decreased production of synovial fluid.
5. Long-term exercise results in an increase in thickness of hyaline cartilage.
6. Long-term exercise makes a person's bones more likely to break if they should fall over.
7. An example of weight-bearing exercise is swimming.
8. The average resting heart rate of an adult male is 120.
9. Hypertrophy is the name given to the increase in lung size through participation in long-term exercise.
10. Stroke volume is the amount of blood ejected from the heart per beat.

Activity 18.7 1–2 hours   P3 P4 M3 D1

The long-term effects of exercise on the body systems

Taking part in exercise or sport is good for our body and helps our body systems adapt so that they become stronger and more able to cope with the demands of our activities.

Task 1

Design a poster or spider diagram that illustrates the long-term effects of exercise on the musculoskeletal, cardiovascular and respiratory systems.

Task 2

Write a report that describes, explains and analyses the long-term effects of exercise on the musculoskeletal, cardiovascular and respiratory systems.

Tip

When you are describing each system, write about what each system is and what it does; for explaining, you will need to write about how each body system does its job and how it adapts to training; for an analysis, you will need to write about why each body system changes in the way it does.

Key learning points

The long-term effects of exercise on the body systems are:

- Skeletal system
  - Bones become stronger
  - Increased thickness of hyaline cartilage
  - Increase in production of synovial fluid
- Muscular system
  - Increase in muscle size (hypertrophy)
  - Increase in tendon strength
- Respiratory system
  - Increase in vital capacity
- Cardiovascular system
  - Decrease in resting heart rate
  - Increase in heart size
  - Increase in stroke volume.

18.3 Energy Systems

Three main energy systems are responsible for producing the energy that allows us to take part in sports. The energy system used is determined by the speed at which the body needs that energy.

1. **Phosphocreatine system** – this energy system supplies energy very quickly for such sporting events as the high jump or long jump. It does not require oxygen and is therefore also known as an anaerobic energy system.

Definitions

Anaerobic **without oxygen.**
Aerobic **with oxygen.**

2. **Lactic acid system** – this system supplies energy quite quickly for sporting events that last between ten and 40 seconds, such as the 400 m. This system produces a waste product called lactic acid that makes our muscles feel sore and eventually stops

us from exercising. This system is also an anaerobic energy system.

3. **Aerobic energy system** – this system supplies energy at a slower rate than the other two systems. It provides energy for longer-lasting events, such as the 5000 ms marathon, and mountain walking. This system uses oxygen, which is why it is called the aerobic energy system.

Energy Requirements of Physical Activity

In order to take part in sports our body uses the food we have eaten, converted by the energy systems to produce energy. Different sports have different energy requirements (see Table 18.1).

Type of exercise	Kilocalories used per hour
Aerobics	450
Aqua aerobics	400
Bicycling	450
Cross-country ski machine	500
Hiking	500
Jogging, 5 mph	500
Rowing	550
Running	700
Skipping with rope	720
Spinning	650
Step aerobics	550
Squash	650
Swimming	500
Table tennis	290
Tennis	350
Walking, 3 mph	280

Table 18.1 Energy requirements for different sports

Activity 18.8 45 mins

P5

M4

Energy systems

All sports require us to use energy so that we can take part in them. For this activity, try to think about sports that you enjoy or have taken part in.

Task 1

Write a report that describes two types of physical activity that use the aerobic system.

Task 2

Write a report that describes two types of physical activity that use the anaerobic energy systems.

Task 3

Look at the list of energy requirements for different sports. Note the one that requires the most kilocalories, the one that requires the least number of kilocalories and two more of your choice. Explain why you think they each require different amounts of energy.

Key learning points

- The anaerobic energy systems are the phosphocreatine energy system and the lactic acid energy system.
- The anaerobic energy systems do not require oxygen.
- Examples of sports that use the anaerobic energy systems are the 100-m sprint, shot put and high jump.
- The aerobic energy system requires oxygen.
- Examples of sports that use the aerobic energy system are marathons, cycling long distances and swimming long distances.

Quick Quiz 3 10 mins ?

Answer the following statements with True or False.

1. The phosphocreatine energy system requires oxygen.
2. The aerobic energy system provides energy for the 100-m sprint.
3. Walking uses more kilocalories per hour than swimming.
4. An example of a sport that uses the lactic acid energy system is the 400 m.
5. A person competing in an iron man triatholon will mainly use the aerobic energy system to supply energy.
6. The phosphocreatine energy system produces lactic acid.
7. Sports that use both the arms and legs use more kilocalories than sports that just use the legs.
8. The energy system used to make the energy is determined by the speed at which the body needs that energy.
9. Anaerobic means with oxygen.
10. Lactic acid makes our muscles feel sore and eventually stops us from exercising.

18.4 The Impact of Drugs in Sport

The issue of drugs in sport has grown and grown since 1988 when Ben Johnson, who had won the 100-m Olympic final, failed a drug test for anabolic steroids. Other scandals have been the use of a drug called nandrolone and the failure of several British athletes to pass drug tests over the last couple of years; scandals that have hit the Tour de France include erythropoietin (EPO) and human growth hormone (hGH). There are even examples of animals being given drugs to try to increase their performance; at the 2004 Olympics Ireland lost an equestrianism medal after a horse failed a drug test!

There is a direct link between the rise of money to be won in sport and the rise of drug use. As the rewards for success increase, so do the risks athletes are willing to take to gain these rewards. Although athletes must know that training is the best path to victory, they are also aware that some drugs can boost their efforts and give them a greater chance of victory even at the expense of their health and their athletic careers. Some of the substances athletes take are illegal, as defined by the International Olympic Committee (IOC), whereas others are perfectly legitimate ways of naturally improving one's performance, such as consuming a sports drink during a game or eating large amounts of pasta the night before an endurance race.

The practice of using banned substances to enhance athletic performance is called doping. The first drug tests on athletes were conducted at the 1968 Olympic Games in Mexico. Since then, drug testing has become a major part of sporting competition and new methods of detecting drugs are always being sought.

There are two main issues with drugs:

1. All drugs have side-effects that damage health.
2. It is cheating by gaining an unfair advantage.

Types of Drugs

The majority of drugs used by athletes today were initially designed by the medical profession in order to treat patients with various illnesses or disorders. Many types of drugs are available to the athlete, and what they take is determined by the sport in which they compete. The main effects of the different groups of drugs are to:

- Build muscle mass
- Increase the delivery of oxygen to exercising tissues
- Provide pain relief
- Stimulate the body
- Relax
- Reduce weight.

Building Muscle Mass

Athletes competing in sports that require a high muscle mass, such as weightlifting, throwing events, sprinting or boxing, may take muscle-building drugs. There is a variety of drugs available that will increase the muscle mass of an athlete, including anabolic steroids, human growth hormone (hGH) and insulin.

Anabolic Steroids

Athletes and others abuse anabolic steroids to enhance performance and improve physical appearance. However, just taking anabolic steroids will not increase muscle bulk; the athlete must still train hard in order to achieve an increase in muscle mass. The main advantage in taking these drugs is that the muscles recover more quickly from training. This will allow the athlete to train at a higher level, and for longer, than if they were not taking the drugs.

Disadvantages

The main disadvantages of taking anabolic steroids are:

- Liver and kidney tumours
- Jaundice

- High blood pressure
- Severe acne
- Trembling.

There are also some sex-specific side-effects.

Males:

- Shrinking of the testicles
- Reduced sperm count, infertility
- Baldness
- Development of breasts
- Increased risk for prostate cancer.

Females:

- Growth of facial hair
- Male-pattern baldness
- Changes in or cessation of the menstrual cycle
- Enlargement of the clitoris
- Deepened voice.

Scientific research also shows that aggression and other psychiatric side-effects may result from the abuse of anabolic steroids. Depression can be experienced when the person stops taking the drugs and may contribute to them becoming dependent on anabolic steroids.

Human Growth Hormone (hGH)

hGH is a naturally occurring protein hormone and is important for normal human growth and development, especially in children and teenagers. Low hGH levels in children and teenagers result in dwarfism. Growth hormone stimulates the development of natural male and female sex hormones.

Advantages

In males, hGH acts to increase testosterone levels and results in increased muscle development, as with anabolic steroids. Excessive hGH levels increase muscle mass by stimulating protein synthesis, strengthen bones by stimulating bone growth and reduce body fat by stimulating the breakdown of fat cells.

Disadvantages

The side-effects of hGH in males are the same as those of anabolic steroids together with enlarged internal organs. The athlete taking the drug may also develop acromegaly, which results in the person's hands, feet and lower jaw growing much larger than normal.

Increasing Oxygen in Tissues

Athletes competing in endurance sports are the principal abusers of drugs that increase the oxygen supply to their muscle tissues. One method of increasing oxgyen supply to tissue is by taking erythropoietin (EPO).

Erythropoietin (EPO)

EPO is a naturally occurring protein hormone. It acts on the bone marrow, where it stimulates the production of red blood cells.

Advantages

Since EPO increases a person's red blood cell count, it will result in higher blood haemoglobin concentrations. Therefore, after taking EPO, a person's blood will have an increased oxygen-carrying capacity, which potentially has the effect of increasing an athlete's performance. Endurance athletes, such as those who compete in marathons, the Tour de France, cross-country skiing and so on can use EPO to increase their oxygen supply by as much as ten per cent.

Disadvantages

The main side-effect of taking EPO is an increase in the 'thickness' of the blood. This thickened blood will not flow through the blood vessels very well because it has a greater resistance. As a result, the heart must work harder to pump blood around the body, which will increase the chances of the athlete suffering from a heart attack.

Providing Pain Relief – Stimulants

The main stimulants used by athletes are amphetamines. Stimulants act to mimic the action of the sympathetic nervous system.

Advantages

Stimulants have the effect of getting more blood to the working muscles and increasing the amount of air that a person can breath in while exercising. They have the effect of increasing a person's mental alertness and also help to conceal feelings of exhaustion. As a result, athletes competing in endurance events, contact sports, or those demanding fast reactions, may take stimulants in order to enhance their performance.

Disadvantages

As stimulants hide feelings of fatigue, it is possible for athletes to overexert themselves to the point where they can suffer heat stroke and cardiac failure. Other side-effects include increased blood pressure and body temperature, increased and irregular heartbeat, aggression, anxiety and loss of appetite.

Relaxation

Beta Blockers

Beta blockers are used to lower heart rate and blood pressure and reduce anxiety.

Advantages

Beta blockers slow the heart rate, relax muscles in blood vessel walls, and decrease the force of heart contractions. Athletes may use these drugs in sport in order to reduce anxiety levels and to prevent their body from shaking. As a result, athletes who take part in sports that require steady nerves and hands (for example snooker, archery, shooting and darts) may abuse this type of drug.

Figure 18.6   An archer

Disadvantages

The side-effects of taking this drug include lowered blood pressure, slow heart rate and tiredness. In extreme cases, the heart may actually stop because it has been slowed down too much.

Weight Reduction

Diuretics

Diuretics act to help to get rid of excess water from the body.

Advantages

The main reason diuretics are misused by competitors in sport is to reduce their body weight quickly in sports where weight categories are involved. Boxers, weightlifters or judo competitors may take this drug in order to remain in their weight category. If their body weight is only slightly above the category lower limit, they will be competing against athletes who are larger than them and, therefore, presumably have a greater muscle mass, which would leave the athlete at a disadvantage.

Disadvantages

Possible side-effects of taking diuretics include dehydration, which could then lead to dizziness and fainting, vomiting and muscle cramps. If the athlete becomes severely dehydrated through taking the diuretics, the effect on the kidneys and the heart could lead to death.

Activity **18.9** 2 hours   **P7** **P8** M4

Drugs in sport

In small groups (two to three) prepare a five to ten-minute presentation about drugs in sport.

Task 1

Select four different types of drugs and, where possible, try to find an athlete that has been found to be using one of each type of drug you have selected.

Task 2

Describe each type of drug together with why and how it is used to increase sports performance.

Task 3

Describe the advantages and disadvantages of taking each type of drug.

Task 4

Examine and then describe the negative effects of drugs in sport – these should include:

- Harmful effects on the body
- The negative effects on sport
- Ethics
- How they have affected society.

Quick Quiz 4 5 mins

Amphetamine	Growth hormone	EPO	Stimulant	Doping
Cheating	Beta blocker	Damage health	Diuretics	International Olympic Committee

Chose a word or words from the boxes above to answer the following questions.

1. **This type of drug could be taken by an athlete who wants to increase the size of their muscles.**
2. **A boxer may take this type of drug to try to get into a lower weight category.**
3. **An archer may take this type of drug.**
4. **An athlete taking part in the Tour de France may take this drug to try to stop feelings of exhaustion.**
5. **An athlete who runs for long distances may take this type of drug to try to improve their performance.**
6. **This type of drug can make a person's jaw larger than usual.**
7. **This is the name of the practice of using banned substances to enhance athletic performance.**
8. **One of the main issues with drugs is that they all have side-effects which can do what to an athlete?**
9. **Taking drugs provides athletes with an unfair advantage over other competitors and is therefore called what?**
10. **This is the name of the committee that determines which drugs are legal and which ones should be banned.**

Key learning points

- Anabolic steroids are used to increase muscle mass.
- EPO is used to increase the number of red blood cells so helps endurance athletes.
- Stimulants increase a person's alertness.
- Beta blockers slow down a person's heart rate.
- Diuretics increase fluid loss.
- All drugs have side-effects and negatively affect a person's health.

Further Reading

Beashel, P., Dibson, A. and Taylor, J., 2001, *The World of Sport Examined*. Cheltenham: Nelson Thornes.

Stafford-Brown, J., Rea, S. and Chance, J., 2003, *BTEC National in Sport and Exercise Science*. London: Hodder and Stoughton.

Useful websites

www.science.org.au/nova/055/055key.htm

Online article published by the Australian Academy of Science, which looks at the use of anabolic steroids, human growth hormone and ePO in sport.

www.bbc.co.uk/schools/gcsebitesize/pe/performance/

In addition to a self-assessed test for students, BBC's GCSE Bitesize online service offers a revision of the most common drugs (and their side-effects) used in sport.

www.getbodysmart.com/

Free American site that offers online demonstrations of how the body works (cardiovascular, respiratory and muscular systems) through quizzes and short animations.

www.medtropolis.com/VBody.asp

A very good interactive website for anatomy with quizzes and tutorials.

www.innerbody.com

Free and informative diagrams of the different body systems, including respiratory, cardiovascular, skeletal and muscular.

Chapter 19
Business Skills in Sport

The sport and active leisure industry is a huge business and one that is continuing to grow. If you are planning to work in the sport and active leisure business you will need good business skills to help you to work effectively and efficiently. As most sport and active leisure industries involve working with customers, all customer-facing staff should possess excellent customer service skills so that the customer feels valued and keeps coming back, which keeps the sport and active leisure facility in business.

In this chapter you will learn a range of different business skills including customer service skills, managing information, verbal and written communication skills and marketing and publicity.

Learning Goals

By the end of this chapter you should:

- Know the business skills needed to support customers in the sport and leisure industry.
- Be able to use the skills required to manage customer service situations.
- Know the skills needed for effective sport and leisure business operation.
- Be able to review the quality of a sport and leisure business.

To achieve a PASS grade the evidence must show that the learner is able to:	To achieve a MERIT grade the evidence must show that, in addition to the pass criteria, the learner is able to:	To achieve a DISTINCTION grade the evidence must show that, in addition to the pass and merit criteria, the learner is able to:
P1 describe the business skills needed to support customers in the sport and leisure industry	**M1** explain how business skills differ to support different customers in the sport and leisure industry	**D1** evaluate business skills and their role in supporting different types of customer
P2 demonstrate use of customer service skills in three different customer service situations	**M2** demonstrate integrated use of customer service skills	
P3 produce guidelines for a selected customer service situation		
P4 identify the skills needed for effective sport and leisure business operation		
P5 review the quality of a selected sport and leisure business, identifying strengths and areas for future development	**M3** review the quality of a selected sport and leisure business, explaining strengths and areas for future development	**D2** review the quality of a selected sport and leisure business, justifying strengths and areas for future development

19.1 Business Skills to Support Customers in the Sport and Leisure Industry P1 M1 D1

Customer Information

Customers need to be provided with a range of different types of information including:

- Sports and activities on offer at the centre
- Prices
- Opening and closing times
- Health and safety
- Unacceptable behaviour in the swimming pool
- Where they can eat and drink
- Cleaning times and checks of toilet facilities
- Types of footwear allowed in different sports halls.

If a centre has lots of information available for its customers, they will be well informed as to what is expected from them and what they can expect from the centre and the staff. This helps to prevent conflict between staff and customers – for example, if a group of 5-a-side football players were eating crisps in the sports hall but there were signs stating 'Do not eat or drink in here', then a member of staff can more easily ask the customers to refrain from eating in the sports hall and point to the sign to emphasise their point and to show that it is the centre's policy.

This information can be displayed in lots of different ways including signs, posters, leaflets and notices.

Ticketing Systems

The type of sport and leisure centre in which you are working will determine what sort of ticketing systems are in place. Many private-sector clubs such as David Lloyd or Virgin Active require members to use their membership card to 'swipe' themselves in so that they can be identified as members and make use of most of the facilities. In public sports centres, customers don't usually need to be members. These centres need to identify a way in which it is clear that the customer has paid for the activity in which they are planning to take part in. Many swimming pools give their customers coloured wristbands to wear – this makes it clear to the lifeguards that they have paid and also allows the centre to control when customers leave the pool – you may have heard over the public-speaking system requests for customers wearing a certain coloured band to leave the pool – this helps to prevent customers from staying for longer than they are allowed, and therefore also helps to prevent overcrowding in the pool area.

Customer Inductions

When a customer joins a gym he or she needs to be well enough to take part in exercise and then they need to be shown how to use the various different types of equipment – a process called an induction. This process is designed to help the customer feel that the gym is familiar and safe, and to make them feel confident about using the gym equipment so that they can achieve their fitness goals.

Figure 19.1 A customer being shown how to use the gym equipment safely

An induction usually incorporates the following parts:

1. Lifestyle and health assessment.
2. Facility tour.
3. Health and safety procedures.
4. Instruction in gym equipment.
5. Planning an exercise programme/goal setting.
6. Booking procedures.

1. Lifestyle and health assessment

The first part of an induction usually requires a written or interview assessment of the customer's current lifestyle, such as diet, current physical activity levels, whether they smoke or not, and also how much alcohol they consume per week. During the whole of this process it is important to handle the information sensitively and not to be judgemental.

After this information has been taken, a variety of physical tests can be administered. These usually include:

- Height
- Weight
- Body mass index
- Blood pressure
- Resting heart rate.

Again, care needs to be taken to remain discreet and sensitive to the data that is collected. The data will also need to be stored securely in line with the Data Protection Act. The centre in which you work will have already devised a method of storing this data securely, so ensure that you follow the guidelines that have been set.

The results of these tests and a PAR-Q (physical activity readiness questionnaire) will help to determine if the customer is ready to take part in exercise. There is always the chance that the results of these tests and questionnaires may show that the customer requires further medical checks from a qualified doctor before joining the gym – if this is the case, try not to alarm the customer by telling them that they have to go and see a doctor immediately! However, do ensure that the customer understands why they need medical clearance prior to taking part in exercise and that it is only something that a qualified medical professional can do. These checks are carried out to look after the health of the customer and also to protect the gym from liability should a customer fall ill while taking part in exercise.

2. Facility tour

Once the health and lifestyle checks have been completed, the next step is to show the customer around the facilities – this would include the toilets, showers, lockers, exercise areas (for example aerobics studio, spinning studio etc), swimming pool, refreshment area etc.

3. Health and safety

Health and safety procedures will also need to be pointed out, including locations of fire exists and the various methods of summoning first aid, such as phones or alarm buttons.

4. Instruction in gym equipment

There is a huge range of different types of gym equipment available and even experienced gym users may not be familiar with the brands of gym equipment that you have in your centre. As a qualified gym instructor you will be aware of the process of instructing customers how to use the equipment:

a demonstrate
b demonstrate with teaching points
c observe the customer using the equipment while providing teaching points.

5. Exercise programme planning/goal setting

Most customers who come to a gym do have some sort of goal in mind; this may be to lose weight, tone up, get fit for a specific event such as a 5 km run etc. While you are working with your customer, ensure that you listen to their goals and help to guide them to a realistic time frame of when they can hope to achieve their goals, together with planning short-term goals that are SMART (specific, measurable, achievable, realistic and time-constrained). Try to include the customer in devising their exercise programme so that you are including exercises that they will enjoy.

6. Booking Procedures

Most sport and active leisure centres offer a wide range of activities, including:

- Swimming lessons
- Aerobics classes
- Spinning classes
- Squash
- Badminton
- Tennis
- Aqua aerobics
- Martial arts.

For many of these activities the customer will need to book in advance to get a place in the class. In many cases the receptionist is responsible for taking bookings by phone or in person as well as greeting customers on their arrival and dealing with other customer requests. During peak periods it may be difficult for the receptionist to fulfill all of these duties, which can then result in customers having to wait for extended periods of time before they are served.

In order to meet customers' needs, centres sometimes provide more staff on reception during peak periods to meet this additional demand. Alternatively centres may incorporate other methods of booking, such as online booking or automated phone bookings that allow customers to respond to structured questions with their telephone key pad to place their bookings.

Customer Trends

Sport and active leisure does lend itself to new trends where various organisations bring out new ways and methods for people to exercise. These are designed to help to keep customers motivated and keep them on their exercise programme. New technology is continually being introduced in gym equipment to try to keep exercising customers engaged and motivated while working out on an exercise bike or treadmill. However, this equipment is expensive and most centres cannot keep updating their technology to keep up with the latest trends.

Exercise classes are highly subject to trends as new things come on to the market. Aerobics was a huge trend in the 80s and it is still being taught. However, there is much more choice today, including the already very popular 'bums and tums', spinning, step, circuits and Pilates.

Some newer and more unusual classes include:

- Stiletto strength – where customers wear high heels and take part in Pilates and strength exercises, finishing with a 15-minute walk in 3-inch high heels.

- Forza – participants use a wooden sword to mimic samurai swordmanship for this workout, which mainly concentrates on exercising the body's core.

Figure 19.2   An exercise class

- Bikram yoga – the class temperature is set at a minimum of 105°F (40°C) and participants perform yoga postures to warm the body inside and out.

Exercise instructors and organisations are blending different types of exercise classes to create new workouts because something like aerobics can become repetitive and therefore boring. As a manager of a sport and active leisure centre it is difficult to keep on top of the new trends and kit the classes out with the correct equipment and have trained instructors for each new initiative. It is therefore necessary to have an understanding of the new trends together with meeting the needs and wants of the customers.

Market Analysis

Market analysis is an important business skill in order for a sport and active leisure facility to plan ahead and provide for its customers appropriately. Details of market analysis will vary from one organisation to another, but usually includes such factors as:

- Staffing
- Equipment – current equipment and future equipment requirements
- Promotional activities
- Ways in which to expand
- Competitors and what they are doing
- Market trends and changes
- Opportunities for market and product development.

Market analysis is carried out through researching what other businesses in the same line of work are doing and offering and assessing customers' needs and wants and working out ways in which the business can meet these needs.

Customer Complaints

How you deal with a customer's complaint is very important. You should always ensure you respect the customer and listen carefully to the complaint. Ensure you give an apology, even when it is not your fault, and try to find a solution to the problem. You should be sure to keep calm and not argue with the customer. If a solution cannot be agreed on, you should bring your manager into the discussion. Once a solution has been agreed, ensure that what you have promised does happen.

Customer Feedback

In order for a manager to understand how well their staff and facilities are providing for their customers there is nothing more valuable than customer feedback. Many centres have a customer feedback box in which customers place any specific feedback or suggestions and still remain anonymous. However, this box is rarely used by customers when they want to provide good feedback; it is usually used when customers want to complain about something! Therefore, this is a useful tool but it is usually used in conjunction with other forms of feedback.

Some centres hand out regular surveys that can target specific aspects of the centre and what it has to offer – for example, they may have introduced a new exercise class and want of find out how well it has been received to determine if it should stay on the class timetable. The only problem with surveys is that they do take time for people to complete so many customers need some sort of incentive. This can be done, for example, by putting all the names of the people who have completed the questionnaire into a draw and the winner receives a free meal from the centre restaurant.

The feedback that has been received needs to be dealt with accordingly – if customers are identifying that they are receiving poor customer service then staff will need to undergo some customer service training in order to rectify this problem.

Another popular method of receiving feedback is to have a mystery customer visit the centre. A mystery customer is someone who appears to be a 'normal' customer and may well 'test out' staff with questions and requests to see what sort of service they receive. They may well also contact the centre by phone to make a booking prior to their visit. The mystery customer can then feed back their findings to the centre manager, for example, were staff knowledgeable and helpful, did the mystery customer have to wait long for the phone to be answered when they made the booking, was the receptionist polite and helpful, were the changing rooms clean and tidy, were the toilet facilities clean, was the induction process appropriate, etc. The centre manager can then act on the feedback accordingly.

Activity 19.1 40 mins P1

Mystery customer M1

Imagine you are a mystery customer and need to write a report on the business skills (including service and facilities) provided at your local sport and active leisure centre. D1

Task 1

Write a list of five things you noticed that were good about the customer service or provision in your centre.

Task 2

(a) Write a list of five things that you think could be improved in your local sport and active leisure centre.
(b) Write a report to suggest ideas on how the centre can improve these five things that you have noticed.

Customers

Working in the sport and leisure industry means you will be dealing with all sorts of different customers and you will therefore need to be able to learn skills in dealing with the public. These skills are very important as you need to be sure you are giving the customers the treatment they expect to ensure that they keep coming back to your leisure facility. You will need to learn what the customers' needs are and how you can meet these requirements or even exceed them.

Definition

Customer service refers to the level of assistance and courtesy given to those who use the facility.

There are many different types of customers who use leisure facilities and you should have a basic understanding of how to deal with every person you meet. Here are some examples of customers you may meet, together with some suggestions on how you should deal with them.

Groups

Dealing with groups means that you rarely get the chance to find out the needs of every customer in the group. You may deal with groups if you are teaching a swimming class, for example, or instructing a step aerobics class. In these cases you will need to communicate clearly to the whole group through speech and demonstrations. You should always ensure you offer the group time to speak to you on a one-to-one basis, either at the start or at the end of the session. You can also communicate to groups through the use of posters, letters and signs etc.

Different Age Groups

In the leisure industry you can expect to deal with people of all ages, from babies and toddlers right through to the over-60s. Therefore, you should be able to have an understanding of their needs; for example, be aware of where the baby-changing facilities are, ensure you know about reduced prices for the over-60s, be aware of special swimming sessions for the over-60s etc.

Different Cultural Backgrounds

You need to be aware of different cultural needs and be able to cater for them accordingly. For example, some cultures will not allow males to see females in their swimsuits. Therefore, you must be able to give these females details of when there are female-only swimming sessions. These sessions would also have to have only female lifeguards on duty. You should be aware of people that use the facility who do not have English as their first language, and ensure there are signs and promotional materials that they can understand.

Specific Needs

A good leisure facility is able to cater for every person in its local area, including people who have specific needs. An example of a person with a specific need is someone with restricted mobility; these people may require the use of a walking stick or wheelchair, for example. In these cases the facility should have appropriate access so that people can enter the building unaided. If the building is on two stories, there must be a lift or ramps to allow the person to move up to the next floor. If the facility has a swimming pool, there must be some form of access available for people with disabilities, such as a chair hoist.

Key learning points

The business skills required to support customers in the sport and leisure industry include:

- Booking procedures
- Customer induction
- Market trends
- Market analysis
- Customer feedback
- Ticketing systems
- Customer information.

Activity 19.2 2 hours

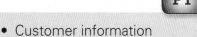

Business skills to support customers in the sport and leisure industry

In the sport and leisure industry there are many different types of customers with a variety of different needs. In any business that deals with customers, customer service and meeting the needs of the customers is very important.

Task 1

Examine and, where possible, visit different types of sport and leisure providers, for example leisure centres, gyms, swim centres, racket centres etc.

Task 2

Examine the different types of business skills used by each sport and leisure provider to support customers; these include:

- Customer information
- Booking procedures
- Customer inductions
- Customer records
- Ticketing systems
- Customer trends
- Market analysis
- Methods of obtaining customer feedback
- Ways of dealing with customer complaints.

Task 3

Write a report that describes, explains and evaluates the business skills that you have investigated and how they support different types of customer in the sport and active leisure industry.

19.2 Skills Required to Manage Customer Service Situations P2 P3 M2

Providing Information and Assistance

As a member of staff in a sport or leisure facility it is important that you are able to provide information and assistance to customers. In order to do this you will need to know who does what within the organisation – for example, if the customer wants to book a badminton court you will need to direct them to the person responsible for making bookings, such as the receptionist. You should also be aware of the range of information leaflets that the centre has available so that you can pass these on to the customer to help to answer their questions.

When you are unable to answer the customer's question it is a good idea to reply in a helpful and positive manner and concentrate on what you will do for the customer and how you can go about addressing their needs. For example, rather than saying 'I don't know' you could say 'I will find out,' or instead of 'I can't sort out that request unless it is in writing' you could say 'I can sort that out for you if you can send me the details in an email.'

You may find that you are dealing with customers who require assistance or support. If this is the case, you should always approach the customer and ask them if they would like some help before giving it!

Where you meet a customer who requires assistance or support you have two options in how you can help them. You can either:

- Remove the cause of difficulty, or
- Support the customer.

For example, if an elderly customer is having difficulty walking up stairs you could assist them by telling them where the lifts are situated.

Activity **19.3** 30 mins P2

Customer service skills M2

Look at the questions and answers below, then try to provide answers that are more positive and helpful:

Question

Can I book a badminton court for next week?

Answer

That's not my job, go and speak to the receptionist.

Question

The toilets are filthy. Why aren't they cleaned more regularly?

Answer

We are short-staffed so it will have to wait until the manger is free to cover one of us.

Question

Do I need to wear trainers for the aerobics class?

Answer

I'm not sure, I expect so.

Question

Why on earth are we paying so much for our gym membership when the air conditioning keeps breaking down?

Answer

I don't have anything to do with that.

Activity **19.4** 10 mins P2

Assisting and supporting customers M2

How would you offer assistance and/or support to the following customers:

- A blind customer having difficulty finding the female changing rooms
- A dyslexic customer having difficulty working out swimming times
- A person with a broken arm trying to get their belongings into their locker
- A parent who has lost their child somewhere in the facility
- A person in a wheelchair having difficulty getting up a ramp.

pleased to see that person, which makes them feel welcome. This service should be in place in both the reception area, as the customer enters the building, and also in the area in which their activity is to take place, for example in the gym, where the gym instructors should make a point of acknowledging the customer's arrival.

When addressing customers you should always ensure that you are using appropriate language and are addressing customers in the appropriate manner – your centre will probably have a policy whereby they address customers as Mr or Mrs/Miss followed by their surname unless the customer has requested that you address them by their first name. Ensure that you are aware of the policy and, if in doubt, it is usually safe to address adults as Sir or Madam if you do not know their surname or Mr/Mrs/Miss followed by their surname if you do. In the workplace, bad or inappropriate language is rarely tolerated, especially when dealing with customers.

Body language can say an awful lot about how we feel, how confident we are and how enthusiastic we are, and people will often form a first impression about someone based on their body language alone. Therefore, it is important to convey the right message by using appropriate body language – such as standing up straight, looking interested, paying attention

Alternatively, if the customer does not wish to use the lifts, you could offer to carry their bag or provide a steadying arm to help them to get up the stairs.

Communication Skills

Making the customer feel welcome is a very important aspect of customer care. A simple greeting with a smile as the customer arrives through the door gives the impression you are to the customer and actively listening to their question. Your body language should also reflect the message that you are sending; for example, when you are greeting a customer with a 'Hello' it will appear much more sincere if you are smiling at the same time!

If you work in a sport and active leisure facility, you should be able to answer questions about the basic operations of this facility, such as opening hours and services the facility has to offer. If, however, you do not know the answer, you must be able to direct the customer to someone who does – never tell a customer that you do not know the answer to their question and then walk away.

Customer Service Situations

Answering the Telephone

If you are involved with dealing with customers over the telephone, it is very important that you have some basic training in telephone communication as the customer's first impression of the centre in which you work will be based upon the conversation they have with you and the service that they receive.

Answer the call with a 'Good morning' or 'Good afternoon' and identify the name of the centre and who you are, for example:

'Good morning, Aqua Vale Swim Centre, James speaking.'

Remember to speak clearly and not to mumble.

Do not eat, drink or chew gum while talking on the phone; the other person will be able to hear you do this and it does not sound professional!

Use appropriate language and address the caller in the appropriate manner, such as Mr Smith or Mrs Neate, unless you have been given prior permission to call them by their first name.

Listen carefully to what the caller has to say – if the caller is leaving a message make sure you write it down clearly and repeat the message to the caller so that they can confirm it is correct – this is especially important if they are leaving

their contact details, such as a phone number or email address.

If you are responsible for answering the phone, you will also need to master such skills as how to transfer the call to another person in the organisation, how to end the call politely when necessary, for example if you have a number of people to deal with who are waiting in a queue, how to cancel or take bookings, and you will need to know the timings of the centre and different activities that are on in the centre etc.

Written Communication

In sport and active leisure centres there are a range of different types of written communication that can be roughly divided into communication for the customer and communication for staff. Whenever using written communication always make sure that you have used the correct spelling and grammar; if there are spelling mistakes or grammatical errors the person reading the information may well make assumptions about the writer, such as that they have not taken sufficient care or time in writing the document and are not really that bothered by the content.

Communication with customers should be professional and the words used should be appropriate for the customer who is going to read it. Customers will view written communication in the form of leaflets, signs, posters and notices. In each of these cases the wording should be clear and concise – customers are put off reading leaflets and posters that are too wordy. With health and safety signs the message should be clear and also contain pictures where appropriate – for example a 'no smoking' sign usually just has a picture of a cigarette with a line through it.

Many staff communicate with each other through emails. A centre manager can send an email to all members of staff very quickly, which is an excellent way of communicating significant

Figure 19.3 No smoking allowed

Activity **19.5** ⏱ 30 mins P2 M2

Verbal communication skills

Mrs Ferguson is interested in joining the new health and fitness centre that has opened up in her local area. She calls the centre to find out more about what the centre has to offer.

Receptionist: Hello, how can I help you?

Mrs Ferguson: Oh hello, I'm interested in joining your fitness centre. However I would like to find out a bit more about what you have to offer.

Receptionist: What do you want to know?

Mrs Ferguson: Well, do you have a swimming pool?

Receptionist: Yes.

Mrs Ferguson: Is it a 25 m pool?

Receptionist: I think so. It does look quite big.

Mrs Ferguson: Do you have lane-swimming sessions?

Receptionist: Sometimes, not all of the time though.

Mrs Ferguson: What times are lane-swimming sessions on?

Receptionist: Hold on a sec, I'll just try and find out.

In the background Mrs Ferguson can hear the receptionist call out to the duty manager: 'Oy, Daz, when's the lane-swimming sessions on ... I dunno, where's the leaflet with the timetables on, here it is ...'

One minute later

Receptionist: They are on every morning from 6 to 8 a.m., lunchtimes and most evenings between 6 and 9 p.m., except when the club swimmers are in.

Mrs Ferguson: And when are the club swimmers in?

Receptionist: Ummmm, just getting to that bit, hang on, ah there it is ... right, it says here that they are in on Mondays, Wednesdays and Fridays.

Mrs Ferguson: How much does it cost to go swimming?

Receptionist: Depends on your age – how old are you?

Mrs Ferguson: I'd rather not say actually.

Receptionist: Well it does make a difference. If you are between the ages of 18 and 50 then it's £4.50. If you are over the age of 50 you can get a discounted rate of £2.50. You can also become a member and just pay a monthly charge and swim as many times as you want.

Mrs Ferguson: Oh, that sounds good. Can you tell me a bit more about the membership scheme?

Receptionist: Not really, I don't deal with that. If you ring back in about 30 minutes our membership person will be back from lunch.

Mrs Ferguson: OK, thank you for your help.

Receptionist: Sorry, what was that, couldn't hear you above the noise of the people waiting in the queue.

Mrs Ferguson: *hangs up the phone.*

Receptionist: How rude, that's the second time someone has hung up on me today.

Tasks

(a) Read through the case study above.

(b) List as many positive things that you can find about how the receptionist dealt with the telephone communication with Mrs Ferguson.

(c) List five ways in which the receptionist did not deal with the telephone communication in a customer-friendly way.

(d) Describe in each of the above five situations what the receptionist could have done or said that would have been a more appropriate method of communication with a customer.

events or day-to-day operating procedures such as:

- Health and safety points
- Staff training
- Problems with cleanliness.

Dealing with Accidents and Issues

In most cases, if you are working in a sport and active leisure centre and a customer is involved in an accident you will need to seek assistance. Ensure you are aware of the different methods of summoning help – some centres have alarm buttons placed around the building – this is usually the case in swimming pools where a lifeguard may need to summon help urgently. When the alarm goes off, the centre manager knows where the alarm is situated and is able to get there quickly to deal with the situation. Where the centre does not have alarms, other methods

of summoning help can usually be found; these can consist of telephones or staff may be issued with walkie-talkies so that they are able to summon help whenever it is required.

You should also be aware of details such as where the ambulance will arrive so that you know where to go to greet the paramedics on arrival, if asked to do so, and take them to the casualty.

Procedures for Dealing with Customer Complaints

If you are working in the sport and active leisure industry and dealing with customers, you are very likely to be in a situation where you have to deal with a customer who has a complaint to make. When a customer does complain they usually do so with an expectation that something will be done about their complaint – this may be as simple as an apology or alternatively something that requires much more time and attention. The main aim for staff dealing with a

---

Activity 19.6 2 hours   P2 P3 M2

Demonstrating customer service skills

You now have a good idea of the types of skills required when dealing with customers in the sport and leisure industry; you just need to be able to put these skills into practice!

Task 1

Visit your local sport or active leisure centre and try to observe their staff dealing with customers. Watch to see how the staff communicate with the customers: are they using clear and appropriate language, is their body language reflecting what they are saying? How do the staff provide information and assistance to their customers, how do they deal with issues such as customer complaints?

Task 2

Make a note of all of the good customer service skills that you observed and also note which skills could be improved and why you think they need to be improved.

Task 3

With a friend, carry out a role-play exercise where you are a member of staff dealing with a customer.

Carry out this role-play exercise for **three** different customer service situations.

Examples of customer service situations could include:

- Customer complaint
- Customer leaving a message by telephone
- Customer trying to find out about exercise classes
- Dealing with an injured customer.

Task 4

Select one of the customer service situations from Task 3 and then write out a set of guidelines that could be used by other members of staff to instruct them in the correct ways of dealing with this particular service situation.

customer who is complaining is to ensure that the customer is satisfied with how the complaint is dealt – if the customer is not satisfied the centre may well lose their business and this customer may well spread the word about how poorly they have been dealt with by this particular centre, which is very bad for business.

The general guidelines for dealing with customer complaints are to:

- Remain calm

- Listen carefully to the complaint and try not to interrupt the customer

- Re-tell the main points of the complaint so that the customer knows that you've understood the reason for their complaint

- Apologise to the customer, even if the complaint has nothing to do with you – you are representing the company

- Resolve the complaint quickly. If you cannot deal with the complaint, find someone who can and take them to the customer.

19.3 Skills Needed for Effective Sport and Leisure Business Operation P4

A number of factors will determine if a sports and leisure business is successful. These factors are shown in Figure 19.4.

Income

This is the amount of money that the business makes. The business will then have to deduct money from their income to pay taxes etc.

Profit

Profit literally means 'to make progress'. If a business is not making a profit after a certain period of time it will usually have to close down.

Figure 19.4   Factors that can affect the success of a sports & leisure business

A business will make a profit if the money coming in to the company is more than the money that is going out. The money going out of the business includes staff salaries, cost of the product or services, tax deductions, rent etc.

Growth

If a business is doing well, it will usually grow in some shape or form. Many successful businesses will grow by taking on more staff to cope with the greater demand for the product or service. Some businesses may open a branch in a different location so that they are able to sell to a larger market. Other businesses may grow by opening a website to either trade their product online or advertise their services.

Customer Satisfaction

All sports businesses require customers to buy their products and/or services. Therefore, in order for the business to succeed, it is vital that the customer is satisfied with the product or service they receive. If the customer is satisfied then the benefits your business will receive include:

- Customer loyalty

- New customers

- Increased sales and profits
- A good image
- Employee satisfaction
- A competitive edge.

The business skills used by the manager and staff in a sport and leisure business will help to determine if these factors are met and whether the business will be successful.

Financial Skills

All businesses involve financial transactions, which is where money comes in to the centre and money is also spent on buying products and paying wages by the centre. In order for a business to make money the income must be greater than the outgoings.

There are many different types of financial transactions within a sport and active leisure centre. These can include:

Figure 19.5 Some of the financial transactions within a sport and active leisure centre

Many sport and leisure centres have systems in place to help with the financial skills in a business and most will employ one or more accountants to keep records of the money transactions.

Health and Safety Skills

Health and safety skills are very important in sport and leisure in order to ensure the safety of both the customers and the staff. As a member of staff there are some key health and safety skills that you will need to be aware of so that you know what to do on a daily basis and in the face of an emergency.

In most large sports facilities, staff are encouraged to qualify in first aid, since the chances of an accident or injury while participating in sport or exercise is quite high. Ensure your first-aid qualification is up to date and, remember, you will need to keep updating this qualification as it runs out after a certain period of time. Qualified lifeguards will have learnt and practised most aspects of first aid as part of their lifeguard training and know how to deal with a range of different pool-related incidents – again, this qualification is one that needs to be taken on a regular basis as it runs out after a period of time (usually three years).

Fire and Evacuation Procedures

Emergency procedures should be in place to evacuate a sports centre, including procedures to deal with fire, chemical release, explosion, terrorist threats etc. It is very important that, in the event of an evacuation, customers and staff are evacuated as quickly and safely as possible. All sports centres should have a policy that shows customers what to do and where to go in an emergency and, for the staff, what everyone's role is in evacuating a building, including muster points and a policy for re-admission to the building. As a member of staff you would be expected to help show customers the way to fire exits and to ensure that they are congregating at a safe and correct muster point.

Security Skills

Leisure facilities are open to the public so, in theory, any person is able to enter the building. It is the duty of the staff within the leisure facility to ensure that the facility is secure so that the customers are protected from abusive and violent behavior. Arrangements should also be made to provide a secure environment for the customer to store his or her belongings

Preventing Violence

The reception area should always be staffed to help to track customers who are entering the building. If the receptionist observes a person who is showing antisocial behaviour or appears to be under the influence of alcohol or drugs on arrival, they can refuse them entry to the facility.

Customers taking part in activities or competitions may become violent towards staff because they are cross with themselves for playing badly or annoyed that their opponent is getting away with cheating. Most centres will provide staff with training on skills to deal with people who are exhibiting unacceptable behaviour.

Preventing Theft

All customer and staff belongings should be stored safely and securely in lockers. In some instances CCTV may be provided in locker areas. This will give additional security to people's belongings. CCTV should also be placed in car parks together with signs telling people not to leave valuables in their cars. Equipment should be kept in an area that can be locked.

Theft of information is also something a leisure facility should take precautions to prevent. Most facilities have a database that contains all their customer information, which they use when sending promotional material etc. This information could be very useful to other leisure providers as it would give them the opportunity to advertise directly to your customers, which

may make them change their leisure provider. Not only this, each facility must adhere to the Data Protection Act (1998), which means that it is illegal to use the information gained from individuals for anything other than its original intention. If the information is stolen, it is highly likely that the data will be used for something other than its original purpose.

> **(k) Key learning points**
>
> The operational side of a sport and leisure business requires a person to have:
>
> - Financial skills for managing different types of money transactions;
> - Health and safety skills to ensure the safety of the staff and customers;
> - Security skills to protect the staff and customers and their belongings.

Activity 19.7 20 mins **P4**

Skills needed for effective sport and leisure business operation

Working in the sport and leisure business requires a number of different types of skills to help ensure that the operational side of the business is effective.

Task

Design a poster that identifies the skills needed for the smooth and effective running of a sport and leisure facility.

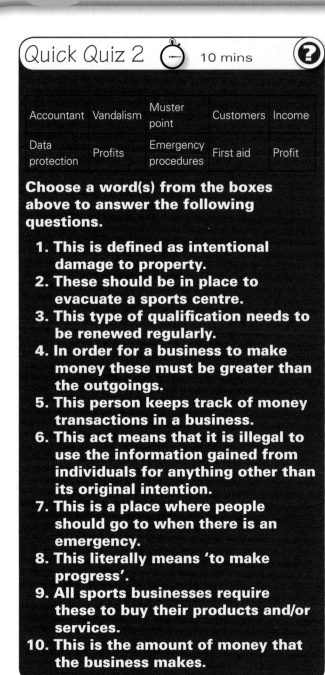

Quick Quiz 2 ⏱ 10 mins ❓

| Accountant | Vandalism | Muster point | Customers | Income |
| Data protection | Profits | Emergency procedures | First aid | Profit |

Choose a word(s) from the boxes above to answer the following questions.

1. **This is defined as intentional damage to property.**
2. **These should be in place to evacuate a sports centre.**
3. **This type of qualification needs to be renewed regularly.**
4. **In order for a business to make money these must be greater than the outgoings.**
5. **This person keeps track of money transactions in a business.**
6. **This act means that it is illegal to use the information gained from individuals for anything other than its original intention.**
7. **This is a place where people should go to when there is an emergency.**
8. **This literally means 'to make progress'.**
9. **All sports businesses require these to buy their products and/or services.**
10. **This is the amount of money that the business makes.**

19.4 Reviewing the Quality of a Sport and Leisure Business [P5] [M3] [D2]

When reviewing the quality of a sport and leisure business there are many different aspects to consider including:

- Customers
- Affordability
- Marketing
- Customer feedback
- Sport and leisure activities
- Facility mix
- Health and safety
- Access for people with disabilities
- Changing facilities
- Customer information
- Quality standard.

We will take a brief look at each to give you ideas on what sort of things demonstrate good practice and ways in which you can investigate each aspect.

Customers

There are many different types of customer who use sport and leisure facilities. The different types of customer can be categorised according to their demographics.

Definition

Demographics information that puts people into different categories based on characteristics such as age, gender, income, race etc.

To work out the customer demographics of a sport and leisure facility you would need to carry out a survey. Surveys are usually in a questionnaire format. They can be carried out in writing, face to face or by telephone. The questionnaire should be brief so that it does not put the customer off. The questions should be relevant to the topic of interest – in this case you would be asking questions about such topics as:

- Age category – it is usually better to allow the customer to place a tick in the box of a certain age range, for example 25–30, rather than asking them to tell you their actual age as this can be deemed sensitive information by some.

Other demographics you may wish to investigate include:

- Income – again, placing a tick in a box for an approximate salary bracket is usually better received, for example:

  £15–20 000

- Race – in line with equal opportunities' policy & legislation, you will need data relating to the ethnic origin of customers.

An example of a survey to work out the demographics of a sport and leisure facility could look like this:

Gender

| Male | ☐ |
| Female | ☐ |

Age

under 12	☐
12–17	☐
18–25	☐
26–35	☐
36–45	☐
46–55	☐
56–65	☐
66 or over	☐

Income

under £5000	☐
£5000–£10 000	☐
£10 000–£15 000	☐
£15 000–£25 000	☐
£25 000–£35 000	☐
£35 000–£45 000	☐
£45 000–£55 000	☐
£55 000–£65 000	☐
over £65 000	☐

Race

Caucasian	☐
Afro Caribbean	☐
Indian Asian	☐
Oriental Asian	☐
Other (please specify)	☐

Sampling

As it is not possible to collect data from every customer, the data collected is going to be used to represent the views of all of the businesses customers. Therefore, the sample of people used in this activity should try to represent a cross-section of all of the customers. For example, in a leisure centre, if the sample was chosen between 10 a.m. to 11 am on a Monday morning it would probably consist mainly of retired people and mothers and children and it would therefore not be a true representation of all of the customers that use the facility. However, if the sampling took place throughout the day say, 6–7 am, 9–10 am, 12 –1 pm, 3–4 pm, 6–7 pm and 9–10 pm it would give a much clearer picture of the views of all of the facilities customers.

Another method of sampling could be to pick every twentieth customer throughout the day. This again would give a good representation of the customers who use this facility.

Affordability

You could also include a question on affordability in your survey to find out if the customers feel that the facility is offering activities at a price that they can afford. Another way of investigating the costing of the activities would be to compare the prices for similar activities at other sports facilities. If the sports facility that you are investigating has prices that are significantly higher for the activities that they are providing, try to find out if they are offering something more than the other facilities. For example, private health clubs are often more expensive to use than public leisure centres; however, the customers are given toiletries to use in the changing areas; there are often additional spa facilities such as a Jacuzzi and steam room; the gym equipment consists of the latest technology etc.

If the facility is not offering anything different from its competitors, then there is the danger that they will start to lose customers as most customers prefer to save money where they can and will use the facilities at the cheaper centre.

Marketing

A sports and leisure facility will need to 'sell' itself to the public so that people will choose to go there. Most businesses take a lot of time and effort to promote a positive image of themselves and the products and services that they have to offer. Posters, leaflets and adverts in the local papers are used to promote the business. Many gyms advertise themselves using photos of good-looking and toned people using their facility. This is done to try and make people think that if they joined that particular gym then they too would look like the people in the advert.

Many businesses will encourage customers to use their facility by offering various promotional discounts; for example, during the first few weeks of January when people are looking to keep to their New Year resolutions of 'getting fit or losing weight', many gyms will offer a 'no joining fee' promotion to encourage potential new customers to join their gym.

Customer Feedback

As discussed previously in this chapter, customer feedback is very important. There are different ways of gaining customer feedback and these can include:

- Questionnaires
- Suggestion boxes
- Interviews
- Phone calls.

It is very important that a centre does seek out customer feedback so that it can ensure that it is meeting the needs of its customers. If customers are not happy then they will seek out a different sport and leisure facility that meets their needs, and the centre will loose their custom, which is bad for business.

Sport and Leisure Activities

The range of sport and leisure activities that a centre runs is also very important. These can include:

- A range of different types of exercise classes
- Racket sports
- Swimming
- Football
- Rugby
- Netball
- Basketball
- Gym.

However, the centre can also provide activities for other types of customer, which may help draw in new customers and meet the needs of the local area – for example, doctors prescribe exercise for different types of people as regular participation in exercise has been proven to increase the health and well-being of most people. If the centre is linked to a doctor's surgery, they can welcome referred patients to their centre and provide their exercise prescription.

Other types of activities could be included for women who are pregnant (antenatal) or women who are keen to try to get their figures back after pregnancy (post-natal) and there are specific exercises classes that are designed for women in these different circumstances. There are also exercise classes suitable for older adults who may have restricted mobility.

Facility Mix

Facility mix means the different types of facility that are available at a centre. These can include the following:

- Sports hall
- Swimming pool
- Aerobics studio
- Spinning studio
- Diving pool
- Fitness gym
- Soft-play area for children
- Cafe

- Jacuzzi
- Sauna
- Beauty rooms.

If the sport and leisure facility is an aquatic centre then you would expect a good range of swim-based facilities such as a competition pool, leisure pool and slides. If the centre does not specialise in a certain type of activity then a usual mix would contain a sports hall, gym and swimming pool. The facilty mix of a sport and leisure facility will also help to determine the demographics of the customer that uses the facility – for example, if the facility has a toddlers' swimming pool and a soft-play area, it would attract people with young children; if the centre just had a sports hall and a gym then it would mainly attract adults.

Health and Safety

There should be regular inspections to ensure the facility is functioning in accordance with health and safety guidelines. These checks may be required on a regular basis throughout the day or some may need to be performed at the start and end of the day. For example, examining the changing facilities to ensure they are clean and tidy, and testing the swimming pool water to assess the chlorine levels, should be carried out once every few hours, but checking that all the lights are working inside and outside the building only really needs to be carried out once or twice a day.

Some checks will be carried out by external agencies or contractors; these will include the fire department who will check such things as the number and functioning of fire extinguishers and that the fire exits are easily accessible. Contractors may have service agreements to ensure plant and equipment such as air-conditioning units are maintained to a safe standard.

Every centre needs to be able to provide evidence that these checks are taking place regularly and they are usually documented in logbooks and files.

Access for People with Disabilities

The Disability Discrimination Act (DDA) requires public facilities to promote equality of opportunity for disabled people. A disabled person as defined by the act is 'someone who has a physical or mental impairment that has a substantial and long-term adverse effect on his or her ability to carry out normal day-to-day activities'.

Sport and leisure facilities should allow access for people with disabilities, such as providing ramps and automatic doors for people in wheelchairs, and also be able to cater to their needs such as by providing information in Braille for blind people.

Changing Facilities

Changing facilities range from communal areas to single-sex changing rooms. They should provide sufficient space for a person to get changed and store their belongings while they are taking part in their selected activity. There should also be an area for customers to shower after having completed their activity. This area should be kept clean and tidy and checked regularly by members of staff. Some provide toiletries such as shampoo or shower gel in the shower area.

Quality Standard

A method of measuring the quality of a sport and leisure facility is to see if it has won any awards – there are lots of different schemes and organisations that provide industries with awards if they are meeting certain standards or providing exceptional service.

When reviewing your selected sport and leisure facility you will also need to take into account the aims of the business – for the majority of businesses their main aim is to make a profit; however, for some businesses, such as those in the public sector, the primary aim is to provide a service to the community.

Key learning points

When reviewing the quality of a sport and leisure business a person should investigate the strengths and areas for improvement in relation to:

- The different types of customers that use the business
- Affordability of the activities/products
- Marketing of the business
- Ways in which it gathers and deals with customer feedback
- Sport and leisure activities
- Facility mix
- Health and safety
- Access for people with disabilities
- Standard and cleanliness of the changing facilities
- Different types and availability of customer Information
- Quality standard awards that the business has received.

Activity 19.8   1.5–2 hours   P5 M3   D2

Reviewing the quality of a sport and leisure business

Select a sport and leisure business of your choice but make sure it is one that you can access easily and visit a number of times. Try to phone the business manager in advance of your visit and seek permission to study the business. If possible, try to arrange a time to speak to the business manager or other members of staff during one of your visits.

Task 1

Design and use a survey to work out the demographics of the customers using your selected sport and leisure business.

Task 2

Examine and write a report that reviews the quality of the different aspects of the business including:

- Different types of marketing for your select-ed sport and leisure business, for example leaflets, posters, adverts in local magazines, website

- Affordability of the activities and/or products
- Methods used to gain customer feedback
- Facility mix
- Sport and leisure activities
- Health and safety
- Access for people with disabilities
- Changing facilities
- Customer information
- Award schemes for quality standard
- Identifying, explaining and justifying the business's strengths.

Task 3

Complete your report by identifying, explaining and justifying areas that you think your selected sport and leisure business could develop in the future.

Quick Quiz 3 15 mins

D	G	N	I	T	E	K	R	A	M	S
U	E	I	M	E	Y	A	E	F	S	E
V	M	M	S	D	C	E	E	I	U	I
L	Y	I	O	C	D	E	V	T	R	T
T	T	A	E	G	D	R	A	R	V	I
T	I	S	D	B	R	C	B	K	U	V
D	S	S	A	C	C	A	I	R	Y	S
O	I	C	T	E	E	D	P	A	A	T
N	K	V	S	S	O	O	H	H	S	C
F	A	C	I	L	I	T	Y	M	I	X
S	E	I	T	I	V	I	T	C	A	C

Find the following words in the wordsearch above:

DEMOGRAPHIC
FACILITY MIX
ACTIVITIES
MARKETING
FEEDBACK
SURVEY
ACCESS

Useful websites

www.sportactivensa.co.uk/howwecanhelpyou/students/iminhigherfurthereducation.ashx

Career advice from the National Skills Academy, including links to sports and active leisure-related degrees and other qualifications.

www.sportengland.org/facilities_planning/design_guidance_notes.aspx

Extensive printable guidance on the appropriate design and requirements for building types and sports activities in the UK

www.health-club.co.uk/

Online industry magazine with news and vacancies for people working in the health and fitness industry updated daily.

www.smallbusiness.co.uk/channels/business-insights

Lots of free video presentations and printable advice covering sound principles for running a business; topics include how to find and keep customers, marketing your business effectively, making presentations, and the importance of having a good website.

Chapter 20
Planning & Running a Sports Event

It is likely that you have been involved in a sports event through your school, college or sports clubs. In the future, depending on what work you choose, it is likely you will be involved in planning or helping to plan some sort of sports event. It may be as small as a pool tournament or as large as an Olympic Games. Sometimes sports events look like they run themselves or are easy to run and this is probably due to the hard work that has been put in planning and organising the event. This is what you should aim for – 'to make it look easy'.

This chapter looks at the planning process or steps you must take to plan a sports event and, in particular, in considering the various resources, such as staff, venue and the amount of money you have to spend (budget). You will also look at the types of sports events that you may have to contribute to during your work. Then we will look at the types of customers that you may be targeting and how you would meet their needs and make the event attractive to them, and then the factors you need to consider when you organise the event. Then we look at the actual running of the sports event and what needs to be done before, during and after it. Finally, we look at the process of reviewing the success of the event and methods you can use to gain information about the event from other people. This is so that you can learn about what you should do and not do the next time you organise a similar event.

Learning Goals

By the end of this chapter you should:

- Be able to plan a sports event.
- Be able to contribute to the organisation of a sports event.
- Be able to contribute to the running of a sports event.
- Be able to review the success of a sports event.

To achieve a PASS grade the evidence must show that the learner is able to:	To achieve a MERIT grade the evidence must show that, in addition to the pass criteria, the learner is able to:	To achieve a DISTINCTION grade the evidence must show that, in addition to the pass and merit criteria, the learner is able to:
P1 produce a plan for a chosen sports event, outlining the planning process to meet given participant or customer requirements	**M1** produce a plan for a chosen sports event, explaining the planning process to meet given participant or customer requirements	
P2 contribute to the organisation of a chosen sports event		
P3 contribute to the running of a chosen sports event		
P4 design and use methods for collecting feedback on the success of a sports event		
P5 assess feedback received, identifying strengths and areas for improvement	**M2** assess feedback received, evaluating strengths and areas for improvement, providing recommendations for future events	**D1** assess feedback received, analysing strengths and areas for improvement, justifying recommendations for future events

20.1 Creating a Sports Event P1

Before we plan the sports event you should consider the range of sports events that could be organised and why they are being organised. Events are organised for many reasons:

● For the enjoyment of the participants

● To create competition and improve individuals' skills

● To raise money for charity or other purposes

● To promote a product or service

● To bring a group of people together

● To teach and educate people.

First, you need to be clear about why you are organising the event and then what the event is going to be. Activity 20.1 gets you to think about what sort of event you might organise.

Activity 20.1 ⏱ 15 mins P1

Sports event

Task

Take a piece of paper and in the middle of it write what the aim of your event is and draw a circle around it. Once you have done this draw five or six lines out of the circle to produce a spider diagram. Now spend five minutes coming up with as many ideas for a sports event as you can. You could do this with someone in your group or with a friend. Then take each idea and think about what would be good about this idea and what would make it difficult.

For example, you may have decided to organise an event to raise money for charity. You could have chosen to organise a 5 K run, a knockout tennis tournament, a day of sports activities for children, a 5-a-side indoor football tournament or a dinner with a celebrity speaker. As you

consider factors such as cost, time, staff needed, to whom it is attractive (customers) and whether it is realistic, you will realise the pros and cons of each – this will help you decide what sports event to choose.

The types of sports events that could be organised are shown in Figure 20.1.

Figure 20.1 Types of sporting event

These are just broad categories of events and they can vary based on the actual detail of the event.

Timing of the Event

When you are deciding on a sports event and planning it you need to be aware of the timescale you will work to. A major sports event, such as the Olympics, takes years to plan. The British Olympic Association (BOA) first started work on the 2012 Olympics in 1997; the government decided to make a formal bid in 2003 and London was awarded the Games in July 2005, giving seven years to plan for 2012. Your event will be on a much smaller scale but you must be realistic about the timescale that your tutor is allowing you to work to.

Customers' Requirements

Activity 20.2 looks at how you can identify your customers and the needs they may have.

This activity gets you to focus on some of the following issues:

- Do they need access to male and female changing rooms/toilets?
- Do I need to make signs in different languages?
- How much can I charge each participant?
- Do I need to lay on transport?
- How can I give them the information they need?
- Do I need more helpers or any special equipment?
- Will they like all the activities I am offering?

You could conduct a survey of your potential customers so that you know what their needs are and whether you are going to meet their needs. You could develop questions using the categories above.

Planning Process

Hopefully, now you have decided on the sports event that you are going to organise and why you are doing it. You need to look at the smaller details of the event now. You need to make decisions about the following aspects of the event:

1. Nature of the event – what size will the event be in terms of the number of participants and the venue?

2. Budget – how much will the event cost to organise and run? What expenses will I incur? How much money do I have and how much will the event raise? How can I raise more money? (By charging participants, obtaining sponsorship?)

3. Staffing – how many people will I need to run the event, will I need to pay them and, if so, how much? How will I look after the staff and give them food and drinks? What roles and responsibilities does each person need to fulfil?

4. Target audience – who are my customers and how can I let them know about the event and make it attractive to them?

Activity 20.2 20 mins   P1

Who are my customers?

Task

You will need to identify your target audience by breaking it down into various groups. Once you have identified the types of customers you will be attracting to your event you can think about what needs they may have.

Complete the following table.

Factor	Category	Needs of the group
Age	E.g. Children aged 8–9	E.g. need to be kept active with exciting activities
Sex		
Ethnic background		
Available income		
Availability of transport		
Access to IT		
Any disabilities or special needs		
Likes/dislikes		

Activity **20.3** 90 mins

Planning a sports event

Task

Part 1

To achieve P1 you need to draw up a plan for your sports event by following the ten stages of the planning process. This can be done by using the following template:

Part 2

To achieve M1 you need to explain this planning process and show how it meets your customers' needs.

Title of the event:
Nature of the event: Venue – Number of participants –
Budget: How much will the event cost to organise and run? – How much have I got? – How much will the event raise? – How will I raise money? –
Staffing: How many people do I need to run the event? – How much will I need to pay them? – How will I look after the staff? – What roles and responsibilities will each person fulfil? –
Target audience: Who are my target customers? –
Promotional activities: How will I let them know abouth the event? – How can I make the event attractive to them?
Contingency plans: What may go wrong? – What will I do if it does go wrong? –

Activity **20.3** Continued

First aid:
Do I need first aid? –
How am I going to provide it? –

Forms and paperwork:
What forms do I need?

Diary:
What do I need to make records of? –

Evaluation:
What will I use to evaluate the event? –

5. Promotional activities – how can I let my target audience know about the event?

6. Contingency plans – what may go wrong and what will I do if it does?

7. First aid – do I need first aid? How am I going to provide it?

8. Forms and paperwork – what forms do I need for staff and participants (for example informed consent, disclaimers, risk assessment)?

9. Diary – to record records of meetings, actions taken and any notes.

10. Evaluation – how am I going to evaluate the event (interviews, forms, cards)?

Now that you have considered the smaller details of the event you can start to make decisions and actually organise the event.

Quick Quiz 1   15 mins   ?

1. **Discuss five aspects of an event that you would need to consider when you are planning it.**
2. **List five customer groups you would target if you were organising a 5-a-side football tournament.**

20.2 Contribute to the Organisation of a Sports Event P2

By now you should have answered the following questions:

1. What is my event?

2. Why am I doing it – what are my aims and objectives?

3. How long have I got to organise the event?

Organising the Event

Now we should have everything we need to organise the event. However, there are many things to remember, all of which will be happening at the same time. Therefore, it is best to prepare a checklist or organisation chart to provide a step-by-step guide for organising and running the event. At this point it is vital to be clear about the timeline. The timeline shows in visual form the amount of time you have and the deadline for each task.

A Gantt chart is a suggested way to lay out the event plan, although there are other options.

The Gantt chart, as shown in Figure 20.2, breaks down each area that needs to be considered and the tasks that need to be completed as well as the date it needs to be completed by timeline.

This has broken down the organisation of the event into smaller manageable areas and the work has been divided across the six weeks of the organisation period. However, it does not state the work that needs to be done each week.

The chart below shows which organisational areas you will focus on each week, but you will need a second chart to show what you will be doing each week. For example:

Week 1

Organisational area/s: Venue and equipment

Tasks:

1. Is my chosen venue available?

2. Do I need to book it? When do I need to book it by?

3. Do they have all the facilities I need?

4. Do they all the equipment I need?

5. Do they have enough changing rooms/toilets?

Organisational area	Week 1	Week 2	Week 3	Week 4	Week 5	Week 6	Progress (Tick when complete)
Date: week ending	6/10	13/10	20/10	27/10	4/11	11/11	
Venue							
Finance							
Transport							
Staffing							
Equipment							
Information/Promotion							
Catering							
Entertainment							
Staffing							
Health and safety							
Contingency plans							

Figure 20.2
(*Source*: Adapted from Running Sports, 2007)

Special Considerations

Budgeting

You must consider whether there will be any expenses that you incur organising and running the event because an event that runs over budget can have serious consequences. Spend some time thinking about what you may spend on:

- Equipment
- Venue hire
- Transport hire
- Staff costs (wages, uniforms, refreshments)
- Trophies/prizes
- Promotional materials and activities
- Refreshments for participants.

Then think about how you may raise money:

- Entrance fees
- Sponsorship
- Donations
- Sales of food and drink
- Spectator fees.

Hopefully these two will be the same or else you need to think of more ways to raise money!

Staffing

Large-scale and small-scale sports events are dependent on volunteers who give their time without charge and enjoy the experience of being involved in the event. You need to decide what roles need to be fulfilled to allow the event to run smoothly and then which skills are needed for these roles. The following roles will need to be considered:

- Event manager
- Reception/hosting staff
- Referees/officials
- People to serve refreshments
- First-aid workers.

There will be more roles specific to your event and it is vital that you get these people on board early on and then keep checking they are available. You will also need to brief the staff and maybe meet their training needs. Further information on the considerations for organising an event can be explored through Activity 20.4.

Child Protection

It may well be that your event will be organised for children to participate in. Therefore, you are required to consider child protection and put

---

Activity **20.4** 30 mins   **P1** P2 P3 P4 P5 M1 M2 **D1**

Additional resources

There are many websites containing resources about how to organise an event. The two stated are specific to organising sports events:

Task

Go to: www.runningsports.org

1. Use the search box and enter 'managing events'.
2. Click on the pdf titled 'managing events' to bring up information that covers all the relevant aspects of managing events.
3. Use the search box and enter 'volunteers'.

4. Click on the pdf titled 'volunteers' to bring up information regarding the roles, recruitment and training of volunteers.
5. On the home page of the Running Sports website click on the link to case studies on the right hand side.
6. Choose a sports event to look at it and see how it was organised.

The following website also contains lots of good information on all aspects of sports event management:

www.ehow.com/how_2062720_organize-sports-tournament.html

in place measures to ensure their protection. These requirements include:

- A clear code of conduct for all staff and volunteers

- Police checks on the staff involved

- Registration details for the young people

- Contact details for the parents or guardians of the children

- Contact details for support services

- Procedure relating to use of photography equipment.

Sports Coach UK provides further information on child protection in their leaflet 'Safeguarding and Protecting Children: A guide for sports people'.

Quick Quiz 2   15 mins

1. **How would a Gantt chart help you during the planning process?**
2. **If you were planning the budget for a swimming gala what expenses would you have?**
3. **When you are deciding on staff for the event what factors would you consider?**

Activity **20.5**   1 hour   P2

Organising the event

Task

Make a record of all the contributions that you have made to the organisation of the event as part of a log or diary. You could use a template like the following:

> Date:
>
> Area of organisation:
>
> Tasks completed:

The following example shows you how you might fill in the log:

> Date: 04/11/10
>
> Area of organisation:
>
> *Staffing*
>
> Tasks completed:
>
> 1. Prepared a list of all the roles required and the available staff.
> 2. Decided which staff would perform what roles.
> 3. Produced a checklist of activities to train the staff.
> 4. Organised a time, date and venue for staff training.

Activity **20.6**   1 hour   P3

Log of contributions to the event

Task

Make a record of all the contributions that you have made to the running of the event as part of a log or diary. You will need to include as much evidence of your involvement as possible, such as records of meetings, witness statements from your tutor or other people involved in the event about what you did on the day.

You could use a template like the following:

> Date:
>
> Stage of the event (pre, during or post event):
>
> Description of contribution:

20.3 Contribute to the Running of a Sports Event   P3

Now that you have planned the event you are ready to run the event on the day. As the event organiser you should have an action plan that

Table 20.1   Event action plan

Phase	Tasks	Complete?
Setting up	• Signs in position • Equipment all set up and checked • Entertainment organised • Food and drink areas ready • Changing rooms/toilets prepared • Spectator facilities ready	
During event	• Customers' requests met • Officials in place • Food and drink always available • Unexpected occurrences dealt with	
Setting down	• All equipment put away • All ancillary areas clean and tidy • All waste disposed of • All signs taken down	

shows you what needs to be done on the day and by whom. It should include the three phases of the event, which are setting up for the event, during the event and setting down from the event. The action plan may look something like Table 20.1.

The running of the event involves ensuring that all your plans are put into place, any problems are dealt with and all the participants are kept happy. This will involve you implementing your personal and social skills including communication, decision-making and team-working. Every event is important in its own right; however, it is also important to learn from the experience of organising and running an event and the next section considers reviewing the event.

20.4 Review the Success of an Event

P4 **P5** **M2** **D1**

It may be that your event has gone perfectly and that everyone has gone home happy, or there may have been certain problems along the way. Either way there is a big opportunity here to learn from what was good about the event and what could be improved. If we can identify what was good then we can repeat it next time

or apply whatever made it good to the areas that were not so good. If we can identify what was not so good we can then develop ways to improve it in the future.

However the event went, there are always things that we can learn from it to help our future performance. This is sometimes called 'reflection' and involves us gathering as much information as we can from as many people involved in the event by asking them well-designed questions.

The Process of Review

Figure 20.3 shows the performance cycle – that is, the stages you will go through when organising a sports event (or, indeed, any other actions you take). It was presented by Steve

Figure 20.3   The performance cycle.
(*Source*: Bull, S, 2006)

Bull (2006), the sport pychologist to the England cricket team, to show the three stages that sports performers go through.

In the review phase of the event we will want to look at what sources of information we have for gaining evidence about the success of the event, how we will gain this information and what we can do with it.

Sources of Feedback

We often think that we know what was good and what was bad and don't need anyone else to tell us; however, there is no way that we can experience the event fully. We cannot fully put ourselves into the shoes of the participants or other staff and see things from their perspective. Therefore, we have to use all sources of information. The following are sources that you could use to gain information:

- Participants
- Staff
- Fellow organisational team members
- Venue staff
- Spectators
- Sponsors
- Self.

However, you will want to ask each group different questions and will have to design different questions for each one.

Methods of Feedback

Feedback can be gained verbally or in writing. Interviewing everyone can be a time-consuming business; however, there may be some key people whose feedback you would consider to be very important and you may interview them.

There are many methods of gaining feedback about an event including the following:

- Questionnaires
- Interviews
- Witness statements

- Customer comment cards
- Observation sheets.

You may choose to use a mixture of the above methods or different methods for different groups. You will also ask very different questions to different groups. For example, when seeking customers' views you will want to know about their experience of participating in the event and which parts they enjoyed. However, when you question your staff you will want to know about the process of organising the event and how they found the skills you used, such as communication, motivation and team-working.

Activity **20.7** 🕐 1 hour   **P4**

Collecting feedback

Task

Choose two methods for collecting feedback and then make each method specific to collect information about the success of your event.

Success of the Event

The aim of the review process is to produce a document that presents a summary of the strengths and weaknesses of the event and the recommendations for any future events. This can only be produced once the event has been fully evaluated. The review summary document is shown in Table 20.2.

Table 20.2   Review summary

Areas of strength
Areas of weakness
Recommendations for future events

This figure can be adjusted to help you achieve P5, M2 and D1. This is shown Activity 20.8.

The recommendations you have made will be the actions that you need to take next time or apply to the next similar event you are involved in.

Activity 20.8 ⏱ 1 hour P5 M2 D1

Assessing strengths and areas for improvement

Task

Use the following template to present the areas of strength and areas that need improvement.

	P5 assess feedback received, identifying strengths and areas for improvement	**M2** assess feedback received, evaluating strengths and areas for improvement, providing recommendations for future events	**D1** assess feedback received, analysing strengths and areas for improvement, justifying recommendations for future events
Areas of strength	• All competitors had a positive experience	•	•
Areas of improvement	• The event was poorly attended	•	•
Recommendations for future events	•	•	•
Justification of recommendations for future events	•	•	•

(k) Key learning points

- Events are planned for different reasons: enjoyment, competition, charity or educational reasons.
- Sports events take many different forms, for example competitions, activity days, training camps, educational events and charity dinners.
- When you are planning an event you need to take into account the budget, staffing, target audience, promotional activities, contingency plans, first aid and methods to evaluate the event.
- When you run an event you need to consider what you will do before, during and after the event.
- It is vital to review the event so that you can analyse its strengths and weaknesses and make recommendations to improve future events.

Further Reading

Allen, J., 2002, *The Business of Event Planning: Behind-the-scenes Secrets of Successful Special Events*. New York: John Wiley & Sons.

Hoyle, L. H., 2002, *Event Marketing: How to Successfully Promote Events, Festivals, Conventions and Expositions*. Wiley Events Management Series. New York: John Wiley & Sons.

Shone, A. and Parry, B., 2004, *Successful Event Management*. Stamford, CT: Thomson Learning.

Supovitz, F. and Goldblatt, J. J., 2004, *The Sports Event Management and Marketing Playbook: Managing and Marketing Winning Events*. New York: John Wiley & Sons.

References

Bull, S., 2006, *The Game Plan: Your Guide to Mental Toughness at Work*. Chichester: Capstone.

Running Sports, 2007, 'Managing events', www.runningsports.org/Resources/Running%20Sports/Documents/Managing%20Events.pdf (accessed 12 September 2009).

Useful websites

www.runningsports.org

Tips and ideas for setting up and running your own sports events; also offers a photo gallery and details of practical training courses.

www.ehow.com/how_2062720_organize-sports-tournement.html

American video presentation showing you how you can organise your own sports event successfully.

INDEX